T0394988

Moygara Castle, County Sligo and the O'Garas of Coolavin

Dedicated to the memory of

Markus Casey, archaeologist,
Paul Kerrigan, architect and architectural historian, and
Frank O'Neill, farmer and landowner,
who all worked in different ways at Moygara Castle.

Moygara Castle, County Sligo and the O'Garas of Coolavin

Kieran O'Conor

EDITOR

FOUR COURTS PRESS

Typeset in 10.5pt on 13.5pt AdobeGaramondPro by
Carrigboy Typesetting Services for
FOUR COURTS PRESS LTD
7 Malpas Street, Dublin 8, Ireland
www.fourcourtspress.ie
and in North America for
FOUR COURTS PRESS
c/o IPG, 814 N Franklin St, Chicago, IL 60610.

© the various contributors and Four Courts Press 2023

A catalogue record for this title is available from the British Library.

ISBN 978-1-84682-797-6

SPECIAL ACKNOWLEDGMENT

This publication has been made possible with financial assistance from
Sligo County Council, the Moygara Castle Research and Conservation Project,
the Heritage Council, the National Monuments Service,
the Publication Fund of the University of Galway and
the Atlantic Technological University.

 An Roinn Tithíochta,
Rialtais Áitiúil agus Oidhreachta
Department of Housing,
Local Government and Heritage

An Chomhairle Oidhreachta
The Heritage Council

 Sligo County Council
Comhairle Chontae Shligigh

 OLLSCOIL NA GAILLIMHE
UNIVERSITY OF GALWAY

 Moygara Castle

RESEARCH AND CONSERVATION PROJECT

 Ollscoil
Teicneolaíochta
an Atlantaigh

Atlantic
Technological
University

Printed by L&C Printing Group,
Kraków, Poland.

Contents

FOREWORD *P.J. O'Neill*   7

LIST OF ILLUSTRATIONS   8

LIST OF ABBREVIATIONS   11

CONTRIBUTORS   12

ACKNOWLEDGMENTS   13

1   Introduction: Moygara Castle and the O'Garas of Coolavin   15
     Kieran O'Conor

2   Moygara Castle: a history   26
     Anne Connon

3   Moygara Castle, Co. Sligo: a siting and map regression study   66
     Phyl Foley and Kieran O'Conor

4   An architectural description of Moygara Castle   78
     Rory Sherlock and Kieran O'Conor

5   Moygara Castle: the wider context   93
     Rory Sherlock, Paul M. Kerrigan and Kieran O'Conor

6   The O'Gara dynasty through time and place   108
     Maura O'Gara-O'Riordan and Máire Ní Chearbhaill

7   Moygara Castle: the topographical and geophysical surveys   133
     Kevin Barton

8   Excavations at Moygara Castle, 2013–17: preliminary results   155
     Christopher Read

9   Dating the mortars of Moygara Castle   171
     Jason Bolton

10   Moygara Castle through time   181
        Kieran O'Conor

APPENDIX 1. A listing and description of the land denominations of the
        half-barony of Coolavin on a parish-by-parish basis as found in
        sixteenth- to nineteenth-century sources   209
        Anne Connon

APPENDIX 2. The regional affiliations of Killaraght   261
        Anne Connon

BIBLIOGRAPHY   263

INDEX   281

Foreword

P.J. O'NEILL

With a building like Moygara Castle, you never really own it. If anything, it owns you. Like my father and his father before him, and for generations before that, the castle has been an integral part of O'Neill family life. The eight acres of pasture land that surround the castle have helped provide a living for my family for many generations in our rural farming community near Gurteen in south Co. Sligo. My interest in the history of the castle was engendered by my late father Frank, who, while he loved to farm its pastures, also encouraged a healthy interest among his children in the castle and its past. It was this interest that led me in 2005 to set up the Moygara Castle Research and Conservation Project, with the help of Maura O'Gara-O'Riordan, the O'Gara Clan and members of the local community.

From my own point of view, I wanted to try to shed light on how the O'Neill family came to own this piece of Sligo history, which was deeply associated with the O'Gara lordship of Coolavin up to the seventeenth century. From the aspect of local history, members of the Moygara Castle Research and Conservation Project wanted to learn as much as possible about the history of the site. There were a number of initial questions that needed to be answered. Who built the castle? When was it first constructed? What was its purpose? Was there more than one phase of construction and occupation? The answers to these questions have in turn posed many new questions, which we are still working on today. When you spend some time within the walls of this magnificent complex and allow your imagination free rein, it is not hard to envision what life must have been like in the Moygara of the past.

Unfortunately, time has taken its toll on the castle and it has become apparent that there is an urgent need to conserve the site. There is an enormous amount of work required to secure the future of the castle and for me to be able to hand it on to the next generation for them to appreciate. The castle is as much a piece of my family history over the last 150 years as it was for the O'Garas during the later medieval and post-medieval periods. Some would say fifteen years of research is a long time to spend on one site. Truthfully, we realize that we have only scratched the surface. I started off by saying that 'You don't own a castle like Moygara', and that's true, you are only custodian of it for a very short time and understand that it really belongs to history.

Illustrations

FIGURES

1.1	An aerial photograph of Moygara Castle, Co. Sligo.	16
1.2	Aerial photograph of Moygara Castle taken from the south-east.	16
1.3	Moygara Castle, Co. Sligo – location map.	17
1.4	William Frederick Wakeman's 1878 watercolour of Moygara Castle.	19
2.1	The topography and parishes of the half-barony of Coolavin.	27
2.2	Detail from Petty's map of Ireland.	28
2.3	Detail from Petty's map of Connacht.	29
2.4	The parishes and townlands of Coolavin.	30
2.5	The diocese of Achonry.	35
2.6	The main medieval routeways in the north Roscommon/south Sligo region.	39
2.7	The moated site at Killaraght, Co. Sligo.	41
2.8	Detail of the 1724 map of the Kingston lands in the vicinity of Moygara Castle.	51
2.9	William Frederick Wakeman's 1878 watercolour of the apotropaic carving that originally was located on the external face of the gatehouse at Moygara Castle.	55
2.10	Tom Cocking's sketch of Moygara Castle dated to 1791.	64
3.1	John Browne I's 1589 map of Co. Sligo.	70
3.2	Detail of the Moygara area, showing 'Moygarre' depicted as a castle, from Browne's 1589 map of Sligo.	71
3.3	Moygara is listed as an important place on John Browne II's 1591 map of Connacht.	72
3.4	Moygara is marked as an important place on the Down Survey map of Co. Sligo.	73
3.5	Detail from the 1777 Taylor and Skinner map of the road from Boyle to Ballaghaderreen (then in Co. Mayo).	74
3.6	Moygara Castle as depicted on the first-edition six-inch Ordnance Survey map.	76
4.1	Plan of Moygara Castle (after Markus Casey).	79
4.2	The interior of the bawn from the east.	80
4.3	The exterior of the south-eastern flanking tower.	82

4.4   Plan of the south-western flanking tower at first-floor level.   83
4.5   Plan of the south-western flanking tower at second-floor level.   83
4.6   Plan of the south-western flanking tower at wall-walk level.   84
4.7   The stairs alcove in the south-western flanking tower.   84
4.8   Plan of the south-eastern flanking tower at first-floor level.   85
4.9   Plan of the north-western flanking tower at first-floor level.   85
4.10   Plan of the north-eastern flanking tower at first-floor level.   86
4.11   Gun loops in the parapet of the south-western flanking tower.   87
4.12   A drip stone on the wall walk of the south-western flanking tower.   87
4.13   Plan of the gatehouse at first-floor level.   89
4.14   The portcullis slot within the gatehouse.   89
4.15   Figurative carving on a stone lying in the gatehouse.   90
4.16   A section of the external façade of the northern wall of the bawn
       showing the join between the earlier structure and the bawn wall.   92

5.1   Parke's Castle, Co. Leitrim.   95
5.2   Castlederg, Co. Tyrone.   96
5.3   Plan of Faugher, Co. Donegal.   98
5.4   Plan of Sir Edward Blayney's fort at Castleblayney, Co. Monaghan.   100
5.5   William Larkin's 1807 map of Manorhamilton Castle, Co. Leitrim.   101
5.6   Plan of Ballinafad Castle, Co. Sligo.   104
5.7   Plan of Ardtarmon Castle, Co. Sligo.   105

6.1   Extract from the O'Gara set of the Annals of the Four Masters
       under the year 964.   131
6.2   Extract from the Louvain set of the Annals of the Four Masters
       under the year 964.   131

7.1   Moygara Castle: outline castle plan with associated fieldwalls, minor
       road and selected loose and ground-fast stones.   135
7.2   Topographic contour map.   136
7.3   Hill-shaded images of the topographic data.   137
7.4   Visualization of the results of the earth resistance surveys carried out
       in 2006 and 2008.   139
7.5   Principal features interpreted from the earth resistance survey.   140
7.6   Electrical resistivity tomography (ERT) survey results.   143
7.7   Visualization of the results of the magnetic gradiometer survey.   147
7.8   Principal features interpreted from the magnetic gradiometer survey.   148
7.9   Ground penetrating radar (GPR) survey results.   150
7.10   Principal features interpreted from the ground penetrating radar.   151

7.11 Summary of the results of the topographic and principal geophysical surveys draped on 3D models of the topographic data. 153

8.1 Moygara Castle: locations of cuttings and principal features. 156

8.2 East-facing section of the Oval Enclosure's ditch, cutting 1. 158

8.3 Section through the Oval Enclosure's ditch in cutting 1, looking west. 158

8.4 Cutting 6: eastern wall and entrance of the tower house, looking west. 160

8.5 Cutting 6: looking south, showing the entranceway lobby and the remains of the stone stairs ascending to the upper floors of the tower house. 161

8.6 Cutting 6: south-facing section showing the external and internal walls of the tower house. 161

8.7 Ground-floor plan of Clara tower house, Co. Kilkenny. 162

8.8 Clara tower house, Co. Kilkenny. 163

8.9 Cutting 5: external wall, cobbling and drain of the later rectangular building. 166

8.10 Cutting 5: fireplace inside the later rectangular western building, looking north. 166

9.1 Sample locations at Moygara Castle. 172

9.2 Dressed limestone re-used among the sandstone rubble inside the north-west tower. 174

9.3 Render basecoat on the external face of the south-west tower. 174

9.4 Sample B from the bawn wall. 177

9.5 Lime lumps 'floating' in the binder matrix. 178

9.6 Sample 5 from the tower house. 178

10.1 The carving in the gatehouse at Kilkea Castle, Co. Kildare. 203

Abbreviations

AConn	Freeman, A. Martin (ed.), *The Annals of Connacht* (Dublin, 1944).
AFM	O'Donovan, John (ed.), *The Annals of the Kingdom of Ireland by the Four Masters*, 7 vols (Dublin, 1848–51).
AH	*Analecta Hibernica*
AHN	Archivo Historico Nacional (Madrid)
ALC	Hennessey, William M. (ed.), *The Annals of Lough Cé*, 2 vols (Dublin, 1871).
ASE	'Abstracts of grants of lands and other hereditaments, under the Acts of Settlement and Explanation, A.D.1666–1684', *Record Commissioners Report*, 15 (London, 1825), pp 130, 258.
ATig	Stokes, Whitley (ed.), 'The Annals of Tigernach', *Revue Celtique*, 18 (1897), pp 9–95, 150–97, 267–303.
AU	Hennessey, William M. and Bartholomew McCarthy (eds), *The Annals of Ulster*, 4 vols (Dublin, 1887–1901).
BAR	British Archaeological Report
BB	Royal Irish Academy, MS 536 (23 P 12: Book of Ballymote)
BL	British Library (London)
BSD	Simmington, Robert C. (ed.), *Books of Survey and Distribution, being abstracts of various surveys and instruments of title, 1636–1703*, i: *Roscommon* (Dublin, 1949).
CS	Hennessey, William M. (ed.), *Chronicum Scotorum: a chronicle of Irish affairs from the earliest times to A.D. 1135: with a supplement containing the events from 1141 to 1150* (London, 1866).
IHS	*Irish Historical Studies*
JGAHS	*Journal of the Galway Archaeological and Historical Society*
JRSAI	*Journal of the Royal Society of Antiquaries of Ireland*
Lec	Royal Irish Academy, MS 535 (23 P 2: Book of Lecan)
LGS	Landscape and Geological Services
NAI	National Archives of Ireland (Dublin)
NLI	National Library of Ireland (Dublin)
PRIA	*Proceedings of the Royal Irish Academy*
SPL	Sligo Public Library
TCD	Trinity College Dublin
TFE	'Abstracts of the conveyances from the trustees of the forfeited estates and interests in Ireland in 1688', *Record Commissioners Report*, 15 (London, 1825), p. 370.
TAB	National Archives of Ireland, Tithe Applotment Books 1834 (microfilm).

CONVENTIONS

The following chronology is used in this volume:

Early medieval	(*c.*400–*c.*1100)
High medieval	(*c.*1100–*c.*1350)
Late medieval	(*c.*1350–*c.*1600)
Later medieval	(*c.*1100–*c.*1600 – i.e., the high and late medieval periods combined)
Post medieval	(*c.*1600–*c.*1700)

Contributors

KEVIN BARTON, geophysicist and director of Landscape and Geophysical Services Ltd.

JASON BOLTON, built-heritage conservator.

ANNE CONNON, historian and adjunct Senior Lecturer, Department of Early and Medieval Irish, University College Cork.

PHYL FOLEY, local historian and independent scholar.

PAUL M. KERRIGAN, architect and architectural historian (RIP).

MÁIRE NÍ CHEARBHAILL, historian and independent scholar (RIP).

KIERAN O'CONOR, archaeologist and Senior Lecturer, School of Geography, Archaeology and Irish Studies, University of Galway.

MAURA O'GARA-O'RIORDAN, historian and independent scholar.

P.J. O'NEILL, chairman of the Moygara Castle Research and Conservation Project Committee and owner of Moygara Castle.

CHRISTOPHER READ, archaeologist and lecturer in archaeology, Atlantic Technological University (formerly IT Sligo).

RORY SHERLOCK, archaeologist and director of the Galway Archaeological Summer School.

Acknowledgments

The Moygara Castle Research and Conservation Project originally stemmed from meetings in 2005 with P.J. O'Neill and Maura O'Gara-O'Riordan. I am grateful to both these individuals, as they have encouraged, supported and helped organize the research over the years. In the process, we have become good friends. Thanks, also, to the late Frank O'Neill and the whole O'Neill family, particularly P.J., who have facilitated access to the castle over the years. I am also indebted to the various members of the Moygara Castle Research and Conservation Project Committee for their help since 2005, namely, its chairman P.J. O'Neill, Maura O'Gara-O'Riordan, John O'Gara, Dan McKeon, Kate O'Neill, Bernard Hunt, Kieran Sherlock, Joseph Cryan, Jimmy Casey, John Crawley, Thomas Waldron, Adrian Tansey, Niamh Doddy and Colm O'Riordan. Funding for the research carried out over the years has generously come from the Heritage Council, the Heritage Council's Adopt A Monument Scheme and the Moygara Castle Research and Conservation Project Committee itself. Generous subventions in support of publishing this book were provided by the University of Galway's Grant-in-Aid of Publication Fund, the Institute of Technology, Sligo (now Atlantic Technological University), Sligo County Council Heritage Office, the Heritage Service, the National Monuments Service and, the Moygara Castle Research and Conservation Project.

This publication has taken a number of years to produce, for various reasons. I am deeply indebted to each of the contributors to the volume and apologize for the delay in publishing it. Special thanks go to Sam Moore, who helped at early and late stages in the editing process. Sam also produced many of the images for this publication and was supportive of the project throughout. His help was invaluable. I am extremely grateful to Dr Rory Sherlock for his work with the images used in this book and for reading a draft of its contents. I would also like to thank Angela Gallagher, University of Galway, for her work on the images and her customary attention to detail, which is much appreciated. A significant stimulus to the book was the Connacht Project at the University of Galway. This is a multi-disciplinary research initiative that examines aspects of the past in the province of Connacht. Thanks go to Professor John Waddell for his support and generosity, as always. I am also extremely grateful to Professor Jimmy Schryver of the University of Minnesota, Morris, for his insightful comments on drafts of the text and, also, to Dr John Soderberg of Denison University. Thanks go to Con Manning for his photograph of Clara Castle. Thanks also to Professor Kevin Whelan for his help in tracking down a plan of Manorhamilton Castle and to Dr Brian Lacey for his plan of Faugher. I am grateful to my colleague Dr Pádraig

Lenihan, University of Galway, for his comments on Moygara Castle and introducing me to the complex history of north Connacht during the mid-seventeenth century. Thanks, also, to Dr Rachel Moss of Trinity College Dublin and Gavin Duffy of RealSim Ltd for the use of various photographs.

I am indebted to the following institutions for providing many of the illustrations and in most cases waiving charges: the Bibliothèque National de France, the National Library of Ireland, Sligo County Libraries, the Board of Trinity College Dublin, the National Monuments Service, Donegal County Council, the National Archives, Kew, Antiquity Publications Ltd/Cambridge University Press, Ordnance Survey Ireland, the UCD-OFM Partnership and the Royal Irish Academy.

I am extremely appreciative to Dr James Lyttleton for his insightful suggestions in 2018 on how to improve the various articles that make up this volume. These were very helpful, coming, as they do, from one of Britain and Ireland's most distinguished post-medieval archaeologists. I would also like to thank Four Courts Press, in particular Martin Fanning and Sam Tranum, for working on and then publishing this volume. I strongly believe that Four Courts Press's contribution over the years to understanding Ireland's past is immense. In this respect, I very much miss Michael Adams who founded Four Courts Press and who died in 2009 just as the idea for this book was forming. Lastly, I would like to thank my wife Dr Karena Morton of the National Museum of Ireland, and my two sons, Eoin and Hugh, for their constant support and love.

CHAPTER ONE

Introduction: Moygara Castle and the O'Garas of Coolavin

KIERAN O'CONOR

RATIONALE BEHIND THE STUDY OF MOYGARA CASTLE

Moygara Castle (Mon. No. SL044-052), with its four towers, gatehouse and high curtain walls, still dominates the countryside of south Sligo (figs 1.1–1.3). It also has excellent views south-eastwards across the great expanse of Lough Gara towards Rathcroghan, a locality famed for its late prehistoric archaeology and its associations with the mythological Táin Bó Cúailnge, and the hill of Fairymount (which is beautifully named Mullach na Sí in Irish) in modern north Roscommon. Moygara Castle is clearly one of the most impressive masonry-built monuments not only within its immediate area but in all of north Connacht. The castle compares well in its dramatic effect to Ballymote Castle, constructed *c.*1300 by the great Richard de Burgh, An Iarla Rua, and the Cistercian abbey at Boyle, built in the late twelfth and thirteenth centuries under MacDermot patronage, which both occur within 15km of it. Moygara Castle was described in 1791 as a 'building of considerable strength and extent, constructed by one of the O'Garas'.[1] Even then, the ruins of the castle managed to impress antiquarians and visitors alike. For example, at a later date, the famed antiquarian and artist William Frederick Wakeman, who was commissioned by Colonel Edward Cooper of Markree Castle from 1876 onwards to record in watercolour drawings much of Co. Sligo's rich archaeological heritage, painted the castle in October 1878 (fig. 1.4). Over a century ago, the Mayo-based historian Hubert T. Knox briefly mentioned Moygara Castle in an article analyzing Anglo-Norman settlement in Connacht. He erroneously dated the castle to the thirteenth century, comparing its architecture to Ballintober Castle in the adjacent county of Roscommon.[2] Despite the size of the castle and its impressive appearance, it may come as a surprise to learn that no detailed academic work has been carried out in modern times on Moygara. There is absolutely no mention of the castle in Tom McNeill's 1997 *Castles in Ireland: feudal power in a Gaelic world*,[3] although to be fair little is said about post-1600 castles in this particular book and, as will be seen, most (but not all) of the standing remains at Moygara seem to date to after that year.[4] Even more surprisingly,

1 F. Grose, *The antiquities of Ireland*, 2 vols (London, 1791), i, p. 58.   2 H.T. Knox, 'Occupation of Connaught by the Anglo-Normans after A.D. 1237 – Part II', *JRSAI*, 33 (1903), pp 58–74.   3 T.E. McNeill, *Castles in Ireland: feudal power in a Gaelic world* (London, 1997).   4 See chapter 5.

1.1 An aerial photograph of Moygara Castle, Co. Sligo. The castle still dominates the local landscape (photograph courtesy of Gavin Duffy).

1.2 Aerial photograph of Moygara Castle taken from the south-east. The Ox Mountains and Knocknarea are visible in the distance (photograph courtesy of Gavin Duffy).

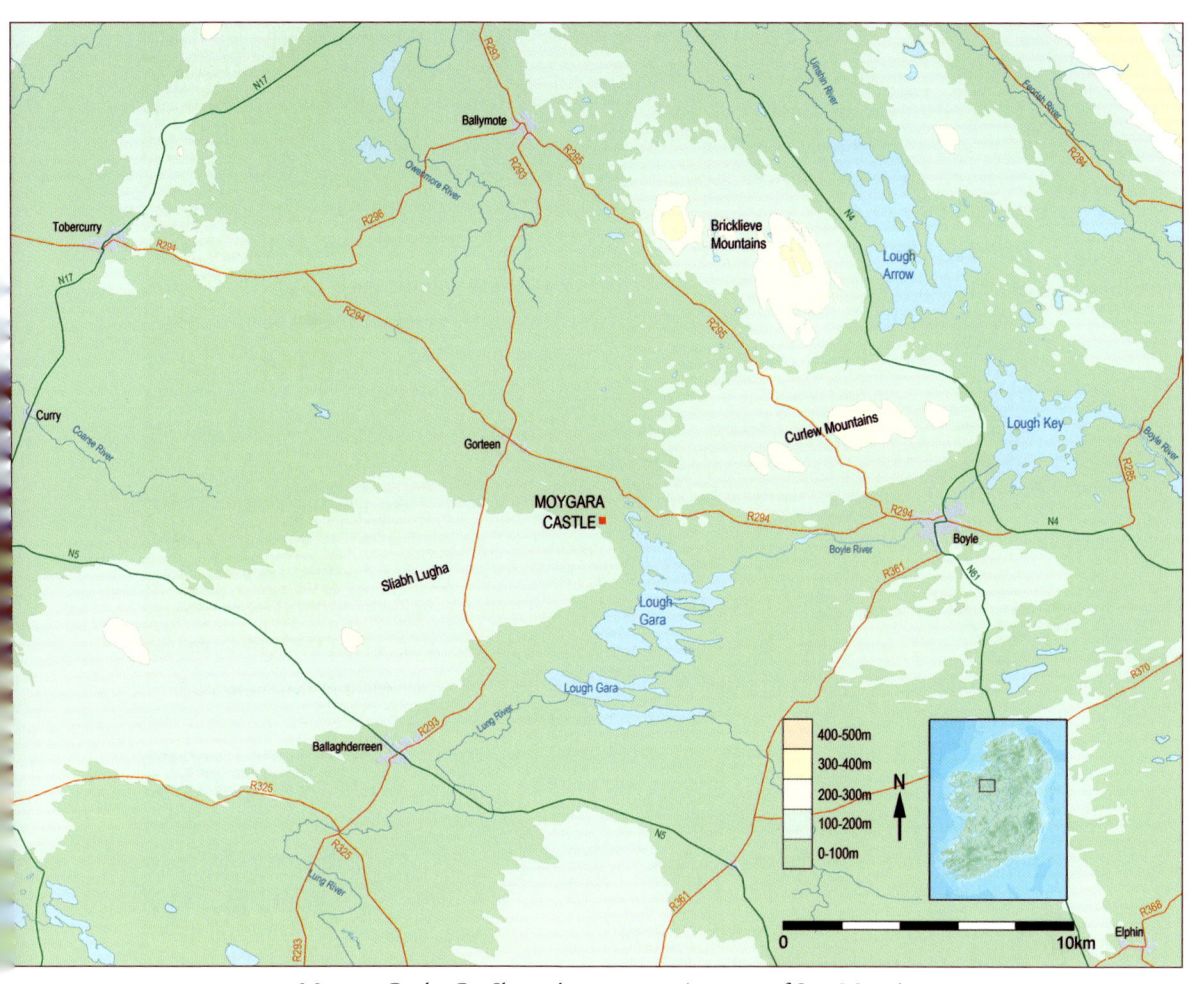

1.3 Moygara Castle, Co. Sligo – location map (courtesy of Sam Moore).

however, given the fact that one of the great strengths of this book is its chapter on late castles, there is no reference to the remains at Moygara in David Sweetman's 1999 *The medieval castles of Ireland*.[5] Neither is there even a mention of the castle in Maurice Craig's *The architecture of Ireland from the earliest times to 1880* published in 1982.[6] There is also no reference to Moygara Castle in the 1995 book *Castles and fortifications in Ireland, 1485–1945*, written by Paul Kerrigan (to whose memory this book is partly dedicated).[7] This is perhaps the most surprising, as this work is the main source of information for fortifications of post-1550 date in this country. The castle is briefly discussed in a brief ten-line description in Salter's 2003 book *The castles of Connacht*,

5 P.D. Sweetman, *The medieval castles of Ireland* (Cork, 1999). **6** M. Craig, *The architecture of Ireland from the earliest times to 1880* (London and Dublin, 1982). **7** P.M. Kerrigan, *Castles and fortifications in Ireland, 1485–*

who interestingly states, without saying why, that the ruins at Moygara, as they now present themselves, are 'early' seventeenth-century in date and that an Anglo-Norman hall house castle lies within the platform feature on the northern side of the site.[8] A brief, if succinct, description of the castle occurs in the 2005 *Archaeological inventory of County Sligo*, although there is little interpretation of its remains.[9] More recently, however, the castle is not mentioned in either Tadhg O'Keeffe's 2015 book *Medieval Irish buildings, 1100–1600* or his 2021 monograph *Ireland encastellated, AD 950–1550* but the main emphasis in these publications is on the standing buildings of the later medieval period that date to before the later sixteenth century.[10] It is not referenced, either, in the late Rolf Loeber's 2019 book *Irish houses and castles 1400–1700* or Vicky McAlister's *The Irish tower house: society, economy and environment, c.1300–1650*.[11] This all shows that Moygara Castle is virtually unknown to modern scholarship and the academy, despite its size and visual impressiveness.

Why is this so? As will be shown, the earliest masonry-castle phase apparent in the architecture at Moygara Castle was probably built at some stage in the fifteenth or early sixteenth century by the Gaelic-Irish (i.e. native Irish) O'Garas and the castle functioned as the centre or *ceann aitt* (literally 'head place') of their lordship of Coolavin.[12] The castle clearly was an important place in the Gaelic-dominated landscape of late medieval north Connacht, or 'Lower Connacht' as it was known by contemporaries. It was noted in 1998, and again in 2001, by the present writer that very little detailed archaeological work had been carried out until then on the settlement, society, landscape, economy and material culture of Gaelic-dominated parts of later medieval Ireland, which would have included most of the west of Ireland.[13] One of the reasons given for this lack of research on Irish-dominated parts of later medieval Ireland was linked to the fact that these regions, which include modern south Sligo and north Roscommon, are located at a distance from the parts of Ireland (namely the east and south-east of the country, especially the Dublin region) that have seen much economic development over the last few decades.[14] Continuing this argument and train of thought, it could be suggested that one reason why Moygara Castle has not figured in the academic literature on Irish castles so far, despite its impressiveness, is because of its location away from the parts of the country that have experienced much in the way of archaeological excavation, fieldwork and research

---

1945 (Cork, 1995).   **8** M. Salter, *The castles of Connacht* (Malvern, 2004).   **9** U. Egan, E. Byrne and M. Sleeman, *Archaeological inventory of county Sligo, i: South Sligo* (Dublin, 2005). In 1992, the archaeologist Markus Casey produced a plan and description of the castle, dating the standing remains there to the late sixteenth century. M. Casey, 'Archaeological report, Moygara Castle, 1992' (unpublished report, Galway 1992).   **10** T. O'Keeffe, *Medieval Irish buildings, 1100–1600*, Maynooth Research Guides for Irish Local History 18 (Dublin, 2015); idem, *Ireland encastellated AD950–1550* (Dublin, 2021).   **11** R. Loeber, *Irish houses and castles 1400–1700* (Dublin, 2019); V. McAlister, *The Irish tower house: society, economy and environment, c.1300–1650* (Manchester, 2019).   **12** See chapters 2 and 10.   **13** K. O'Conor, *The archaeology of medieval rural settlement in Ireland* (Dublin, 1998), pp 73–4; idem, 'The morphology of Gaelic lordly sites in north Connacht' in P.J. Duffy, D. Edwards and E. FitzPatrick (eds), *Gaelic Ireland, c.1250–c.1650: land, lordship and settlement* (Dublin, 2001), pp 329–31.   **14** O'Conor, 'The morphology', p. 331.

1.4 William Frederick Wakeman's 1878 watercolour of Moygara Castle, which was commissioned by Colonel Edward Cooper of Markree Castle (© Sligo County Libraries).

in recent times. Castles like Ballymote and abbeys like Boyle, which both occur in the same general locality as Moygara, as noted, have been subject to quite intensive studies over the years, despite being located in the west of Ireland.[15] However, the difference between Ballymote Castle and Boyle Abbey, on the one hand, and Moygara Castle, on the other, is that the two former sites occur within towns and are located beside railway lines and main roads. Moygara Castle, meanwhile, is situated today in the 'deep' countryside of south Sligo and is surrounded by fields, being approached by a narrow laneway or boreen. Remoteness, therefore, seems to be the major reason why Moygara has not been studied by scholars to date and why its remains have not made any impact on the academic literature on later medieval and post-medieval fortifications in this country, despite the grandeur and impressiveness of its ruins.

It has been suggested that anything up to seven thousand castles of different types were built in Ireland between the late twelfth century and *c.*1650, with a large majority of these being late medieval tower houses.[16] It might be added that there are no visible surface remains of many of these castles and this large figure is based partly on the

15 J.E. Fitzpatrick, 'Ballymote Castle', *JRSAI*, 57 (1927), pp 81–99; McNeill, *Castles in Ireland*, pp 101, 198, 233; Sweetman, *The medieval castles of Ireland*, pp 105–8; B. Kalkreuter, *Boyle Abbey and the School of the West* (Bray, 2001); R.A. Stalley, *The Cistercian monasteries of Ireland* (New Haven, 1987), passim. See, also, P.D. Sweetman, 'Archaeological excavations at Ballymote Castle, Co. Sligo', *JGAHS*, 40 (1985–6), pp 114–24. **16** T.B. Barry, 'Rural settlement in Ireland in the Middle Ages: an overview', *Ruralia,* 1 (1996), p. 140; see, also, K. O'Conor and J. Williams, 'Ballinagare Castle, Co. Roscommon' in L. Gibbons and K. O'Conor (eds), *Charles O'Conor of Ballinagare, 1710–91: life and works* (Dublin, 2015), pp 60–4.

evidence from early maps and the surviving historical sources, particularly the colonial sources of late sixteenth- and seventeenth-century date. Given these numbers, Ireland was clearly one of the most castellated parts of later medieval Europe, especially by the year 1600.[17] Again, considering these figures and, indeed, the many fine examples of fortresses that can be seen on the island of Ireland whose architecture can compare well with the best in Britain and Europe, it comes as yet another surprise to learn that comparatively little detailed research has been carried out on castles in this country over the years – in particular over most of the twentieth century. Part of the problem lay in the perception among many people in the last century that castles were physical symbols of English domination and oppression since the late twelfth century.[18] This may partly explain why many professional archaeologists in Ireland prior to the 1980s concentrated their research and work on the early medieval and prehistoric periods, as these were seen as eras free from English interference in Ireland's affairs and were believed to have been halcyon days of great cultural and spiritual achievement for the Irish people.[19] It was only from the late 1980s and early 1990s that castle studies in Ireland really developed and were placed on more solid ground. In a 2008 review of castle studies in Ireland, the present writer, while noting the sterling research that had been carried out on Irish castles over the previous couple of decades, argued that there was still room for a large amount of improvement. In particular, it was noted that comprehensive monographs on individual castles were lacking for Ireland, unlike the situation on the neighbouring island of Britain and across large parts of mainland Europe.[20] This echoed McNeill's earlier 1997 plea that more data about castles in Ireland needs to be collected to bring castle studies in Ireland onto a much firmer footing.[21] Despite the advances made in castle studies on this island since *c.*1990, it was argued that many theories about castles in Ireland were based on nothing more than short visits to these sites, which could 'be measured in terms of hours rather than weeks or months'.[22] It was suggested that more comprehensive monographs on individual castles or groups of castles should be published and then used as reliable data from which old ideas on castles could be questioned, proved or disproved and from which new questions could be asked.[23] In all, it was felt in 2008 that castle studies in Ireland suffered from a lack of dependable, peer-reviewed, in-depth analyses of individual castles and that this, in turn, had hindered the intellectual development of castle studies in Ireland.[24] These circumstances have now changed, with a number of peer-reviewed monographs on important castles published since then, which add substantially to our knowledge about them in this country. The Archaeological Monograph Series of the National Monuments Service, now in the Department of

17 K. O'Conor, 'Castle studies in Ireland: the way forward' in P. Ettel, A.-M. Flambard Héricher and T.E. McNeill (eds), *Château Gaillard, 23: Bilan des recherches en castellogie* (Caen, 2008), pp 329–32. **18** Ibid., p. 332. **19** T.B. Barry, *The archaeology of medieval Ireland* (London and New York, 1987), p. 1; O'Conor, *The archaeology*, pp 10–11; idem, 'Castle studies in Ireland', p. 332. **20** O'Conor, 'Castle studies in Ireland', p. 333. **21** McNeill, *Castles in Ireland*, pp 2–3. **22** O'Conor, 'Castle studies in Ireland', p. 333. **23** Ibid. **24** Ibid.

Housing, Local Government and Heritage, not only presents the results of the excavations of various castles, abbeys and churches in state care, but also includes detailed examinations of the architecture and history of these places. They are, in fact, in-depth, multi-disciplinary studies of these sites. Six monographs produced in this series since 2003 have been on important castles located in different parts of Ireland. These are Roscrea Castle, Co. Tipperary, Glanworth Castle, Co. Cork, Trim Castle, Co. Meath, Parke's Castle, Co. Leitrim, Clogh Oughter Castle, Co. Cavan, and Barryscourt Castle, Co. Cork.[25] James Lyttleton's book on Blarney Castle in Co. Cork is also a valuable and comprehensive addition to castle studies in Ireland.[26] Lyttleton has also published a book entitled *The Jacobean plantations in seventeenth-century Offaly* and it includes much useful information on fortified houses and the late use of tower houses.[27] Comprehensive multi-disciplinary studies of Dunluce Castle, Co. Antrim, and Portumna Castle, Co. Galway, appeared in 2012.[28] Furthermore, a number of peer-reviewed articles outlining the architectural development of individual castles have also been published in the last decade or so.[29] Nevertheless, many, if not most, important castles in Ireland still lack a detailed multi-disciplinary, published analysis. Therefore, such a publication for Moygara Castle is to be welcomed as being another, comprehensive publication on an important but hitherto little-understood castle that will hopefully play a small but important part in bringing the academic study of castles in Ireland onto a firmer footing. Furthermore, castle studies in Ireland have been aided by three recent publications, all briefly alluded to above. These are O'Keeffe's comprehensive 2015 book on medieval architecture in Ireland, his recent book on medieval Irish castles and McAlister's very useful tome on tower houses.[30] These three general studies help give greater context to the research at Moygara Castle.

25 C. Manning (ed.), *Excavations at Roscrea Castle* (Dublin, 2003); idem, *The history and archaeology of Glanworth Castle, Co. Cork* (Dublin, 2009); idem, *Clogh Oughter Castle, Co. Cavan: archaeology, history and architecture* (Dublin, 2013); A.R. Hayden, *Trim Castle, Co. Meath: excavations, 1995–8* (Dublin, 2011); C. Foley and C. Donnelly, *Parke's Castle, Co. Leitrim; archaeology, history and architecture* (Dublin, 2012); D. Pollock, *Barryscourt Castle, Co. Cork: archaeology, history and architecture* (Dublin, 2017). **26** J. Lyttleton, *Blarney Castle: an Irish tower house* (Dublin, 2011). **27** J. Lyttleton, *The Jacobean plantations in seventeenth-century Offaly* (Dublin, 2013). **28** C. Breen, *Dunluce Castle: archaeology and history* (Dublin, 2012); J. Fenlon (ed.), *Clanricard's Castle; Portumna House, Co. Galway* (Dublin, 2012). **29** For example, see R. Sherlock, 'An introduction to the history and architecture of Bunratty Castle' in R.A. Stalley (ed.), *Limerick and south-west Ireland: medieval art and architecture,* Transactions of the British Archaeological Association XXXIV (Leeds, 2011), pp 202–18; T. O'Keeffe, 'Building lordship in thirteenth-century Ireland: the donjon of Coonagh Castle, Co. Limerick', *JRSAI,* 141 (2011), pp 91–127; idem, 'Lohort Castle: medieval architecture, medievalist imagination', *Journal of the Cork Historical and Archaeological Society,* 118 (2013), pp 24–34; K. O'Conor, P. Naessens and R. Sherlock, 'Rindoon Castle, Co. Roscommon: a border castle on the Irish frontier' in P. Ettel, A.-M. Flambard-Héricher and K. O'Conor (eds), *Château Gaillard, 26: L'environment du château* (Caen, 2014), pp 313–23; K. O'Conor and P. Naessens, 'Temple House; from Templar castle to New English mansion' in M. Browne and C. Ó Clabaigh (eds), *Soldiers of Christ: the Knights Hospitallers and the Knights Templar in medieval Ireland* (Dublin, 2016), pp 124–50; K. O'Conor, P. Naessens and R. Sherlock, 'Rindoon Castle, Co. Roscommon: an Anglo-Norman castle on the western shores of Lough Ree' in B. Cunningham and H. Murtagh (eds), *Lough Ree: historic lakeland settlement* (Dublin, 2016), pp 83–109; K. O'Conor and B. Shanahan, *Rindoon Castle and deserted medieval town* (Roscommon, 2018). **30** O'Keeffe, *Medieval Irish buildings, 1100–1600*; idem, *Ireland encastellated AD 950–1550;*

The study of Moygara Castle since 2005, furthermore, was also a catalyst for the academic study of its original owners, the O'Garas, and their territory, Coolavin. In this respect, the situation concerning the lack of archaeological work on later medieval Gaelic Ireland has also changed in the last numbers of years, as a large number of publications have appeared in the last twenty years or so that examine this important aspect of Ireland's past.[31] Elizabeth FitzPatrick's 2004 *Royal inauguration in Gaelic Ireland, c.1100–1600* was a comprehensive study of later medieval Gaelic inauguration sites and practices and also examined aspects of the material culture of the indigenous Irish during the period.[32] Colin Breen's 2005 book *The Gaelic lordship of the O'Sullivan Beare: a landscape cultural history* was the first major archaeological and landscape study of a later medieval Gaelic lordship ever to be published.[33] The 2010 *Medieval Lough Ce: history, archaeology and landscape*, edited by Tom Finan of St Louis University, can be described as a multi-disciplinary study of the later medieval MacDermot lordship of Moylurg, which has very strong archaeological and landscape components within it.[34] A major aspect of the work of the Discovery Programme's Medieval Rural Settlement Programme, which was under the directorship of Niall Brady, examined the archaeology of later medieval central Roscommon, a region dominated throughout the latter period by the O'Conors.[35] The ongoing excavations at the MacDermot centre on the island fortress known as the Rock of Lough Key, Co. Roscommon, and its service site on the adjacent Rockingham shore are also extremely important.[36] The excavation of the cashel at Caherconnell in Co. Clare has shown that this site, which was originally built in the tenth century, was continuously occupied throughout later

McAlister, *The Irish tower house*. **31** For a review of the archaeological study of later medieval Gaelic Ireland since the very late 1990s, see K. O'Conor, '*Crannóga* in later medieval Ireland: continuity and change' in E. Campbell, E. FitzPatrick and A. Horning (eds), *Becoming and belonging in Gaelic Ireland, AD c.1200–1600: essays in identity and cultural practice* (Cork, 2018), pp 149–51; see, also, T. O'Keeffe, *The Gaelic peoples and their archaeological identities AD 1000–1650* (Cambridge, 2004). **32** E. FitzPatrick, *Royal inauguration in Gaelic Ireland, c.1100–1600* (Woodbridge, 2004). **33** C. Breen, *The Gaelic lordship of the O'Sullivan Beare: a landscape cultural history* (Dublin, 2005). **34** T. Finan (ed.), *Medieval Lough Cé: history, archaeology and landscape* (Dublin, 2010). **35** N. Brady, 'The Medieval Rural Settlement Project: an overview for 2002–2004', *Discovery Programme Reports 7* (Dublin, 2005), pp 1–2 ; R. McNeary and B. Shanahan, 'Medieval settlement, society and land use in medieval Roscommon, 1100–1650 AD', *Discovery Programme Reports 7* (Dublin, 2005), pp 3–22; N. Brady, A. Connon, R. McNeary, B. Shanahan and R. Shaw, 'A survey of the priory and graveyard at Tulsk, Co. Roscommon', *Discovery Programme Reports 7* (Dublin, 2005), pp 40–64; N. Brady and P. Gibson, 'The earthwork at Tulsk: topographical and geophysical excavations and preliminary excavations', *Discovery Programme Reports 7* (Dublin, 2005), pp 65–76; R. McNeary and B. Shanahan, 'Settlement and enclosure in a medieval Gaelic lordship: a case study from the territory of the O'Conors of north Roscommon' in R. Compatangelo, J.-R. Bertrand, J. Chapman, and P.-Y. Laffont (eds), *Landmarks and socio-economic systems: constructing of pre-industrial landscapes and their perception by contemporary societies* (Rennes, 2008), pp 187–97; R. McNeary and B. Shanahan, 'The March in Roscommon, 1170–1400: culture, contact, continuity and change' in J. Ní Ghrádaigh and E. O'Byrne (eds), *The March in the islands of the medieval West* (Leiden and Boston, 2012), pp 195–226; see, also, N. Brady, *Discovering Irish medieval landscapes* (Dublin, 2003). **36** For interim reports on these two separate but related excavations, see T. Finan, 'The Rock of Lough Key and the moated site at Rockingham: components of a lordly landscape' in P. Ettel, A.-M. Flambard-Héricher and K. O'Conor (eds), *Château Gaillard 28: l'environment du château* (Caen, 2018), pp 143–45; idem, 'Living in Gaelic castles: inter-disciplinary advances in 13th-century Irish castle studies' in P. Ettel, A.-M. Flambard-Héricher and K. O'Conor (eds), *Château Gaillard*

medieval times down to the seventeenth century. These excavations have thrown further light on the material culture and economy of later medieval Gaelic Ireland.[37] The excavation of burials from Ballyhanna graveyard in south Co. Donegal has produced a large amount of important, new information about the lives of ordinary people in this part of later medieval Gaelic Ireland.[38] Archaeological fieldwork and further research since the year 2005, when the Moygara Castle Research and Conservation Project began, has identified, discussed and analyzed individual Gaelic Irish elite centres, inauguration and assembly sites, hunting landscapes, habitation sites of ordinary people and cultural landscapes of general later medieval date.[39] The work at Ballyhanna graveyard, for example, has culminated in the publication of McKenzie and Murphy's recent book *Life and death in medieval Gaelic Ireland*. This publication

29: *vivre au château* (Caen, 2020), pp 107–13.   **37** M. Comber and G. Hull, 'Excavations at Caherconnell Cashel, the Burren, Co. Clare: implications for cashel chronology and Gaelic settlement', *PRIA*, 110, pp 133–73; M. Comber, *Caherconnell Archaeological Project: summary of fieldwork to date* (Burren, 2014); idem, 'Central places in a rural landscape', *Journal of the North Atlantic*, 36 (2018), pp 1–12; idem, 'The tale of items lost … what items tell us about the life of a medieval family at Caherconnell Cashel, Co. Clare' in J. Fenwick (ed.), *Lost and Found III* (Dublin, 2018), pp 95–102.   **38** C. McKenzie, E.M. Murphy and C.J. Donnelly (eds), *The science of a lost medieval graveyard: the Ballyhanna Research Project* (Dublin, 2015).   **39** For example, see P. Naessens, 'Gaelic lords of the sea: the coastal tower houses of South Connemara' in L. Doran and J. Lyttleton (eds), *Lordship in medieval Ireland: image and reality* (Dublin, 2007), pp 217–35; E. FitzPatrick, 'Native enclosed settlement and the problem of the Irish "ringfort"', *Medieval Archaeology*, 53 (2009), pp 271–307. K. O'Conor, N. Brady, A. Connon and C. Fidalgo-Romo, 'The Rock of Lough Cé, Co. Roscommon' in T. Finan (ed.), *Medieval Lough Cé: history, archaeology and landscape* (Dublin, 2010), pp 15–40; S. McDermott, 'The archaeology of the Twelve Tates of McKenna, *c.*1591', *Clogher Record*, 20:2 (2010), pp 373–406; E. FitzPatrick, E. Murphy, R. McHugh and C.J. Donnelly, 'Evoking the White Mare; the cult landscape of Sgiath Gabhra and its medieval perception in Gaelic Fir Mhanach' in R. Schot, C. Newman and E. Bhreathnach (eds), *Landscapes of cult and kingship* (Dublin, 2011), pp 163–91; P. Naessens and K. O'Conor, 'Pre-Norman fortification in eleventh- and twelfth-century Connacht' in P. Ettel, A.-M. Flambard-Héricher and K. O'Conor (eds), *Château Gaillard*, 25: *L'origine du château médiéval* (Caen, 2012), pp 259–68; E. FitzPatrick, '*Formaoil na Fiann*: hunting preserves and assembly places in Gaelic Ireland', *Proceedings of the Harvard Celtic Colloquium*, 32 (2013), pp 95–118; idem, 'The landscape and settlements of the Uí Dhálaigh poets of Muinter Bháire' in S. Duffy (ed.), *Princes, prelates and poets in medieval Ireland: essays in honour of Katharine Simms* (Dublin, 2013), pp 460–80; A. Horning, 'Challenging colonial equations? The Gaelic experience in early modern Ireland' in N. Ferris, R. Harrison and M.V. Wilcox (eds), *Rethinking colonial pasts through archaeology* (Oxford, 2014), pp 293–314; T. Finan, 'Moated sites in County Roscommon, Ireland: a statistical approach' in P. Ettel, A.-M. Flambard-Héricher and K. O'Conor (eds), *Château Gaillard*, 26: *L'environnement du château* (Caen, 2014), pp 177–80; E. FitzPatrick, 'Assembly places and elite collective identities in medieval Ireland', *Journal of the North Atlantic*, 8 (2015), pp 52–68; P. Naessens, 'Murchadh Ó Flaithbheartaigh and the aggrandizement of Aughanure Castle' in R. Oram (ed.), *Tower Studies 1 & 2: 'A house that thieves might knock at':* proceedings of the 2010 Stirling and 2011 Dundee Conferences (Donington, 2015), pp 214–30; J.J. McDermott and K. O'Conor, 'Rosclogher Castle: a Gaelic lordship centre on Lough Melvin, County Leitrim', *Breifne*, 13:50 (2015), pp 470–97; E. FitzPatrick, 'The last kings of Ireland: material expressions of Gaelic lordship, *c.*1300–1400' in K. Buchanan, L.H.S. Dean and M. Penman (eds), *Medieval and early modern representations of authority in Scotland and the British Isles* (Oxford, 2016), pp 197–213; T. Finan, 'The Rock of Lough Key and the moated site at Rockingham: components of a lordly landscape' in P. Ettel, A.-M. Flambard-Héricher and K. O'Conor (eds), *Château Gaillard*, 28: *L'environnement du château* (Caen, 2018), pp 143–5; K. O'Conor and T. Finan, 'Medieval settlement in north Roscommon, *c.*1200AD–*c.*1350AD' in R. Farrell, K. O'Conor and M. Potter (eds), *Roscommon history and society: interdisciplinary essays on the history of an Irish county* (Dublin, 2018), pp 105–32; K. O'Conor, and C. Fredengren, 'Medieval settlement in Leitrim, 1169–*c.*1380AD' in Liam Kelly and Brendan Scott (eds), *Leitrim history and society: interdisciplinary essays on the history*

is really the first comprehensive study of a skeletal population from later medieval Gaelic Ireland and provides detailed insights into the health, diet and lifestyles of the largely invisible lower classes of Gaelic Ireland during the latter period.[40] The 2018 volume *Becoming and belonging in Gaelic Ireland, AD c.1200–1600: essays in identity and cultural practice*, edited by Eve Campbell, Elizabeth FitzPatrick and Audrey Horning, has a large number of essays within it dealing directly with the archaeology of later medieval Gaelic Ireland.[41] Very recent articles have outlined the evidence for elite settlement in Gaelic-dominated parts of medieval Ireland prior to *c.*1350, primarily making the important point again that crannogs and different forms of ringforts, such as the cashel, continued to be occupied by native lords long after *c.*1100, down in some places to *c.*1600. This fact needs to be fully recognized and acknowledged or the archaeological study of large parts of medieval Ireland will be compromised and grind to a halt as a result.[42] This discussion indicates that quite a bit more is known about the settlement archaeology and material culture of later medieval Gaelic Ireland than was the situation in 2005. Our knowledge of this aspect of medieval archaeology in Ireland will hopefully be strengthened in the relatively near future when the work of the Discovery Programme's Medieval Rural Settlement Project is fully published. Nevertheless, despite this published work and ongoing research, it can still be stated that much more is known about the archaeology of eastern and south-eastern Ireland during the later medieval period, meaning that we know more about the lifeways, settlements and material culture of the Anglo-Normans and their late medieval descendants than we do about Gaelic Ireland.[43] Therefore, it can be stated that another justification for the work at Moygara Castle outlined in this book is that it produces additional and important new evidence about life and society in later medieval Gaelic Ireland.

A multi-disciplinary approach is taken in this study of Moygara Castle, combining evidence from architectural survey,[44] excavation,[45] the surviving historical sources,[46] geophysical survey,[47] aerial photography and early maps[48] and the dating of lime mortars.[49] It is abundantly clear from various, mostly recent studies that this approach, bringing together data from different disciplines and methods, represents the most efficient way to carry out research on the medieval period, as these strands of evidence

of an Irish county (Dublin, 2019), pp 79–101.   **40** C.J. McKenzie and E.M. Murphy, *Life and death in medieval Gaelic Ireland* (Dublin, 2018).   **41** E. Campbell, E. FitzPatrick and A. Horning (eds), *Becoming and belonging in Gaelic Ireland, AD c.1200–1600: essays in identity and cultural practice* (Cork, 2018).   **42** D. Curley, 'Reconstructing the Lough Croan *cenn áit* of the medieval Ó Cellaig lordship of Uí Maine', *JRSAI*, 150 (2020), pp 201–24; idem, '*Le triúcha chéd in Chalaidh a màeraidecht idir mincís mórthobach*: multidisciplinary approaches to recovering an Ó Cellaig *cenn àit* in later medieval Uí Maine', *Eolas: the Journal of the American Society of Irish Medieval Studies*, 13 (2021), 2–42; K. O'Conor, 'Settlement in Gaelic Ireland, 1100–1350', *Eolas: the Journal of the American Society of Irish Medieval Studies*, 13 (2021), pp 43–71.   **43** See M. Gardiner and K. O'Conor, 'The later medieval countryside lying beneath' in M. Stanley, R. Swan and A. O'Sullivan (eds), *Stories of Ireland's past: knowledge gained from NRA roads archaeology* (Dublin, 2017), pp 133–52.   **44** See chapters 4 and 5.   **45** See chapter 8.   **46** See chapters 2 and 6.   **47** See chapter 7.   **48** See chapter 3.   **49** See chapter 9.

can combine to give a relatively clear picture of how a building, site or landscape developed over time. It is the best way, furthermore, of isolating important questions that can be answered by targeted excavation(s) in the future.[50]

CONCLUSIONS

The rationale behind the publication of the recent work at Moygara Castle has been outlined in this introductory chapter. This research can hopefully contribute to knowledge in three ways. Firstly, a comprehensive, multi-disciplinary analysis of the castle is clearly the only way to understand its development through time and elucidate the important part it played in the settlement history of south Sligo. Secondly, this research will join the growing body of similar, peer-reviewed studies of individual castles that have appeared in recent years. The evidence from these comprehensive studies will eventually combine to create a mass of reliable data that will help put castle studies in Ireland onto a firmer footing than at present, allowing questions to be posed and answered with more confidence and reliability. Thirdly, a study of Moygara Castle, which functioned as the centre of O'Gara power in south Sligo, will provide much-needed information about life in a later medieval Gaelic lordship and throw some light on the history of a prominent Irish sept.

50 O'Conor, 'Castle studies in Ireland', p. 333; T. Finan, 'Introduction: Moylurg and Lough Cé in the later Middle Ages' in Finan (ed.), *Medieval Lough Cé*, p. 11; see, also, H. Anderson, B. Scholkmann and M.S. Kristiansen, 'Medieval archaeology at the outset of the third millenium: research and teaching' in J. Graham-Campbell with M. Valor (eds), *The archaeology of medieval Europe*, i: *eighth to twelfth centuries AD* (Aarhus, 2007), pp 19–20, 25, 27–8.

CHAPTER TWO

Moygara Castle: a history

ANNE CONNON

INTRODUCTION

Situated on the north-east slopes of Mullaghthee, overlooking the waters of Lough Gara, stand the remains of Moygara Castle. The epithet 'Moygara' refers to the plain (*magh*) of the O'Gara (Ó Gadhra) dynasty, a branch of an ancient people known as the Luighne. From at least the sixteenth century, Moygara was the *caput* or *ceann áitt* – that is to say, the centre – of the O'Gara lordship of Cúil Ó bhFind, the region corresponding to the half-barony of Coolavin in southernmost Sligo. Moygara Castle's place within the history of that lordship is the subject of this chapter.

Discussion will focus first on the earlier tower house phase of the castle, now embedded into the upstanding remains of the second and most impressive phase of masonry construction activity at the site: a very impressive bawn with four flanking towers and a gatehouse.[1] The chapter will then proceed to an investigation of the bawn phase itself, which has been dated generally on architectural grounds to somewhere between the late sixteenth century and early to mid-seventeenth century. On analogy with castles and fortifications elsewhere in north-west Ireland, however, a more specific date was suggested for this phase: somewhere between *c*.1610 and the mid- to late 1630s, but possibly as late as the 1640s.[2] An attempt to determine who was responsible for building the bawn phase of Moygara Castle lies at the heart of this part of the discussion. Before grappling with the history of either phase of the castle, though, the chapter will first outline the territory of Coolavin and the successive waves of peoples who occupied it.

COOLAVIN

The half-barony of Coolavin came into being in the latter half of the sixteenth century when the province of Connacht underwent shiring by the Tudor government. In addition to delimiting the borders of the various counties, the shiring process included the creation of a series of baronies whose boundaries were based on those of pre-existing lordships. In this way, the half-barony of Coolavin was created out of the territory of the O'Gara lordship. The civil parishes of Kilfree and Killaraght and the

---

1 See chapter 4.   2 See chapter 5.

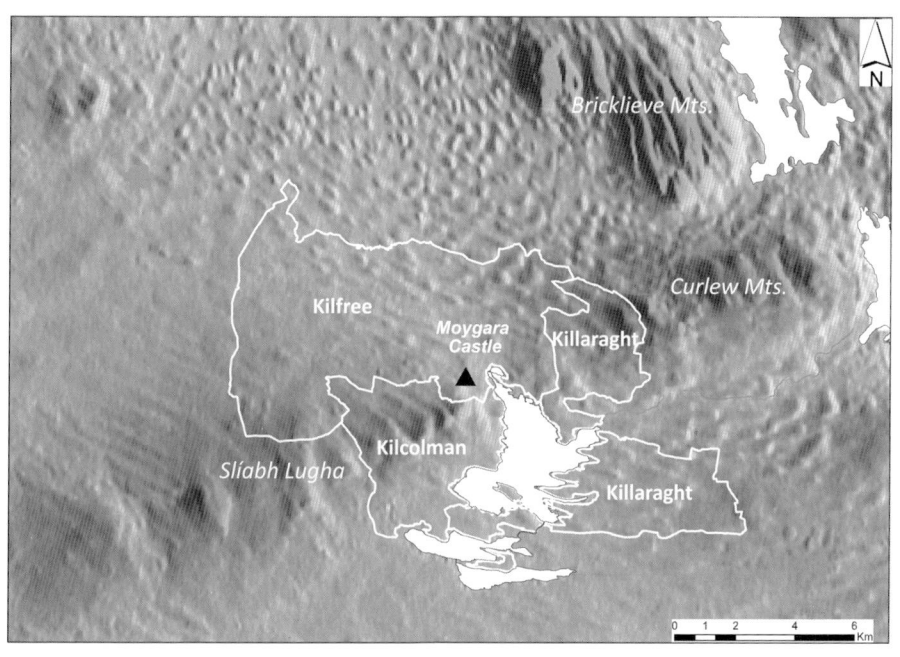

2.1 The topography and parishes of the half-barony of Coolavin (© Anne Connon).

easternmost portion of the civil parish of Kilcolman lay within Coolavin (fig. 2.1); the rest of Kilcolman lay in the barony of Costello.[3] When creating the baronies, adherence to the boundaries of the lordships on which they were based took precedence over maintaining the integrity of the older parish boundaries that lay within them. Since the parish of Kilcolman had been split between the O'Gara and Mac Costello lordships, so was Kilcolman split between the baronies of Coolavin and Costello. All three of the Coolavin parishes are now located in Co. Sligo, but cartographic evidence from the late sixteenth to mid-seventeenth centuries suggests that the part of Killaraght lying to the east of Lough Gara – that is, all of Killaraght except the townlands of Lomcloon and Clooncuny – originally lay in Co. Roscommon (figs 2.2 and 2.3; see fig. 2.4 for a map of townlands in Coolavin).[4] Over the centuries, control of the Killaraght region appears to have shunted back and forth between the O'Gara lordship of Coolavin and the MacDermot lordship of Moylurg, a dynamic that likely informed the alternative name by which Killaraght was known: Na Ranna,

3 The Kilcolman portion of the barony of Costello is found today in Co. Roscommon. Before the late nineteenth century, though, this portion, like the rest of Costello, was part of Mayo. **4** It is possibly for this reason that Killaraght was not included in the survey of Sligo taken *c.*1635 (see the section of this chapter dealing with the implications of the 1635 survey). For maps, see: John Browne's map of Connaught and Thomond, TCD, MS 1209/68 (AD 1591), now reprinted in J.H. Andrews, 'Sir Richard Bingham and the mapping of western Ireland', *PRIA*, 103C (2003), pp 61–95, pl. v; see chapter 3, fig. 3.3; William Petty, 'Map of Sligo', 'Map of Connaught' in *Hiberniae delineatio: atlas of Ireland* (London, 1685; Newcastle-upon-Tyne, 1968).

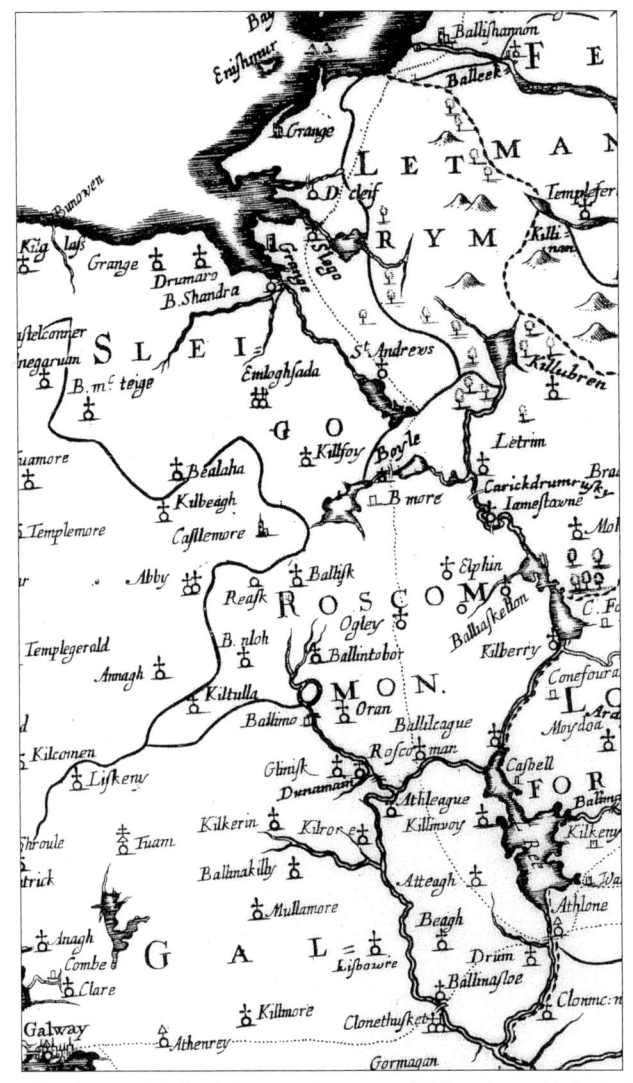

2.2 Detail from Petty's map of Ireland showing that most of Killaraght parish lay in Co. Roscommon in the late sixteenth and mid-seventeenth century (William Petty, *Hiberniae delineatio: atlas of Ireland*, 'A general mapp of Ireland' (London, 1685; Newcastle upon Tyne, 1968)).

'The Divisions'.[5] The earliest known evidence, which dates to the twelfth and thirteenth centuries, however, points to Killaraght as originally belonging to Coolavin.[6]

The earliest known occurrence of the place-name Cúil Ó bhFind – the Irish form of Coolavin – is in the long saga tale about Fionn mac Cumhaill and St Patrick known as *Acallam na senórach*, which translates as 'The Colloquy of the Ancients'. The text,

5 K.W. Nicholls, 'Rectory, vicarage and parish in the Western Irish dioceses', *JRSAI*, 101 (1971), p. 82.   **6** See appendix 2.

2.3 Detail from Petty's map of Connacht showing that most of Killaraght parish lay in
Co. Roscommon in the late sixteenth and mid-seventeenth century (William Petty, *Hiberniae
delineatio: atlas of Ireland*, 'Map of Connaught' (London, 1685; Newcastle upon Tyne, 1968)).

which likely dates to the first third of the thirteenth century, makes numerous
references to Cúil Ó bhFind, one of which states that it was located in Luighne.[7]
Another passage in the saga describes Cúil Ó bhFind as lying on the outskirts of Slíabh
Lugha.[8] It has been argued that the *Acallam* was written in the Augustinian monastery
of Roscommon, which, if correct, would make these Cúil Ó bhFind mentions quite
local references.[9]

7 W. Stokes (ed.), 'Acallamh na senórach' in W. Stokes and E. Windisch (eds), *Irische Texte*, series 4 (Leipzig,
1900), i, p. 207; A. Dooley and H. Roe (eds and trans.), *Tales of the elders of Ireland: a new translation of Acallamh
na senórach* (Oxford, 1999), p. 208.   **8** Stokes, 'Acallamh na senórach', p. 203. The equivalent passage in Dooley
and Roe, *Tales of the elders of Ireland*, is found at p. 205.   **9** A. Connon, 'The Roscommon *locus* of *Acallam na
senórach* and some thoughts as to *tempus* and *persona*' in A. Doyle and K. Murray (eds), *In dialogue with the
Agallamh* (Dublin, 2014), pp 21–59.

2.4 The parishes and townlands of Coolavin (© Anne Connon).

Evidence indicating that Cúil Ó bhFind once designated a more specific area than the general Kilfree/Killaraght/Kilcolman region is found in the Ecclesiastical Taxation of 1306. In the section for the diocese of Achonry, the Taxation has a separate entry for the church of Coolavin ('Culonyn') in addition to those for Kilfree (Kelnafriych), Killaraght (Kellethratha) and Kilcolman (Kellcalman).[10] The rural rectory of 'Cuilofind and Ranna', meanwhile, is referred to several times in papal letters dating to the first half of the fifteenth century. Here, the rectory of 'Cuilofind and Ranna' is defined variously as either the parish church of Kilfree[11] or as the parish churches of Kilfree together with Killaraght.[12] As the parish of Coolavin is not included in the seventeenth-century list of parishes within the half-barony, it was clearly absorbed by that time into one of the other parishes, most likely Kilfree. Perhaps the eponymous

10 H.S. Sweetman and G.F. Handcock (eds), *Calendar of documents relating to Ireland preserved in her majesty's Public Record Office, London 1302–1307* (London, 1866; repr. Nendeln, Liechtenstein, 1974), p. 219.   **11** W.H. Bliss and J.A. Twemlow (eds), *Calendar of entries in the papal registers relating to Great Britain and Ireland*, v: *1396–1404* (London, 1904), p. 453.   **12** J.A. Twemlow (ed.), *Calendar of entries in the papal registers relating to Great Britain and Ireland*, viii: *1427–1447* (London, 1909), p. 109.

church of the archaic townland of Clonehagglishe,[13] 'the meadow of the church' – now the modern townland of Cuilprughlish in eastern Kilfree – represented the old parish church of Coolavin. If Coolavin truly did originally designate the eastern part of Kilfree, a quick glance at the region's topography may provide insight into the derivation of its name. 'Cúil Ó bhFind' means the nook, corner, or recess of the Ó Finn family, and *cúil* seems a rather appropriate description of a region that is curled around the top of Lough Gara and tucked between Slíabh Lugha to the west and the Curlew Mountains to the east (fig. 2.1).

THE PEOPLES OF COOLAVIN

The Greagraighe

The earliest known associations of the Coolavin/Lough Gara region were with the people known as Greagraighe, whose numerous branches were scattered throughout Ireland, most notably in Connacht and in Munster.[14] The Connacht Greagraighe first appear in the seventh-century life of St Patrick by Tírechán in an episode describing how the saint entered the territory of Greagraighe and founded a church at Drummae (now the townland of Warren or Drum in the civil parish of Boyle, barony of Boyle, Co. Roscommon).[15] That same episode then mentions that St Athracht (Attracta), the eponym of the parish of Killaraght ('the church of Athracht'), received the veil from Patrick himself. The version of this episode found in the possibly ninth-century life of Patrick known as the Vita Tripartita specifically describes the Greagraighe as 'the Greagraighe of Loch Techet'; Loch Techet was the ancient name for Lough Gara.[16] The Vita Tripartita further claims that Ceall Athrachta, the church of Athracht, was in Greagraighe also.[17] From this version of the episode, it is apparent that Greagraighe was an earlier name for at least the south-eastern portion of Coolavin. The Vita Tripartita asserts that Athracht herself belonged to the Greagraighe, although her pedigree in the saints' genealogies claims that she was a distant relation of St Comhgall of Bangor, who belonged to the Uí Echach Coba of Co. Down.[18] The latter pedigree might possibly be a reflection of later links between Bangor and Killaraght.[19]

---

13 See appendix 1, entry for 'Cloonehaghlishe'. 14 D. Ó Corráin, *Ireland before the Normans* (Dublin, 1972), p. 13; T. Shingurova, '"This is why it is unlawful for a man from the Eóganachta to kill a man from the Crecraige": the origins and status of the Crecraige in medieval Ireland', *Eolas: the Journal of the American Society of Irish Medieval Studies,* 12 (2019), pp 26–42. 15 L. Bieler (ed. and trans.), *The Patrician documents in the Book of Armagh* (Dublin, 1979), p. 148. The identification of Drummae with Drum in the parish of Boyle is made by K.W. Nicholls, 'Some Patrician sites of eastern Connacht', *Dinnsenchas,* 5 (1972–3), p. 116. The foundations of a church (Mon. No. RO006-026001) can be seen in the townland of Warren or Drum today. 16 Edmund Hogan, *Onomasticon Goedelicum locorum et tribuum Hiberniae et Scotiae: an index, with identifications, to the Gaelic names of places and tribes* (Dublin, 1910; repr. 1993), p. 450. 17 K. Mulchrone (ed.), *Bethu Phátraic: the tripartite life of Patrick* (Dublin, 1939), p. 67; W. Stokes (ed. and trans.), *The tripartite life of Patrick*, 2 vols (London, 1887), i, p. 109. 18 P. Ó Riain (ed.), *Corpus genealogiarum sanctorum Hiberniae* (Dublin, 1985), §398.1; P. Ó Riain, *A dictionary of Irish saints* (Dublin, 2011), pp 81–2. 19 For a discussion of the relationship

Other Connacht locations said to lie in Greagraighe were the churches of Ceall
Churcaighe (Kilcorkey, barony of Ballintober North, Co. Roscommon) and 'Ráith
Ríoghbhaird' (barony of Tireragh, Co. Sligo, perhaps in the townland of Carrowmably,
parish of Kilmachalgan).[20] Since these locations span a wide area, it is possible that
different branches of the Greagraighe were settled in different areas of Connacht.
Possible support for this supposition lies in the obit of a late ninth-century abbot of
Clonmacnoise, Maol Tuile Ó Cúana (d. 877). The Chronicon Scotorum describes
Maol Tuile as being from the Luighne of Connacht and glosses this location with
'Greagraighe Arda'.[21] Another abbot of Clonmacnoise, this one from the mid-seventh
century, is described by a different set of annals as belonging to the Greagraighe of
Loch Techet.[22] Donnchadh Ó Corráin thought that the original extent of the
Greagraighe's Connacht territory probably ran from the barony of Leyny to
Frenchpark, which lay south of Lough Gara (Frenchpark is one of the most westerly
baronies in Co. Roscommon, encompassing the civil parishes of Tibohine and the
Roscommon portions of Kilcolman and Castlemore).[23] Paul MacCotter, meanwhile,
has suggested that in the ninth century the territory of the Greagraighe of Loch Techet
may have grown following the collapse of the Uí Ailella, expanding eastwards from
Coolavin to encompass Magh Luirg (roughly corresponding to the barony of Boyle,
Co. Roscommon) and possibly northwards into Tír Ailella (corresponding to the
barony of Tirerrill, Co. Sligo).[24]

The two obits just discussed comprise half the annalistic entries related to the
Greagraighe. The other half include: an entry for the year 753 relating that the
Greagraighe devastated the Uí Ailella, the dynasty who gave their name to the barony
of Tirerrill in south-east Sligo, not far from Coolavin; and an entry under the year 816
that records the burning and destruction of 'Foibrén in the territory of Greagraighe'.[25]
As Foibrén has plausibly been identified as Foyren in the civil parish of Fore (barony
of Fore) in north Co. Meath, just south of Lough Sheelin, this annal entry appears to
indicate that there was also a branch of the Greagraighe in Mide.[26] The notice of the
destruction of Foibrén is included in the same entry as a notice of the defeat of the
dynasty of Uí Fhiachrach Muirsce by the Síl Muireadhaigh king of Connacht,
Diarmait mac Tomaltaigh, although it is unclear if the events were meant to be
connected.[27] No further mention of the Greagraighe is found after the 877 obit for
Maol Tuile Ó Cúana; they were likely demoted after the end of the ninth century to

between the Greagraighe and the cult of Athracht, see P. MacCotter, 'Diocese of Achonry: church, land, and
history', *Peritia*, 24–5 (2013–14), pp 261–3.   **20** N. Ó Muraíle (ed. and trans.), *An leabhar mór na ngenealach:
the great book of Irish genealogies, by Dubhaltach Mac Fhirbhisigh*, 5 vols (Dublin, 2004), iv, p. 475.   **21** *CS*
s.a. 877.   **22** *ATig* 665.   **23** Ó Corráin, *Ireland before the Normans*, p. 13.   **24** MacCotter, 'Diocese of
Achonry', p. 162; see, also, Paul MacCotter, *Medieval Ireland: territorial, political and economic divisions* (Dublin,
2014), p. 211.   **25** 'loscadh 7 orggain Foibrein i crich Graicraigi', *AU* 816.8.   **26** E. Moore, 'Foibrén in Mide',
JRSAI, 142–3 (2012–13), pp 188–90.   **27** The Uí Fhiachrach Muirsce were based in the barony of Tireragh in
north-west Sligo, near the mouth of the Moy, and it is not immediately obvious why a battle fought between
them and Síl Muireadaigh would have been linked to a location in north-west Mide.

the status of a subject people of the Síl Muireadhaigh, the dynasty later led by the Ó Conchobhair (O'Conor) kings of Connacht.

The Uí Dhiarmada and Corcu Fhir Trí

Diarmait mac Tomaltaigh, the king of Connacht whose victory is recorded immediately before the destruction of Foibrén, was the ancestor of a sept of the Síl Muireadhaigh known as the Uí Dhiarmada. The Uí Dhiarmada, whose ruling line was the Ó Con Cheannáin (O'Concannon) family, are traditionally associated with the region around the barony of Tiaquin in east Co. Galway. A section of the Uí Dhiarmada genealogies, however, claims that they were originally based in the territory of 'Anarta and In Caladh', close to the territory of Diarmait's foster father, the king of Corcu Fhir Trí.[28] The Corcu Fhir Trí were a people who intermittently held the kingship of the Luighne of Connacht throughout the late ninth and tenth centuries. The fact that their eponymous ancestor Fear Trí is sometimes referred to as 'Lughna Fear Trí' would seem to reflect an attempt to link them genealogically with the Luighne.[29] However, the earliest genealogies give them a different pedigree, tracing their descent to Fiachu Súighde, son of Feidhlimidh Reachtmhár, alleged ancestor of the Déisi and Corcu Roídhe, and brother of Conn Céatchathach, ancestor of the Connachta.[30]

The Corcu Fhir Trí were based in the ancient territory of Corann, a region partially but not completely represented by the barony of Corran in south Sligo.[31] Given that the original territory of Uí Dhiarmada supposedly lay close to that of Corcu Fhir Trí, one possible location for 'In Caladh' is the townland of Callow or Runawillin, lying on the southern shores of Lough Gara (in the civil parish of Kilnamanagh, barony of Frenchpark, Co. Roscommon).[32] Further place-name evidence that might support this identification includes the possibility that the townland of Cloonmacmullan in east Kilnamanagh reflects the name of a branch of the Uí Dhiarmada known as the Ó Mothláin (O'Mullen),[33] while the obsolete townland of 'Cloondermot' in

---

28 *Lec*, 67vc23; *BB*, 101c27; *An leabhar mór na ngenealach*, i, §236.8, p. 534. **29** D. Ó Corrain, 'Historical need and literary narrative' in D. Ellis Evans, J.G. Griffith and E.M. Jope (eds), *Proceedings of the Seventh International Congress of Celtic Studies* (Oxford, 1986), p. 149. **30** T. Ó Raithbheartaigh (ed. and trans.), *Genealogical tracts 1* (Dublin, 1932), §183, p. 190; Ó Corráin, 'Historical need', p. 150. **31** Hogan, *Onomasticon Goedelicum*, pp 291, 294; MacCotter, *Medieval Ireland*, p. 137. **32** Nollaig Ó Muraíle suggests that the 'In Chaladh' meant here is the Callows region in southern Co. Roscommon i.e. Callowbeg in the parish of Drum (*An leabhar mór na ngenealach*, iv, p. 414). The Locus project has recently suggested that 'In Chaladh' is to be identified with the townland of Callow in the civil parish of Killasser, barony of Gallen, Co. Mayo. See D. Ó Murchadha, K. Murray and P. Ó Riain (eds), *Historical dictionary of Gaelic placenames/Foclóir stairiúil áitainmneacha na Gaeilge*: 'Letter A' of revised *Onomasticon* (London, 2003), i, p. 57. This identification is in line with an interpretation of Corann in its broadest sense as extending to Mayo; however, the north Roscommon identification of 'In Chaladh' being located on the southern shore of Lough Gara would seem to be a better fit with Síl Muireadhaigh holdings at this point in time. A crannog, known as Bawn Island, occurs in this Callow townland on Lough Gara, just offshore from a late sixteenth-century stone-walled enclosure or bawn – see K. O'Conor, 'English settlement and change in Roscommon during the late sixteenth and seventeenth centuries' in A. Horning, R. Ó Baoill, C. Donnelly and P. Logue (eds), *The post-medieval archaeology of Ireland, 1550–1850* (Dublin, 2007), pp 197–8. **33** For the Ó Mothláin, see *Lec*, 67Rb8; *BB*, 100c8; *An leabhar mór na ngenealach*,

Kilnamanagh (possibly represented today by the modern townland of Cloonacarrow) may have originally been Cluain Úa Diarmada, 'the meadow of Uí Dhiarmada'.[34]

If the claim of the genealogies is accurate, and if the Kilnamanagh identification of 'In Caladh' is correct, then the Uí Dhiarmada would have been in control of the southern shores of Lough Gara around the mid-ninth century. If so, it is extremely interesting to note that another branch of Uí Dhiarmada, closely related to the Ó Mothláin line, is none other than the Ó Finn line.[35] It is certainly tempting to identify this family with the eponymous O'Finns of Cúil Ó bhFind and surmise that the Uí Dhiarmada also controlled the northern shores of Lough Gara. An alternative suggestion previously put forward as to the identity of the O'Finns is the ruling O'Finn line of the Calraighe of Lough Gill (near the civil parish of Calry, barony of Carbury, Co. Sligo).[36] While the north Sligo location of the Calry O'Finns makes the latter identification not implausible, the possible Lough Gara associations of the Uí Dhiarmada O'Finns would seem a better fit for Coolavin. Regardless of the identity of the O'Finns, however, by the first third of the thirteenth century, and possibly considerably earlier, Coolavin was considered to be in Luighne territory. This conclusion can be drawn from *Acallam na senórach*'s description of Cúil Ó bhFind as being located in Luighne.[37] The Strafford Survey notes for Sligo, dated to 1635, which detail the possessions of a Finn family in the parishes of Emlaghfad, Kilmorgan, Kilshalvy and Toomour, all in the barony of Corran, suggests that the O'Finns of Coolavin did not move very far away after their displacement.[38]

The Luighne of Connacht in the pre-Norman era

Although accorded a Munster origin by the genealogists, during the early medieval period the Luighne were to be found in the northern kingdoms of Mide and Connacht. Paul MacCotter explains that Luighne was the name of both a larger regional kingdom in Connacht and one of the three smaller local kingdoms that lay within it. The regional kingdom of Luighne roughly corresponded to the diocese of Achonry, which encompasses the Sligo baronies of Leyny (which took its name from 'Luighne') and Corran, and the half-barony of Coolavin, as well as most of the barony of Gallen and the northern half of Costello, both in Co. Mayo (fig. 2.5). The more local kingdom, meanwhile, would have corresponded to the baronies of Leyny and Gallen.[39]

The first king of the Luighne of Connacht named in the annals is Taichleach, son of Cenn Faoladh, who died in 734.[40] From Taichleach descended Sóergus, son of Bécc,

i, §234.4, p. 528.   **34** R.C. Simmington (ed.), *Books of Survey and Distribution, being abstracts of various surveys and instruments of title, 1636–1703*, i: *Roscommon* (Dublin, 1949), p. 130.   **35** *Lec*, 67rc29; *BB*, 101a24; *An leabhar mór na ngenealach*, i, §235.4, p. 530.   **36** E. MacLysaght, *Irish families: their names, arms, and origins* (Dublin, 1991). For the O'Finns of Calry, see J. Carney (ed.), *Topographical poems by Seaán Mór Ó Dubhagáin and Giolla-Na-Naomh Ó hUidhrín* (Dublin, 1943), p. 25.   **37** See fn 5.   **38** W.G. Wood-Martin, *History of Sligo, county and town, from the earliest ages to the close of the reign of Queen Elizabeth* (Dublin, 1882), p. 175.   **39** MacCotter, *Medieval Ireland*, pp 139–40; Hogan, *Onomasticon Goedelicum*, pp 507–8.   **40** *AU* 734.9, 771.7.

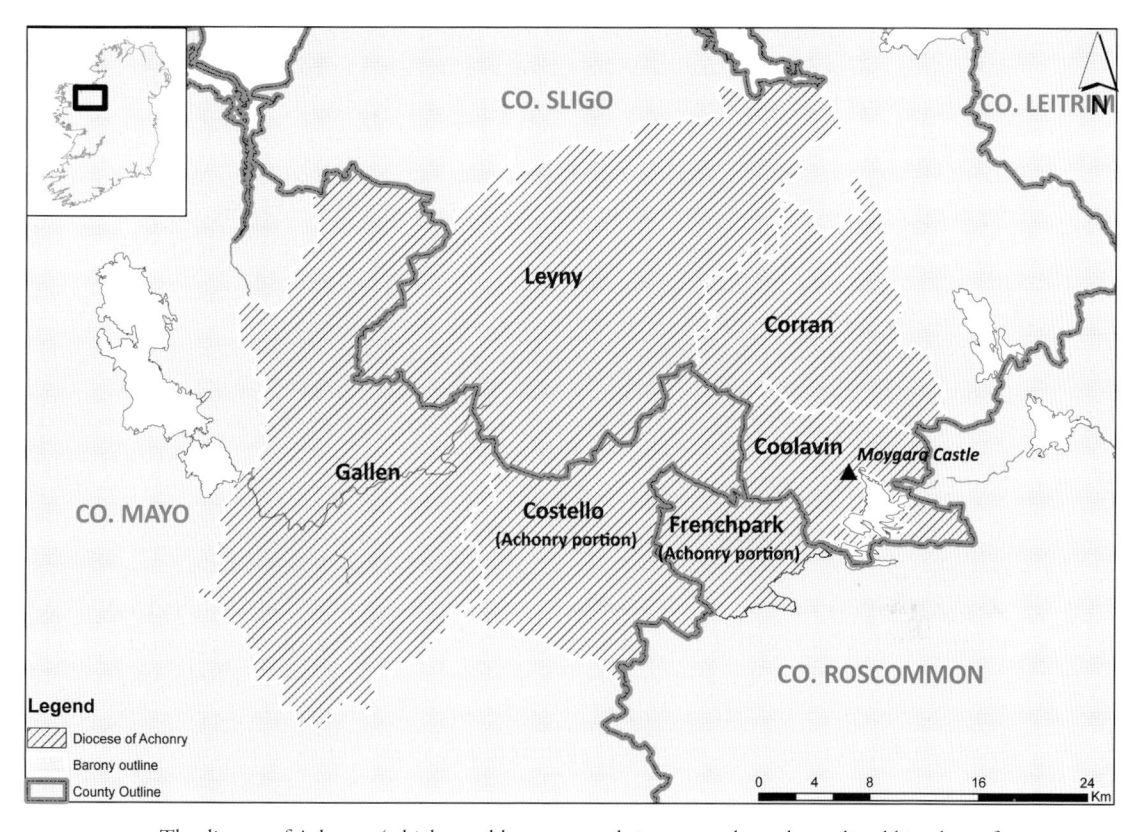

2.5 The diocese of Achonry (which roughly corresponds in area to the early medieval kingdom of Luighne) (© Anne Connon).

mutual ancestor of both the O'Hara (Ó hEaghra) and O'Gara (Ó Gadhra) dynasties of Sligo.[41] Although the O'Gara line provided a king of Luighne in the tenth century and another in the twelfth century,[42] it was the O'Hara dynasty, together with the Ó Doibhiléin dynasty of the Corcu Fhir Trí of Corann,[43] who were to dominate the Luighne kingship. The O'Gara line appear to have been compensated for their demotion from the overall kingship with a sub-kingship alternatively referred to in the second half of the tenth century as the kingship of Gaileanga[44] and the kingship of South Luighne;[45] from the late twelfth to the late thirteenth centuries, their title changes to 'king of Slíabh Lugha'.[46] Gaileanga corresponds to the barony of Gallen in Co. Mayo, while the territory of Slíabh Lugha would have encompassed Coolavin together with the civil parishes of Kilmovee, Kilbeagh, Kilcolman and Castlemore in

41 S. Pender (ed.), 'The O'Clery Book of Genealogies', *AH*, 18 (1951), §2043; see chapter 6.   **42** *AFM* 931, 1128.   **43** *AFM* 885, 928; *CS* 921 [*recte* 922], 945 [*recte* 946]; *ATig* 985, 989, 1031; *AU* 994.1 [*ATig* 994]. **44** *AFM* 993 [*ATig* 994].   **45** *AFM* 964 [*recte* 966]. The *Chronicon Scotorum* refers to the same individual as 'Righ Luigne', without qualifying him as king of only south Luighne.   **46** *AU* 1181.7; *ALC* 1208.1; *AConn*

the northern half of the baronies of Costello, Co. Mayo, and Frenchpark, Co. Roscommon.[47] It is uncertain whether the O'Gara sub-kingship of South Luighne contained both Gallen *and* Slíabh Lugha or if the twelfth-century switch in title connoted a similar switch in territory.

In 1333, the Norman cantred of Slíabh Lugha (Sleoflow) contained not only Slíabh Lugha but also the territories of Airtech (Tibohine in the southern half of the barony of Frenchpark, Co. Roscommon), Ciarraige Locha na nAirnead and Ciarraige Uachtarach (the civil parishes of Knock, Aghamore, Bekan and Annagh in the southern part of the barony of Costello).[48] It may be that these additional three regions were likewise included in the O'Gara kingship of Slíabh Lugha; however, the fact that none of the three were part of the diocese of Achonry – and thus less likely to have been part of the original kingdom of Luighne – may tell against this possibility.

The Luighne in the Anglo-Norman period

With the coming of the Anglo-Normans, the lands of the O'Gara dynasty were reduced to a fraction of their original size. After 1235, the kingdom of Luighne – like all of Connacht with the exception of the 'king's Five Cantreds'[49] – fell under the control of the Anglo-Norman lord, Richard de Burgh. De Burgh granted the cantreds of Luighne and Slieve Lugha to Hugh de Lacy, together with the cantreds of Corran, Carbury-Drumcliff and Tireragh on the Moy.[50] De Lacy, in turn, made several large sub-grants of territory to his own supporters, splitting up the kingdom of Luighne in the process. He granted the northern half of the cantred of Luighne, together with the cantred of Carbury, to Maurice Fitz Gerald, while the southern half of the cantred – the O'Gara half – went to Jordan of Exeter.[51] Jordan then divided his half of Luighne in two and gave one of the sections to Fitz Gerald. This part of the southern half of Luighne, together with Fitz Gerald's original northern half of the cantred, constitute the modern barony of Leyny. Jordan's remaining part of the southern half of Luighne constitutes the modern barony of Gallen.[52] The O'Gara cantred of Slieve Lugha, meanwhile, was granted to Miles de Nangle (De Angulo) (d. 1259), possibly as part of the marriage agreement between Miles and Hugh de Lacy's daughter.[53] The cantred of Slieve Lugha was to become the northern half of the present-day barony of Costello,

1227.4, 1256.4, 1285.6.   **47** K. Nicholls, 'Rectory, vicarage, and parish', p. 75; MacCotter, *Medieval Ireland*, p. 146.   **48** MacCotter, *Medieval Ireland*, pp 146–7.   **49** The five cantreds 'nearest to Athlone', which King John reserved for himself, were granted to the O'Conor kings and basically represented the O'Conor patrimonial kingdom of Síl Muireadhaigh (Sil Murray). This kingdom is roughly approximated by the modern diocese of Elphin. It is also important to remember that the present county of Leitrim was not included in this grant to de Burgh, as it was then part of Breifne. For a recent publication outlining the history and archaeology of the Five Cantreds, see T. Finan, *Landscape and history on the medieval Irish frontier: the king's cantreds in the thirteenth century* (Turnhout, 2016).   **50** G.H. Orpen, *Ireland under the Normans, 1169–1333* (Dublin, 2005), pp 378–9; see, also, K. O'Conor, 'Introduction' in U. Egan, E. Byrne and M. Sleeman, *Archaeologial inventory of Co. Sligo, i: South Sligo* (Dublin, 2005), pp ix–xii.   **51** Orpen, *Ireland under the Normans*, pp 380–1.   **52** Ibid., p. 380.   **53** Ibid., p. 382.

the lordship controlled by Miles' descendants, the Mac Costellos (see fig. 2.5 for the boundaries of modern baronies).

By the middle of the fourteenth century, the O'Haras had once again taken control of Leyny,[54] but the O'Garas were not to be so fortunate. Deprived of the majority of their territory by the Anglo-Normans, they became restricted to the most easterly part of their original domain: the region of Coolavin. As Orpen notes, there is no record of hostilities between the O'Garas and the Mac Costellos during this transitional period;[55] however, the annals do record conflict between themselves and the Anglo-Norman figure David, son of Richard Cúisín (Cushing). In 1256, Cushing treacherously killed Ruaidrí Ó Gadhra, 'king of Sliabh Lugha' and destroyed his castle (*a chaslen*).[56] The fact that Cushing is described as O'Gara's 'gossip' or foster-father, however, suggests that relations had not always been so strained between the two, but rather that the O'Garas had attempted to come to some sort of *modus vivendi* with their Norman supplanters. Later that year, Aodh O'Conor, son of Felim O'Conor, 'son of the king of Connacht, took eye-for-an-eye type revenge on Cushing for his treatment of O'Gara, not only killing him but also destroying his castle and all those in it.[57] The annals add that O'Conor then took control of all 'Loch Dechet' (i.e. Lough Gara), a statement that implies that Cushing's castle lay close by the lake. Although the annals do not locate Cushing's castle in any more detail, onomastic evidence suggests his castle lay to the north-west of Lough Gara: according to O'Donovan's Ordnance Survey letters, there was a fort known as Lios a Chúisín in Greyfield, a townland on the northern border of the civil parish of Kilfree.[58]

The location of the O'Gara fortress destroyed by Cushing is unknown; Máire Garvey suggests that it might have been at Castlemore, later the site of the great Mac Costello castle.[59] The same author suggests that it was at about this period that the O'Garas were confined to the territory of Coolavin, with Cushing's destruction of their castle having been a factor in their expulsion to the area.[60] Although the first instance of the title 'Lord of Coolavin' in connection with an O'Gara does not occur until almost two hundred years later in 1434,[61] a much earlier record may connect the family with the Coolavin area by at least the end of the thirteenth century. This is an entry under the year 1285 in the Annals of Connacht and the Annals of Loch Cé that relates that 'Ruaidhrí Ua Gadhra, king of Slíabh Lugha' (a different Ruaidhrí than the

---

54 Ibid., p. 380. **55** Ibid., p. 382. **56** *AConn* 1256.4. **57** *AConn* 1256.18; *ALC* 1256. **58** M. O'Flanagan (ed.), *Letters containing information relative to the antiquities of the county of Sligo* (Bray, 1927), p. 94, 229, Special Collections, National University of Ireland, Galway copy. Two ringforts can be seen in Greyfield townland today. There was a third fort standing in the townland in 1835 but the location of this earthwork is presently unknown, indicating that it has been levelled since the latter year. See Egan, Byrne and Sleeman, *Archaeologial inventory of Co. Sligo*, pp 220–1. **59** M. Garvey, *Mid-Connacht: the ancient territory of Sliabh Lugha* (Dublin, 1995), p. 14; a hall house castle of thirteenth-century date survives at Castlemore today, so this is a possibility. See C.J. Lynn, 'Some 13th-century castle sites in the west of Ireland: notes on a preliminary reconnaissance', *JGAHS*, 40 (1985–6), pp 98–100. **60** M. Garvey, *Mid-Connacht*, p. 14. **61** *AConn* 1434.2.

one slain by Cushing) was killed by the Anglo-Norman Mac Feorais 'on his own lake';[62] the version of this entry found in the early seventeenth-century Annals of the Four Masters specifically identifies that lake as Lough Gara.[63] Since the Four Masters elsewhere contain many O'Gara entries not found in other annals – Fergal O'Gara was the patron of the Four Masters and may have made available to its compilers otherwise unknown records concerning the area – it is quite possible that the annalists were drawing on a contemporary source that has not survived to the present day for their additional information. It is also possible, however, that the name Lough Gara was a retroactive gloss based on the annalists' knowledge of the family's later whereabouts.

HISTORICAL REFERENCES TO AN EARLIER CASTLE AT MOYGARA

Annal references

The first references explicitly linking the O'Garas to a castle at Moygara occur in 1538. In an entry discussing a hosting made by Manus O'Donnell, king of Tir Connell, into Lower Connacht, the Annals of Connacht state that O'Donnell's son, Niall Garbh, was killed by a gunshot at 'Magh h. Gadhra' (i.e. Moygara). His death occurred while O'Donnell's forces were going around Moygara on the way back to Donegal after capturing the castle of Sligo and destroying the country of Moylurg.[64] The version of this entry in the Annals of Loch Cé reports that O'Donnell's son was killed while the host was going around *caislein I Gadhra*, 'the castle of O'Gara'.[65] The seventeenth-century Annals of the Four Masters combine the two versions and add some additional information, claiming that Niall Garbh was killed when O'Donnell took *c-caislén dian h-ainm Magh Uí Ghadhra*, 'the castle called Magh Uí Ghadhra'.[66] The main road during the whole medieval period between Roscommon and Sligo (which was also the Dublin/Sligo road, which came via Athlone) went across the Boyle River at Boyle Abbey and then through the pass in the Curlews at Bealach Buidhe (Ballaghboy in the civil parish of Aghanagh, Co. Sligo).[67] This routeway was known as *Bóthar an Iarla Ruaidh* and bits of it can still be made out. An alternative route across the Curlews into the Sligo area, known as *Bóthar an Corann*, veered off north-westwards from this main road at Boyle.[68] However, the 1538 annal entry indicates that the gap between Sliabh Lugha and the Curlews at Lough Gara was yet a third alternative route between Sligo and Roscommon (fig. 2.6). Moygara Castle, overlooking the lower land between the

62 *AConn* 1285.6; *ALC* 1285. **63** *AFM* 1285. **64** *AConn* 1538.5. **65** *ALC* 1538.5. **66** *AFM* 1538. **67** M. O'Dowd, *Power, politics and land: early modern Sligo 1568–1688* (Belfast, 1991), pp 2, 12; S. Moore, 'The Bealach Buidhe, the Red Earl's Road and Bóthar an Corann in Counties Sligo and Roscommon: an overview', *Journal of the Sligo Field Club*, 1 (2015), pp 65–88; see, also, C. Ó Lochlainn, 'Roadways in ancient Ireland' in J. Ryan (ed.), *Féil-sgríbhinn Eoin Mhic Néill: essays and studies presented to Professor Eoin MacNeill on the occasion of his seventieth birthday, May 15th 1938* (Dublin, 1940), pp 465–74. **68** Moore, 'The Bealach Buidhe, the Red Earl's Road and Bóthar an Corann', pp 60–1.

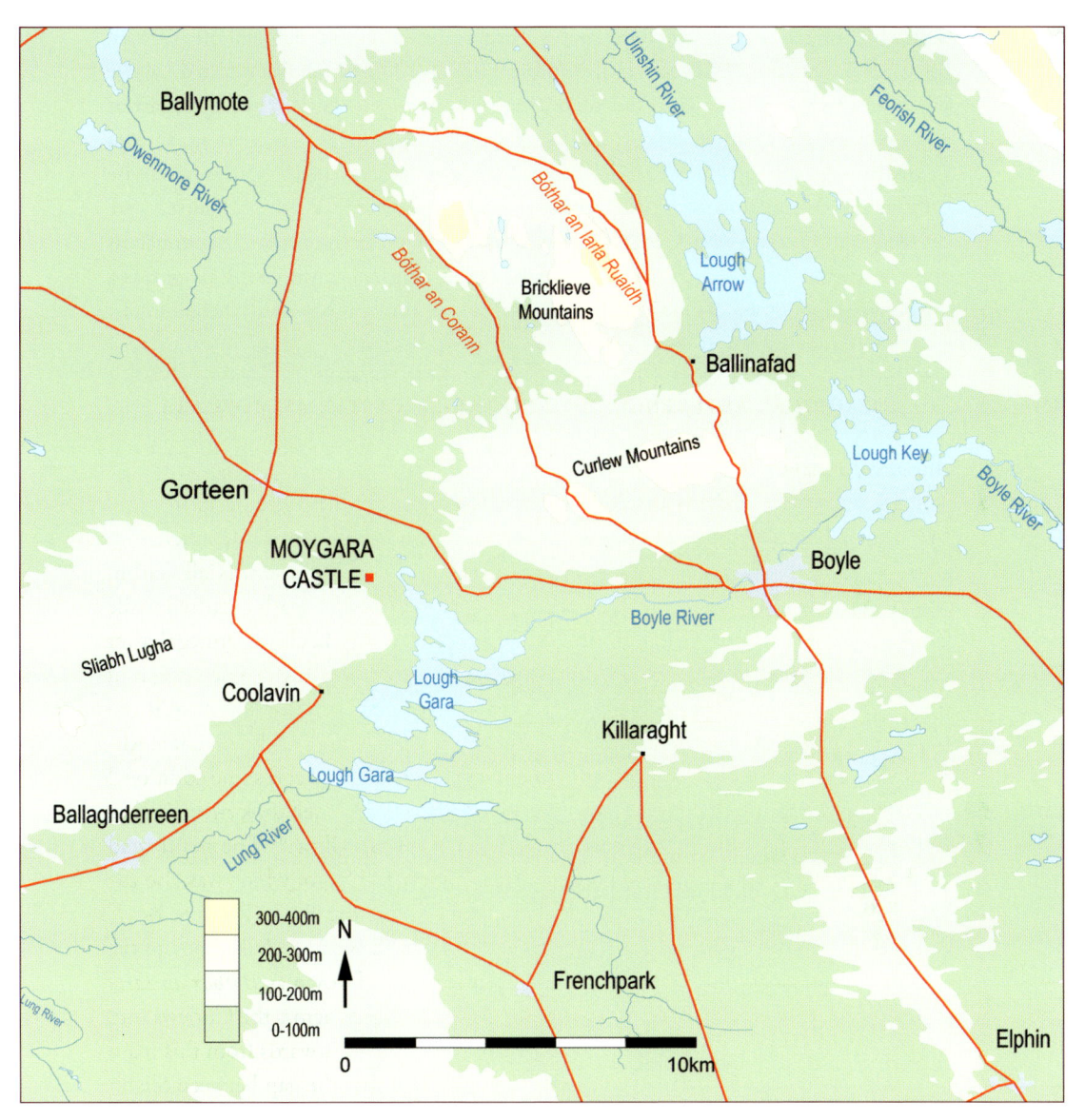

2.6 The main medieval routeways in the north Roscommon/south Sligo region. Moygara Castle lay near one of these important routeways into the Sligo area (map courtesy of Sam Moore).

outskirts of Sliabh Lugha and the lough, would thus have been of considerable strategic importance.[69]

A second reference to the castle at Moygara occurs fifty years later in a description of an encounter between O'Conor Sligo, Cathal Óg O'Conor, and a number of Gaelic

69 See chapter 3.

lords of Connacht on the one hand and a 'great army' of Scottish mercenaries sent by the English president of Connacht, Captain Nicholas Malby, on the other. In 1581 O'Conor and his men attacked the Scots at Loch Feeny in Corran and the mercenaries retreated up to Coolavin. There, the latter attacked the local Gaelic lords, killing Diarmait Óg, son of Cian O'Gara, among others, and burned Caislén Mhaighe h-Í Ghadra, 'Moygara Castle'.[70]

The final reference to Moygara in the annals yet again involves an O'Donnell. In 1602, when the English of Roscommon and Upper Connacht mustered an army to march against Rory O'Donnell, they stopped at Boyle Abbey. O'Donnell and O'Conor Sligo gathered their own army in turn, and went across the Curlews, pitching their camp on the other side of Boyle from the English. In order to alleviate plundering of their lands while they were gone, the Annals of the Four Masters report that O'Donnell and O'Conor took their people, property and cattle with them 'from Moy O'Gara in Cúil Ó bhFinn to the eastern extremity of the Coirrshliabh'.[71] The sense of this phrase appears to be that the annalist is indicating the western and eastern limits of the territory from which O'Conor Sligo and O'Donnell gathered their people.[72]

While this last annal reference is to Moygara the place, rather than to Moygara the castle, the two earlier sixteenth-century annal entries are specifically about Caislén Mhaighe h-Í Ghadra. The *caislén* they speak of presumably refers to the fifteenth- or sixteenth-century structure, the first recognizable masonry phase at the site. This seems to have been a tower house, whose much disintegrated remains are embedded into the north wall of the current castle bawn as a near featureless rectangular structure.[73] It is also possible that they refer to the later bawn, though, as discussed in greater detail later on, it is argued throughout this volume that it is much more likely that this structure was not built until the seventeenth century.[74] The memory of this earlier tower house castle is likewise embedded into the archaic townland name 'Carrowcaslan', the quarter of the *caislén*. 'Carrowcaslan' is one of two quarters of land that comprise the modern day townland of Moygara.[75]

It is uncertain where exactly the chief O'Gara stronghold lay prior to the construction of the tower house. At the start of this project, it was thought that the tower-house site might also have been the location of the earlier stronghold since geophysical survey had revealed an oval enclosure underlying the current castle, perhaps indicating continuity of settlement at the site.[76] However, subsequent excavation has shown that this enclosure, certainly at first glance, was not really defensive or domestic in nature.[77] Another possible location for the earlier O'Gara *ceann áitt* or *caput* could have been one of the moated sites scattered throughout

---

70 *ALC* 1581.18.   **71** *AFM* 1602.   **72** At that time, O'Donnell's people and cattle were spread throughout Sligo (*AFM* 1602).   **73** See chapters 8, 4 and 10.   **74** See chapters 4 and 5.   **75** The other is the quarter of Killnaskorny. See appendix 1.   **76** See chapter 7.   **77** See chapter 8; see, also, chapter 10.

2.7 Moated site, Killaraght, Co. Sligo (courtesy of the National Monuments Service, Dublin).

Coolavin: the area around Lough O'Gara has been identified as one of three clusters of moated sites in south Sligo. More than a fifth of the twenty-eight moated sites in south Sligo are in the civil parish of Killaraght (two in the townland of Killaraght (see fig. 2.7), and one each in the townlands of Ardsoreen, Cuppanagh and Derrymore island), while another is found at Gortygara in the civil parish of Kilfree.[78] While moated sites have traditionally been identified as having been the residences of Anglo-Norman and English settlers, particularly those settlers who lived in frontier areas, a number of scholars have argued that they were also the homes of high-ranking Gaelic nobles in north Connacht during the thirteenth and fourteenth centuries.[79] Of the moated sites in Coolavin, the one located in Gortygara in the north-west of Kilfree is

78 Egan, Byrne and Sleeman, *Archaeological inventory of County Sligo*, pp 467–70.   **79** K. O'Conor, *The archaeology of medieval rural settlement in Ireland* (Dublin, 1998), p. 98; idem, 'The morphology of Gaelic lordly sites in north Connacht' in P. Duffy, D. Edwards and E. FitzPatrick (eds), *Gaelic Ireland, c.1250–c.1650: land, lordship and settlement* (Dublin, 2001), pp 338–40; T. Finan and K. O'Conor, 'The moated site at Cloonfree, Co. Roscommon', *JGAHS*, 54 (2002), pp 72–87; see, also, R. McNeary and B. Shanahan, 'Settlement and enclosure in a medieval Gaelic lordship: a case study from the territory of the O'Conors of north Roscommon, Ireland' in R. Compatangelo, J-R. Bertrand and P-Y. Laffront (eds), *Marqueurs des paysages et systemes socio-economiques actes de colloque COST de Le Mans: landmarks and socio-economic systems: constructing of pre-industrial landscapes and their perception by contemporary societies* (Rennes, 2008), p. 191; R. McNeary and B. Shanahan, 'Roscommon landscape' in *The Discovery Programme/An Clár Fionnachtana: 2008 Annual Report* (Dublin, 2008), p. 23; K. O'Conor, N. Brady, A. Connon and C. Fidalgo-Romo, 'The Rock of Lough Cé' in T. Finan (ed.), *Medieval Lough*

perhaps the most likely to have been an O'Gara stronghold. The moated site may be the eponymous *lios* of Lissoshinagh, an archaic quarter of land now subsumed within the modern townland of Gortygara. This townland, which bears the O'Gara name, is consistently listed as part of the O'Gara landholdings in the seventeenth century.[80] The most probable candidate for the location of the earlier main O'Gara stronghold, however, is in fact a crannog out on Lough Gara. Research in recent years has clearly shown that crannogs continued to be used as fortified residences by Gaelic princes and lords long after the end of the early medieval period (the era that they were traditionally associated with by Irish scholarship) right down to the early seventeenth century.[81]

As witnessed by the fact that there are several references made by the governor of Connacht, Sir Richard Bingham, to staying in Moygara Castle ('the castle of Moygharee') in September of 1586, the earlier castle was evidently repaired and put back into use after being burnt by the Scots in 1581.[82] After Bingham's stay at Moygara, he went on directly to Castlemore, which he refers to as 'a place as commodious to answer the service as the other was'. It is quite plausible that 'the other' here refers to Moygara Castle; if so, then Bingham's remarks suggest that Moygara Castle was fairly large.[83]

Moygara Castle next appears in a deed dated to the 21 May 1603, between Irriel O'Gara, Lord of Coolavin, and Donogh O'Conor Sligo. The deed granted all Irriel's interest 'forever' in the castles of Moygara, Cuppanagh and Derrymore to O'Conor Sligo, along with 'all the lands, tenements, lordships, mill, territories, etcetera to the

Cé: history, archaeology and landscape (Dublin, 2010), pp 30–1; R. McNeary and B. Shanahan, 'The March in Roscommon, 1170–1400: culture, contact, continuity and change' in J. Ní Ghrádaigh and E. O'Byrne (eds), *The March in the islands of the medieval West* (Leiden and Boston, 2012), p. 210; T. Finan, 'Moated sites in County Roscommon, Ireland: a statistical approach' in P. Ettel, A.-M. Flambard-Héricher and K. O'Conor (eds), *Château Gaillard, 26: L'environment du château* (Caen, 2014), pp 177–80; E. FitzPatrick, 'The last kings of Ireland: material expressions of Gaelic lordship, *c.*1300–1400' in K. Buchanan, L.H.S. Dean and M. Penman (eds), *Medieval and early modern representations of authority in Scotland and the British Isles* (Oxford, 2016), p. 204; K. O'Conor and T. Finan, 'Medieval settlement in north Roscommon, *c.*1200AD–*c.*1350AD' in R. Farrell, K. O'Conor and M. Potter (eds), *Roscommon history and society: interdisciplinary essays on the history of an Irish county* (Dublin, 2018), pp 116–22. **80** See appendix 1, entry for 'Lissoshinagh'. **81** O'Conor, *The archaeology of medieval rural settlement*, pp 79–85; idem, 'The morphology of Gaelic lordly sites in north Connacht', pp 337–8; A. O'Sullivan, *The archaeology of lake settlement in Ireland* (Dublin, 1998), pp 152–5, 167–76; idem, 'Crannogs in late medieval Gaelic Ireland, *c.*1350–*c.*1650' in P. Duffy, D. Edwards and E. Fitzpatrick (eds), *Gaelic Ireland c.1250–c.1650: land, lordship and settlement* (Dublin, 2001), pp 397–417; C. Fredengren, *Crannogs* (Dublin, 2002), pp 265–76, 282, 287; N. Brady and K. O'Conor, 'The later medieval usage of crannogs in Ireland', *Ruralia*, 5 (2005), pp 127–36; C. Foley and B. Williams, 'The crannogs of County Fermanagh' in M. Meek (ed.), *The modern traveller to our past* (Belfast, 2006), pp 53–64; K. O'Conor, '*Crannóga* in late medieval Ireland' in E. Campbell, E. FitzPatrick and A. Horning (eds), *Becoming and belonging in Gaelic Ireland, AD 1200–1600: essays in identity and cultural practice* (Cork, 2018), pp 148–66; O'Conor and Finan, 'Medieval settlement in north Roscommon, *c.*1200AD–*c.*1350AD', pp 113–16; K. O'Conor and C. Fredengren, 'Medieval settlement in Leitrim, 1169–*c.*1380AD' in L. Kelly and B. Scott (eds), *Leitrim history and society: interdisciplinary essays on the history of an Irish county* (Dublin, 2019), pp 88–94. **82** H.C. Hamilton (ed.), *Calendar of state papers, Ireland, Elizabeth, 1586–1588,* 126 (London, 1877), pp 164, 177. **83** I owe this point, as well as the Bingham references, to Maura

same belonging'.[84] The castle also appears repeatedly as 'the castle, town, and lands of Moygara' or as the 'manor, castle, town, and lands of Moygara' in landholding records dated between 1614 and 1617.[85] Since the records in question detail the possessions of Irriel O'Gara, and of his grandson and heir Fergal, the O'Gara claim to Moygara evidently was not 'forever' lost to O'Conor Sligo after all.

Mary O'Dowd has suggested that Irriel O'Gara made over his estate to O'Conor Sligo as a way of actually protecting his land. O'Conor had the support of the crown and O'Gara may have reckoned that he would have been able to protect the lands of Coolavin from any aggressively interested English, both Old and New English.[86] One of the men that O'Gara would most likely have needed protection from was Sir William Taaffe. The Taaffes were an Old English family from the Pale in Co. Louth who acquired such extensive lands in Sligo in the sixteenth and seventeenth centuries that they became the largest resident landlords in the county.[87] Sir William Taaffe, an official of the English government in Sligo, had first imprisoned Irriel in 1586 for allegedly harbouring Scottish soldiers, and then forced the tenants of the imprisoned Irriel to leave Coolavin and move to his own lands instead.[88] According to a post-mortem inquisition of Irriel's lands taken in 1614, O'Gara had leased most of his property to Taaffe.[89] O'Dowd comments:

> Considering Taaffe's dubious land acquisitions in other baronies, it is likely that his 'lease' of the seventeenth century was a means of concealing the chicanery by which Taaffe benefited from O'Gara's lands in the sixteenth century.[90]

Regardless of their motivations, though, neither O'Conor Sligo nor Taaffe held onto O'Gara lands in the long-term. While the inquisition of 1614 acknowledges that Roger Jones, the 'heir' to O'Conor Sligo's possessions, claimed 'through a certain enfeoffment, the whole semi-barony of Coolavin', it nonetheless affirmed O'Gara ownership of Moygara Castle and the associated lands.[91]

The lands of Moygara Castle

The various landholding records indicate that the demesne lands associated with Moygara Castle – that is to say the lands from which no composition rent were due to the crown – were the quarter of Carrowcaslan itself, the quarter of Kilnaskorny (the two of which together comprise the modern townland of Moygara), the quarter of Mahanagh and the quarter of Mullaghroe. All three of the latter townlands were contiguous to Carrowcaslan, and it seems that Carrowcaslan, Kilnaskorny and

O'Gara-O'Riordan.   **84** M.C. Griffiths (ed.), *Calendar of the Irish patent rolls of James I* (Dublin, 1965), p. 475 (pat. 18, Jas. I, LXXV).   **85** See appendix 1, entry for 'Carrowcaslan' or 'Moygara'.   **86** O'Dowd, *Power, politics and land*, p. 75.   **87** Ibid., p. 95.   **88** M. O'Dowd, 'Landownership in the Sligo area, 1585–1616' (PhD, UCD, 1978), p. 436.   **89** NAI, MS RC 9/15, inq. 17, p. 515 (69).   **90** O'Dowd, 'Land ownership in the Sligo area', p. 437.   **91** NAI, MS RC 9/15, inq. 17 and inq. 19, p. 515 (69).

Mahanagh constituted the actual *magh* or plain of Moygara.[92] In addition to this core demesne, the O'Garas controlled a much larger swathe of land in Coolavin, on which they owed both composition rent to the crown and an annual return of £10 to O'Conor Sligo, the overlord of Lower Connacht.[93]

In the context of land division, a 'quarter' is the English translation of *ceathramha*, usually anglicized as 'carrow'. In many, but not all, cases, the modern townland is equivalent to one of these medieval quarters. *Ceathramha*, which corresponds to approximately 120 acres of land, refers to a quarter of a *baile. Baile*, anglicized as 'bally', is the basic territorial unit underpinning the land division of Connacht. Hard to translate, the word originally meant simply 'place', but came to mean something along the lines of 'homestead'. It was later used to translate the English word 'town'.[94] The exact number of quarters held by the O'Garas varies according to different sources. In the *Compossicion Booke of Conought*, which dates to 1585, the half-barony of Coolavin was said to contain twenty quarters.[95] Inquisitions dating to 1614 and 1615, however, enumerate over forty different quarters formerly in the possession of Irriel O'Gara.[96] Between 1614 and 1641, the precise townlands named as belonging to the head of the O'Gara family continue to vary, but the territory basically amounted to almost all of the civil parishes of Kilfree and Kilcolman (Coolavin portion), excepting church land. During Fergal's tenure at least, the O'Gara possessions also included the northern portion of Killaraght.[97] Much of the southern portion of Killaraght east of Lough Gara – excluding a small strip at the bottom of the parish in the hands of the MacDermot family – seems to have originally belonged to Boyle Abbey.[98] This portion of Killaraght eventually fell into the hands of the King family by 1616, although its ownership had earlier been contested between Theobald Dillon and Christopher Nugent.[99]

While the terms of the Composition of Connacht, agreed upon in 1585, stipulated that the head of the O'Gara family – first Irriel, and, later, Fergal – technically owned all the O'Gara lands in Coolavin, there is evidence to suggest that in the early seventeenth century, different branches of the O'Gara family either owned or were linked to specific lands within the half barony. In 1614, the patent rolls and crown rentals record that the quarter of Rinnasharragh and Caronwentyhane, now subsumed into the modern townland of Cuilmore in the civil parish of Kilfree, had been the property of Tadg ne Gann O'Gara, before he was slain in rebellion.[100] This Tadg is not to be confused with Tadg bane O'Gara, son of Irriel and father of Fergal O'Gara, who

92 See appendix 1, entry for 'Moygara'.   **93** See A.M. Freeman (ed.), *The compossicion booke of Conought* (Dublin, 1936), pp 130, 135, 137–8.   **94** T. McErlean, 'The Irish townland system of landscape organization' in T. Reeves-Smyth and F. Hamond (eds), *Landscape archaeology in Ireland*, BAR 116 (1983), pp 315–39. **95** *Compossicion booke of Conought*, p. 130.   **96** NAI, MS RC 9/15, inq. 17 and inq. 19.   **97** See all of appendix 1 for a detailed account of the lands of Coolavin and their owners, organized by parish.   **98** TCD, MS 570, f. 36v.   **99** O'Dowd, 'Landownership in the Sligo area', p. 435.   **100** TCD, MS 570, f. 285v; *Calendar of Irish*

likewise seems to have been associated with a distinct, but unspecified, block of either ten or thirteen quarters of land.[101] Finally, according to an inquisition of 1614, a certain Edmund Og, son of Cormac O'Gara, claimed four of the quarters listed in the possessions of Irriel O'Gara. The inquisition does not specify which four quarters these were, but perhaps they correspond to the four quarters of Carrogortinenearny (Gorteen), Carrowcowlskeaghan (Kilstraghlan or Ragwood), Cloonsillagh and Carrontobber (now subsumed into the townland of Kilfree) out of which Irriel received an annual return.[102] All of the aforementioned lands, save Derrymore, are included in the later possessions of Fergal O'Gara.[103] Fergal himself shared ownership of some of his lands in Kilfree with Owen O'Gara.[104]

The association of different branches of the O'Gara family with different, specific lands in Coolavin is also reflected in pardons granted to various O'Garas in the 1590s for their participation in the Nine Years War, though these individuals may have been tenants rather than landowners.[105] The pardons, recorded in the Elizabethan fiants, included Shean glasse, Ferall and Shane og O'Gara, all of whom lived in Bonnenedan (Monasteredan, Kilcolman),[106] Ferriell m'Tomultogh and Tadg boy O Garie of Shrowe (Shroove, Kilcolman),[107] and Dualtagh m'Shane oge O Gary m'Brian m'Dermot of Dirremore (Derrymore, Killaraght).[108] Derrymore seems to have been subjected to a particularly high turnover in ownership. In 1586 Irriel O'Gara granted the castle of Derrymore, as well as five *baile* of 'na rand', to Theobald Dillon.[109] In 1603, as we have seen, the castle seemed to be back in O'Gara hands once again, only to be made over to O'Conor Sligo. Finally, Sir John King's lands in Killaraght in 1617 are referred to as the manor of 'Derrimore', suggesting that the castle had become his property;[110] this suggestion is confirmed by a reference in the Books of Survey and Distribution for Sligo to 'Derrimore Island on the Lough with an old Castle and chappell wall within it' in the possession of Sir Robert King, son of Sir John.[111]

---

patent rolls of James I, p. 264.   **101** The reference to Tadg's possession of ten quarters of land, which were granted to John Baxter, is found in the *Calendar of Irish patent rolls of James I*, p. 266 (pat. 11, Jas I = 1615). The reference to Tadg's possession of thirteen quarters of land, which were granted to Sir John King, is found in the crown rentals contained in TCD, MS 570, f. 285v. The reference in an inquisition of 1614 to ten quarters of land, set aside from Irriel O'Gara's thirty other quarters of land, is likely to this same portion of Tadg's. See NAI, MS RC 9/15, inq. 17, p. 512 (66).   **102** NAI, MS RC 9/15, inq. 17, p. 514 (68).   **103** See appendix 1.   **104** Books of Survey and Distribution: Sligo, p. 132. See appendix 1 for details.   **105** I owe this point to Kieran O'Conor. **106** K.W. Nicholls (ed.), *The Irish fiants of the Tudor sovereigns: during the reigns of Henry VIII, Edward VI, Philip and Mary and Elizabeth I*, 4 vols (Dublin, 1994), iii, p. 100, no. 5420.   **107** *Fiants*, p. 128, no. 5498. **108** *Fiants*, p. 229, no. 5848.   **109** *ALC* 1586. The editor of the annals translates 'na rand' literally as 'the divisions'; however, given that the *Calendar of papal letters* refers to the rectory of 'Cuilofynd and Ranna' as a synonym for the parishes of Kilfree and Killaraght, 'na rand' would seem to be a place-name. Although not certain, it is likely that 'Na Ranna' referred to Killaraght since this was the part of Coolavin in which Dillon was known to have acquired territory (see O'Dowd, 'Land ownership in the Sligo area', p. 435). It is also the parish to which Derrymore Island is affiliated. Appendix 2 discusses 'Na Ranna' in more detail.   **110** *Calendar of Irish patent rolls of James I*, p. 321 (pat. 14, Jas. I).   **111** NAI, Books of Survey and Distribution: Sligo (microfilm).

Castle life

A fascinating glimpse into what daily life at the O'Gara castle might have been like in the late sixteenth and early seventeenth centuries is afforded by a list of pardons to figures connected with Moygara (both townland and castle) in 1604. These pardons, which absolved participants in the Nine Years War, detail the names, occupations and residences of the individuals concerned. In addition to the high-ranking 'gentlemen' such as Irriel O'Gara and his relatives (sons?) Rory, Fergananim, Owen, Tadg and Cian O'Gara, the pardons list farmers or husbandmen, labourers, kerne (foot soldiers of the light infantry variety), a shot (presumably a musketeer), two harpers, a friar, a 'rymer' (poet) and a surgeon all living at Moygara. In this way, the pardons provide a window into the multi-faceted military, agricultural, cultural and spiritual life of the early seventeenth-century castle:

> General Pardon to … Irriell O'Garie of Moygarie, gent., Rory O'Garie of the same, gent. Farginannyne O'Garie of the same, gent. Owen O'Garie of the same, gent., Teige O'Garie of the same, gent. Manes Keogh McBrien Reogh O'Garie of the same, horseman, Gilligroma McDermot of the same, kerne, Hugh boy McManus Keogh of the same, kerne, Ferrill Mc Tomoltogh of the same, kerne, Dermot roe Mc Moellronye of the same, kerne, Edw. oge McEdward of the same, husbandman, Brien McOwen McRorie of the same, husbandman, Gillegroma McRiccard of the same, shot, Brian McManes O'Garie of the same, kerne, Connor McBrien of the same, husbandman, Rorie roe McBrien of the same, husbandman, Thomas Duffe McDermot Reogh of the same, husbandman, Kyen O'Garie of the same, gent. Manes O'Garie of the same, kerne, Owen boy McFearagheir of the same, surgeon, Cahell O'Cahasey of the same, husbandman, Brin O'Spillane of the same, labourer, Melaghlin O'Coman of the same, labourer, Irriell McDonell Keogh O'Higgin of the same, harper, Irriell McMoelrony O'Higgin of the same, friar, Donnell oge O'Higgen of the same, husbandman, Owen O'Higgin of the same, harper, Fearfasse O'Dwgenaine of the same, rymer, Edw. O'Cahasie of the same, husbandman …[112]

Most of the names in the list are those of local south Sligo and north Roscommon families, many of which can be seen in the Sligo Hearth Money Roll of 1665 to be still living in the general area over fifty years later.[113] One such name on the list is that of 'Brin O'Spillane'. O'Spillane is described as a labourer, but the certainty that his family were once landowners is enshrined in the name 'Levalleispallan' given as an alias for the two quarters of Lomcloon and Clooncunny in Killaraght.[114] 'Levalleispallan' would

---

112 *Calendar of Irish patent rolls of James I*, p. 24 (pat. 1, Jas. 1).   113 E. MacLysaght (ed.), 'Seventeenth-century hearth money rolls with full transcript relating to County Sligo', *AH*, 24 (1967), pp 1–89.   114 NAI, RC 9/15, inq. 17 and inq. 19; BL, Harleian MS 2048, Coolavin, p. 2. This surname was anglicized to Spellman, which is

appear to be the anglicization of Leth-Bhaile Uí Spealláin, 'the half-*baile* of the Ó Spealláin'. It is also interesting to note the presence in the pardons of individuals from not one but two of the hereditary learned families of Lower Connacht (the O'Higgins and O'Duignenans), an indication of an emphasis placed on cultural life by the O'Garas that prefigures the patronage of the Annals of the Four Masters by Irriel's grandson, Fergal, thirty years later. The surgeon, Owen boy McFearagheir, is of interest as well since the McFearagheirs are an otherwise unattested medical family. In the early sixteenth century, it was the great hereditary medical kindred, the Mac an Leagha (literally 'son of the surgeon'), who were linked to the O'Garas: in 1509 Connla Mac an Leagha (fl. 1496–1512) treated Tomaltach O'Gara in Killaraght after his foot was dangerously cut by Cormac, son of Brian Óg O'Hart.[115]

In terms of the castle's spiritual life, it is worth noting that the parish church of Kilfree, located in the modern townland of Carrowntemple at the opposite end of the parish from the castle, is described as an 'old church' by the seventeenth-century Books of Survey and Distribution.[116] The church at Cloonehagglishe, on the other hand, located in the modern townland of Cuilpruighlish to the immediate north of the castle demesne lands, is described in a survey of the county taken in 1635 as the church where 'they burey the dead of this halfe Barrony'.[117] Furthermore, the survey of 1635 gives 'Clonohighlish Parish' as a synonym for Kilfree parish.[118] It thus seems that the ecclesiastical centre of the parish was shifted eastwards from Kilfree to Cloonehagglishe, probably to bring it more in line geographically with the region's secular centre.

Also likely located close to the castle was a mill: a map of Moygara townland found in the eighteenth-century maps of Lord Kingston's estate (copied in 1770 from one drawn in 1724) refers to the middle section of the western half of Moygara townland as 'Culmullen'.[119] Here, the 'mullen' element of the place-name probably derives from the Irish *muillenn* 'a mill'. This mill was doubtless the one referred to in the deed of 1603 between Irriel O'Gara and O'Conor Sligo.[120] The same map shows a small settlement within Moygara townland located just to the south of the castle (fig. 2.8).[121] While the antiquity of that settlement is not known, it seems reasonable to suggest that some of the people listed in the pardons may have lived if not in that exact settlement then in one very similar. The continuing presence of a settlement in Moygara from the time of the pardons is confirmed by the 'census' of Ireland for 1659,

quite a common name in south Sligo today. **115** RIA, MS 23 N 29, f. 4r, transcribed in K. Mulchrone, T.F. O'Rahilly, E. FitzPatrick and A.I. Pearson, *Catalogue of Irish manuscripts in the Royal Irish Academy* (Dublin, 1926–70), p. 1221. I owe this reference, and thanks, to Prof. Aoibheann Nic Donnchadha. **116** Books of Survey and Distribution: Sligo, p. 131. **117** BL, Harleian MS 2048, Coolavin barony, p. 3. **118** Ibid., p. 1. **119** NLI, MS 21 F 13, no. 39. This map was copied in 1770 by Cuttle from a map by Garret Hogan dating to 1724. **120** See discussion above. *Calendar of the Irish patent rolls of James I*, p. 475 (pat. 18, Jas. I, LXXV). A good-sized stream can be seen today about 600m to the west of Moygara Castle. The mill may have been located somewhere along this watercourse. In fact, there is a local tradition of a mill once being located beside the only bridge over this stream (P.J. O'Neill, pers. comm.). **121** See chapter 3.

which records thirty-eight people – all Irish – in the townland of Moygara, the second largest return for any of the townlands in Coolavin.[122] As will be discussed, the Sligo Hearth Money Roll for 1665 similarly confirms such a settlement, recording eleven separate households in Moygara townland.[123]

HISTORICAL REFERENCES TO THE LATER CASTLE

The implications of the Strafford Survey of 1635

Some idea of the role played by Moygara Castle within Coolavin can thus be garnered from the historical evidence. The problem is trying to understand which castle the historical sources discussed above – the sixteenth-century annal entries and letters from Bingham; the 1604 pardon to the occupants of Moygara Castle; and the English land-holding records dating to between 1603 and 1621 – were talking about: the tower house embedded within the wall of the later bawn and rectangular platform, or the later bawn itself (from here on, the bawn, gatehouse and four flanking towers will often be referred to as 'the later castle'). The difficulty here is that in the absence of a direct historical reference to the construction of the bawn, or, indeed, to the other phases of the castle, there is uncertainty over the date at which the bawn was built. On analogy with other castles, the best date for the building of the bawn from an architectural point of view is the period 1610 to the late 1630s, even possibly the 1640s; however, it could be earlier, possibly as early as *c.* 1580.[124]

In the mid-1630s a detailed survey of Connacht, known as the Strafford Survey, was conducted in preparation for a projected plantation of the province. That plantation never took place and the survey itself has been almost entirely lost; however, what appears to be a detailed set of notes originally made by one of the surveyors or officials involved in the survey has survived for Co. Sligo.[125] This document has been dated to 1635.[126] According to these survey notes, the quarter of Moygara contained some good arable land and a great 'scope' of mountain, yielded good shelter and firewood, would sustain seven days' worth of mowing hay and would graze 205 cows. Most importantly for the purposes of this study, the survey adds that upon the quarter of Moygara stood an 'ould castle'.[127] Given the architecture of the bawn and four

---

122 S. Pender (ed.), *A census of Ireland circa 1659, with supplementary material from the poll money ordinances 1660–1661* (Dublin, 1939), pp 602–3. The largest return for Coolavin was the seventy-one people recorded in Seefin ('Sexifind' in the census, p. 602). See, also, appendix 1. 123 Mac Lysaght (ed.), 'Seventeenth-century hearth money rolls', pp 26, 28, 46, 54, 63, 70, 75, 79. 124 See the discussion in chapter 5. 125 On a parish-by-parish basis, the Strafford Survey notes provide a detailed account of most of the quarters of land in the county, listing the name, owner, and rent due for each quarter as well as a description of the land itself. Most of the descriptions refer to qualities such as topography, whether the land was suitable for arable use, the number of cows it would graze, the number of days' mowing of hay that it would sustain, and the degree to which it was wooded. In addition, the survey notes the presence of significant buildings. 126 O'Dowd, *Power, politics and land*, p. 64. 127 BL, Harleian MS 2048, Coolavin barony, p. 3.

flankers, which most closely matches those of fortifications constructed between *c.*1610 and the late 1630s, it is rather unlikely that such a structure would have been considered 'old' in 1635. With its myriad of gun loops and its spear-shaped, flanking towers making it an extremely well-defended fortification, it was very much up-to-date for the early seventeenth century.[128] The castle referred to by the 1635 survey, therefore, is in all probability the earlier O'Gara tower house castle, possibly fallen into disrepair or even disuse.

In further support of this conclusion is the fact that Moygara is assessed by the survey to have the same monetary value as its neighbouring quarter of Carrownekillscorny, that is £21.[129] Apart from the presence of the castle on Moygara, the two quarters are said to have nearly identical qualities.[130] Elsewhere in the Strafford Survey of 1635, though, a quarter is specifically said to have been worth more because of the presence of a castle upon it.[131] Since Moygara and Carrownekillscorny were otherwise so similar, if the castle had been a modern, functioning structure one would have expected Moygara to have been valued more highly than its neighbour. An additional piece of evidence pointing to the possibility that the earlier castle at Moygara had become obsolete or was in disrepair by 1635 is that the survey makes a point of saying that the quarter of Cuppanagh (on the east side of Lough Gara) was kept in Fergal O'Gara's own hands.[132] As all the other quarters under Fergal's control, including Moygara, were let to undertenants, perhaps this reference suggests that Fergal was living in Cuppanagh, rather than Moygara, at this date. According to a deed from 1621, there was a castle at Cuppanagh;[133] its presence on lands known to have been kept in Fergal's own hands adds weight to the suggestion that this maybe have been his residence *c.*1635.[134] That said, it should be noted that the dedication of the Annals of the Four Masters, dated to 1634, refers to Fergal as 'Lord of Magh Ui-Ghadhra and Cuil-O-bhFinn'.[135] Even if Fergal might not have been physically dwelling at Moygara at this specific point in time, the site still very much symbolized the *caput* or centre of the lordship.

Based on the fact that the survey makes no reference to another castle within Moygara, two conclusions are possible. The first is that the Strafford Survey was indeed referring to the bawn, complete with embedded earlier structure, despite the apparent incongruity of such a castle being referred to as 'ould' in 1635. If so, then in order to merit the categorization 'ould', the castle would probably have been built in the late sixteenth century or the very early years of the seventeenth. The second possible conclusion is that the 'ould castle' was, in fact, the earlier structure and that the later

---

128 See chapter 5. **129** BL, Harleian MS 2048, Coolavin, p. 3. **130** See appendix 1. **131** Wood-Martin, *History of Sligo*, i, p. 177 (castle of 'Dewlarge'). **132** BL, Harleian, MS 2048: Coolavin, p. 2. **133** M.C. Griffiths (ed.), *Irish patent rolls of James I: facsimile of the Irish Record Commissioners' calendar prepared prior to 1830* (Dublin, 1966), p. 475. See also the entry for Cuppanagh in appendix 1. **134** See chapter 6, where the authors also come to this conclusion. **135** *AFM*, i, p. lv.

bawn had not yet been built. Of the two, the latter conclusion seems by far the most likely. Taking 1635 as a possible *terminus post quem*, however, edges the date of the construction of the bawn and flankers rather close to the period of the Cromwellian confiscations. In the eyes of the British government these confiscations theoretically were backdated to 1641 – the start of the Irish rebellion – but practically speaking were likely to have taken place *circa* the mid-1650s.[136] Accordingly, the thorny question of who actually was responsible for building the later Moygara Castle, with its bawn, flankers and gatehouse, raises its head. In light of the fact that the bawn has many features in common with early seventeenth-century plantation bawns built by incoming English or Lowland Scots settlers,[137] this question becomes particularly pressing: were the upstanding remains of Moygara Castle originally built by an owner of Gaelic or New English extraction?

THE LANDOWNERSHIP HISTORY OF MOYGARA TOWNLAND IN THE SEVENTEENTH CENTURY

Before attempting to answer this question, it will first be helpful to examine the land-ownership history of Moygara townland in the seventeenth century. The later bawn stood, as did the earlier castle, upon the quarter of Carrowcaslan, now subsumed into the modern townland of Moygara. This townland can be shown to be in the direct possession of the head of the O'Gara family – first Irriel, and then his grandson Fergal – from at least as early as 1585 (the date of the Composition of Connaught), though undoubtedly much earlier[138] – until at least as late as 1641 (the date taken as the baseline of landownership in the Books of Survey and Distribution).[139] The date 1641 represents the beginning of the Irish rebellion. After 1641 the lands of those who participated in the rebellion, or rather of those who were adjudged to have participated in the rebellion, were considered by the English government to be attainted and eligible for confiscation, although the actual confiscations did not take place until some years later, as stated (also, see below). In 1641 Carrowcaslan/Moygara was owned by Fergal O'Gara, and after the Cromwellian confiscations, it was in the hands of John, Lord Kingston (also known in some sources as Sir John King), the governor of Connacht in 1666.[140] Kingston, whose family were already substantial landowners in Coolavin before 1641, received the lion's share of O'Gara's confiscated lands, while the remainder went to one Bryan Magrath.[141] The exact date at which the confiscation

---

136 W.A. Maguire, 'The land settlement' in W.A. Maguire (ed.), *Kings in conflict: the revolutionary war in Ireland and its aftermath, 1689–1750* (Belfast, 1990), pp 139–56.   **137** See chapter 5.   **138** *The compossicion booke of Conought* states that 'Urrill o gary of Moygary shall have hold possess and enjoy to him and his heries 3 qrs of land adioning to his said towne of Moygary in Culavin freely exonerated and discharge of and from this compossicon to be holden of the queens Matie as is aforesaid'. See *Compossicion booke of Connaught*, pp 137–8. **139** Books of Survey and Distribution: Sligo, p. 131.   **140** Ibid.   **141** Ibid., pp 130–2.

2.8 Map of the Kingston lands in the Moygara area, first drawn in 1724, showing the castle and a small nucleated settlement to its south (NLI, MS 21 F13, no. 39, courtesy of the National Library of Ireland).

took place is very hazy. Kingston's allocation of the O'Gara lands was enrolled in his possession on 18 January 1667, while Magrath's ownership was not confirmed until the considerably later date of 16 February 1678.[142] These dates, however, represent the official dates at which the new owners' possession was confirmed, not the actual date at which the lands were confiscated. Considering that Sligo finally surrendered to Cromwell's army in 1652,[143] that date is likely to be sometime around the mid-1650s.

The landownership history of Moygara townland then takes a rather complicated turn. On 27 April 1663, four years before John, Lord Kingston, even had O'Gara's

142 'Abstracts of grants of lands and other hereditaments, under the Acts of Settlement and Explanation, A.D. 1666–1684', Record Commissioners Report 15 (London, 1825), pp 130, 258.   **143** O'Dowd, *Power, politics and land*, p. 130.   **144** 'Abstracts of the conveyances from the trustees of the forfeited estates and interests in

former lands officially enrolled in his possession, he demised a number of them, plus a number of non O'Gara-related lands in Roscommon, to Sir Richard Talbot, later the earl of Tyrconnell. The lands were to be collateral security for a deal amounting to the sum of £1,193. The lands in question included the four demesne quarters of the castle – Moygara (Carrowcaslane and Killneskorny), Mahanagh and Mullaghroe – as well as the townlands of Clooneagh, Cloontycarn, Lomcloon, Clooncunny, Tawnymucklagh, Falleens, Cuilpruglish, Cloonsillagh, Cuppanagh, Tuine-Coylehagan, Colloghbegg and Colloghmore (the modern equivalent of these last three quarters is uncertain, although Colloghbegg and Colloghmore appear to have been in Killaraght).[144] The complications arose because Talbot was none other than the commander of James II's army in Ireland, and the king's representative after James fled the country following his defeat at the Battle of the Boyne in 1690. Talbot died of a stroke during the Siege of Limerick in 1691, by which date Kingston's heirs had paid less than half the £1,193 owed to him. Subsequently, when Talbot was deemed attainted after the Williamite War, the Coolavin lands demised to him by Lord Kingston had not yet been redeemed. Accordingly, the lands were confiscated along with Talbot's other possessions and put into the hands of trustees. These lands were then sold to George Gore of Dublin on 22 June 1703.[145] Prior to the sale, however, Lord Kingston's brother and eventual heir, Sir Robert King, first baronet of Rockingham, pleaded his case for family retention of the lands.[146] Eventually it was agreed that upon payment of the remainder of the £1,193, plus interest, King could redeem the territory. It would seem that King did in fact pay the balance of the money owing, since some the lands in question, including Moygara, appear on Kingston estate maps dating to the 1720s (see fig. 2.8).[147]

WHO BUILT THE LATER MOYGARA CASTLE?

Having unravelled the landownership history of Moygara townland, we are now in a somewhat better position to assess the probable identity of the individual responsible for the construction of the later bawn, gatehouse and four flankers. If the 'ould castle' referred to by the Strafford Survey was the later bawn, then Irriel O'Gara, who died in 1613, is one possible candidate; however, as noted above, the bawn's similarities to structures which all post-date *c.*1610 strongly limit the likelihood that it was the structure referred to as 'ould'. If, on the other hand, as is much more likely, the 'ould castle' was the earlier structure and the bawn was built after 1635, then based on the landownership history outlined above, the three possible candidates are:

Ireland in 1688', Record Commissioners Report 15 (London, 1825), p. 370.   **145** 'Abstracts of the conveyances … in 1688', p. 370.   **146** John, Lord Kingston's direct heir was his son, Robert, Lord Kingston. When Robert died childless in 1693, his estate reverted to his uncle, Sir Robert King, John's brother.   **147** NLI, MS 21 F 13,

1) Fergal O'Gara
2) John, Lord Kingston or his heirs
3) Sir Richard Talbot, earl of Tyrconnell.

The case for Fergal O'Gara

The first of the three possible candidates for a post-1635 builder of the later castle is Fergal O'Gara, the last Lord of Coolavin. Were Fergal to have been responsible for its construction, the chronological limits for the erection of the later structure are approximately 1635 – the date of the survey which referred to the castle as 'ould' – on one end and the mid-1650s – the probable date at which Fergal's lands were confiscated – on the other. During the second half of the 1630s and early 1640s, Fergal would have been a figure of considerable standing. The financial difficulties that had likely contributed towards his grandfather, Irriel O'Gara, having to let most of his lands to William Taaffe do not appear to have been a problem for Fergal:[148] not only had he recovered his grandfather's lands, but the evidence of the Survey of 1635 and of the Books of Survey and Distribution indicates that he now controlled some additional lands in Killaraght not listed in his grandfather's original possessions.[149] Indeed in her tabulation of rental income owed to Gaelic landlords, Mary O'Dowd places Fergal at the top of the list.[150] O'Dowd sees the valuable woodlands covering much of Coolavin as the natural resource most responsible for Fergal's wealth.[151] The fact that Fergal was able to act as patron to the very considerable compilation project of the Annals of the Four Masters, undertaken between 1632 and 1636, is an indication of the disposable means under his control.[152] Fergal's appointment in 1634 as one of two members for Sligo in the Dublin parliament is an additional indication of his status during this period.[153]

It would seem, then, that Fergal possessed the wealth, and perhaps the status-consciousness, necessary to build such a major structure as the bawn at Moygara. Although the castle's plantation-style architecture might not be what one would automatically envisage for the home of an Irish lord so intimately in tune with his Gaelic heritage, the style of the castle need not necessarily pose an obstacle to the argument that Fergal commissioned it. The examples of a fortified house at Ballymooney, Co. Offaly, which is known to have been built by Donnell O'Carroll in 1622, and the plantation-style castle at Faugher, Donegal, built by Tirlagh Roe O'Boyle in the period 1611 to 1619, are concrete proof that Gaelic lords were capable of building colonial-style strongholds.[154] Furthermore, while Renaissance-influenced

no. 39. **148** NAI, MS RC 9/15 [Jas. I], no. 17, pp 512 (66)–514 (68). **149** See appendix 1. Mary O'Dowd credits the successful recovery and retention of Fergal's estate to its custodianship by Sir Theobald Dillon during Fergal's minority. See O'Dowd, *Power, politics and land*, p. 81. **150** Ibid., p. 78. **151** O'Dowd, 'Landownership in the Sligo area', p. 439. **152** *AFM*, i, pp ix, xi, lv–lxi; See, also, B. Cunningham, *The Annals of the Four Masters: Irish history, kingship and society in the early seventeenth century* (Dublin, 2010), pp 295–8. **153** R.P. Mahaffy (ed.), *Calendar of state papers relating to Ireland, 1633–47* (London, 1901), p. 66. **154** See chapter 5;

fortified houses were initially associated with New English officials, clerics and settlers in late sixteenth-century Ireland, Lyttleton has clearly demonstrated that nine out of the seventeen mostly early seventeenth-century fortified houses identified in west and south Co. Offaly were built by Gaelic-Irish gentlemen; these fortified houses were often attached onto or at least beside earlier tower houses.[155]

Even without the parallels from Offaly and Faugher, though, it would not be surprising for Fergal to have been open to colonial influences. After Fergal's father, Tadg, son of Irriel O'Gara, died in 1598,[156] the two year-old Fergal became the ward of Theobald Dillon. Dillon, an Old English magnate who had recently acquired Castlemore and half the lordship of Costello, was allegedly responsible for sending Fergal to Trinity College between the ages of twelve and eighteen.[157] The exposure to English influence that Fergal would have experienced during both his wardship and his possible enrolment at Trinity would have been further augmented by his marriage, at age nineteen, to one of the daughters of Sir John Taaffe.[158]

In Fergal, then, we have a figure who appears to have comfortably straddled two worlds, operating effectively within an English milieu, while taking great strides to preserve Gaelic culture. This duality recalls one of the features of the later bawn highlighted in the architectural report on Moygara Castle: a number of tapering corbels decorated with carvings of human figures that lie, quite literally, cheek by jowl with the highly defensive architecture of the bawn (fig. 2.9). It has been suggested that these corbels, which today lie on the ground in the passageway through the gatehouse, may have originally belonged to the earlier O'Gara castle and were incorporated into the later structure to form part of a box machicolation over the entrance way of the gatehouse.[159] In his account of the ruins of Moygara Castle published in 1889 as part of his history of Sligo, Terence O'Rorke claims that these stones in the machicolation bore the arms and mottos of the O'Garas.[160] If his claim is accurate, it would certainly constitute evidence in favour of an O'Gara origin for the later castle. No such insignia

C. O'Brien and P.D. Sweetman, *Archaeological inventory of County Offaly* (Dublin, 1997), pp 159–60, §877; J. Lyttleton, *The Jacobean plantation in seventeenth-century Offaly* (Dublin, 2013), pp 134, 262. I am grateful to Prof. Elizabeth FitzPatrick for first supplying me with the Ballymooney reference.   **155** Lyttleton, *The Jacobean plantations in seventeenth-century Offaly*, pp 108–60, 262–4.   **156** NAI, MS RC 9/15, inq. 19, p. 520 (74). **157** *ALC* 1586; Calendar of Irish patent rolls of James I, p. 311 [pat. 14, Jas. 1 = 1617]. There is some debate over whether Fergal actually attended Trinity College. Although the conditions of Dillon's wardship of Fergal, as recorded in the Calendar of Patent Rolls, include Fergal's attendance at Trinity, there is no record of his actually having gone. For further discussion, see O'Dowd, 'Landownership in the Sligo area', pp 439–40.   **158** O'Dowd, *Power, land and politics*, p. 97.   **159** See chapter 4. Alternatively, they could have been keystones of the arches over the main gateway and the gateway at the rear of the gatehouse that led into the interior of the bawn. **160** 'This fine ruin is not cared as it should be, and is, consequently, crumbling away fast. Portions of the bold central tower of the west wall have been pulled down, obviously for stones to block up the chief entrance, and thus to secure the court-yard for cattle; and it is little to the credit of people, living on the spot, to find, in piles of rubbish, fragments of elaborately carved stones, which bore the arms and motto of the [p. 366] O'Garas, but which were broken into pieces by the rough handling they received when hurled down on the ground from their place in the tower.' See T. O'Rorke, *The history of Sligo: town and county*, 2 vols (Dublin, 1889), ii, p. 365.

2.9 William Frederick Wakeman's 1878 watercolour of the apotropaic carving that originally was located on the external face of the gatehouse at Moygara Castle, which was commissioned by Colonel Edward Cooper of Markree Castle (© Sligo County Libraries). This seems to have been located on one of the tapering corbels that seem to have been part of the original machicolation over the gateway there.

is now visible, however, and it is possible that his claim was a misinterpretation of the vestiges of the carvings representing human figures.[161] Perhaps, then, the conundrum presented by a modern, plantation-style castle being associated with the *caput* or *ceann áitt* of a Gaelic lordship of considerable antiquity can best be resolved by

161 It is, of course, possible that the stones with the figures carved on relief on them which are extant today, one of which was drawn by Wakeman in 1878, are in fact different to the ones identified by O'Rorke as representing the O'Gara coat of arms in the 1880s. These latter stones may have since been lost, either because they are buried

understanding how the two traditions were reconciled within the figure of Fergal himself.

Musings about Fergal's liminality quite aside, however, the strongest point in favour of the later castle being an O'Gara creation is, ironically, the very style of the plantation-style architecture itself. As noted, the close parallels between Moygara Castle and a number of bawns built in the north and north-west of Ireland between 1610 and the late 1630s, but perhaps as late as *c.*1640, suggests that the bawn at Moygara was built sometime in this roughly thirty-year period.[162] If this was in fact the case, then, given the strong likelihood that the bawn was not the 'ould' castle referred to in 1635 – and thus probably built sometime after that date – it could be argued that the bawn and flankers at Moygara, the dominant phase of architecture at the site, would need to have been built at some point between 1635 and the 1640s. As Fergal O'Gara was very much in control of Moygara and Coolavin at this time, he could have been the only one responsible for the castle's construction during this period.

The case against Fergal O'Gara

The problem with a *c.*1640s date of construction from an historical point of view, however, is that between 1635 and 1688 not one of the multiple sources that one would expect to mention such a fortification makes any reference to Moygara Castle whatsoever. Instead, after its description as an 'ould castle' in the Survey of 1635, Moygara Castle abruptly drops out of sight in the records for over fifty years, only to re-emerge in 1689 during the Williamite War. An account dated to 1689 describes the Jacobites as 'taking Moygara a considerable strength in a bogueish country and turning out the Lord Kingston's tenants there'.[163] Several years later, a letter dated to 1691 writes of the Jacobites establishing a garrison at Moygara.[164] The significant lacuna in the history of the fortification between 1635 and 1689 raises the possibility that the reason for Moygara Castle's absence in the records of this period was that the later bawn might not yet have been built.

The earliest of the sources in which one might expect to find mention of Moygara Castle is a list, dated to 1646, of the principal fortifications held by Parliamentarian forces in Connacht. The list's author, Sir Robert Hannay, writes that the Parliamentary forces had reduced all of Leitrim and Sligo, save about six strongholds, to obedience, and then lists those fourteen Sligo forts that were under Parliamentary control.[165] Moygara Castle is not one of them; however, given how hard it would have been to

---

in rubble on the site or were taken by someone for 'safekeeping' in the 130 years since O'Rorke's time.   **162** See chapter 5.   **163** M. Ó Duigeannáin, 'Three seventeenth-century Connacht documents', *JGAHS*, 17 (1936–7), p. 156. The document is referred to in W.G. Wood-Martin, *Sligo and the Enniskilliners from 1688–1691* (Dublin, 1880), p. 28.   **164** Letter from Toby or Theobald Mulloy, sheriff of Co. Roscommon, to Colonel Lloyd, Sept. 4, 1691, quoted in D. Mac Dermot, *Mac Dermot of Moylurg: the story of a Connacht family* (Manorhamilton, 1996), p. 236.   **165** J. Hogan, *Letters and papers relating to the Irish rebellion between 1642–46* (Dublin, 1936),

take in light of its strong defensive structure, perhaps Moygara Castle was one of the six strongholds in Leitrim and Sligo still in Confederate hands.

More puzzling is the castle's absence from the description of Moygara townland found in the Books of Survey and Distribution for Sligo, the parish-by-parish, townland-by-townland record of landownership in Ireland both before and after the Cromwellian land confiscations. The component of the Books of Survey and Distribution dealing with the pre-Cromwellian period was mainly based on the no longer extant Down Survey conducted by Sir William Petty in the 1650s; Sligo was surveyed in 1657.[166] One of the interesting aspects of Coolavin's treatment in the Books of Survey and Distribution is that their account of lands in Coolavin – particularly those in the parishes of Kilfree and Kilcolman – is considerably more detailed than their treatment of the rest of the county. Achonry is the only other Sligo parish where the level of detail even comes close to that exhibited in the Coolavin section.[167] Among the details found in the Coolavin section are several specific references to significant buildings upon the land denominations in question. One mentions the old church of Kilfree in the quarter of Carrowntemple, while the other notes an 'old Castle and chappell wall within it' on Derrymore Island in the parish of Killaraght.[168] Of Moygara Castle, presumably a quite recent and imposing structure, though, there is no mention. While Moygara Castle is not the only Sligo castle which the Books of Survey and Distribution fail to record, the level of detail in the sections containing the sites of these omitted castles nowhere near approaches that of the Coolavin section.[169] At first glance, the omission of Moygara Castle from the Books of Survey and Distribution might thus be taken as evidence that the bawn, gatehouse and four flanking towers at Moygara had not yet been built when the Down Survey was conducted in 1657.

Closer examination of the two Coolavin entries that provide details about buildings, however, reveal that they both refer to lands that were *not* forfeited after the 1641 rebellion; Carrowntemple was church land, owned by the bishop of Achonry, while Derrymore already belonged to John, Lord Kingston, before the confiscations. This is important because while the Books of Survey and Distribution encompassed both forfeited and non-forfeited lands, the Down Survey covered the forfeited lands alone. For the non-forfeited lands, the Books of Survey and Distribution had to draw upon other sources.[170] This is a crucial point in regard to the absence of Moygara

pp 193, 195. I owe this reference to the late Paul Kerrigan.   **166** W. Smyth, *Map-making, landscapes and memory: a geography of colonial and early modern Ireland, c.1530–1750* (Cork, 2006), pp 179, 181.   **167** Books of Survey and Distribution: Sligo.   **168** Books of Survey and Distribution: Sligo, pp 130, 131.   **169** The castles listed by the Books of Survey and Distribution for Sligo are: Court Abbey, Doneally, Bayynechowne, Roslee, Rathlee, Castletowne, Pollkenny, Iniskrowen, Leackan and Castleconnor.   **170** For Connacht, the source of information about the non-forfeited lands is usually understood to be the Strafford Survey (Simmington, *Books of Survey and Distribution: Roscommon*, p. xxxix); however, comparison of the Books of Survey and Distribution for Sligo with the Coolavin section of the notes for the Sligo section of Strafford Survey (Harleian MS 2048) reveals that the details about the church and old castle in Derrymore are not found in Strafford and must come from a different

Castle from its pages since it means that those entries that included more detailed references to key buildings in Coolavin were taken from an entirely different source than the entry dealing with Moygara. The fact that the Moygara entry does not mention a castle while the Derrymore entry does may thus simply reflect the different recording styles and criteria of the surveyors. Given that the entry for the forfeited quarter of Cuppanagh in Kilfree likewise omits any reference to a castle, despite the fact that there is a record of a castle there in 1621,[171] the Coolavin section of the Down Survey clearly did not put the same priority on the recording of buildings as did the surveyor for the non-forfeited lands. The omission of Moygara Castle from the Books of Survey and Distribution for Sligo is thus not nearly as significant as it first seems, and cannot be taken as evidence that the later castle had not yet been built.

Petty's quite detailed map of Co. Sligo, which uses small icons to mark a number of important castles and ecclesiastical institutions, similarly fails to note the presence of Moygara Castle, although it does indicate the location of Moygara townland. Petty's map of Ireland and his county maps, published in the atlas *Hiberniae delineatio*, were based on his Down Survey of the 1650s.[172] Although not published until 1685, Petty's map of Ireland was almost complete by 1659, and engraved in the mid-1660s.[173] The absence of a castle icon for Moygara on Petty's county map of Sligo is perhaps the least surprising of the omissions of the castle from the various mid-seventeenth sources. A close comparison of the map with other records of Sligo castles reveals that icons for a number of fortifications, including the large castle at Collooney, are also absent.[174] Unfortunately the level of detail enshrined in the county map is the highest one available for the parishes of Coolavin. Although a copy made of Petty's parish maps for Sligo survived the destruction that befell the other parish maps,[175] the half-barony of Coolavin is unfortunately the one part of the county not included in the mapping.[176]

The final mid-seventeenth century source to omit Moygara Castle is the Sligo Hearth Money Roll of 1665. For the purpose of enabling the collection of a tax based on the number of fireplaces owned, this source details the names, townland addresses and number of hearths of individuals – of both Irish and English extraction – throughout Sligo. For Moygara townland, the roll enumerates eleven different households – including those of several O'Garas – all of which appear to have had only one hearth.[177] As indicated by the architectural report on Moygara Castle, however, the four flanking towers of the seventeenth-century bawn contain not less than six

source.　**171** *Calendar of Irish patent rolls of James I*, p. 475.　**172** Petty, *Hiberniae delineatio*, 'Map of Sligo'; see chapter 3, fig. 3.4.　**173** Smyth, *Map-making*, p. 24.　**174** In almost all cases, though, the townland name in which the castles are located is included on the map.　**175** Not included in the published atlas were a series of highly detailed parish maps, most of which were burned either in the Custom House fire of 1711 or the Four Courts fire in 1922 during the Civil War. See Y.M. Goblet, *A topographical index of the parishes and townlands of Ireland in Sir William Petty's MSS. barony maps (c.1655–9)* (Dublin, 1932), p. v.　**176** SPL, 'Down Survey Co. Sligo parish maps (1654–7): 38 sheets'.　**177** Mac Lysaght (ed.), 'Seventeenth century hearth money rolls', pp 26, 28, 46, 54, 63, 70, 75, 79. I am grateful to Maura O'Gara-O'Riordan for compiling – from the original

fireplaces between them, possibly more originally.[178] Nothing in the Hearth Money Roll for Sligo thus indicates the footprint of the castle in the townland. As mentioned earlier, the Hearth Roll's documenting of eleven different buildings in Moygara is consistent with the number of thirty-eight individuals recorded as living at Moygara by the 1659 census of Ireland.[179] All thirty-eight of these individuals are recorded as Irish, with no Englishmen said to be in the townland. The absence of any Englishmen in Moygara correlates with the fact that the only 'titulado' (one Henry Tifford [*recte* Clifford?]) whom the census records for Coolavin is listed as living not in Moygara but in the townland of Killaraght.[180] The absence of a titulado or any Englishmen in Moygara at the time of the census strongly suggests that if there was in fact a castle at Moygara in 1659, it was not functioning as an English garrison at the time.[181]

A comparison of the Hearth Money Roll with a list of major Sligo castles reveals that several other important fortifications similarly leave no footprint in the Roll in terms of having multiple hearths listed. The absence of a structure with multiple hearths in Moygara cannot, therefore, be taken as proof in itself that the castle was not in place by 1665. Indeed, as indicated above, plausible explanations for the exclusion of Moygara Castle can be found for all of the mid-seventeenth century sources included in this discussion. Taken individually, the negative evidence of each source is worth noting but perhaps no more than that. Taken *collectively*, however, the absence of Moygara Castle from the sources covering the period between 1646 and 1665 seems worthy of further consideration. There are three possible explanations for this exclusion. The first is that Moygara Castle's absence from all four sources is just a coincidence and that the bawn, gatehouse, and four flankers were in place by this period as a going concern. The second is that the bawn had ceased to be a functional castle by the mid-1660s, either having already slipped into obsolescence by 1635, if we are to believe that it was the 'ould castle' of the Strafford Survey, or if it was built after 1635, as is most likely, destroyed sometime shortly thereafter, most likely as a consequence of the Confederate and Cromwellian wars. The third possible explanation is that the bawn, gatehouse and four flanking towers were not, in fact, built until *after* the mid-1660s.

Of these three explanations, the first, which would see Moygara's absence from all four sources as a coincidence, and the second – that the later castle had already been destroyed by the mid-seventeenth century – would be compatible with the argument that Fergal O'Gara built the later bawn after 1635. The third explanation – that the bawn and its flanking towers were not built until at least the mid-1660s, i.e. at a time

---

manuscript – and making available to me a detailed list of all residences with multiple fireplaces. **178** See chapter 4. **179** *Census of Ireland, 1659*, pp 602–3. **180** In the 1659 census the term 'titulado' was used to describe the most prestigious people in any area – landowners, merchants, and professionals – who were usually, but not always, of English extraction. **181** For discussion of the term 'titulado', see Smyth, *Map making*, pp 195, 211.

after Fergal O'Gara had lost control of his lands – would not. Instead, it would mean that the later castle was an English fortification.

Although it is uncertain exactly when Fergal O'Gara lost possession of Moygara, it seems probable that his lands had been confiscated by the late 1650s. Certainly, as indicated by his demise of the lands to Talbot, John, Lord Kingston, was in at least de facto possession of Moygara by 1663. If the later castle was built after the mid-1660s, then the most likely candidates for its erection would presumably be: John, Lord Kingston, (d. 1676); his younger brother, Sir Robert King (d. 1707), who administered Kingston's Boyle estates for him from 1666;[182] and John's oldest son and successor, Robert, Lord Kingston (d. 1693). While it is not impossible that Sir Richard Talbot, to whom Moygara was demised, could have built the bawn, it seems much less likely; the identification of the people expelled from Moygara by the Jacobites in 1689 as 'Lord Kingston's tenants' suggests that Kingston remained in control of his lands after their demise.

The case for the King family or Talbot

When considering whether the King family or Talbot were responsible for the construction of the bawn phase of Moygara Castle, one must first consider why they would have built such a structure. The King family's principal residence had long been the fortified former abbey of Boyle, Co. Roscommon, just a few miles east of Moygara, while Talbot's family home was in Talbotstown in west Co. Wicklow. A further local home recorded in the possession of the King family was at Knocklough in the civil parish of Toomour in the barony of Corran.[183] Building a bawn at Moygara as a fortified home does not, therefore, appear an obvious choice for either the Kings or Talbot. This is particularly true given the legal status of the townland after 1663. It does not seem particularly practical for either the owner of the lands, or the person to which they were demised, to invest large sums of money in building a structure on territory which neither was guaranteed to have in their possession. What, though, if the motivation behind the construction of the bawn phase at Moygara Castle was not, in fact, to build a fortified home? One of the most noted features of the seventeenth-century bawn is its very markedly defensive character, particular with regard to the large number of gun loops present within the structure and its flanking towers.[184] We know that the castle was used as a Jacobite garrison during the Williamite War of 1689–91. If the bawn was indeed built after the mid-1660s, could it have been intended primarily as a barracks all along? Lord Kingston and his son were both highly

---

182 Kingston moved to Co. Cork at this point to administer the large Mitchelstown estate he had inherited through his wife (T. Clavin, 'King, Sir John', *Dictionary of Irish biography*, dib.ie/biography/king-sir-john-a4563, accessed 26 Apr. 2021).   **183** The census of Ireland for 1659 records 'Robert King gent' as the titulado for 'Cnockloch'. The Robert King in question is likely the brother of John, Lord Kingston. This Sir Robert became the first baronet of Rockingham in 1682. (John, Lord Kingston, also had a son called Robert King (d. 1693) but he would have just been a baby at the time of the census). *Census of Ireland, 1659*, p. 602.   **184** See chapters 4

experienced military commanders, as indeed was Talbot, and one could easily envision them in charge of a purpose-built barracks at Moygara.[185]

In light of this theory, it is extremely interesting to note that the Books of Survey and Distribution record that immediately after the Williamite confiscations, the two quarters of Moygara were in the possession of 'The Trustees of the Barracks'.[186] The same is said of several other nearby townlands in Kilfree and Kilcolman.[187] Tellingly, all the lands designated in this way were part of the territory demised by Lord Kingston to Talbot and thus put in the hands of trustees when Talbot's property was confiscated at the end of the war. One interpretation of this statement is simply that the proceeds arising from these confiscated townlands were intended for the general support of military barracks throughout the county, perhaps even the country. Against this interpretation, however, is the fact that the phrase 'Trustees of the Barracks' is found *only* in conjunction with the aforementioned townlands in Coolavin. None of the other townlands in Sligo, nor indeed any of the townlands in any of the counties for which we have published editions of the *Books of Survey and Distribution*, are similarly noted as being in the possession of such trustees. Even those Roscommon and Galway lands belonging to Lord Kingston that were demised to Talbot at the same time as the Coolavin territories are not associated with the trustees of the barracks. Instead, they are simply noted as being in the possession of Gore, the individual to which Talbot's confiscated lands were sold in 1703.[188] This evidence strongly suggests that it was not a coincidence that the word 'barracks' appears in conjunction with the site of a heavily fortified structure and known garrison. Instead, a good argument can be made that the 'barracks' in question was in fact the seventeenth-century bawn at Moygara.

The possibility that such a barracks may have been an ongoing concern after the Williamite victory is suggested by the fact that one Colonel Manus O'Donnell is recorded as the tenant of Moygara townland in 1697.[189] Manus O'Donnell was the son of Rory O'Donnell, the figure responsible for leading a group of transplanted Donegal settlers to Mayo following the Cromwellian wars. During the Williamite War, Manus had been an officer in the earl of Antrim's infantry, eventually returning to the lands in Mayo that he had been allowed to keep by the terms of the Treaty of Limerick. In the 1720s he moved into Newport, where the family thrived, eventually taking a leading place among the surviving Catholic gentry of Mayo.[190] What was a man with his own small estate in Mayo doing as a tenant at Moygara in 1697? It seems plausible to suggest that he might have been in charge of the barracks there. Although Manus had fought on the Jacobite side, the Williamites were keen to retain soldiers

and 5. **185** Clavin, 'King, Sir John'; G. Goodwin, 'King, Robert (d. 1693)' in S. Lee (ed.), *Dictionary of national biography*, 31 (1885–1900), pp 155–6. **186** Books of Survey and Distribution: Sligo, p. 131. **187** Books of Survey and Distribution: Sligo, pp 131–2. **188** See the landownership discussion above. **189** SPL, 'Surveys and rentals of lands in County Sligo in the 17th & 18th cc', Mac Donagh MS xiii S/R. **190** J. D'Alton, *Illustrations, historical and genealogical of King James's Irish army list (1689)* (Dublin, 1855; repr. Limerick, 1997),

O'GARAS CASTLE.

2.10 Tom Cocking's sketch of Moygara Castle, dated to 1791, which is entitled *O'Gara's Castle* (after Grose 1791, i, p. 58, pl. 102).

been built by the English as a barracks shortly after Fergal O'Gara's lands were confiscated following Sligo's surrender in 1652? Telling strongly against this proposition is Moygara's profile in the 1659 census. Were Kingston to have had a purpose-built barracks erected on his newly acquired lands following the rebellion, it almost certainly would have been garrisoned with at least some English soldiers or officers. As noted earlier, though, the fact that the census records thirty-eight Irish but neither a titulado nor any English as living in the townland militates against it having functioned as an English garrison in 1659.

Accordingly, the weight of the evidence suggests that the bawn, gatehouse and four flankers at Moygara – the second and most extensive phase of masonry building at the site – were indeed built by an O'Gara. While the bawn phase could have been erected by Irriel O'Gara or perhaps even by his predecessor, Diarmait, son of Eóghan O'Gara (d. 1579), it is most likely that it was built by Fergal O'Gara sometime between 1635 and the 1640s, although no conclusions on this point can be absolute. The view that Fergal rebuilt the castle, apparently an earlier tower house, turning it into a modern fortification for its time, fits the architectural evidence as well.[199] Despite being a

also, O'Conor, 'English settlement and change in Roscommon', p. 194. **199** See chapter 5.

conservative man who was only reluctantly drawn into rebellion in the 1640s,[200] Fergal may nonetheless have built such a heavily fortified home as a safeguard against the prospect of troubled times ahead. Presumably Fergal had been cognizant of the survey of his territory in 1635, and would have been all too aware of its potential implications for his continued possession of the lands of Coolavin. It is also quite possible that he built the later castle after the war had already begun, not just as a defence against the Parliamentarian army but also as protection from the general instability in Sligo at the time.[201] The notion that it might always been primarily intended as a military fortification would fit with the apparent reference to it as 'the barracks' in the Williamite confiscations. If, as seems plausible, the bawn-style castle had then fallen into disuse by the mid-seventeenth century, it later appears to have been resurrected and given a new lease of life as a Jacobite garrison and possibly a Williamite barracks in the late seventeenth century, only to fall into disuse again by at least as early as the second half of the eighteenth century. Taylor and Skinner categorize Moygara Castle as 'Castle Ruins' in their road map of the route from Boyle to Ballaghaderreen dated to 1783, while the 1791 drawing of the castle in Grose's *Antiquities of Ireland* portrays it in better condition than today's upstanding remains, but a romantic ruin nonetheless (see fig. 2.10).[202] Moygara Castle's day as a defensive fortification was done.

---

200 O'Dowd, *Power, politics, and land*, p. 124. **201** For discussion of the chaos in Sligo in this period, see O'Dowd, *Power, politics and land*, pp 125–30. **202** George Taylor, *Taylor and Skinner's maps of the roads of Ireland, surveyed 1777 and corrected down to 1783* (Dublin, 1783; repr. Shannon, 1969), p. 240; see chapter 3, fig. 3.5.

CHAPTER THREE

Moygara Castle, Co. Sligo: a siting and map regression study

PHYL FOLEY AND KIERAN O'CONOR

THE SITING OF MOYGARA CASTLE

The landscape setting of the castle at Moygara is in a townland of the same name at an elevation of approximately 80m above sea level.[1] It is sited at the eastern end of a ridge on the lowermost north-eastern slopes of Mullaghthee (a low mountain at the north-eastern end of the Sliabh Lugha range) and overlooks and has exceptional views of Lough Gara to its south-east and south.[2] The ground slopes away steeply from the northern edge of the castle but falls more gently to the site's east and south. The ground is level to the west of the castle and this is clearly the natural line of approach to it. A small turlough or seasonal lake (in size, really no more than a pond) occurs at the base of the slope 100m to the north of the castle and this usually dries up during summertime.

There are panoramic views from Moygara Castle across the drumlin country of south Sligo to the north as far as Knocknarea Mountain, near Sligo town, which lies on the horizon, as do the Ox Mountains to the north-west. Keshcorran, the Bricklieves and the Curlew Mountains can all be seen just to the north-east of the site. The famed Benbulben, with its steep slopes dropping almost vertically westwards to Donegal Bay, can be observed to the north on good days. The nearest part of the north-western end of Lough Gara, before its drainage in the 1950s, occurred about 650m to the east of the site. There are also excellent views south-eastwards across the latter lough towards the higher ground of Rathcroghan and Fairymount in modern north Co. Roscommon. The outflow of the Boyle River from the lough is visible to the east of the site. Presumably this river (which is a tributary of the mighty Shannon) was navigable in the past for small craft such as cots and wherrys, although portages may have been needed in places.[3] It is clear that transporting goods, which included animal hides,

---

1 See appendix 1, entries for 'Carrowcaslan' and 'Moygara'. The part of Moygara townland that the castle is located within today was called Carrowcaslan (i.e. the 'Castle Quarter') in colonial sources of seventeenth-century date.   **2** See, also, chapter 1, especially fig. 1.3.   **3** See H. Murtagh, 'Boating on Lough Ree' in B. Cunningham and H. Murtagh (eds), *Lough Ree: historic lakeland settlement* (Dublin, 2015), pp 200–1; K. O'Conor and Paul Naessens, 'The medieval harbour beside Rindoon Castle, Co. Roscommon' in P. Ettel, A.-M. Flambard-Héricher and K. O'Conor (eds), *Château Gaillard, 27: Château et commerce* (Caen, 2016), pp 237–42. Remarkably little detailed research has been carried out to date on the archaeology and history of riverine and lacustrine trade in

grain, barrels of fish and wine, building stone and timber, was far cheaper and more efficient in later medieval Ireland when moved by boat along rivers and lakes than by carting the same goods by road. Even quite insignificant rivers were used to transport goods during this whole period and one of the reasons why castles were sited close to or beside rivers and large lakes was to take advantage of their navigable qualities for both travel and economic purposes.[4]

In all, this analysis of its siting shows that Moygara Castle is clearly a very dominant feature in the landscape of the Lough Gara area and can be seen for miles around. This visibility was probably deliberate and was at least partly linked to a desire by its elite occupants to demonstrate their power, wealth and status to the world. Examples of castles that were deliberately placed to be observed from and to dominate their landscapes are numerous throughout Britain and Ireland. In this respect, these structures were often not located in what were the most naturally defensible sites in their immediate vicinities but in ones with a high degree of visibility. In the case of Moygara, it is clear that a natural island out on adjacent Lough Gara or higher up the slopes of Mullaghthee would have been a more effective choice of siting for the castle from a purely military point of view and yet such a site was not chosen. Castles like Moygara were partly sited to impress and overawe locals, visitors and travellers of all ranks and their siting in prominent positions was a form of power display by their owners.[5]

Both the design and the location of the castle raise a number of questions. It appears that light beer (known as small beer) and to a lesser extent wine, cider and mead, rather than water, would have been the everyday drink of people living in castles during the whole later medieval and post-medieval periods. Yet even in peacetime water was essential for cooking and fire prevention. Livestock and horses, stabled within the precincts of any given castle or beside it, would also have needed water in large quantities every day.[6] In times of war, an adequate supply of water was also essential to a castle's ability to withstand a siege of even a few days, as the same livestock and horses needed to be watered and it was also required to douse fires started by enemy action.[7] There is no well visible within Moygara Castle today, nor is there a

later medieval Ireland.   **4** V.L. McAlister, *The Irish tower house: society, economy and environment, c.1300–1650* (Manchester, 2019), pp 125–35. See, also, J.A. Galloway, 'The economic hinterland of Drogheda in the later Middle Ages' in V.L. McAlister and T.B. Barry (eds), *Space and settlement in medieval Ireland* (Dublin, 2015), pp 167–85. This article focusses on the agricultural economy of the Drogheda region in eastern Ireland but it is also clear from it that the Boyne and its tributaries were used to transport goods, particularly vital firewood, by boat down to the latter town from its hinterland, particularly from Trim with its great castle, throughout the later medieval period.   **5** See, for example, R. Liddiard, '*Landscapes of lordship': Norman castles and the countryside in medieval Norfolk, 1066–1200*, BAR (Oxford, 2000), pp 49–51, 60–4; O.H. Creighton, *Designs upon the land: elite landscapes of the Middle Ages* (Woodbridge, 2009), pp 157–8. See, also, O.H. Creighton, *Castles and landscapes: power, community and fortification in medieval England* (London, 2005); R. Liddiard, *Castles in context: power, symbolism and fortification in medieval England* (Macclesfield, 2005); M. Hansson, *Aristocratic landscape: the spatial ideology of the medieval aristocracy* (Lund, 2006).   **6** N.A. Ruckley, 'Water supply of medieval castles in the United Kingdom', *Fortress*, 7 (1990), p. 16.   **7** R. Allen Brown, *English castles* (London, 1976), p. 190.

stream within the immediate vicinity of the site – the nearest one lies 400m to the west
of the castle. The turlough just to the north may have been a source of water in winter
for the castle but not for the rest of the year, as it dries up in summer, except in very
wet years. It could be that any wells or cisterns at Moygara Castle have been blocked
up by collapsed rubble or were deliberately closed up at some stage in the past. For
example, there was no well visible at Carlow Castle prior to its excavation in 1996.
However, the excavation uncovered the remains of a well at ground level in the north-
eastern corner of the early thirteenth-century corner-towered donjon at the site. This
well appears to have been blocked up at some stage in the seventeenth century.[8]
However, geophysical survey has not produced any evidence for a filled-in well or
cistern within Moygara Castle.[9] With no obvious water source evident today, it is
difficult to understand at first glance how the castle's occupants sourced their water
supply without going to considerable trouble. However, the water-levels in this area
have changed on a number of occasions in recent times. Two drainage schemes in the
area of the lake, one which took place in 1859 and the second which was carried out
during the 1950s, have resulted in a drop in water-level of approximately one metre.[10]
This may have altered the water table in the area around Moygara Castle and should
be taken into consideration when thinking about water-levels in the past. Alternatively,
one strong possibility for water storage at Moygara was that rainwater was channelled
in gutters and pipes from the tops of the castle's corner towers down into a tank,
wooden barrels or an above-ground cistern, all located at ground level. Evidence
for such a system, for example, was found during the excavation of the later
twelfth-century phase at Hen Domen motte-and-bailey castle on the modern
Powys/Shropshire border, just inside Wales.[11]

A lot of evidence exists for the continued use of crannogs as fortified residences and
estate centres by members of the Gaelic elite beyond the early medieval period up to
the very first years of the seventeenth century.[12] It has been shown that a number of
crannogs on Lough Gara had occupation layers on them that suggest that they were
inhabited during later medieval times. The crannogs that had these late habitation
layers on them were distinguished from ones solely occupied in earlier times by the
higher heights of the stone dumps that made up these artificial islands. These crannogs

---

8 K. O'Conor, 'The origins of Carlow Castle', *Archaeology Ireland*, 11:3 (1997), pp 13–16.   **9** See chapter 7.
10 C. Fredengren, *Crannogs* (Dublin, 2002), p. 65.   **11** R. Higham and P. Barker, *Hen Domen, Montgomery: a
timber castle on the English-Welsh border: a final report* (Exeter, 2000), p. 18.   **12** K. O'Conor, *The archaeology of
medieval rural settlement in Ireland* (Dublin, 1998), pp 77–84; idem, 'The morphology of Gaelic lordly sites' in
P.J. Duffy, D. Edwards and E. FitzPatrick (eds), *Gaelic Ireland, c.1250–c.1650: land, lordship and settlement*
(Dublin, 2001), pp 337–8; A. O'Sullivan, *The archaeology of lake settlement in Ireland* (Dublin, 1998), pp 152–5,
167–76; idem, 'Crannogs in late medieval Gaelic Ireland, c.1350–1650' in P.J. Duffy, D. Edwards and
E. FitzPatrick (eds), *Gaelic Ireland, c.1250–c.1650: land, lordship and settlement* (Dublin, 2001), pp 397–417;
N. Brady and K. O'Conor, 'The later medieval usage of crannogs in Ireland', *Ruralia*, 5 (2005), pp 127–36;
K. O'Conor, '*Crannóga* in later medieval Ireland' in E. Campbell, E. FitzPatrick and A. Horning (eds), *Becoming
and belonging in Gaelic Ireland, AD c.1200–1600: essays in identity and cultural practice* (Cork, 2018), pp 148–66.

with evidence for later medieval habitation on them have been named 'high-cairn' crannogs for classification purposes.[13] Presumably some of these inhabited crannogs on the lough were visible from Moygara Castle, especially during its earlier, pre-1600 phases of occupation. Derrymore Castle, which was located on Derrymore Island on the lake, and the castle at Cuppanagh, both owned by the O'Garas and which were probably tower houses, would also have been visible from Moygara Castle, when it was in use.[14]

<h2 style="text-align:center">MOYGARA CASTLE: A MAP REGRESSION STUDY</h2>

This study also examined maps of the area surrounding Moygara Castle, which were drawn at different times in the past starting in the late sixteenth century. Map regression can be used for a variety of purposes including determining and understanding which cultural and natural features of the landscape have changed over time and those that have not. A regression study can also be used to locate sites which were recorded on earlier maps but are no longer marked on modern ones. This type of study can also be tentatively used to determine the phases of any given building. It can also be a means of identifying early field boundaries, trackways, roads, settlements and other features that no longer exist. Basically, a map regression study of Moygara may shed information on the landscape context of the castle when it was occupied.

A 1589 map of Sligo, drawn by an anonymous hand, apparently at the behest of Sir Richard Bingham, the then English governor of Connacht, provides the first cartographic reference to Moygara Castle.[15] The castle is represented stylistically on this map, not accurately, and is marked 'Moyegarre' on it (figs 3.1 and 3.2). This map was probably sketched from an original drawn by one John Browne (the elder), a well-known English or Anglo-Irish mapmaker and military commander in Connacht at the time.[16] Browne held a number of military and administrative posts in Mayo, owned

---

13 Fredengren, *Crannogs*, pp 265–76, 282, 287.   **14** U. Egan, E. Byrne and M. Sleeman, *Archaeological inventory of County Sligo* (Dublin, 2005), pp 486–7. The Archaeological Survey of Ireland wrongly states that Derrymore Castle was built and owned by the O'Haras and that Cuppanagh Castle belonged to the MacDermots. References in the surviving historical sources clearly show that these were O'Gara castles. The remains of both castles are too ruinous today for their original form to be discerned with any certainty. However, studies have shown that while relatively few castles (or at least fortifications that European contemporaries then and modern scholars now classify as castles) were built in Gaelic Ireland prior to the late fourteenth century, large numbers of tower houses were built by native lords like the O'Garas after the latter date, especially in the fifteenth and sixteenth centuries. See O'Conor, *The archaeology of medieval rural settlement in Ireland*, pp 75–7, 102–4. Literally hundreds of tower houses were built across Ireland in these two centuries and it is felt that most of the unclassified castles in the Irish countryside today, like Cuppanagh and Derrymore, were originally tower houses. See T.B. Barry, 'Rural settlement in Ireland in the Middle Ages', *Ruralia*, 1 (1996), p. 140; see also K. O'Conor and J. Williams, 'Ballinagare Castle, Co. Roscommon' in L. Gibbons and K. O'Conor (eds), *Charles O'Conor of Ballinagare, 1710–91: life and works* (Dublin, 2015), pp 60–4.   **15** PRO, MPF 91; J.H. Andrews, 'Sir Richard Bingham and the mapping of Western Ireland', *PRIA*, 103C (2003), pp 79–81; M. Swift, *Historical maps of Ireland* (London, 1999), p. 42.   **16** Andrews, 'Sir Richard Bingham and the mapping of Western Ireland', p. 74.

3.1 John Browne I's 1589 map of Co. Sligo. Moygara Castle is marked on it
(PRO, MPF 91, courtesy of the National Archives, Kew).

an estate at the Neale in that county and was killed in action in very early 1589. This
all meant that Browne was familiar with Connacht, particularly north or Lower
Connacht.[17] However, this map of Sligo shows a number of inaccuracies, including the
origin and size of both the Shannon and the Boyle rivers and does not mention or even
mark Lough Allen, Lough Arrow or Lough Key. These inaccuracies point to this map,
which was endorsed by Sir Richard Bingham, the English governor of Connacht at the
time, as being the work of a copyist as Browne was known for his attention to detail.[18]

17 Ibid., pp 79–81.   18 Ibid., p. 79.

3.2 Detail of the Moygara area, showing 'Moygarre' depicted as a castle, from Browne's 1589 map of Sligo (PRO, MPF 91, courtesy of the National Archives, Kew).

Anyway, the fact that Moygara Castle is drawn and marked on this map is an indication that it was regarded as a castle of importance by the English colonial administration at the time. For example, Derrymore Castle and Cuppanagh Castle, which were both O'Gara fortresses, are not marked, nor are many other tower house castles in the Sligo area. A subsequent map of Connacht (and Clare) drawn or completed in 1591 for Bingham by John Browne's nephew of the same name identifies Moygara as a place, though it does not comment on the castle (fig. 3.3).[19] The fact that Moygara is the only spot marked in the Coolavin area on these two maps is an indication that the castle was the principal place within the O'Gara lordship at this particular time and the main residence of its chief.[20] Moygara is also marked as a place on the Down Survey map of Co. Sligo – the data for which was collected in the 1650s

---

19 TCD, MS 1209/68; Andrews, 'Sir Richard Bingham and the mapping of Western Ireland', pp 84–92.
20 See Andrews, 'Sir Richard Bingham and the mapping of Western Ireland', p. 92.

3.3 Moygara is listed as an important place on John Browne II's 1591 map of Connacht (TCD, MS 1209/ 68, courtesy of Trinity College Dublin).

as part of the Cromwellian conquest, though only published in 1685. This suggests that it was still regarded as an important centre at a local level during the 1650s (fig. 3.4). The castle is also depicted on an originally 1724 map of Lord Kingston's lands in the Moygara area. The gatehouse is not depicted on this map and it is not clear whether the castle is ruined or still occupied at this time.[21]

In 1777 the Irish House of Commons commissioned George Taylor and Andrew Skinner to map and survey the roads of Ireland. Taylor and Skinner published their results in the following year. These maps were noted for their accuracy and depicted roads, crossroads, rivers, forests, mills, mountains, houses, bridges and churches. They also named the principal landlords in any given area and marked the location of their houses – distances were listed in both English and Irish miles.[22] An updated second edition of this book was published in 1783.[23] The importance of these maps lies in the fact that they essentially depicted the road network of the country prior to the infrastructural changes to Ireland's roads that took place from the nineteenth century onwards. Many of the roads depicted on Taylor and Skinner's maps reflect the road

21 See chapter 2, especially fig. 2.8.   **22** G. Taylor and A. Skinner, *Maps of the roads of Ireland, surveyed 1777* (1st ed., London and Dublin, 1778), map 240.   **23** G. Taylor and A. Skinner, *Maps of the roads of Ireland, surveyed 1777, corrected down to 1783* (2nd ed., London and Dublin, 1783; Shannon, 1969).

3.4 Moygara is marked as an important place on the Down Survey map of Co. Sligo
(courtesy of the Bibliothèque National de France).

networks of earlier times, particularly those of the later medieval period. In this
respect, one of the maps drawn by Taylor and Skinner depicts the road from the town
of Boyle to Ballaghaderreen. This road skirted the northern and western edges of
Lough Gara, in contrast to the modern route between these two towns which goes via
the village of Frenchpark. The location of Moygara Castle is marked as a ruined castle
on this map, close to a junction where the road from Boyle forked, with one road
turning west for Ballaghaderreen and the other continued on for Tubbercurry
(fig. 3.5).

It was noted in the introduction to this book that Moygara Castle lies in the depths
of the south Sligo countryside today, away from towns and main roads.[24] The evidence

---

24 See chapter 1.

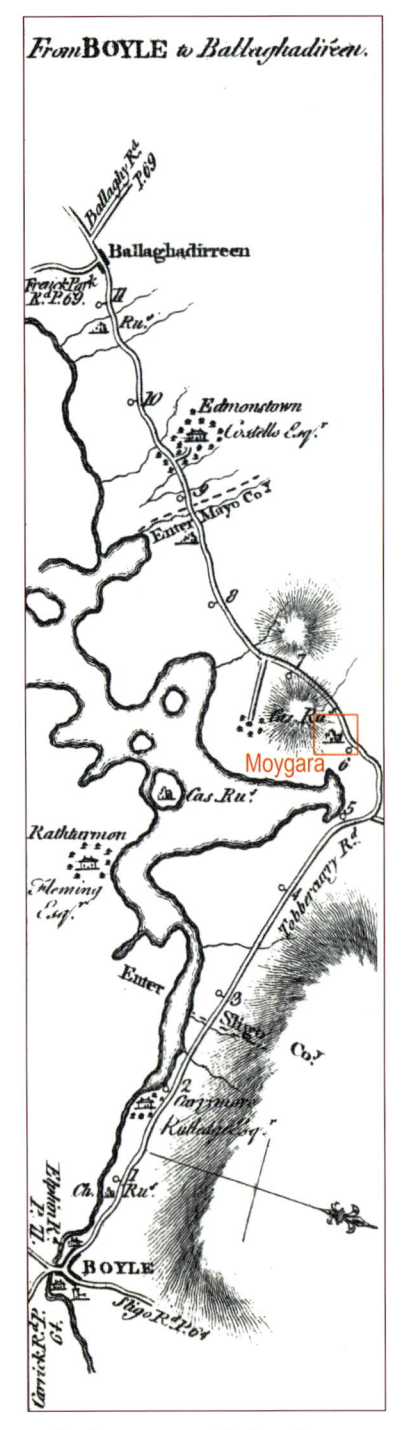

from Taylor and Skinner's eighteenth-century map suggests that this was not the case in the past. As just noted, the castle appears in the eighteenth century to have been located close to a junction of locally important roads which linked at least three prominent settlements – Boyle, Ballaghaderreen and Tubbercurry – and their hinterlands to one another. It is highly likely that this was a reflection of the road network in the area during later medieval times. In fact, it has been suggested that the Boyle/Tubbercurry road (the modern R294), depicted on the Taylor and Skinner map, which runs through a gap that lies very close to Moygara Castle between the Sliabh Lugha range and the Curlews at the north-western end of Lough Gara, was one of the three most important routes into the whole Sligo region during later medieval times.[25] The castle lies only 150m to the west of what appears to have been the main Boyle/Ballaghderreen road in the eighteenth century and presumably the later medieval period. This road is now only a very minor road (the L4103) – really no more than a boreen or lane linking farms and houses. In all, the evidence from the Taylor and Skinner map suggests strongly that Moygara during later medieval and post-medieval times was not the relatively isolated place it appears to be today, but lay beside routeways that were quite important, at least at a local and regional level.

3.5 Moygara Castle was depicted as a ruined castle on the 1777 Taylor and Skinner map of the road from Boyle to Ballaghaderreen (then in Co. Mayo) (courtesy of Trinity College Dublin).

25 See chapter 2, especially fig. 2.6.

THE FIRST-EDITION SIX-INCH ORDNANCE SURVEY MAP OF 1837

In 1824 the Ordnance Survey was given the task of mapping all of Ireland at a scale of six inches to the mile. These comprehensive maps of the Irish landscape were to be used by the government for taxation purposes and planning roads and, later, railways. The first-edition of the six-inch series of maps for all Irish counties were published between 1833 and 1846. Various later editions of these maps, adding new developments, buildings and roads, were published during the course of the second half of the nineteenth century and the early twentieth century. Antiquities of all dates were also depicted on these maps.[26]

While ruined, Moygara Castle is depicted on the 1837 first-edition Ordnance Survey map for the area as being in a relatively reasonable state of repair, not unlike today. The towers at each of the corners of the castle are shown and the gatehouse is marked clearly. A small unplanned, nucleated, clachan-type settlement of about eight to ten houses and outhouses is shown a couple of hundred metres to the south-east of the castle (fig. 3.6). Some sort of small nucleated settlement existed here in the very early eighteenth century also, as it is depicted on a map of Moygara townland, in this case to the south of the castle.[27]

It has been argued that there was little in the way of nucleated villages in the countryside of the Gaelic-dominated parts of later medieval Ireland, with dispersed settlement of single farmsteads and hamlets being the norm.[28] To a certain extent, this model is open to question. Certainly there was much dispersed settlement in later medieval Gaelic Ireland but it is now clear that there were also quite large nucleated settlements that can be best described as small towns in both their form and function, as was the situation at Roscommon throughout the later medieval period.[29] In the present context, however, while the debate continues as to the number of large, nucleated villages and small towns in later medieval Gaelic Ireland, it is generally accepted that small, unplanned clusters of houses existed beside many castles, particularly tower houses, during the sixteenth and early seventeenth centuries at least, all over Ireland, including Gaelic and gaelicized parts of the island.[30] It is possible that

26 J.H. Andrews, 'Ordnance Survey' in B. Lalor (ed.), *The encyclopaedia of Ireland* (Dublin, 2003), p. 840. **27** NLI, MS 21 F 13, no. 39.k; see chapter 2, particularly fig. 2.8. **28** See O'Conor, *The archaeology of medieval rural settlement*, pp 74, 104. **29** R. McNeary and B. Shanahan, 'The March in Roscommon, 1170–1400: culture, contact, continuity and change' in Jenifer Ní Ghrádaigh and Emmett O'Byrne (eds), *The March in the islands of the medieval West* (Leiden and Boston, 2012), pp 212–19; K. O'Conor and B. Shanahan, *Roscommon Abbey: a visitor's guide* (Roscommon, 2013), passim. **30** See K.W. Nicholls, 'Gaelic society and economy in the high Middle Ages' in A. Cosgrove (ed.), *A new history of Ireland*, ii: *Medieval Ireland, 1169–1534* (Oxford, 1987), p. 404; T.B. Barry, 'Late medieval Ireland: the debate on the social and economic transformation, 1350–1550' in B.J. Graham and L.J. Proudfoot (eds), *A historical geography of Ireland* (London, 1993), p. 118; W. Smyth, 'Property, patronage and population: reconstructing the human geography of mid-17th-century County Tipperary' in W. Nolan (ed.), *Tipperary: history and society* (Dublin, 1985), pp 118–30; O'Conor, *The archaeology of medieval rural settlement*, p. 104; see, also, McAlister, *The Irish tower house*, 51.

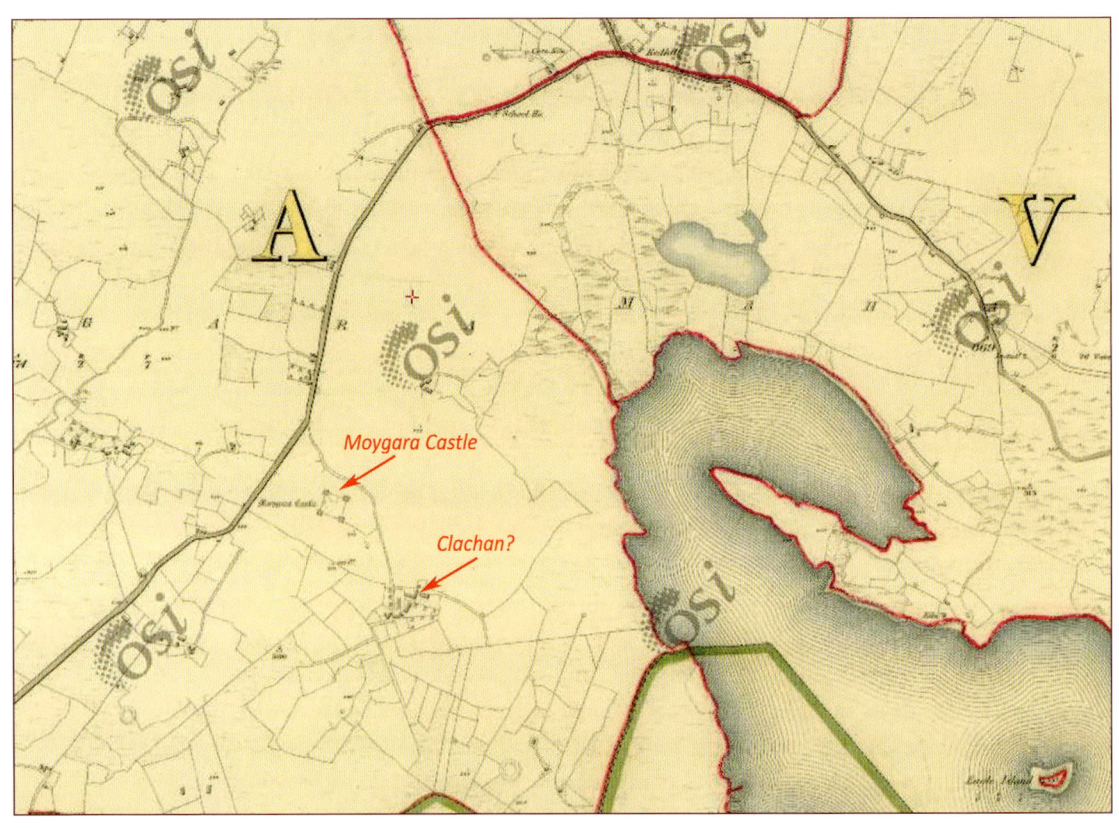

3.6 Moygara Castle as depicted on the first-edition six-inch Ordnance Survey map for the area (sheet 44), which dates to 1837. Note the clachan-type settlement to the south-east of the site (© Ordnance Survey Ireland/Government of Ireland, copyright permit no. MP 003520).

the small, unplanned nucleated settlement marked on both the early eighteenth-century map of Moygara townland and the first-edition Ordnance Survey map represent the remains and location of what originated as a small castle-centred village close to Moygara Castle at some stage in the sixteenth century or even earlier. It might be added that the surviving historical sources seem to confirm this and also suggest that a small village of some description existed beside the castle in the late sixteenth and early seventeenth centuries.[31] Presumably the inhabitants of this clachan-like village/hamlet provided services for O'Gara lords of the castle, being the place where some servants, soldiers and craftsmen lived with their families. Some of the people living in this settlement would have laboured on the O'Gara agricultural estate which lay in the immediate vicinity of the castle.[32]

31 See chapter 2.   **32** See McAlister, *The Irish tower house*, 65–89 for a useful discussion on late medieval tower houses and agriculture. The demesne lands of Moygara Castle seem to have consisted of the present townlands of Moygara, Mullaghroe and Mahanagh – see appendix 1; see, also, chapter 2.

CONCLUSIONS

There are three conclusions about Moygara Castle that can be made from this map regression study. Firstly, the fact that the castle was chosen to be depicted on Browne's map of 1589 show that the English administration in Connacht regarded it as one of the most important places in the whole Sligo area at that time. It must be remembered that the great majority of castles occupied in the county were not marked on the map – only the most important centres were depicted by Browne. Secondly, while Moygara Castle is arguably located in a quiet, secluded part of Co. Sligo today, the evidence suggests that it lay beside a junction of locally important routeways in later medieval times. Thirdly, there are hints from the historical sources and later maps that a small, unplanned village or large hamlet once existed very close to the castle when it was in use.

CHAPTER FOUR

An architectural description of Moygara Castle

RORY SHERLOCK AND KIERAN O'CONOR

Moygara Castle is essentially composed of the well-preserved remains of a large square bawn with four corner towers and a two-storey gatehouse (fig. 4.1). Three of the corner towers stand to two storeys in height, while the fourth, at the south-western corner of the bawn, stands to three storeys (fig. 4.2). Other notable features of the site include a rectangular stone-revetted platform on the northern side of the bawn and the foundations of a rectangular house-like structure along the inner face of the bawn's western wall. The aim of this paper is to describe and phase the standing visible remains of Moygara Castle. In chronological terms, the earliest structure on the site is the raised platform, which appears to have within it the base of a substantial building. The second phase of building at the site consists of the building of the bawn wall, gatehouse and corner towers. This second phase, while essentially one extended building episode, has at least two sub-phases within it. The rectangular house represents a third phase.

THE RAISED PLATFORM (PHASE 1)

The raised platform that dominates the northern end of the site is defined by a poorly preserved stone wall that has clearly been repaired and rebuilt in a number of places. The platform is located to the west of centre on the north side of the site and the northern wall of the bawn was built in line with the northern wall of the earlier structure, so that the platform is now enclosed by the later bawn.

The platform itself is a rather featureless grass-covered mound that clearly contains within it surviving masonry from an earlier structure,[1] though much of the platform's bulk is likely to be made up of rubble from this building. The original masonry of this earlier structure appears to survive best on the northern side where it may be seen to be distinctly different from the masonry of the later bawn. The only feature of note is what appears to be a latrine shaft towards the western end of the north wall of the

---

1 Read's subsequent excavation has indicated that the existing structure within this raised platform appears to be the base of a tower house. See chapter 8. The function of this raised platform, which seems to be mostly composed of the base of this tower house and collapsed masonry from its upper storeys, is discussed in the concluding article to this book, see chapter 10.

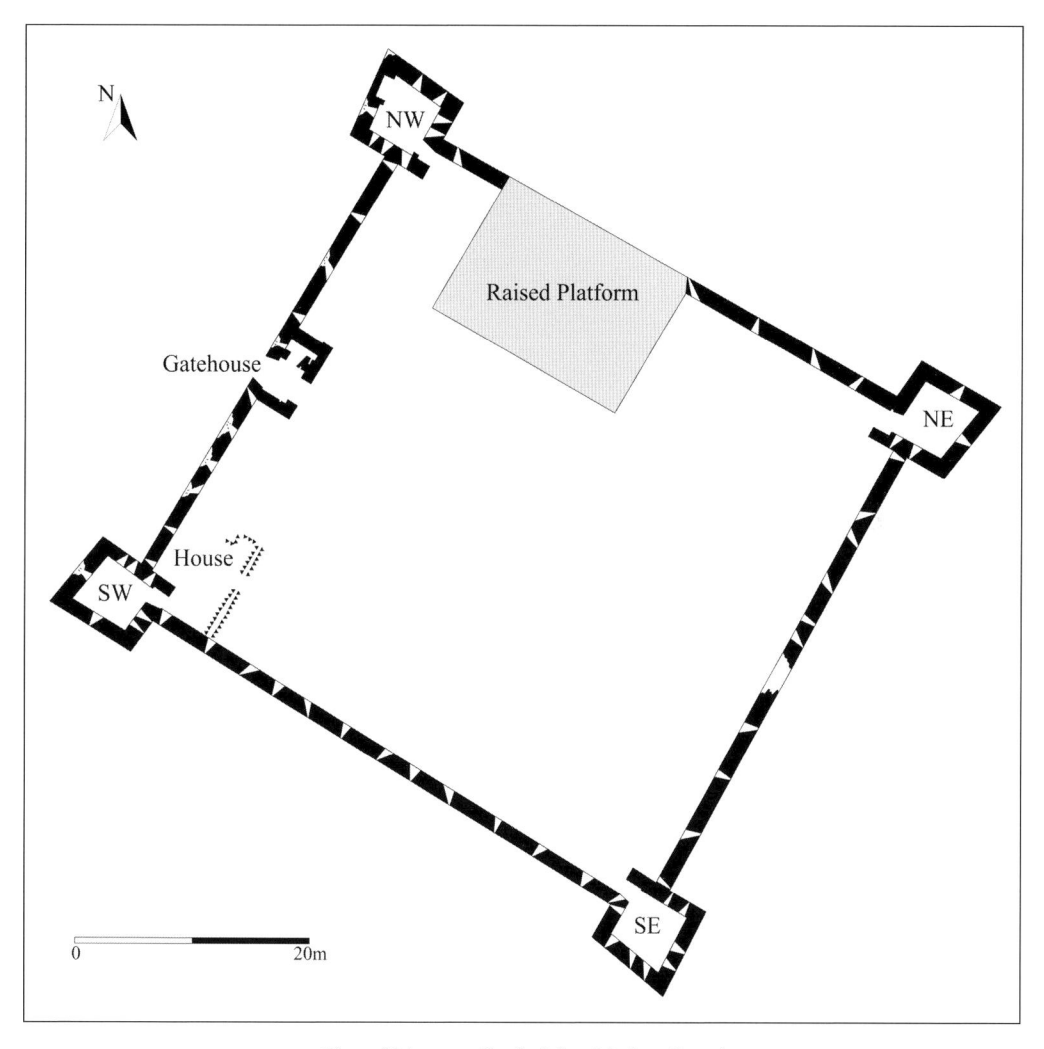

4.1 Plan of Moygara Castle (after Markus Casey).

structure and this well-constructed vertical chute in the thickness of the masonry measures 1.41m long by 0.56m wide.

It is interesting to note that the later bawn was built to the south of the platform in order to incorporate the earlier structure in the most efficient manner possible, while at the same time developing a new complex on a level site. The north-eastern, north-western and south-western corners of the new bawn were built as far away as possible from the earlier structure in order to maximize the size of the bawn while simultaneously avoiding steep falls in ground level, maintaining the square plan of the bawn and efficiently utilizing one of the long sides of the existing structure.

4.2 The interior of the bawn from the east, with the south-western flanking tower and the gatehouse evident (© Rory Sherlock).

THE BAWN, FLANKING TOWERS AND GATEHOUSE (PHASE 2)

The bawn

The bawn at Moygara Castle measures *c.* 50m square and is defined by a well-preserved stone wall pierced by at least thirty-seven gun loops, which are original features of the structure. Many further gun loops are found at all levels in the flanking towers and gatehouse and, in this respect, it can be said that bawn had quite formidable defences. The interior of the bawn slopes down gently to the south from the raised platform at the north, which occupies the highest point of the east-west ridge upon which the castle is located.

The eastern and southern walls of the bawn are exactly 4ft (1.22m) thick[2] and the use of foot-based measurements is evident elsewhere in the castle also, as many of the tower walls measure exactly 3ft (0.92m) in thickness. It would appear that initially the bawn's builders desired a simple gateway in its western wall to be the main entranceway to the castle.[3] This wall, with its gateway, was raised to a height of *c.*1.95m before it was decided to also build a two-storey gatehouse, complete with a portcullis, to its rear. The ground floor of the gatehouse (with its entrance passage) was then built to almost its first-floor level to match the height of the existing bawn wall. This explains why the walls of the ground floor of the gatehouse are not bonded into the western wall of the bawn. Anyway, once the walls of the gatehouse were built level with the existing partly completed bawn wall, work was recommenced on it. Thereafter, the upper levels of gatehouse and this western bawn wall were built together to completion. This can be seen by the fact that the stones of the gatehouse's first floor (and, actually, the very uppermost part of its ground floor) and the upper portion of the bawn's wall are tied in together and were, therefore, constructed as one. The gatehouse will be discussed in more detail below.

The remains of a distinct building line can be seen in many places about 2.30m–2.70m above ground level in the bawn's walls today. This seems to have been at least partly done to create a level line from which to build the wall walk, which is corbelled out 0.25m–0.4m in two steps on the inner face of the wall. This corbelling allowed for a wider wall walk to be built above it. This double-step feature is not seen on the northern wall of the bawn, but is evident on the full lengths of the eastern and southern walls and also runs along the western wall from the south-western tower towards the gatehouse before terminating abruptly. Very little survives of the upper sections of the bawn wall above the level of the double-step courses, though the southern wall does retain up to 1m of walling above this point. In a number of locations where the bawn wall joins the flanking towers, evidence can be seen on the tower façade for a tall parapet wall that once rose from the outer edge of the bawn wall. It is probable that this parapet wall originally had crenellations and gun loops in its merlons.[4]

The flanking towers

The four flanking towers of the castle are not square in plan, as the outermost angle is slightly acute, which gives each tower a subtle spearhead-shape in plan (figs 4.1 and 4.3). The towers are remarkably similar to each other in terms of their general

2 This makes Moygara Castle's curtain wall thicker than the average bawn wall (James Lyttleton, pers. comm.) **3** The western wall is the side of Moygara Castle that was closest to the then main Ballaghaderreen/Boyle Road and faced the natural line of approach to the site. See chapter 3.   **4** Gun loops can be seen in profusion in the merlons surviving at a number of other late bawns, such as in the crenellations extant at Pallas Castle, Co. Galway or Parke's Castle, Co. Leitrim. The fact that the merlons on the battlements of the well preserved south-west tower at Moygara Castle have gun loops suggests that the now-destroyed ones on the bawn's curtain wall were similar.

4.3 The exterior of the south-eastern flanking tower (© Rory Sherlock).

form and in their particular features. Each tower would appear to have had two entrance doorways, one at ground-floor level and another at first-floor level, and the lack of evidence for steps leading up to the elevated doorways would suggest that they were probably accessed by fixed timber stairs originally. It appears likely that these external staircases also gave access to the wall walks atop the adjacent bawn walls. It is unclear if direct access was possible between the ground-floor levels and the first-floor levels of the towers, as the internal staircases begin at first-floor level in each of the towers. The staircase within the south-western tower gave access from the first floor to the second floor and then the wall walk and was provided with a series of gun loops at each level (figs 4.4–4.7). While the south-western tower stands to three storeys in height, as noted, the remaining three towers now stand to just two storeys and it is unclear if this was their original height or if they once stood the full three storeys also (figs 4.8–4.10).

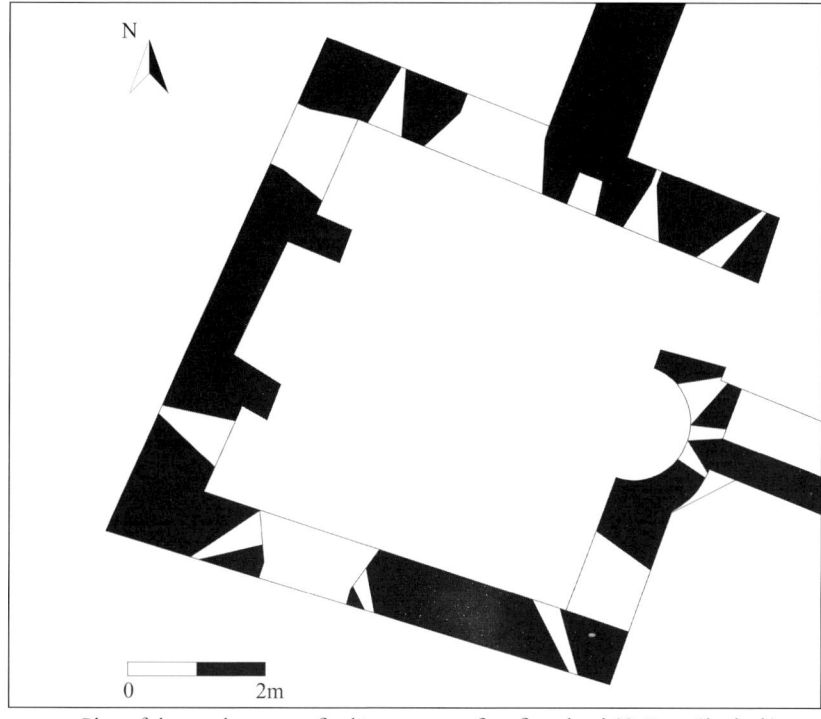

4.4 Plan of the south-western flanking tower at first-floor level (© Rory Sherlock).

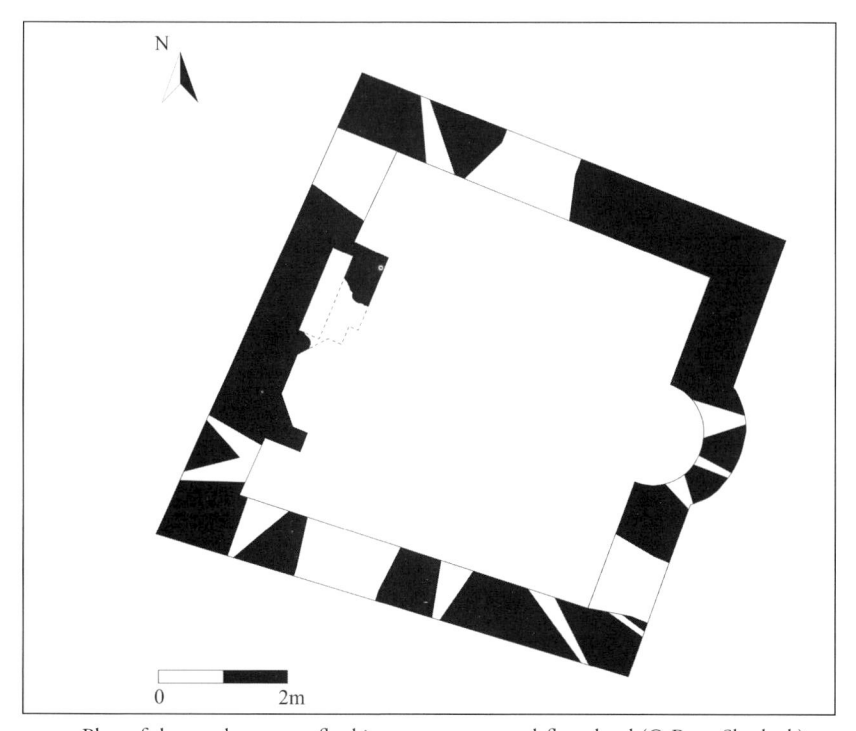

4.5 Plan of the south-western flanking tower at second-floor level (© Rory Sherlock).

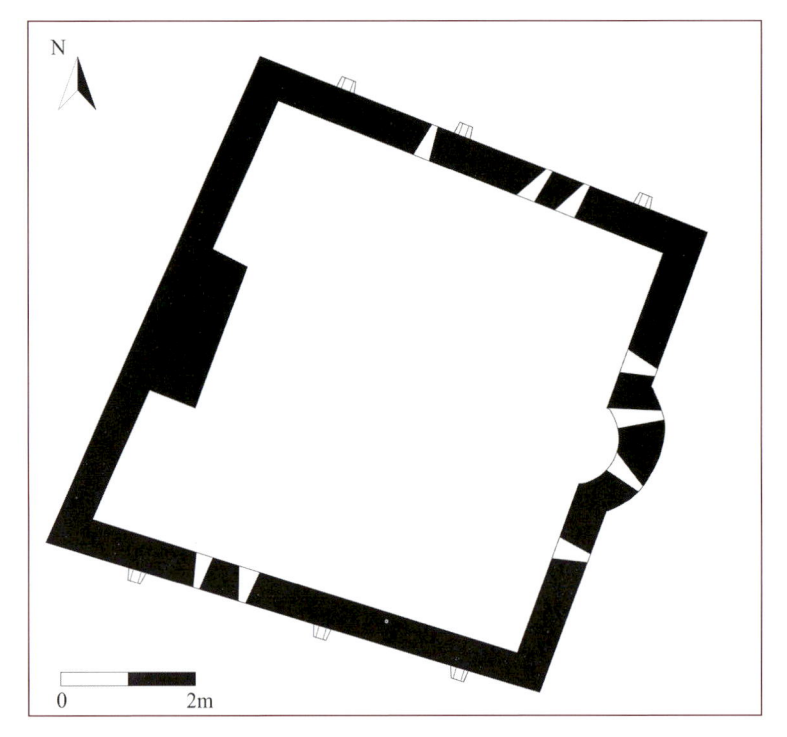

4.6 (*above*) Plan of the south-western flanking tower at wall-walk level (© Rory Sherlock).

4.7 The stairs alcove in the south-western flanking tower (© Rory Sherlock).

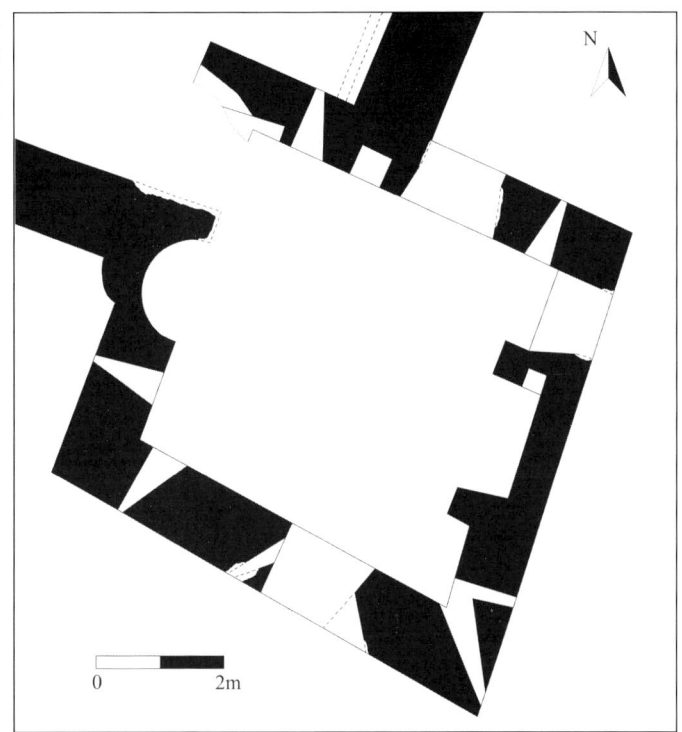

4.8 Plan of the south-
eastern flanking tower at
first-floor level
(© Rory Sherlock).

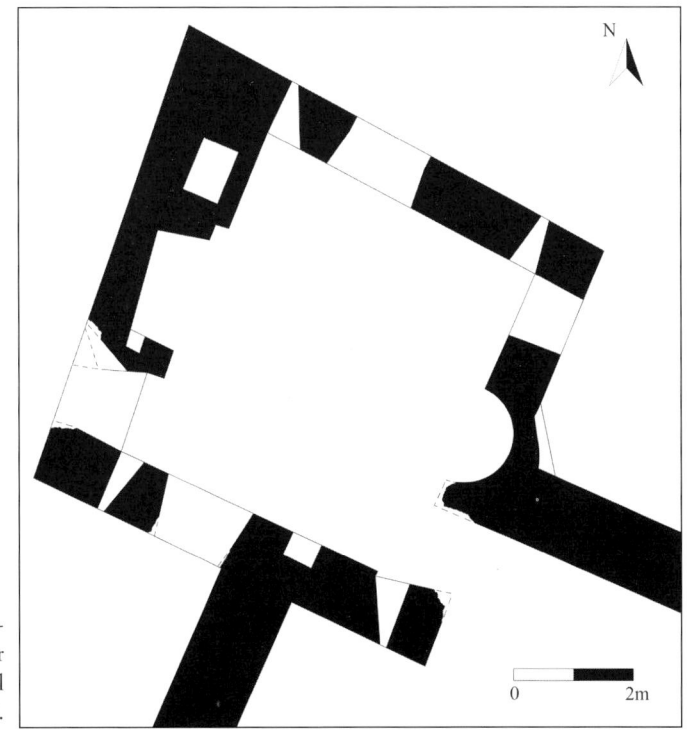

4.9 Plan of the north-
western flanking tower
at first-floor level
(© Rory Sherlock).

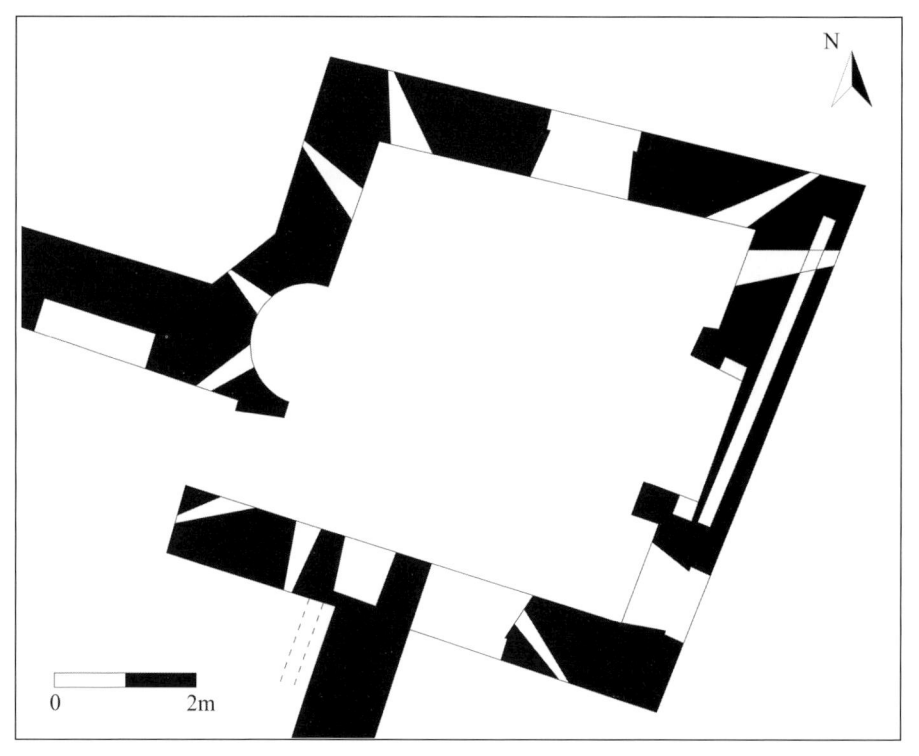

4.10 Plan of the north-eastern flanking tower at first-floor level (© Rory Sherlock).

It is notable that the tower doorways face in just two directions – the doorways of the eastern towers face west and the doorways of the western towers face east, with no tower doorways facing either north or south. Similarly, the stairs turrets that project from each tower are found only on either the western or eastern facades. In each case, they rise from first-floor level and are partially supported by the bawn wall beneath them and partially carried on a squinch arch or angle lintel spanning the gap between the latter wall and the wall of the tower.

All four towers have large original fireplaces at first floor level and similar fireplaces are also found at second-floor level in the south-western tower and at ground-floor level in the north-western tower. The presence of a fireplace at ground-floor level in the north-western tower may suggest that this chamber served as a kitchen. This theory finds some support in the presence of a large slop stone in the north wall of the room. The fireplaces are quite large, measuring 1.25m–1.4m in height from the surface of the hearth to the underside of the lintel, and all fireplaces are located in the wall opposite the doorway into the room.

Three types of window or ope occur in the flanking towers and their locations were, upon detailed analysis, found to follow a certain pattern. The three types noted are: large wide windows at first- and second-floor levels; vertical loops measuring *c.*0.45m

4.11 Gun loops in the parapet of the south-western flanking tower (© Rory Sherlock).

4.12 A drip stone on the wall walk of the south-western flanking tower (© Rory Sherlock).

high and *c*.0.12m wide, which were fitted with well-cut limestone jambs; and simple gun loops.

The first type of window is usually found in at least three walls of the first- or second-floor rooms in the towers. In fact, the western towers have or had four windows in each room on their upper floors, while the eastern towers have just three in each. Just one such window is found in each wall and they are normally positioned centrally in the wall unless the presence of another mural feature, such as a stair alcove or a fireplace, dictated that the window should be positioned off-centre in it.

The deployment of the second type of ope, the narrow vertical loop, also seems to follow a strict pattern. They are usually found looking into the bawn at ground- and first-floor levels from the sides of the flanking towers that project into the bawn but which do not contain the doorways and are therefore found in the southern walls of the northern towers and the northern walls of the southern towers. In addition, further examples are found, or are likely to have been found, looking outside the castle at ground-floor level in the eastern walls of the eastern towers and the western walls of the western towers.

The third form of ope, the simple gun loop, is found at all levels in all four towers and examples may be found that look into the bawn, though the majority look outwards (figs 4.11 and 4.12). The fact that some gun loops in the towers cover the interior of the bawn means that each individual tower had the potential to hold out independently, even if the rest of the castle had fallen to attackers.

The gatehouse

The sequence of the way in which this poorly preserved two-storey gatehouse, the gateway and the adjacent bawn wall were built has been discussed above. The gateway itself is *c*.2.2m in width. The gatehouse behind it has a central gate passage running through it at ground-floor level from the latter gateway eastwards into the bawn and this passage was protected by the original wooden gate and an inner portcullis which was operated from the upper level of the gatehouse (figs 4.13 and 4.14). A portcullis was an openwork defensive gate of iron or wood (or wood sheeted in iron) that was able to slide up and down in grooves cut into the walls of castle gate passageways or the jambs of castle gateways. It was operated by a lever in the room over the gate passage (as at Moygara, as just noted) and its importance was that it could be dropped to provide an instantaneous barrier to stop a surprise attack. A second, inner wooden gate may also have been positioned at the inner end of the gate passage in this gatehouse.

There is evidence to suggest that there was a large box machicolation over the entrance gate too, but this no longer survives (fig. 4.15). Certainly the 1791 sketch of Moygara Castle by Cocking shows one.[5] A machicolation can be defined as an opening

5 See chapter 2, fig. 2.10.

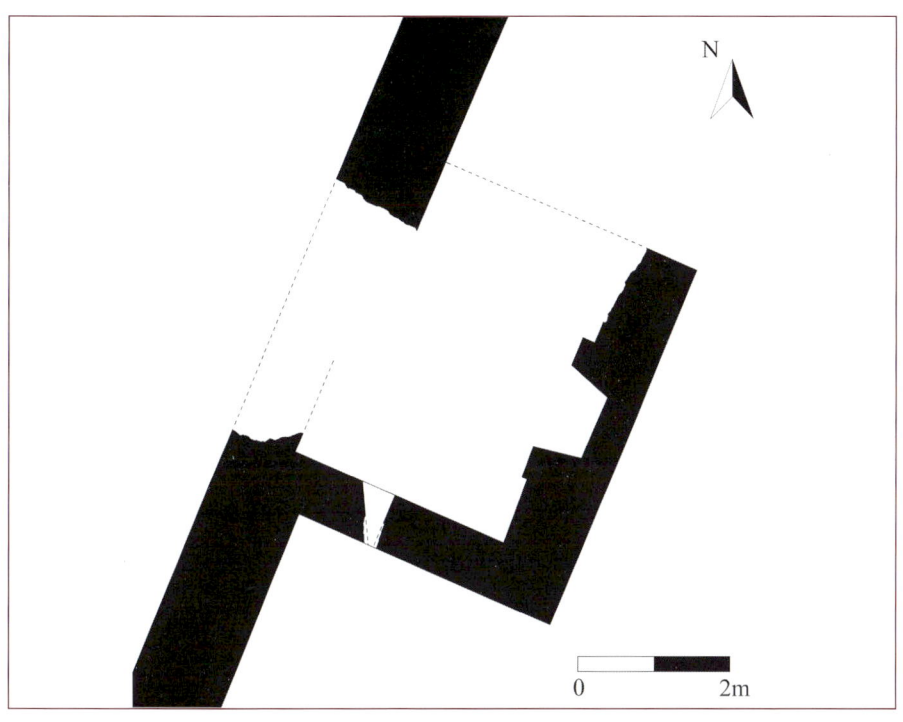

4.13 (*above*) Plan of the gatehouse at first-floor level (© Rory Sherlock).

4.14 The portcullis slot within the gatehouse (© Rory Sherlock).

4.15 Figurative carving on a stone lying in the gatehouse. This stone was once part of the
machicolation over the gateway (© Rory Sherlock).

between the supporting corbels of a projecting parapet through which missiles could
be dropped down on attackers at the base of a wall, tower or, as in the case of Moygara,
gatehouse. The first-floor level of the gatehouse would appear to have been occupied
by a single room within which the mechanism for raising and lowering the portcullis,
the access to the box machicolation and a fireplace were probably located, though it is
difficult to envisage how the fireplace could have been used if the portcullis was raised.

THE HOUSE (PHASE 3)

The foundations of a rectangular building extend along the inner face of the western
wall of the bawn from its southern wall and the south-western tower almost as far
north as the gatehouse located midway along the western side of the bawn. This
rectangular structure, which appears to be later in date than the bawn because it blocks
a gun loop in its western wall, is likely to have been a one- or two-storey domestic
structure. It probably dates to the seventeenth or eighteenth centuries, but is not
clearly indicated on the first-edition six-inch Ordnance Survey map, which dates to

the late 1830s. It appears to have been built across the access route to the ground-floor doorway of the south-western tower and it remains unclear if it was built to extend the accommodation available in this tower or if it functioned as an independent entity after the abandonment of the tower.[6]

CONCLUSIONS

This architectural description of Moygara Castle has shown a number of things. Firstly, it demonstrated (even before the excavation by Christopher Read) that the northern platform seems to represent the remains of an early building (which has a latrine), whose northern wall was incorporated into the later bawn (fig. 4.16). The bawn, with its four flanking towers, represents the second phase of masonry construction at the castle. While the gatehouse, with its portcullis, was not initially planned as part of this second phase, a decision was made to build it when the bawn wall was almost 2m high. The upper portions of the gatehouse and the western bawn wall were then built together. This all suggests that the gatehouse should be seen as part of the second phase of building at Moygara, albeit started a little later than the bawn wall adjacent to it with its entranceway. A third phase is represented by the rectangular building whose foundations can still be seen on the south-western side of the site. The fact that there are three phases of masonry construction visible in the architecture at Moygara highlights the point made in the introduction to this volume that castles and, for that matter, other medieval and post-medieval buildings, such as parish churches, chapels-of-ease, abbeys, friaries and undefended gentry houses, were often re-modelled to suit contemporary needs.[7] The fact that a number of architectural phases are visible in buildings, such as Moygara Castle, is also an indication that many of them were occupied for long periods of time, often for several centuries.

Nevertheless, it is the second phase of building activity at the site – the fine bawn, with its distinctive spear-shaped flanking towers, and the gatehouse – that dominates people's perception of the place and is the most visible and spectacular today. This is the castle that people, in particular the O'Gara clan, with their proud and ancient past, are romantically attached to because of the power of its architecture. Therefore, it may come as a surprise for them to learn that there is more to the castle than just one construction phase, but, again, it must be emphasized that there is nothing unique about this – castle after castle across Ireland, Britain and Europe, when analyzed in depth by archaeologists and architectural historians, show evidence for continued re-building and re-modelling.[8] The evidence from Moygara Castle fits a pattern.

---

6 See chapter 8.   7 See chapter 1.   8 See W. Meyer, 'Castle archaeology: an introduction' in M. Carver and J. Klápště (eds), *The archaeology of medieval Europe*, ii: *twelfth to fifteenth centuries* (Aarhus, 2011), pp 234–5.

4.16 A section of the external façade of the northern wall of the bawn showing the join between the earlier structure (left) and the bawn wall (right) (© Rory Sherlock).

There are other things of note about the architecture of this highly impressive second phase at Moygara Castle. The architectural arrangements, windows and use of space in each of the towers are almost exactly similar in detail and this regimentation of design stands out. It is also clear from the numerous gun loops in both the bawn wall and the towers, from the box-machicolation over the gateway, and from the added gatehouse, with its portcullis, that the castle in this phase was very well defended. If properly and stoutly held by men armed with the latest firearms, it would have proved a difficult place to capture.

CHAPTER FIVE

Moygara Castle: the wider context

RORY SHERLOCK, PAUL M. KERRIGAN AND
KIERAN O'CONOR

INTRODUCTION

In general terms, following on from the last chapter, the remains of the second phase of building activity at Moygara Castle are clearly the most visible today. This phase consisted of a bawn wall with four substantial flankers, a gateway with a machicolation over it and a gatehouse to its rear. The architecture of these elements is characteristic of Irish castle architecture of the late sixteenth and early to mid-seventeenth centuries and in particular of the bawns built during the establishment of the Ulster Plantation and later plantations in north-west Ireland by incoming English and Lowland Scots settlers, but also by some native Irish grantees, in the second, third and fourth decades of the seventeenth century.

The profusion of gun loops throughout the bawn walls and flanking towers at Moygara is, perhaps, more reminiscent of a military fortification than a castle designed for residential use and it is important to note in this regard that the early seventeenth century saw the development of a clear differentiation between military forts and private lordly residences, where before these two functions would have been easily accommodated with the walls of a medieval castle.[1] The means by which the space at Moygara was used in the seventeenth century is difficult to establish, as it cannot even be determined, for example, if the north-eastern, north-western and south-eastern towers were originally of two storeys, as they now stand, or if they were originally three storeys in height, as the south-western tower currently stands. This simple question has significant implications for the interpretation of the remains at Moygara and one should note that the current pre-eminence of the south-western tower based on its height may simply be a modern misreading of the architecture of the castle made, quite understandably, on the basis of surviving evidence rather than original form.

To place the dominant second phase of building activity at Moygara Castle in its wider architectural and chronological context, comparisons may be made between certain notable architectural features at Moygara and similar features found elsewhere. The principal motifs that allow Moygara to be compared to similar sites are:

---

1 See K. O'Conor, 'Fortifications in the North (1200–1600)' in M. Carver and J. Klápště (eds), *The archaeology of medieval Europe*, ii: *twelfth to sixteenth centuries AD* (Aarhus, 2011), pp 243, 250–2, for the wider European context.

- The erection of a plantation-style bawn on the site of an earlier Gaelic castle.
- The general layout of the bawn with four flankers and gatehouse.
- The shape of the flankers (i.e. the acute outermost angle).
- The form of the stairs in the flanking towers.

IMPOSITION OR ADOPTION?

The architectural and archaeological evidence, when considered in conjunction with the available historical evidence, suggests that the earlier platform at the northern edge of the site, which represents the first recognizable masonry-building activity at Moygara, seems to be the remains of the late medieval O'Gara castle, apparently a tower house, which is known to have existed in 1538.[2] While no direct historical references have been found to confirm that much of the remains seen at Moygara Castle today represent a bawn of late sixteenth- or early to mid-seventeenth-century date, the bawn clearly belongs to a secondary phase of construction at the site – one that saw a massive remodelling of the castle, although the exact impetus behind the construction of this second, later phase is somewhat unclear and a matter of debate.[3] The scenario whereby Gaelic strongholds were taken over, re-modelled or re-established by either settlers or Irish or Old English gentry as plantation-style castles is not uncommon and several comparable examples may be identified in the region, though it cannot be suggested based on the evidence currently available that similar events led to the construction of the bawn at Moygara. However, it may be useful to outline the changes that befell certain Gaelic sites in the north-west of Ireland between *c.*1580 and *c.*1650 in order to more fully understand the wider context of the bawn at Moygara.

In the O'Rourke lordship of West Breifne (i.e. much of the present county of Leitrim), several important strongholds were taken over by incoming New English settlers in the late sixteenth and early seventeenth centuries. The abandoned O'Rourke tower house at Newtown on the shores of Lough Gill was destroyed and a plantation bawn (which was re-modelled out of the pre-existing O'Rourke tower house bawn) was established on the site. Shortly afterwards, *c.*1630, a fortified house (fig. 5.1) was built within the bawn by Captain Robert Parke and the site is now known as Parke's Castle.[4] In a similar case from the same lordship, the principal seat of the O'Rourkes at Dromahair, Co. Leitrim, is known to have been a very important site and to have had a tower house and a large hall at its core. The late medieval hall of the O'Rourkes survives but after the site was taken by the earl of Clanricarde and Sir Richard

---

2 *AConn* 1538.5; *ALC* 1538.5; *AFM*; see chapters 2, 4 and 8.   3 See chapter 10.   4 See C. Foley and C. Donnelly, *Parke's Castle, Co. Leitrim: archaeology, history and architecture* (Dublin, 2012); M. Salter, *The castles of Connacht* (Malvern, 2004), p. 66.

5.1 Parke's Castle, Co. Leitrim (© Rory Sherlock).

Bingham, the tower house was subsequently levelled to be replaced by a fortified house constructed by one of the Villiers family in 1628, probably William Villiers.[5]

Moving further afield, the castle of Castlederg in west Co. Tyrone provides further evidence for the takeover of Gaelic strongholds by settlers in the early seventeenth century. A bawn (fig. 5.2), measuring 34m by 30m, which originally had four square flankers attached and a house within, was built *c.*1615 by Sir John Davies, the famous

---

5 M. Moore, *Archaeological inventory of County Leitrim* (Dublin, 2003), p. 213; Salter, *The castles of Connacht*, p. 64; see, also, K. O'Conor and C. Fredengren, 'Medieval settlement in Leitrim, 1169–*c.*1380AD' in L. Kelly and B. Scott (eds), *Leitrim history and society: interdisciplinary essays on the history of an Irish county* (Dublin, 2019),

5.2 Castlederg, Co. Tyrone (© Rory Sherlock).

Welsh writer and attorney general for Ireland.[6] During excavations undertaken by Conor Newman in 1991, the foundations of a tower house were found in the centre of the bawn and indeed the plantation bawn appears to have incorporated parts of the earlier bawn associated with the tower.[7] The tower house was controlled by the O'Donnells and the O'Neills at various periods during the fifteenth and sixteenth centuries.[8] In another comparable example from Co. Tyrone, a large bawn was built at Benburb in 1611 by Sir Richard Wingfield on the site of an earlier O'Neill stronghold.[9]

pp 82–4. **6** M. Salter, *The castles of Ulster* (Malvern, 2004), p. 66. **7** C. Newman, 'Castlederg Castle' in I. Bennett (ed.), *Excavations 1991: summary accounts of archaeological excavations in Ireland* (Bray, 1992), pp 43–4. **8** Salter, *The castles of Ulster*, p. 66. **9** P.M. Kerrigan, *Castles and fortifications in Ireland, 1485–1945* (Cork, 1995), p. 72.

THE BAWN AT MOYGARA

The distinctive plan of Moygara Castle, with a stone-walled bawn defended by four corner flankers and accessed via a gateway and gatehouse, is not unique and can be compared to many other sites in the north-west of Ireland. The aforementioned castle of Castlederg, Co. Tyrone, is comparable to Moygara in terms of general plan form and so too are, for example, the early seventeenth-century bawns of Tully, Aghalane and Portora, Co. Fermanagh, Faugher, Co. Donegal, Lismore, Co. Tyrone (called 'Favour Royal' by Salter), Castleblaney, Co. Monaghan, Clegna, Cootehall, Co. Roscommon, and Manorhamilton, Co. Leitrim (see table 5.1).[10]

Table 5.1 Builders and construction dates of bawns comparable to Moygara Castle

Site	County	Builder	Date
Tully	Fermanagh	Sir John Hume	1615–18
Aghalane	Fermanagh	Thomas Creighton	*c.*1615–18
Portora	Fermanagh	Sir William Cole	*c.*1615
Faugher	Donegal	Tirlagh Roe O'Boyle	1611–19
Castlederg	Tyrone	Sir John Davies	*c.*1615
Lismore	Tyrone	George Ridgeway	1611–18
Castleblaney	Monaghan	Sir Edward Blayney	*c.*1611
Cootehall	Roscommon	Sir Charles Coote	*c.*1620
Manorhamilton	Leitrim	Sir Frederick Hamilton	1622–38 (but probably built post-1635)

Tully, Aghalane, Portora, Faugher, Castlederg and Lismore were all built by beneficiaries of the Plantation of Ulster, who were required, under the terms of the plantation scheme, to build strong bawns on the lands granted to them. Under the terms of the plantation scheme, the baronies of counties Donegal, Tyrone, Fermanagh, Armagh and Cavan were assigned to one of three types of people: English undertakers and servitors; Lowland Scots undertakers and servitors; approved native Irish gentry. Accordingly, the baronies of Magheraboy and Knockninny in Co. Fermanagh, within which Tully, Aghalane and Portora were built, had been granted to Scottish undertakers, while Castlederg and Lismore were built by English undertakers in the

---

10 See B. Lacey, *Archaeological inventory of County Donegal* (Lifford, 1983), pp 367–9; Kerrigan, *Castles and fortifications in Ireland*, p. 80; Salter, *The castles of Ulster*, pp 52, 57, 66–7; idem, *The castles of Connacht*, pp 65, 90; K. O'Conor, 'English settlement and change in Roscommon during the late sixteenth and seventeenth centuries' in A. Horning, R. Ó Baoill, C. Donnelly and P. Logue (eds), *The post-medieval archaeology of Ireland, 1550–1850* (Dublin, 2007), p. 198.

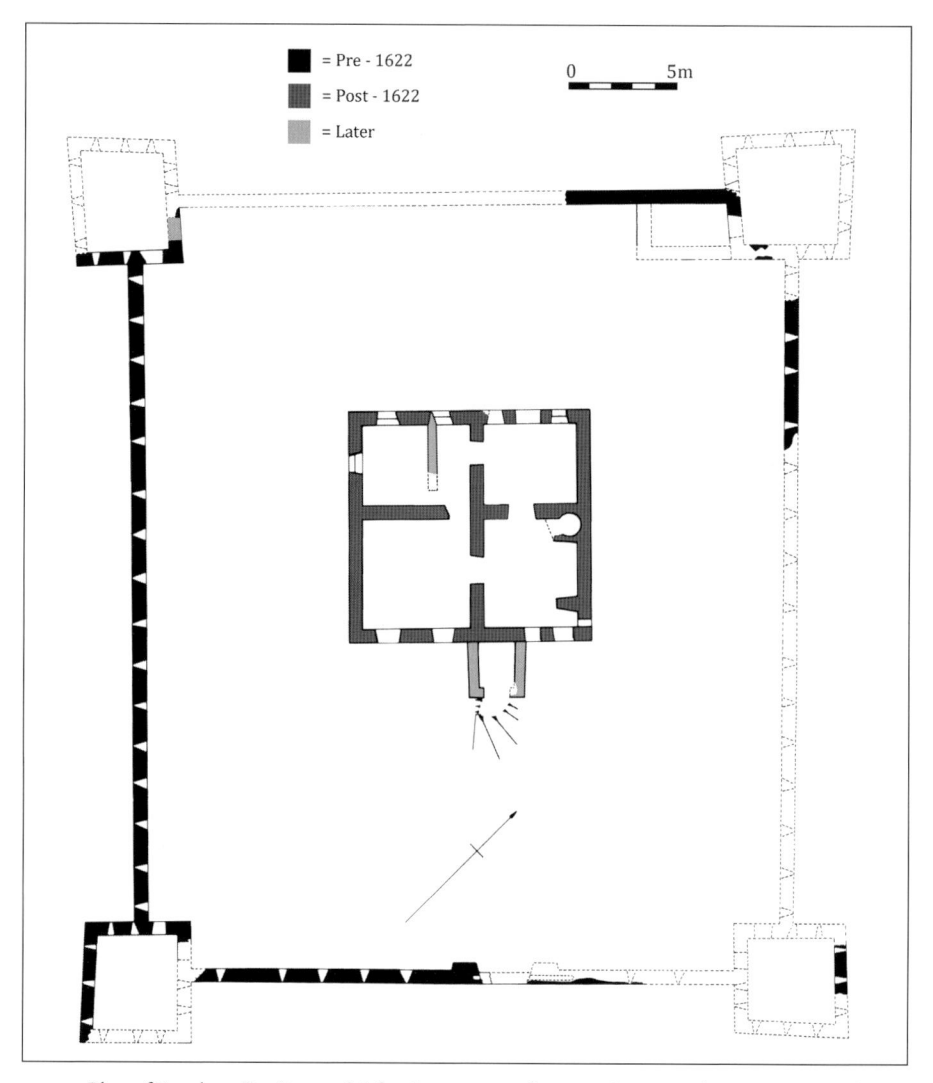

5.3 Plan of Faugher, Co. Donegal (after Laccy 1983, fig. 193; © Donegal County Council).

baronies of Omagh and Clogher in Co. Tyrone, though it appears that it was actually an Englishman, Captain William Cole, who built the bawn at Portora after he purchased it from the original Scottish grantee, Jerome (or Jeremy) Lindsey.[11]

The case of Faugher (fig. 5.3), in the barony of Kilmacrenan in Co. Donegal, is of considerable interest also, in that this plantation bawn is one of few surviving such

---

11 G. Hill, *An historical account of the Plantation in Ulster at the commencement of the seventeenth century, 1608–1620* (Belfast, 1877), pp 266–7, 271, 299–305, 494; R.J. Hunter, 'Sir William Cole, the town of Enniskillen and Plantation County Fermanagh' in E. Murphy and W.J. Roulston (eds), *Fermanagh history and society: interdisciplinary essays on the history of an Irish county* (Dublin, 2004), pp 122, 133.

structures which were built by native Irish landholders in the distinctive style of architecture associated with the Plantation of Ulster. Hill records that one Tirlagh O'Boyle was granted 2,000 acres in the Plantation but the strict tripartite separation of settlers under the terms of the plantation had a profound effect upon him, as the lands of his late father, the lord of Boylagh, were assigned to Scottish undertakers.[12] This meant that O'Boyle could not be granted land in the area. Instead, O'Boyle had to move northwards from the homelands he had lost in the barony of Boylagh in order to occupy his newly acquired lands in the old MacSweeney lordship of Doe in what later became the barony of Kilmacrenan. As a result, O'Boyle found himself settled immediately to the south of Sir Mulmory McSweeney na Doe and though he was now in the old territory of the MacSweeneys, he was essentially on equal terms with his new neighbour.[13] It is interesting to note, in fact, that these two figures were among just six native landholders who received large estates in Donegal under the terms of the plantation and of these six, O'Boyle and the heads of the three branches of the MacSweeneys each received 2,000 acres to hold forever in common socage at a rent of £21 6s. 8d. On the other hand, the fifth native recipient of a large estate, Walter McLaughlin McSweeney, was given less than 900 acres and the sixth, Hugh McHugh Duffe O'Donnell, was given 1,000 acres for the duration of his life after which the land would revert to Sir Richard Hansard.[14] It appears that O'Boyle moved relatively quickly to fulfil certain terms of the plantation scheme, though he was clearly less enthusiastic about others, and Pynnar, who undertook a survey of the progress of the plantation in 1618 and 1619, reported that:

> Tirlagh Roe O'Boyle hath 2,000 acres, called Caroghbleagh and Clomas. He hath built a good Bawne and a House of Lime and Stone, in which he, with his Family dwelleth. He hath made no estates, and all his Tenants do plough after the Irish Manner.[15]

Sir Edward Blayney built two bawns in Co. Monaghan in the early seventeenth century, at some stage after 1607, and though these sites no longer survive, both are illustrated on contemporary plans.[16] Both of these bawns, at Castleblayney (fig. 5.4) and Monaghan town, are essentially composed of a stone wall enclosing an area measuring c.67m square and while the bawn at Monaghan has just two spearhead-shaped flankers positioned at opposing corners of the structure, that at Castleblayney, built c.1611, has four flankers, two of which are circular and two of which are spearhead shaped.[17]

12 Hill, *An historical account of the Plantation in Ulster*, pp 328–9.   **13** Ibid.   **14** Ibid., pp 327–30; R.J. Hunter, 'Plantation in Donegal' in W. Nolan, L. Ronayne and M. Dunlevy (eds), *Donegal history and society: interdisciplinary essays on the history of an Irish county* (Dublin, 1995), p. 292.   **15** Hill, *An historical account of the Plantation in Ulster*, p. 526.   **16** TCD, MS 1209 (32).   **17** See P.M. Kerrigan, 'Seventeenth-century fortifications, forts and garrisons in Ireland: a preliminary list', *Irish Sword*, 14 (1980), pl. 16; idem, *Castles and*

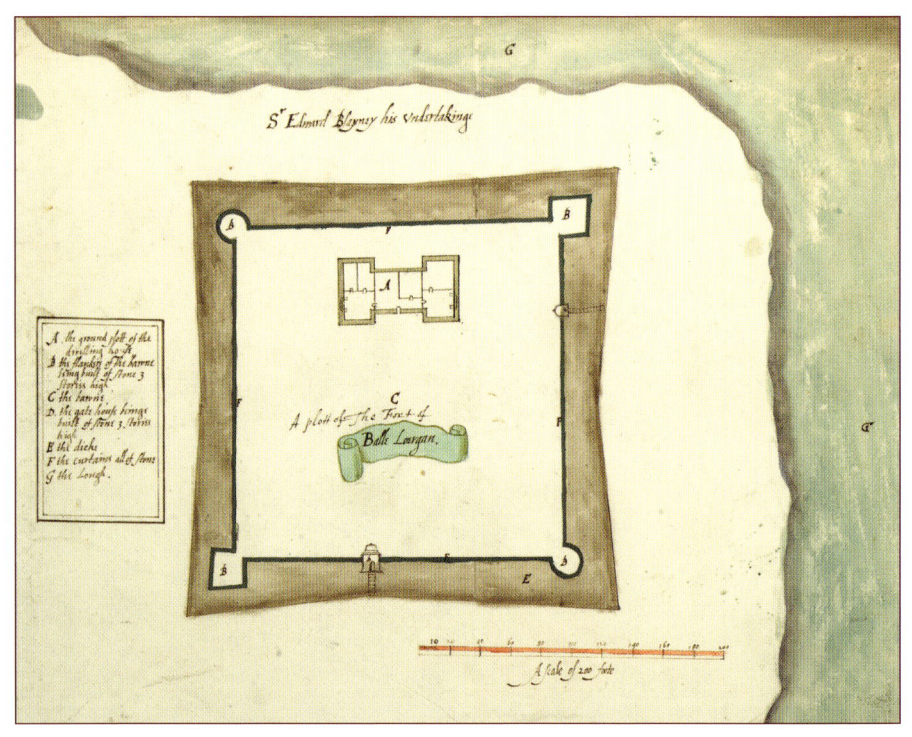

5.4 Plan of Sir Edward Blayney's fort at Castleblayney, Co. Monaghan (TCD, MS 1209/32, by permission of the Board of Trinity College Dublin).

It has been suggested that the fortified house and bawn, which originally had four flankers, still largely visible today in Manorhamilton, Co. Leitrim, was built by the Scottish nobleman Sir Frederick Hamilton in 1638.[18] Direct evidence to support this claim, however, is hard to find. It is possible, too, that Hamilton built his house and bawn there in the early to mid-1620s after he had been granted 5,500 acres in the plantation scheme designed for Leitrim. This consisted of two parcels of land centred on the Glenfarne area and what was to become Manorhamilton.[19] Under the terms of his grant, dated 18 March 1622, Hamilton agreed to build a castle surrounded by a bawn on his lands within three years or forfeit £780.[20] This may well have been the spur to the building of Manorhamilton Castle but again direct proof of this has not been forthcoming. In fact, it has been noted that there was a remarkable degree of non-compliance by the grantees of the Leitrim plantation with the terms of their land grants. Little seems to have been built in the county in the immediate years after

fortifications in Ireland, p. 80.   **18** D. Mac an Ghallóglaigh, 'Sir Frederick Hamilton', *Breifne*, 3:9 (1966), pp 59–60; Moore, *Archaeological inventory of County Leitrim*, p. 312.   **19** D. Rooney, 'Sir Frederick Hamilton (1590–1647), Leitrim planter' in L. Kelly and B. Scott (eds), *Leitrim history and society: interdisciplinary essays on the history of an Irish county* (Dublin, 2019), p. 262.   **20** M.C. Griffiths (ed.), *Irish patent rolls of James I: facsimile of the Irish Record Commission's calendar prepared prior to 1830* (Dublin, 1966), p. 539.

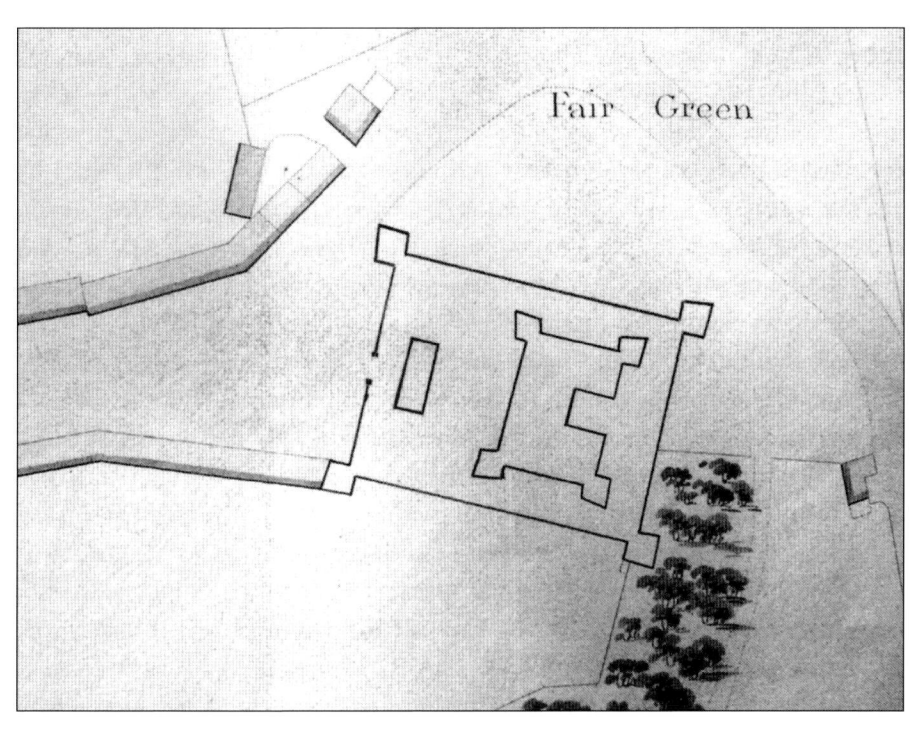

5.5 William Larkin's 1807 map of Manorhamilton Castle, Co. Leitrim (NLI, MS 16 F11, by courtesy of the National Library of Ireland).

1622.[21] Furthermore, however, it seems that when Sir Frederick moved with his young wife to Leitrim during the summer of 1622, they resided on the Glenfarne portion of their new land grant and not at Manorhamilton.[22] Sir Frederick proceeded to expand his Leitrim holdings throughout the 1620s, buying up lands between Glenfarne and Manorhamilton from both English grantees of the Leitrim plantation and native Irishmen. This meant that his lands in Leitrim were considerably more extensive by 1630 than they had been in 1622, now amounting to over 15,000 acres.[23] This enlarged estate was to act as the basis for further plans by him to extend his lands even further and to build a suitable residence with gardens, orchards and deer park in true aristocratic style.[24] However, this plan seems to have been delayed for a number of years, as Sir Frederick spent the next couple of years campaigning in Germany and then resided at court in England.[25] It appears that it was not until the mid-1630s that he really had the time and resources to build his castle at Manorhamilton, move his main residence to it and found a settlement of up to fifty houses there.[26] While it is

21 R. Loeber, *Irish houses and castles, 1400–1740* (Dublin, 2019), pp 125–6. **22** Rooney, 'Sir Frederick Hamilton (1590–1647), Leitrim planter', p. 263. **23** Ibid., pp 264–5. **24** Ibid., p. 265. **25** Ibid., pp 265–7. **26** Ibid., p. 267.

possible that the castle at Manorhamilton was built sometime between 1622 and 1625, on balance, this outline of Sir Frederick's activities in the 1620s and 1630s suggests that the castle at Manorhamilton, whose bawn bore much similarity to the one at Moygara, as its flankers were also apparently spearheaded in shape originally and seem to have been three storeys in height,[27] was constructed after the mid-1630s and was probably completed by 1638 (fig. 5.5). It might be added that the most recent published statement on Manorhamilton, while not giving an exact date for the construction of the castle there, believes that it was built 'in the 1630s' after Sir Frederick came back 'from the Thirty Years War in Germany'.[28]

The historical evidence associated with these sites serves to strongly support the contention that large open bawns with four corner flankers were a characteristic feature of the architecture associated with incoming settlers in west Ulster and parts of north Connacht in the early seventeenth century. However, it appears likely that, in certain cases, these new and distinctive architectural forms were also adopted by Gaelic Irish and Old English landholders and there is some historical evidence to suggest that this was the case at Moygara.[29] Similar conclusions have been noted in other parts of Ireland – not just in its north-western part. O'Conor has briefly noted that certain Gaelic lords in Co. Roscommon began to adopt ultimately English-style architectural forms and features, including bawns replete with gun loops, and inserted large transomed-and-mullioned windows into earlier castles, in the early seventeenth century. This seems to have been a physical manifestation of the fact that although these men were Catholic, spoke Irish as their home language and patronized native culture,[30] they now held their land as English-style landowners who could pass on their estates directly to their eldest sons by the law of primogeniture.[31] James Lyttleton's comprehensive research in Offaly is especially important in the present context. He noted that scholarship in Ireland has traditionally associated fortified houses of late sixteenth- to mid-seventeenth-century date with English and Lowland Scottish settlers.[32] However, in direct contrast to this long-held view, he demonstrated that out of the seventeen fortified houses recognized to date across south and west Offaly, documentary evidence suggests that nine of them seem to have been built by native

---

27 Loeber, *Irish houses and castles 1400–1740*, pp 153–4. This is not so clear today as much of the bawn wall and its flanking towers are either gone, extremely ruined or have been heavily rebuilt in recent centuries. See Moore, *Archaeological inventory of County Leitrim*, pp 212–13. Manorhamilton Castle would surely benefit from an in-depth study to properly understand its original form.   **28** Ibid.   **29** See chapter 2.   **30** Many of whom rebelled in 1641.   **31** O'Conor, 'English settlement and change in Roscommon during the late sixteenth and seventeenth centuries', pp 199–201; see, also, D. Curley, 'Observations from remote sensing of the earthwork at Dundonnell Castle, Co. Roscommon' in R. Farrell, K. O'Conor and M. Potter (eds), *Roscommon history and society: interdisciplinary essays on the history of an Irish county* (Dublin, 2018), pp 133–56. Curley suggests that the Gaelic MacKeoghs built this plantation-type stronghouse at Dundonnell at some stage in the early seventeenth century. **32** J. Lyttleton, *The Jacobean Plantations in seventeenth-century Offaly* (Dublin, 2013), p. 262. Indeed, Lyttleton has suggested that this perception that fortified houses were only built by English and Scots settlers is the reason why the study of this particular type of castle was limited throughout the twentieth century (ibid., p. 160).

Irishmen.[33] These fortified houses in Offaly were set in similar square or rectangular bawns to the one at Moygara, having numerous gun loops, corner flanking towers and gatehouses/gateways.[34] The available evidence suggests that these Gaelic-built fortified houses and bawns in Offaly date to the early to mid-seventeenth century. For example, the fortified house and bawn at Ballymooney Castle was erected by Donnell O'Carroll in 1622 and was, in fact, one of the grandest residences in the Offaly of its day.[35] Using this evidence for the adoption of English-influenced architectural styles and features by Gaelic Irish lords and gentlemen, Lyttleton reminds us that material culture was and is in a continual process of transformation due to changing social, economic and political contexts.[36] This evidence certainly suggests a far higher degree of interaction, even friendship, between native and settler families in the early seventeenth century than perhaps later nationalist and, indeed, unionist interpretations of Irish history have allowed for in the past.

In any case, on the basis of architectural comparisons, the best time to see the bawn at Moygara, with its four flankers and gatehouse (i.e. Phase 2 at the site), being built was between *c.*1610 and the very late 1630s, or even into the 1640s.

THE BAWN FLANKERS

The bawn flankers at Moygara are not square in form as suggested by Salter's plan,[37] but can, in fact, be described as 'spearhead-shaped'.[38] Flanking towers with acute outermost angles are a characteristic feature of late sixteenth and early seventeenth-century defensive architecture in Ireland and may be seen both on bawn flankers and on the corner towers of some fortified houses. Examples may be found from across the country and, as noted, include the bawn flankers at Faugher, Co. Donegal, Castleblaney, Co. Monaghan, and Manorhamilton, Co. Leitrim, and the corner towers of the fortified houses at Raphoe, Co. Donegal, Mountjoy, Co. Tyrone, Rathfarnham, Co. Dublin and, again, Manorhamilton. Craig, when writing of the flankers at Rathfarnham, states that such 'spearhead-shaped' flankers have 'defensive advantages' and that the form is 'found both in multi-storey buildings such as [Rathfarnham] and in artillery-fortifications of large area and low profile'.[39] The aforementioned plan of Castleblaney, Co. Monaghan (fig. 5.4), indicates that both the circular flankers and the spearhead-shaped flankers were three storeys in height.[40] The surviving evidence at Manorhamilton also suggests that the spearhead-shaped flankers there were originally three storeys in height. Indeed, this may lend some support to the suggestion that all four of the flankers at Moygara may originally have stood to this height. The presence

33 Ibid., p. 262. 34 Ibid., pp 141–7. 35 Ibid., pp 150–1. 36 Ibid., 262–3. 37 Salter, *The castles of Connacht*, p. 100. 38 See chapter 4. 39 M. Craig, *The architecture of Ireland from the earliest times to 1880* (Dublin, 1982), p. 117. 40 Kerrigan, *Castles and fortifications in Ireland*, p. 80.

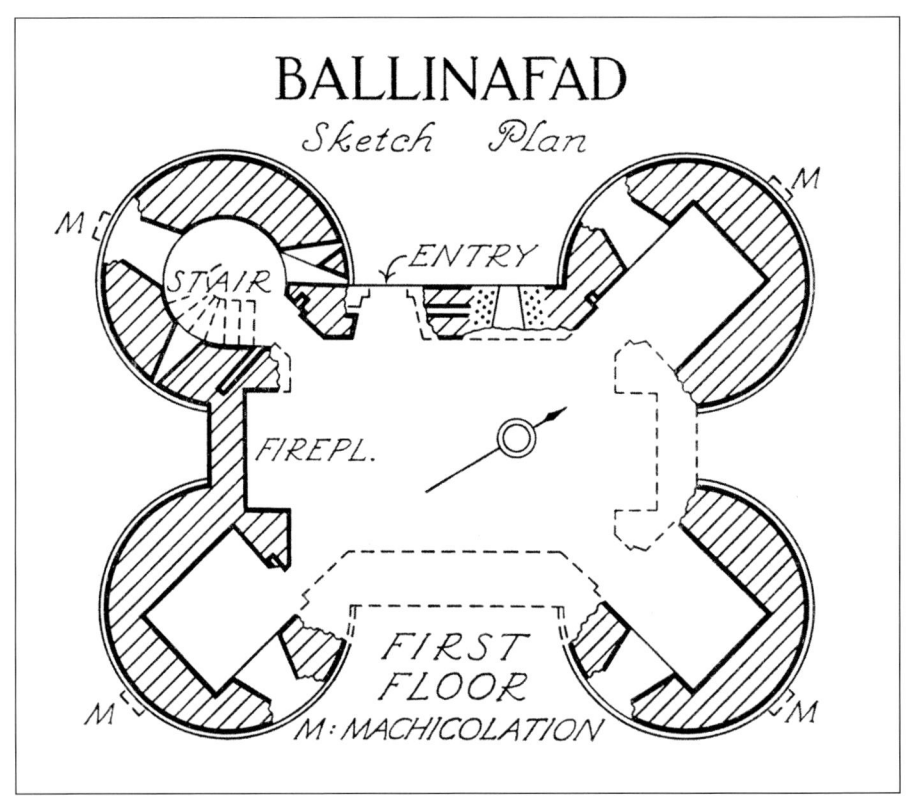

5.6 Plan of Ballinafad Castle, Co. Sligo (after Waterman 1961, fig. 14.6; © Antiquity Publications Ltd/Cambridge University Press).

of bawn flankers with acute outermost angles at Moygara supports the argument that the bawn dates to somewhere in the first four decades of the seventeenth century.

Other architectural features of note at Moygara Castle include the form of the staircases in the flanking towers, the presence of a portcullis within the gatehouse and the use of intra-mural beams in the construction of the castle's walls. The tower staircases would appear to have been contained within semi-circular alcoves in the walls and rose upwards from first-floor level. While mural provision was made for the staircases in the form of the semi-circular alcoves, it is notable that the stairs themselves were not constructed with stone steps, as was normal in earlier buildings, but with timber. This arrangement, using timber steps to construct a spiral stair in a stone building, would appear to be a transitional form between medieval and post-medieval arrangements and has only been noted by the authors at three other sites in the country: a castle or barracks at Ballinafad, Co. Sligo, a late tower house at Emmel West, Co. Offaly, and a fortified house at Ardtarmon on the west coast of Sligo. At Ballinafad, the Castle of the Curlews was built *c*.1590 to accommodate a small

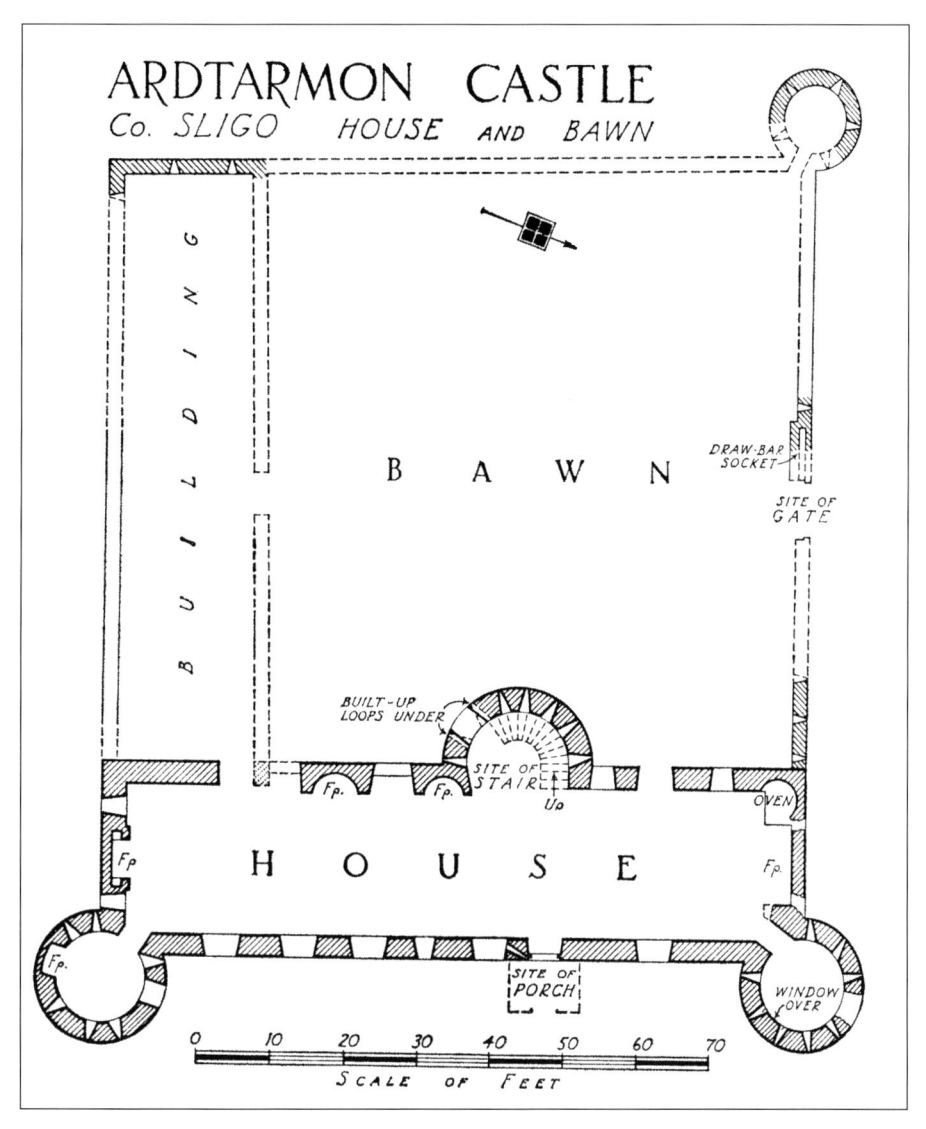

5.7 Plan of Ardtarmon Castle, Co. Sligo (after Waterman 1961, fig. 14.5; © Antiquity Publications Ltd/Cambridge University Press).

government garrison to control an important route through the Curlew Mountains.[41] It is composed of a central rectangular block and four relatively large circular corner turrets (fig. 5.6), one of which contained a timber stair. At Emmel Castle, the oak

41 D.M. Waterman, 'Some Irish seventeenth-century houses and their architectural ancestry' in E.M. Jope (ed.), *Studies in building history: essays in recognition of the work of B.H. St J. O'Neil* (London, 1961), pp 251–74, at pp 270–2. It might be added that the routeway that this government fortification at Ballinafad guarded was, in fact, the main Dublin to Sligo Road.

treads of the spiral stair remain *in situ* within a circular stair turret and dendro-chronological analysis has indicated they were felled in the winter of 1624–5, thereby suggesting that the tower house was built shortly after this date.[42] At Ardtarmon, which has been dated to *c.*1640 by the National Inventory of Architectural Heritage,[43] the timber stairs serving the house was contained within a curved masonry projection, which, though larger than those evident at Moygara, was essentially similar in form and function and was also provided with numerous gun loops (fig. 5.7).[44]

The portcullis within the later gatehouse at Moygara is also an interesting feature. While portcullises may be found in Irish castles of various dates from the early thirteenth century onwards, the closest comparable feature in chronological and geographical terms may be that in the gatehouse which provides access to the bawn enclosing the fortified house at Dromahair, Co. Leitrim. This fortification appears to have been built by a member of the Villiers family sometime around 1628, as stated.[45] The box machicolation that seems to have once existed over the gateway in the western wall of the bawn at Moygara is also to be noted. Stone machicolations like this date from the very late thirteenth century but were common features of tower houses and their associated bawns. However, machiciolations were regularly seen on fortified houses, stronghouses and their bawns. For example, the postern gate in the bawn associated with the fortified house at Kilcolgan More, Co. Offaly, has a box machicolation over it. This castle has been tentatively dated to the late 1640s.[46] Machicolations and portcullises, therefore, can be associated with castles of seventeenth-century date and not just earlier ones.

The use of intra-mural timber beams in the walls of the flanking towers and in the bawn walls is also noteworthy and this practice may have been used much more extensively at Moygara than can now be appreciated. In the north-eastern tower, a small hole at the rear of the first-floor fireplace allows one to investigate the empty intra-mural beam slot in the eastern wall of the tower and other such slots were also noted in the eastern wall of the bawn. This practice, which would appear to derive from a wish to strengthen the walls using internal reinforcements, has been noted elsewhere. For example, this feature was also seen at Ballymote Castle, Co. Sligo, which was built *c.*1299–1300 by Richard de Burgh, *An Iarla Rua*, and which lies about 14km to the north of Moygara Castle.[47]

---

42 N.W. Alcock, 'Tree-ring date lists 2010', *Vernacular Architecture*, 41 (2010), p. 121.   **43** A. Coey, B. Turner and E. Flegg, *An introduction to the architectural heritage of County Sligo* (Dublin, 2007), p. 14.   **44** Waterman, 'Some Irish seventeenth-century houses', pp 268–70; D. Sweetman, *The medieval castles of Ireland* (Cork, 1999), pp 196–8. A semi-circular stair tower, replete with gunloops, juts out of the rear of the fortified house at Gowly, Co. Leitrim. This may have had a timber stairs as well. This house seems to have been built in the 1620s by John Reynolds of the Gaelic MacRannell sept. See Moore, *Archaeological inventory of County Leitrim*, p. 213. **45** Moore, *Archaeological inventory of County Leitrim*, p. 213.   **46** Lyttleton, *The Jacobean Plantations in seventeenth-century Offaly*, pp 124, 143.   **47** D. Sweetman, 'Archaeological excavations at Ballymote Castle, Co. Sligo', *JGAHS*, 40 (1985–6), pp 114–24.

A series of clearly identifiable features noted at Moygara Castle also support a date in the first half of the seventeenth century. Such features include the absence of latrines in the towers despite the fact that they were clearly used for domestic accommodation, the proliferation of original fireplaces in the towers, the absence of stone vaulting in the towers, the proliferation of gun loops throughout the bawn and the flanking towers, the use of timber lintels over the window embrasures and the absence of stone staircases. Such architectural traits clearly link the bawn and towers at Moygara Castle to the architecture of Irish fortified houses of the late sixteenth and early to mid-seventeenth centuries and set it apart from the architecture of the fifteenth- and sixteenth-century tower houses that preceded it.

CONCLUSIONS

This discussion indicates that the second phase of building activity at Moygara Castle – which dominates the architecture of the place today – has architectural features that date it in a very general way to the late sixteenth to mid-seventeenth centuries. However, by comparing the castle to architecturally similar fortifications seen elsewhere in north Connacht and west Ulster, a more detailed analysis of the architecture of this second phase of building at Moygara fine tunes the evidence and suggests that it was most likely built between *c.*1610 and the very late 1630s (but possibly into the 1640s based on shared architectural features with Ardtarmon Castle in north Sligo and Kilcolgan More, Co. Offaly). Furthermore, while similar castles of this date were mostly built by incoming English and Lowland Scots settlers, it is clear that some were also built by native Irish gentry, including Faugher in Donegal – a bawn that bears a lot of architectural similarity to this second phase of building at Moygara Castle. It was shown that the gatehouse behind the gateway in the western wall of the bawn at Moygara appears to have not been included in the original building plan for the site. However, when the bawn wall was partially built to a height of just under 2m, a decision was made to include a gatehouse.

The flanking towers and bawn wall, replete with scores of gun loops, along with the gatehouse with its portcullis and the gateway in front of it with the box machicolation over it, meant that Moygara Castle was extremely well defended during this dominant second architectural phase at the site. This evidence is also a reminder that portcullises, so often associated with castles and urban gatehouses of thirteenth- and fourteenth-century date, and machicolations can be built as late as the seventeenth century.

CHAPTER SIX

The O'Gara dynasty through time and place

MAURA O'GARA-O'RIORDAN AND
MÁIRE NÍ CHEARBHAILL

INTRODUCTION

The history of the O'Gara (Ó Gadhra in Irish) family of north Connacht, or Lower Connacht as it was known in late medieval times, unfolds from records that stretch back to the eighth century. Genealogies, the various annals, church documents, state papers and other official sources, as well as the findings of modern scholarship and technology, all contribute to the story of this ancient dynasty.

The territories where the O'Garas ruled and held their lands are associated with present-day Co. Sligo, but also included parts of Mayo and Roscommon. Ecclesiastical sources from the twelfth century confirm their presence in these areas, with references to O'Gara churchmen in the dioceses of Achonry, Elphin, Killala and Tuam.

From a study of the various sources, it is possible to gain a picture of where the O'Garas were located through different stages of their history, to examine their status as rulers, and their patterns of intermarriage with other leading families, and to trace their declining fortunes in times of war and political change. Some of the sources also allow for a closer personal look at individual families, such as the generation of O'Garas who were born in France and spent their lives in Europe. In its concluding section, this chapter also looks at how modern-day technology is contributing to an enhanced understanding of the centuries-old O'Gara history.

Place-names especially associated with the O'Gara clan include Coolavin, Gurteen Cuppanagh and Moygara townlands, all in south Sligo, and the district around Lough Gara with its O'Gara castles. Moygara Castle lies about 44km south-east of Sligo town and about 10km west of Boyle in Co. Roscommon. Lough Gara spreads over an area of 5.3km from north to south and its maximum width is about 3.3km.[1]

CASTLES, LAKE AND TOWNLANDS

The O'Garas built three castles on the shores of Lough Gara, to act as their residences and estate centres. These were strategically located to survey and protect the surrounding territory. The principal castle, now a ruin, was built in Moygara townland

---

[1] See chapter 3 for the landscape context of Moygara Castle.

on high ground above the north-western end of Lough Gara and is the focus of the research outlined in this volume. From this ruin, looking across the lake to the east, there is a view of Cuppanagh townland, where the second castle was built.[2] Derrymore Island contained the third castle.[3] Dates for the building of the O'Gara castles are not known, but there are references in several annals to an attack on the 'castle of O'Gara' at Moygara in 1538 by the O'Donnells.[4]

Fergal (Fearghal)[5] O'Gara (Ó Gadhra) was the last member of the O'Gara dynastic line to own Moygara Castle. Born in 1596, Fergal was the son of Tadhg and the grandson of Irriel (Oilill) O'Gara. His father died in 1598 but his grandfather lived on for several more years, and on his death, Fergal inherited the O'Gara title and patrimony in 1613/14. His inheritance included the castle of Moygara, referred to in 1538 as the '*caislen I Ghara*' ('castle of O'Gara')[6] and in a drawing by Thomas Cocking in 1791 as 'O'Garas Castle',[7] and surrounding townlands in the half-barony of Coolavin.[8]

O'GARA (Ó GADHRA) ANCESTRY AND SURNAME

Fergal O'Gara's ancestry can be traced back in the male line to the eighth century. The death of Taichleach, king of Luighne, was recorded in the year 734. Taichleach is recorded in all genealogical tables relating to the Luighne of Connacht, a population group that is noted as being of Munster origin in the prehistoric era, along with the Gailenga of Connacht.[9] During the tenth century a Gadhra and an Eaghra belonged

---

2 U. Egan, E. Byrne and M. Sleeman, in the *Archaeological inventory of County Sligo*, i: *South Sligo* (Dublin, 2005), p. 486, incorrectly state that Cuppanagh was a MacDermot castle.   **3** W.G. Wood-Martin, *History of Sligo, county and town, from the earliest ages to the close of the reign of Queen Elizabeth* (Dublin, 1882), p. 322, n. 2 rightly refers to the Derrymore Island castle as an O'Gara castle. However, in citing this source, it appears that Egan, Byrne and Sleeman, *Archaeological inventory of County Sligo*, p. 487, have incorrectly printed 'O'Gara' as 'O'Hara'.   **4** *AU* 1538.20; *AConn* 1538.5; *ALC* 1538.5; *AFM* 1538.5. See, also, chapter 2. It has been argued that the great majority of the unclassified castles seen in the Irish countryside today, particularly in north Connacht, are in fact tower houses of mainly fifteenth- or sixteenth-century date. See K. O'Conor, 'Castles studies in Ireland: the way forward' in P. Ettel, A.-M. Flambard Héricher and T.E. McNeill (eds), *Château Gaillard*, 23: *Bilan des recherches en castellogie* (Caen, 2008), pp 329–32; K. O'Conor and J. Williams, 'Ballinagare Castle, Co. Roscommon' in L. Gibbons and K. O'Conor (eds), *Charles O'Conor of Ballinagare, 1710–91: life and works* (Dublin, 2015), pp 60–4.   **5** Also referred to as Farrill, Farrell, Farell, ffarrill, Ferrall and Farroll. Fearghal is the spelling used in RIA, MS 23 F 16 (Book of O'Gara), f. 126 *i*. Genealogy of Ó Gadhra, beginning with Fergal (son of Tadhg, son of Irriel); see, also, N. Ó Muraíle, 'The autograph manuscripts of the Annals of the Four Masters', *Celtica*, 19 (1987), p. 75: B. Cunningham, *The Annals of the Four Masters: Irish history, kingship and society in the early seventeenth century* (Dublin, 2010), p. 26 and throughout the publication: D.P. McCarthy, *The Irish annals: their genesis, evolution and history* (Dublin, 2008), pp 328, 334–5; P. Ó Macháin, '"One glimpse of Ireland": the manuscript of Fr Nicolás (Fearghal Dubh) Ó Gadhra' in R. Gillespie and R. Ó Huiginn (eds), *Irish Europe, 1600–1650: writing and learning* (Dublin, 2013), pp 135–62; note that some modern historians also spell Fergal as 'Fearghal'.   **6** *AU* 1538.20.   **7** F. Grose, *The antiquities of Ireland* (London, 1791), i, p. 58, pl. 102; see chapter 2, fig. 2.10.   **8** See chapter 2, figs 2.2, 2.4; see, also, chapters 4 and 5.   **9** F.J. Byrne, *Irish kings and high-kings* (London, 1973; repr. Dublin, 2001), p. 291.

to the Luighne and their descent from Taichleach is recorded in genealogical tables compiled in the fourteenth century.[10] Gadhra and Eaghra were the respective ancestors of the O'Garas and O'Haras.[11]

A tenth-century reference to the O'Gara dynasty in the Annals of the Four Masters records how Eaghra, lord of Luighne, in Connacht, died in 926, and Eaghra's son, also lord of Luighne, was slain in 928.[12] Gadhra's son, Domhnall, who took over the title of Luighne, was slain in 931.[13] An entry in Chronicum Scotorum for 966 records the death of Taichlech ua Gadhra, king of Luighne, in battle.[14] The Luighne dominated smaller tribes, and their territory was recognized as an over-kingdom in the twelfth century, when their lands were located in the newly erected diocese of Achonry. The ruling families of O'Gara and O'Hara remained prominent in the south Sligo area well into the seventeenth century.[15]

The surname O'Gara, an anglicization of 'Ua Gadhra', is one of the earliest surnames established in Ireland. It was introduced in the tenth century,[16] when surnames commenced by placing 'Ua' (Ó) before a first name. It became the custom from this time for descendants to continue to use the surname of their forefathers. Over forty such surnames are found by the end of the latter century.[17] O'Gara was the first surname recorded from the Luighne dynastic family in 964/966.[18] Despite sharing a common ancestry, as will be seen below, the O'Hara surname was not recorded until 1023, almost sixty years after O'Gara.

THE O'GARAS IN THE TERRITORY OF LUIGHNE

The Annals of the Four Masters (UCD, MS A 13 (the Louvain set))[19] described Toichleach Ó Gadhra's territory as 'Luigne' in AD 964. The entry in the Annals of the Four Masters (RIA, MS 1220 (C iii 3)),[20] on the other hand, recorded that Ó Gadhra was lord of Luighne *deisc[eir]t* [south] at that time. As will be shown later in this paper, the additional word '*deisc[eir]t*' was an incorrect insertion that had been added after the original manuscript was written. It was not until the twelfth century that the territory of the Luighne was divided,[21] when the O'Garas retained the southern share of the territory, while the O'Haras took the northern section and kept the title of Luighne.[22]

---

10 Eaghra's father was Saergusa and Eaghra had a brother Gleidneachain who was father to Gadhra. Therefore Gadhra was a nephew to Eaghra and grandson to Saergusa: RIA, MS 23 P 12 (The Book of Ballymote), f. 109r; RIA, MS 23 P 2 (The Book of Lecan), ff 223r and 223v; RIA, MS D II 1 (Leabhar Uí Maine), f. 33v, isos.dias.ie, accessed 17 June 2014. **11** See chapter 2. **12** *AFM* 926, 928. **13** *AFM* 931. **14** *CS* 966, ucc.ie/celt/publishd.html, accessed 17 June 2014. **15** Byrne, *Irish kings and high-kings*, p. 233. **16** J. MacNeill, 'Early Irish population-groups', *PRIA*, 29C (1911–12), p. 82. **17** Ibid. **18** See Byrne, *Irish kings and high-kings*, p. 233. **19** UCD-OFM, MS A 13. **20** RIA, MS 1220 (C iii 3). **21** At some date between 1128 and 1181. **22** *AFM*, 1059: Ruaidhri Ua Gadhra, heir to the lordship of Leyny, died; *ATig*, 1059: Ruaidrí h-Ua Gadhra, rígdomna Luigne, occisus est; *AFM*, 1067: RIA, MS C iii 3, f. 438r, isos.dias.ie; *AFM*, 1067: UCD-OFM, MS

With the division in the twelfth century, part or all of the O'Gara southern region appears to have been renamed Sliabh Lugha. The extent and location of the divided territory is unclear. The late nineteenth-century scholar William Wood-Martin claimed that the O'Garas retained the Mayo portion of the territory, together with the half-barony of Coolavin in Gurteen, Co. Sligo.[23] A more recent work, however, places the centre of the territory in the country north of Castlemore and Ballaghaderreen in modern Co. Roscommon.[24] Whatever the exact location and size of their district, the O'Garas were to remain in that area and ruled as kings of Sliabh Lugha for a period of up to 150 years.

Why the Luighne territory that had been ruled by the O'Gara and O'Hara dynastic lines was divided is not known, but rivalry over the title of kingship may have been a factor. There were also wider political upheavals taking place in Ireland at this time. Traditionally, provincial kings could not interfere with the accession rights of the petty kingdoms, but this practice was changing by the twelfth century, as some of the larger rulers expanded their territories. Turlough O'Conor, who ruled as king of Connacht from 1106 until his death in 1156, 'not only deposed kings; he divided kingdoms and created new ones'.[25] As the division of the Luighne territory occurred sometime between 1128 and 1181, it is possible that it came about as a result of these changes in Ireland.

O'GARAS IN SLIABH LUGHA AND COOLAVIN

The first reference in the annals to the district of Sliabh Lugha[26] is recorded towards the end of the twelfth century with the announcement of the death of 'Dondslebi ua Gadra, rí Slebi Luga', in 1181.[27] Several annals also record the deaths of other O'Garas throughout the thirteenth century, with the final entry for an O'Gara 'king' in 1285.[28]

Richard de Burgh, the first Anglo-Norman lord of Connacht, had conquered much of Connacht by the late 1230s, including most of what is now modern Co. Sligo, granting out a lot of it to his most important followers and supporters. It appears, however, that Sligo Gaelic septs like the O'Garas and O'Haras held on to much of their old territories at this time, presumably paying tribute and providing military

---

A 13, f. 440r, isos.dias.ie. Donnsleibhe Ua Gadhra, tanist of Luighne, was killed by Brian Ua hEaghra; *AFM* 1128: Ua Gadhra, lord of Luighne slain; *ATig* 1151: Conchobhar Ciabach Ó hEaghra, king of Luighne, died; *ATig* 1155: Aodh Ó hEaghra, king of Luighne, died; Annals in Cotton MS Titus A. XXV (Cottonian Annals: Annals of Boyle) 1155: Aed ua h-Egra rí Lugni mortuus est; *AFM* 1177: Aed ua h-Egra rí Luigne, mortuus est; *ATig* 1177: Domhnall Ó hEaghra, king of Luighne, died. **23** W.G. Wood-Martin, *History of Sligo, county and town, from the accession of James I to the revolution of 1688* (Dublin, 1889), p. 21. **24** D. MacDermot, *MacDermot of Moylurg: the story of a Connacht family* (Manorhamilton, 1996), p. 412. **25** J. Lydon, *The lordship of Ireland in the Middle Ages* (Dublin, 2003), p. 16. **26** Also written *Slebi Luga* and *Sliab-Lugu*. **27** Annals in Cotton MS Titus A. XXV (Cottonian Annals: Annals of Boyle), ucc.ie/celt/publishd.html, accessed 8 Sept. 2014; *AU* 1181: *ALC* 1181. **28** *AU* 1285; *AConn* 1285.6; *ALC* 1285; *AFM* 1285.

service to these new Anglo-Norman lords.[29] Actual Anglo-Norman settlement in a physical sense, as opposed to just political overlordship, seems to have been relatively light over most of Connacht. For example, it has been argued that a minor branch of the O'Conors of Connacht were encouraged by the de Burghs and the FitzGeralds in the late thirteenth century to settle in the Carbury area of what is now north Co. Sligo in return for rent and military service.[30] This branch of the O'Conors were the ancestors of the O'Conor Sligo line who were to dominate the Sligo region throughout the fifteenth and sixteenth centuries.[31]

The Gaelic Resurgence was to see Anglo-Norman settlement in what is now Co. Sligo collapse by the mid-fourteenth century.[32] As a result of this Gaelic revival, O'Conor Sligo became the most powerful lord in the Sligo area by the late fourteenth century and, as noted, was to retain this hegemony for the next two centuries.[33] The O'Garas did not benefit from the Gaelic Resurgence as much as the latter sept but regained control of some of their former pre-Norman territory in what was to become the half-barony of Coolavin.[34] In effect, the O'Garas were reduced from their pre-1169 position as kings of Sliabh Lugha to being lords of Coolavin, a much smaller territory.[35]

CHURCH RECORDS AS A SOURCE

Although there are references in the annals to the activities or deaths of members of the O'Gara sept between 1285 and 1434, there is no indication of where their territory was located during this time.[36] It is from ecclesiastical records for the diocese of Achonry that the O'Gara presence in Coolavin in the first quarter of the fourteenth century can be revealed.

Diocesan structures were formally established in Ireland in the twelfth century, but the older practice of associating a bishop with an area occupied by a population group appears to have continued for some time. In 1170 a churchman was recorded as 'bishop of Luighne-Chonnacht' rather than of the newly erected diocese of Achonry.[37] The O'Garas are credited with being patrons of a friary built at Knockmore for the Carmelite Order about the year 1320. This friary was located in what was to become the barony of Coolavin.[38] Again, it is ecclesiastical sources rather than the annals that provide accounts of the O'Garas in the Coolavin district during the later fourteenth

29 M. O'Dowd, *Power, politics and land: early modern Sligo 1568–1688* (Belfast, 1991), p. 15; K. O'Conor, 'Introduction' in U. Egan, E. Byrne and M. Sleeman, *Archaeological inventory of County Sligo*, i: *South Sligo*, p. x. **30** G.H. Orpen, *Ireland under the Normans, 1169–1333* (Dublin, 2005), p. 394; O'Conor, 'Introduction', p. x. **31** O'Dowd, *Power, politics and land*, pp 15–20. **32** Ibid.; O'Conor, 'Introduction', p. xi. **33** O'Dowd, *Power, politics and land*, pp 15–20. **34** Ibid., p. 15; O'Conor, 'Introduction', p. xi. **35** O'Dowd, *Power, politics and land*, p. 15. **36** See *AConn* 1434; *AFM* 1435. See, also, *AU, AConn, ALC, AFM* 1325; *AConn, ALC, AFM* 1328; *AU, AConn, ALC, AFM* 1329; *AU, AConn, ALC, AFM* 1359; *AU* 1397; see, also, *Mac Carthaigh's Book, Miscellaneous Irish annals*, Fragment III, ucc.ie/celt/publishd.html, accessed 1 Oct. 2014. **37** *AFM* 1170. **38** A. Gwynn and R.N. Hadcock, *Medieval religious houses: Ireland* (London, 1970), p. 290; P. O'Dwyer,

century and fifteenth century.[39] In the ninety years between 1396 and 1486, members of O'Gara families were noted in the dioceses of Achonry, Elphin and Killala. For example, one Dermot O'Gara held the position of canon in the archdiocese of Tuam in 1487–8.[40]

The papal records name several O'Gara men who served in ecclesiastical positions from an unknown date before 1397 to at least 1486/7. Four served in the diocese of Achonry in 'the rural rectory of Cuilofind (Coolavin) and Ranna ... of the patronage of laymen'.[41] Two served as clerks of Achonry, Rory in 1428[42] and Eugenius in 1447.[43] A Cornelius O'Gara was a clerk of the diocese of Achonry,[44] and a Charles O'Gara was assigned to 'the canonry and prebend of Druymcliab [Drumcliff] in Elphin' in 1414.[45]

In the late fourteenth and early fifteenth century, references are made to vacancies in the diocese of Achonry caused by the death of Bernard O'Gara, who held a number of positions at the perpetual vicarage of Coolavin and Ranna, 'which became void and reserved to the apostolic see' following his death before 2 February 1397.[46] The fact that the O'Gara surname is associated with appointments in the rural rectory of Coolavin and Ranna may indicate that the O'Garas had been contributors to the lay patronage of the rural lands for the parish churches of Killfree and Killaraght in that area. Ranna is listed under the barony of Boyle in the Composition of Connacht, which dates to 1585.[47]

'Carmelites in Pre-Reformation Ireland', *Carmelus*, 16 (1969), fasc. 2, p. 270. **39** The *Calendar of papal registers relating to Great Britain and Ireland* consist of fourteen volumes covering the years 1198 to 1492. The O'Gara name appears in nine of the fourteen volumes – 4, 5, 6, 7, 8, 9, 10, 12, 14 – which are all available at *British History Online*, british-history.ac.uk/cal-papal-registers/brit-ie. **40** 'Vatican Regesta 730: 1487–1488' in J.A. Twemlow (ed.), *Calendar of papal registers relating to Great Britain and Ireland*, xiv: *1484–1492* (London, 1960), pp 211–18. **41** 'Lateran Regesta, 383: 1441' in J.A. Twemlow (ed.), *Calendar of papal registers relating to Great Britain and Ireland*, ix: *1431–1447* (London, 1912), pp 188–201. **42** 'Lateran Regesta 278: 1428' in J.A. Twemlow (ed.), *Calendar of papal registers relating to Great Britain and Ireland*, xiii: *1427–1447* (London, 1909), pp 8–16. **43** 'Lateran Regesta 433: 1447' in J.A. Twemlow (ed.), *Calendar of papal registers relating to Great Britain and Ireland*, x: *1447–1455* (London, 1915), pp 278–87. **44** 'Lateran Regesta 701: 1470' in J.A. Twemlow (ed.), *Calendar of papal registers relating to Great Britain and Ireland*, xii: *1458–1471* (London, 1933), pp 775–7. **45** 'Lateran Regesta 169: 1413–1414' in J.A. Twemlow (eds), *Calendar of Papal Registers Relating to Great Britain and Ireland*, vi: *1404–1415* (London, 1904), pp 422–30; 'Lateran Regesta 232: 1422–1423' in J.A. Twemlow (ed.), *Calendar of papal registers relating to Great Britain and Ireland*, vii: *1417–1431* (London, 1906), pp 263–71; 'Lateran Regesta 277: 1428' in J.A. Twemlow (ed.), *Calendar of papal registers relating to Great Britain and Ireland*, viii: *1427–1447*, pp 1–8; 'Lateran Regesta 282: 1427–1428' in J.A. Twemlow (ed.), *Calendar of papal registers relating to Great Britain and Ireland*, viii: *1427–1447* (London, 1909), pp 50–62; 'Lateran Regesta 286: 1428–1429' in J.A. Twemlow (ed.), *Calendar of papal registers relating to Great Britain and Ireland*, viii: *1427–1447*, pp 83–95; 'Lateran Regesta 290: 1428–1429' in J.A. Twemlow (ed.), *Calendar of papal registers relating to Great Britain and Ireland*, viii: *1427–1447*, pp 112–22. **46** 'Lateran Regesta 39: 1396' in W.H. Bliss and J.A. Twemlow (eds), *Calendar of papal registers relating to Great Britain and Ireland*, iv: *1362–1404* (London, 1902), pp 529–31; 'Lateran Regesta 49: 1397' in W.H. Bliss and J.A. Twemlow (eds), *Calendar of papal registers relating to Great Britain and Ireland*, v: *1398–1404*, pp 79–80; 'Lateran Regesta 84: 1400–1401' in W.H. Bliss and J.A. Twemlow (eds), *Calendar of papal registers relating to Great Britain and Ireland*, v: *1398–1404* (London, 1904), pp 342–4; 'Lateran Regesta 96: 1400–1401' in W.H. Bliss and J.A. Twemlow (eds), *Calendar of papal registers relating to Great Britain and Ireland*, v: *1398–1404*, pp 449–55; 'Lateran Regesta 278: 1428' in J.A. Twemlow (ed.), *Calendar of papal registers relating to Great Britain and Ireland*, viii: *1427–1447*, pp 8–16. **47** MacDermot, *MacDermot of*

KING, LORD OR CHIEF OF THE NAME?

Titles in the annals for the heads of the ruling families gradually changed over time from king, to lord, to chief of the name. They were often referred to simply by the use of their surname, such as O'Gara and O'Dowd in Co. Sligo or MacDermot in Co. Roscommon. The O'Conors, the most powerful Gaelic family in Connacht at one time, had divided into three distinct dynastic groups by *c.*1400.[48]

The system of primogeniture was practised by the O'Garas from at least 1434, according to 'a small but distinguished tree for this family' published in the Book of MacDermot.[49] The information is supported by entries in various annals.[50] In 1469, the Annals of Connacht have recorded that 'O Gadra, that is Eogan, son of Tomaltach Oc, son of Tomaltach Mor, king[51] of Coolavin died between the two autumnal feasts of Mary. The son of this same O Gadra, and a son worthy of him, namely Eogan, died of a sudden sickness. Diarmait, son of Eogan O Gadra, succeeded to his father's lordship, and may it prosper for him.'[52]

For much of the fifteenth and sixteenth centuries the position of the head of the O'Gara ruling family passed from father to son. The ownership of the land of the family followed a similar pattern throughout the early seventeenth century. The result was that the 'O'Gara' had control of all of the lands of his lordship during this whole period.[53]

Various references to the O'Gara (Ó Gadhra) ruling family are found in annal entries dating to the fifteenth and sixteenth centuries.[54] The fact that these entries occur in greatest numbers in the Annals of Loch Cé in the sixteenth century is likely to have been due to family connections with the MacDermots of Moylurg. Brian MacDermot, who died in 1592, was patron, owner and part compiler of the latter annals, and was a first cousin to Sadhbh MacDermot, wife of the O'Gara chief of the name at that time, Diarmaid.[55] Surprisingly, the Annals of the Four Masters, with Fergal O'Gara as its patron, is almost silent on the O'Garas, with only one entry for the ruling family – O'Gara lord of Coolavin[56] – and one entry for the castle called Magh-Uí-Ghadra (i.e. Moygara) in the sixteenth century.[57]

Moylurg, p. 495. The Composition of Connacht of 1585 was an agreement between the Gaelic and gaelicized chiefs of Connacht and the English administration that replaced existing levies with a single tax on land holdings. A form of 'surrender and regrant', the Composition was a part of the Tudor reconquest of Ireland.   **48** The three O'Conor dynastic groups in late medieval Connacht were O'Conor Don, O'Conor Roe (both having adjacent lordships in what is now north Roscommon) and O'Conor Sligo, whose main lands were in Carbury in modern-day north Co. Sligo. See C.O. O'Conor (O'Conor Don), *The O'Conors of Connaught* (Dublin, 1891), passim. **49** MacDermot, *MacDermot of Moylurg*, p. 413.   **50** *AConn, AFM, ALC, AU*; 1469 *AFM, AConn, ALC, AU*; 1495, *AConn, AFM, ALC*, 1537; *ALC* 1577; *ALC*, 1579; *ALC*, 1584.   **51** The title 'king' was recorded in *AConn*, the title 'lord' in *AFM*; there was no title recorded in *AU* or *ALC*. Historians would regard the word 'king', when used in the annals, as an anachronism by the fifteenth century.   **52** *AConn* 1469.8.   **53** O'Dowd, *Power, politics and land*, p. 71.   **54** *AConn, ALC, AFM* 1469; *AU, AConn, ALC* 1495; *AConn, ALC, AFM* 1537; *ALC* 1577; *ALC* 1579; *ALC* 1584.   **55** MacDermot, *MacDermot of Moylurg*, p. 446.   **56** *FM* 1537.   **57** *AFM* 1538. See chapter 2.

CHANGE IN THE TUDOR PERIOD

The O'Conor Sligo sept had expanded out from their lands in Carbury and what is now north Sligo and had acquired Sligo Castle by the mid-fourteenth century as part of the Gaelic Resurgence in the area.[58] The castle remained in hands of O'Conor Sligo well into the sixteenth century and was this sept's main base.[59] On occasion, however, in the second half of the latter century, the castle was taken from O'Conor Sligo by the O'Donnells of Tyrconnell and the English administration.[60] Nevertheless, O'Conor Sligo remained the dominant Gaelic family in the Sligo area well into the early seventeenth century.[61]

As stated, O'Conor Sligo became overlord of the Sligo area from the late fourteenth century onwards and their sublords throughout the late medieval period included the O'Haras of Leyny and the O'Garas of Coolavin. Nevertheless, their overlordship was relatively mild and consisted of little more than asking for military service on occasion. Sublords such as the O'Garas had considerable autonomy and were 'the real lords of the land, acting as both military lords and landlords as well as literary and ecclesiastical patrons' in what were small lordships.[62] The relationship between the O'Conor Sligo and his sublords was also strengthened through marriage alliances.[63]

Henry VIII introduced into Ireland the system known as 'surrender and regrant' in the early 1540s in an attempt to extend his control over the island. Gaelic chiefs were encouraged to surrender their lands, to pay rent under a royal charter and to swear loyalty to the monarch by adopting English laws and customs. In return, they would be protected in their holdings and could enter the parliament of Ireland.[64]

Surrender and Regrant continued during the reign of Elizabeth I, and by the 1560s, O'Conor Sligo had embraced the new system. In 1566, on a tour of Connacht, the lord deputy of Ireland, Sir Henry Sydney, was entertained by the latter at Sligo Castle and was able to report:

> O'Conor (O'Conor Sligo) made me great cheer. O'Ghare (O'Gara) vowed to go into England, which he performed. I took the great abbey of Aboyle (Boyle) in Connaught. MacDermode (MacDermot of Moylurg) submitted.[65]

58 O'Dowd, *Power, politics and land*, p. 16; K. O'Conor, 'Sligo Castle' in M. Timoney (ed.), *A celebration of Sligo: first essays for Sligo Field Club* (Carrick-on-Shannon, 2002), pp 183–4. The O'Conor Sligo takeover of Sligo Castle was important for this sept as it meant control of the rich port of Sligo. **59** O'Conor, 'Sligo Castle', pp 183–4. **60** Ibid. **61** O'Dowd, *Power, politics and land*, p. 66. **62** Ibid., p. 23. **63** Genealogical Office, *Registered Pedigrees*, v, MS 162, p. 114. F. Richard-Maupillier, 'The Irish in the regiments of Duke Leopold of Lorraine 1698–1729', *Archivium Hibernicum*, 67 (2014), p. 97, fn 24; B. MacDermot, *Ó Ruairc of Breifne* (Manorhamilton, 1990), p. 221; MacDermot, *MacDermot of Moylurg*, p. 388; P. O'Connor, *The royal O'Connors of Connaught* (Swinford, 1997), p. 68. **64** C. Maginn and S. Ellis, *The Tudor discovery of Ireland* (Dublin, 2015), pp 157, 185–9. **65** J.S. Brewer and W. Bullen (eds), *Calendar of the Carew manuscripts, 1575–1588* (London, 1868), Sir Henry Sydney to Sir Francis Walsingham (A summary in relation to all his services in Ireland), p. 335, Entry number 501, 1 Mar. 1583.

In November 1567, O'Conor Sligo travelled to England to formalize his relationship with the queen by signing an indenture:

> On 8 November, 9 Eliz., the said O'Conor Sligo came to the Queen at her palace of Hampton Court, and there in his Irish tongue by an interpreter declared to her Majesty that the chief cause of his coming was to see and speak to the powerful and illustrious Princess whom he recognized as his Sovereign Lady …
>
> He not only submits his life, lands, and goods to the Queen's mercy, but also surrenders and resigns his office of captain of O'Conor Sligo into her hands, with all the castles, manors &c., which he holds as O'Conor Sligo, in the countries of Charbery (Carbury), Tire-Eraghe (Tirreragh, Moay(?), Layen (Leyny), Cowlavin (Coolavin), Cormer (Corran) and Tire-Irell (Tirerrill), in Connaught imploring the Queen's pardon and grace, and that he may henceforth be reputed as an Englishman and praying her to grant him his said country and lands, to be held of her Majesty, and that he may be for ever exempted from subjection and servitude, and from all other burdens to be exacted by O'Donnell or any other.[66]

A second account of Sir Donal O'Conor Sligo's journey to London is a report on O'Conor Sligo from the Calendar of State Papers Ireland:

> On 8 November 1567, the said O'Connor Sligo came to the queen at Hampton Court and submitted to her. He acknowledges her as his ruler and will persecute all her rebels. He submits his life, lands and goods to her mercy and surrenders his office of O'Connor Sligo with all its lands and castles in Connacht, imploring the queen's pardon and grace, and asks to be reputed as a natural born Englishman. He wishes to hold his lands of Her Majesty and not to suffer exactions from O'Donnell or an other. Lord Deputy Sidney has confirmed that the said O'Connor Sligo has constantly refused to join with Shane O'Neill. The queen accepts his surrender and resignation. An inquiry will be made of his lands and he shall then receive them by letters patent at a rent not exceeding £100 Irish. For observation of these premises, he binds himself to the queen for £10,000.[67]

With O'Conor Sligo's signing of this indenture, all sublords ruling the areas were committed to his agreement with the queen, including O'Gara of Coolavin. The indenture was intended to protect the sublords from O'Donnell of Tyrconnell and

---

66 J.S. Brewer and W. Bullen (eds), *Calendar of the Carew manuscripts, 1515–1574* (London, 1867), Sir Henry Sydney to Sir Francis Walsingham, p. 378, entry number 255 (vol. 614, p. 151).　　**67** B. Cunningham (ed.), *Calendar of state papers, Ireland: Tudor period, 1568–1571* (Dublin, 2010), 63/23, no. 12, p. 7.

other incursions into Connacht by Ulstermen, which included great cattle raids. By signing the indenture, O'Conor Sligo put himself and his followers firmly on the side of the English and committed himself to aiding and assisting the English forces in actions against Irish rebels.[68]

A 'Memorandum of the division of O'Connor Sligo's country' was recorded shortly after the signing of the indenture. The surnames listed were identical to a listing of the Gaelic families of Sligo back in 1549. The one exception was the acknowledgment by the English authorities of the division of the barony of Leyney between the O'Haras into two separate septs, although the exact lands of each were not indicated.

> O'Gara has 12 town[land]s equal to 48 ploughlands. 14 horse, 100 kerne.
> O'Hara Roe: 96 ploughlands.
> O'Hara Boy: 96 ploughlands, 6 horse, 300 kerne.
> MacDonogh, Corran: 192 ploughlands.
> MacDonogh, Tirerrill: 192 ploughlands.
> O'Dowd, Tireragh: 192 ploughlands.
> O'Conor Sligo, Carbury: 192 ploughlands.
> Totals to pay amongst them: £240 sterling.[69]

SPANISH INVASION: INTERROGATION AND IMPRISONMENT

Three years after O'Conor Sligo promised loyalty to the English crown – and as a result committed the O'Garas to the same agreement – Kean O'Gara of Tirerrill in Sligo returned to Ireland from a voyage to Spain. The ship anchored in Co. Kerry, first at Smerwick and then at Tarbert and, lastly, further up the Shannon estuary.[70]

Kean's journey coincided with a period of heightened tensions in Ireland as fears circulated that opponents of Elizabeth I were seeking allies abroad for a Spanish invasion of the country.[71] There is no documentary evidence to indicate why O'Gara had visited Spain at this time. It is possible that he may have been connected to trade in some way – merchants and businessmen regularly travelled back and forth between the two countries in the sixteenth century.[72] On arrival in Ireland, Kean O'Gara was one of six passengers to be interrogated by Sir John Perrot, the president of Munster.[73] O'Gara's responses to his interrogators suggest that he was not in sympathy with the political and religious movements operating against Queen Elizabeth. However, these

---

68 O'Connor, *The royal O'Connors of Connaught*, p. 29.　**69** B. Cunningham (ed.), *Calendar of state papers, Ireland: Tudor period, 1566–1567* (Dublin, 2009), pp 250–51.　**70** M. O'Dowd (ed.), *Calendar of state papers, Ireland: Tudor period, 1571–1575* (Dublin, 2000), entry 259, SP 63/36, no. 29, pp 163–5.　**71** C. Lennon, *Sixteenth-century Ireland* (Dublin, 1994; repr. 2005), pp 216, 233.　**72** Ibid., pp 6, 40, 49.　**73** The six interrogated were listed as Kean (Cian) O'Gara of Tireowell (Tirerrill) in Connacht, William Bonsfield of Limerick, George Harrold Fitz Piers of Limerick, M. Browne, R. Walshe and Nicholas Rice.

responses may have been prompted by fear for his life. The punishment for those considered to be plotting against the queen was execution. Alternatively, he may have wanted to avoid causing trouble for O'Conor Sligo, who had signed the indenture with the queen in 1567, on his own behalf and on behalf of the ruling lords of Co. Sligo, including O'Gara of Coolavin.

When the interrogators asked O'Gara how many passengers had left Spain with him and what were their names, he replied that he knew none but the mariners and the merchants of Limerick and Waterford, and John O'Grady,[74] brother to Fr David Wolfe,[75] now a prisoner in Dublin. He explained that although they had cast anchor at Smerwick, none had landed there. They had proceeded to Tarbert, where John O'Grady was landed.

Among other questions put to O'Gara were whether he knew anything of the 'pretended' archbishop of Cashel,[76] or of Thomas Stukeley[77] or others who had fled the country. 'The pretended archbishop is gone to Paris upon a breach between him and Stukeley, and Stukeley is with the king of Spain who gives him great living', he replied. O'Gara also admitted that he had heard Spaniards speak against Queen Elizabeth.

Despite his interrogation and the fact that he appeared to have knowledge of the movements of some of those involved in seeking Spanish aid for an invasion, there is no evidence to suggest that Kean O'Gara was subsequently charged or implicated in any way in the conspiracies of the time. Apart from the record of his interrogation in 1572, nothing further has come to light in official sources about him. A clue to his identity is an obituary notice in the Annals of Loch Cé in 1577 in which it states that 'The son of O'Gadhra, i.e. Cian, the son of Diarmaid, son of Eoghan O'Gadhra, died.'[78]

By the late 1580s, the Spanish were engaged in the conflict in Ireland, and Irriell[79] O'Gara, lord of Moygara, was less fortunate than his kinsman. He was accused of harbouring Spaniards after the wreck of Armada ships off the coast of Sligo and imprisoned for sixteen weeks in Ballymote Castle.[80] He had to pay Richard Bingham, the president of Connacht, eighty cows to secure his release. While O'Gara was confined, William Taaffe, 'who had land adjacent to O'Gara's territory, enticed O'Gara's tenants to his lands'.[81] A rebellion in 1589 against Bingham's harsh treatment of the Mayo region was supported by Sligo men including Irriel O'Gara.

---

74 John O'Grady had gone to Coimbra in Portugal to seek money to help release his brother, Fr David Wolfe, who had been imprisoned in Dublin Castle. There is no explanation given for the different surnames. One suggestion is that they were half-brothers, step-brothers or maybe brothers-in-law.   75 Fr David Wolfe SJ was appointed papal legate to Ireland by Pope Pius IV in 1560. He left Ireland in 1572, having spent five years in prison in Dublin Castle: see Lennon, *Sixteenth-century Ireland*, pp 314–16.   76 The 'pretended archbishop' was Maurice MacGibbon [Fitzgibbon], archbishop of Cashel and emissary of Irish leaders to the Spanish court. In 1569 James Fitzmaurice Fitzgerald led a revolt in support of MacGibbon's campaign to seek the aid of Phillip II. See Lennon, *Sixteenth-century Ireland*, p. 318.   77 Stukeley was an English Catholic mercenary who plotted against Queen Elizabeth. See Lennon, *Sixteenth-century Ireland*, p. 225.   78 *ALC* 1577.   79 Also written as Oilill, Iriel, Irill, Irril, Irriel and Oliver.   80 O'Dowd, *Power, politics and land*, p. 39.   81 Ibid.

In his report on the complaints against Bingham's actions, which had caused many families to flee their homes in terror, the lord deputy wrote:

> in the county of Sligo most pitiful complaints have been made unto us of the hard course of government used there by Sir George Bingham and William Taaff, by mean whereof many of the inhabitants of that county had dispersed themselves and left their habitations, and now, albeit upon our words most of them came unto us to declare their griefs … we had much ado either to persuade them to trust ourselves or to return to their dwellings upon our protection … we brought back to their houses four several septs of that country, viz., of the Harts, of some of the O'Connors, McDonoughs, and of the O'Garies, which before were fled into O'Rourke's country and elsewhere.[82]

The rebellion and other incidents, such as the Nine Years War, had repercussions for Irriel O'Gara, and as a protection against losing his estate, he is recorded in the patent rolls of James I, 21 May 1603 as having mortgaged his three castles (i.e. Moygara, Cuppanagh and Derrymore) and all his estate to Donogh O'Conor Sligo.[83] This was ultimately successful and O'Gara kept his lands.[84] There was a family connection between Irriel and the O'Conor Sligo family according to the pedigree of O'Gara in O'Ferral's *Linea Antigua*: Irriel's grandfather was married to a daughter of Cathal O'Conor Sligo, a close relative of Donogh.[85]

Irriel died in 1614 but as his heir Tadhg had died in 1598, the next in line eligible to inherit the O'Gara property was Tadhg's eldest son, Fergal, who was a ward of court at that time. Wards of court were the young inheritors, not yet of age, of important estates, put under the guardianship of persons whom the English administration considered to be reliable.[86] Fergal's guardian was Sir Theobald Dillon, one of the most important people in Connacht at that time. A guardian was granted an allowance for looking after the ward and was allowed to enjoy the benefit of the land of the estate until the latter came of age.[87] In some instances the guardian influenced the choice of a marriage partner for his ward.[88] Both of these privileges appear to have been availed of by Sir Theobald, Fergal's guardian.

Following Irriel's death in 1614 at 'Clontycarna' (Cloontycarn is situated around 2km from Moygara Castle), two inquisitions[89] were held, one on 12 April 1614 when it was noted that Fergal, the heir to Gara lands, was eighteen years old and unmarried and the second on 28 October 1615 when the latter was nineteen-and-a-half years and

82 H.-C. Hamilton (ed.), *Calendar of state papers, Ireland: Tudor period, 1588–92, 146* (London, 1885), pp 230–44. **83** M.C. Griffiths (ed.), *Calendar of the Irish patent rolls of James I* (Dublin, 1965), p. 475 (pat. 18 Jas. I, LXXV); O'Dowd, *Power, politics and land*, p. 75. **84** See chapter 2. **85** R. O'Ferrall, *Linea Antigua* (Genealogical Office, Dublin, 1709), MSS 482–5, pp 150–1. **86** MacDermot, *MacDermot of Moylurg*, appendix 6, p. 512. **87** O'Dowd, *Power, politics and land*, p. 74. **88** MacDermot, *MacDermot of Moylurg*, appendix 6, p. 512. **89** National Archives, Dublin, MSS R.C. 9/15, *Inquisitions James I*, nos. 17 and 19.

married. At the first inquisition it was noted that Irriel had settled by indenture 'for a term of years' the letting of many townlands, including the castle at Moygara, to William Taaffe. In the late 1580s, Irriel had been in conflict with William Taaffe, who was an agent of the president of Connacht. It is very likely that negotiations took place between Irriel and Fergal's guardian, Sir Theobald Dillon, regarding the letting of the O'Gara lands to Sir William Taaffe, whose centre was at Ballymote Castle. Sir Theobald Dillon's daughter Anne was married to John, Taaffe's son. According to the Taaffe genealogical chart, published in the *Memoirs of the family of Taaffe* in 1856, Sir William's daughter Elizabeth, sister of John, married Ferrall (i.e. Fergal) O'Gara, *Armigeri* (a person entitled to bear heraldic arms).[90] Alternatively, it has been claimed that it was John's daughter, not his sister, who married Fergal O'Gara but the source for this statement has not been quoted.[91] In addition, it is possible that Fergal O'Gara's marriage to Elizabeth (Isobel) Taaffe, daughter or granddaughter of Sir William, was also arranged by his guardian. At the time of the inquisitions, claims were made against the O'Gara estate but Fergal was granted most of the property, with the exception of Irriel's bequest of 'six quarters devised to his wife Uny ny Donnogh alias Gara'. A number of people contested Irriel's will, including Roger Jones, as the heir of Daniel O'Conor Sligo. Eight years later, on 31 December 1623, a letter of complaint was received by the Lord Deputy of Ireland:

> Whereas complaint is made unto us by the Countesse Dowager of Desmond, that her late husband Sir Donnogh O'Connor Sligoe, knight, having among other thinges assured unto her by fine and recoverie for her jointure the castle, towne, and land of Copponagh, being one quarter of the land lying in the county of Sligo in that kingdome, shee had quietly in joyed the same the space of 12 yeares and upwardes, but of late one Farrell O'Gara pretending right unto the same and taking advantage of her sollicitor's absence out of that realme, who had the charge and custody of her evidence and was onely instructed in her affaires, hath surreptitiously (as is informed) recovered from her the possession of the said quarter of land without any defence made against him, whereby shee doubteth that others encouraged by his example will goe about to take the like advantage for the rest of her said jointure.[92]

LOSS OF ANCESTRAL LANDS IN THE SEVENTEENTH CENTURY

In the early seventeenth century, Fergal O'Gara (Fearghal Ó Gadhra), grandson of Irriel and patron of the Annals of the Four Masters, lived in Cuppanagh, Co. Sligo. An

90 K. Taaffe, *Memoirs of the family of Taaffe* (Vienna, 1856). This source contains the *Genealogia familie de Taaffe*, compiled by the Ulster king at arms, William Bethan, in 1836.   **91** O'Dowd, *Power, politics and land*, p. 60.
92 J.V. Lyle (ed.), *Acts of the privy council of England, 1621–1623*, 38 (London, 1932), p. 385.

entry reads: 'O'Gara, Farrell, Sligo, Copnagh, gentry: gent, 7 June 1624'.[93] Another source also suggests that Fergal was living in Cuppanagh townland on the shores of Lough Gara. We hear that:

> Coppenogh 1 quar. The inheritance of ffarrill ó Gara who keepes it in his own hands, it is good arbl land & heathey ground, it hath some shelter & good turffe 10 days it will grase 200 cowes, & it is worth £20 p. Annum.[94]

Fergal remained in a prominent position in the west of Ireland. In March 1650, Farell (i.e. Fergal) was named as one of the thirteen leading men of Connacht who signed a petition, addressed to the pope, to have Fr Francis O'Connor, OFM, promoted to the see of Elphin. The other men involved were: three O'Conors; MacDermots; two O'Rourkes O'Conor Don, O'Conor Sligo, O'Dowd, O'Flaherty and O'Hara.[95]

The Confederate and Cromwellian wars and subsequent confiscation of land in the 1650s brought huge change in the fortunes of Irish landowners, including Fergal O'Gara, who, with Tadhg O'Conor Sligo, half-brother to Donogh (to whom the O'Gara land was mortgaged in 1603), were the two MPs appointed to represent Co. Sligo in 1634.[96] The historian Brendan Jennings has stated that Fergal was openly on the side of the Catholic Confederates and sent his son, Captain John, with a company of men, to assist Eoin Roe O'Neill.[97] After the wars, articles of agreement were drawn up between Major General Luke Taaffe and the president of Connacht and were concluded in 1652. The only way that the army could pay the victorious Parliamentarian soldiers for their services was to grant them land. In spite of an earlier agreement that Connacht was to remain in Irish hands, much of Co. Sligo land was eventually confiscated and redistributed to Cromwellian officers and soldiers, and English officials.[98] In 1653, the tenants of Coolavin, where Fergal O'Gara owned most of the land, were ordered to leave the district. People, cattle and goods were to vacate the area by the following year.[99] Following the loss of their lands with the Act of Settlement in 1662, many landlords appealed unsuccessfully to have their estates restored. As agent for some of the dispossessed, Richard Talbot of Malahide (created baron of Talbotstown, Viscount Baltinglas, and earl of Tyrconnel in 1685)[100] conducted a deal with Lord Kingston in April 1663, by which he acquired a number of townlands in Coolavin, formerly the property of Fergal O'Gara, including Moygara

93 J. Ohlmeyer and É. Ó Ciardha (eds), *The Irish statute staple books, 1596–1687* (Dublin, 1998), p. 269. **94** BL, MS 2048, 'The halfe barronie of Coollavin Harleian', ff 124–7 or 331–4, f. 332r or (f. 125r). In fact, there is evidence for Fergal living at Cuppanagh in 1623. See T. O'Rorke, *The history of Sligo: town and county*, 2 vols (Dublin, 1889), i, p. 140. **95** C. Giblin (ed.), 'Vatican Archives', *Archivium Hibernicum*, 31(1973), p. 115. **96** O'Dowd, *Power, politics and land*, p. 60. **97** B. Jennings, *Michael Ó Cleirigh, chief of the Four Masters and his associates* (Dublin, 1936), p. 144. **98** O'Dowd, *Power, politics and land*, pp 131–4. **99** The confiscation of Fergal O'Gara's land is confirmed from 1667 in the Books of Survey and Distribution, SPL, Co. Sligo micro film, MF/R.18. **100** P.W. Sergeant, *Little Jennings and Fighting Dick Talbot: a life of the duke and duchess of Tyrconnel*, 2 vols (London, 1913), i, p. 297.

and Cuppanagh. Talbot returned to England 'to prosecute the work which he had undertaken, carrying with him £18,000 in bonds and other securities from fellow-countrymen desirous of restoration to their estates'.[101]

There is no evidence that Talbot was successful in restoring any of the former O'Gara townlands which had been purchased from Lord Kingston. 'Farroll O Gara of Moygara'[102] (i.e. Fergal O'Gara) was named among the twenty-eight former Co. Sligo landowners who lodged an appeal in 1664 to have their lands restored. When a name was included in the appeals list, it was not proof that the person was alive at that time, but in the case of 'Farroll O Gara', late of Cuppanagh and Moygara, it is plausible that he was still living at the time of the appeal in 1664. A 'Farrell O'Gara' was recorded in the townland of Ardconnell, parish of Emlaghfad, Co. Sligo, a few miles north of Moygara and Cuppanagh as the only person with a hearth in the tax rolls of 1663.[103]

All but one of the former landowners lost their appeals for the restoration of their lands. The Catholic landlord to survive was Theobald Taaffe. He was either a nephew or a grandnephew of Elizabeth Taaffe, wife of Fergal O'Gara of Moygara.[104]

Fergal O'Gara's land holdings in Coolavin were distributed between John, Lord Kingston, Bryan Magrath and Phillip Ormsby. Lands that had been held jointly by Fergal and Owen O'Gara in the same barony became the property of Lord Kingston and Bryan Magrath.[105]

In the barony of Corran, which lies north of Coolavin, two O'Gara men also lost land. Owen O'Gara held Cloonena townland in the parish of Kilshalvey, which was transferred to Theobald Taaffe, the earl of Carlingford. Many former Gaelic and Old English landowners became tenants under the new landlords and there is evidence that a number of O'Gara families remained as such in the Coolavin district, although records for tenants are scarce for seventeenth-century south Sligo.

It is possible to trace the continued presence of some O'Garas in Sligo in the latter half of the seventeenth century by reference to two official surveys. In the Civil Survey of 1659 fourteen O'Gara names are recorded in the baronies of Corran and Coolavin, although no addresses or first names are given.[106] A more detailed study, carried out for the purpose of levying a tax based on the number of hearths in each house, was commenced in 1662. Twelve O'Gara households were taxed in the half-barony of Coolavin, each with one hearth.[107]

101 Ibid., p. 134.   **102** Anonymous, 'The dispossessed landowners of Ireland, 1664 (lists given to the duke of Ormonde to select his nominees for restoration), part 1, Leinster and Connacht', *Irish Genealogist*, 4:4 (Nov. 1971), p. 300. 'The lists which follow were copied from the Prendergast MSS, vol. iv at the King's Inns Library, Dublin, by E.G. More O'Ferrall in 1970, and are published by kind permission of the committee of that library.' (The Editorial committee: Lt-Col. H.D. Gallwey, Hon. Editor; Revd Laurence O'Donoghue, CC; and J.C. Walton, Esq., MA).   **103** NLI, MS 2165, Hearth Money Roll, Co. Sligo.   **104** Taaffe, *Memoirs of the family of Taaffe*. As stated, this source contains the *Genealogia familie de Taaffe*, compiled by the Ulster king at arms, William Bethan, in 1836.   **105** Books of Survey and Distribution: County of Sligo. Microfilm/Reference SUR 006.   **106** S. Pender (ed.), *A census of Ireland circa 1659, with supplementary material from the poll money ordinances 1660–1661* (Dublin, 1939).   **107** NLI, MS 2165, Hearth Money Roll, Co. Sligo.

SERVICE IN THE REGIMENTS OF FRANCE AND SPAIN

Although generations of O'Garas continued to live in Sligo, Mayo and Roscommon, some went abroad, either to further their education or due to the political unrest in Ireland.

Col. Oliver O'Gara was the grandson of Fergal O'Gara and Elizabeth (Isobel) Taaffe. His parents were Captain John O'Gara and Mary O'Conor, grand-aunt to Charles O'Conor of Ballinagare, 1710–91, the historian and activist for Catholic rights, whose grandson Owen inherited the title of O'Conor Don in 1820 from a cousin.[108] During the Williamite War, fighting for James II, Oliver had commanded a regiment of infantry at the Battle of Aughrim in 1691. He was one of the witnesses at the signing of the Articles of Galway on 21 July 1691.[109] Oliver was one of nearly 3,000 Irish troops who left for France in the early 1690s following the defeat of James II. He went into exile with his wife, Mary Fleming, daughter of Randal, Lord Slane of Co. Meath. They settled with many other Irish Jacobites at St Germain, outside Paris, where their eleven children were born. James Patrick, the eldest, born in 1692, had Patrick Sarsfield as one of the sponsors at his baptism.[110]

Oliver initially served with the Irish Guards of James II as lieutenant colonel but by 1696 he had been appointed colonel of the Queen's Regiment of Dragoons.[111] Later, he would receive a pension for his military duty as colonel, and Mary, his wife, was awarded a pension of 25 livres per month from the queen, Mary of Modena, wife of James II.[112] Three of the O'Gara sons joined Irish regiments in Europe in the first decades of the eighteenth century. Many members of former Jacobite regiments first served in France and later in Spain. Those who fought with the Irish regiments under Louis XIV in the War of the Spanish Succession, 1701–14, and who wished to continue their military careers, transferred to the Irish regiments in Spain to serve under Philip V.[113] Fergal O'Gara's great grandson Oliver O'Gara was listed as one of the colonels of the Regiment of Hibernia, which was serving under the Spanish crown.[114]

Oliver and Mary's eldest son, eighteen-year-old John, had already embarked on the life of a soldier in France by 1710. Later he would serve in Spain, where he was awarded a knighthood in 1722,[115] and had reached the rank of lieutenant colonel in the Irlanda Regiment by the time of his death in the late 1730s. James Oliver, their

---

108 L. Gibbons and K. O'Conor, 'Introduction: Charles O'Conor of Ballinagare (1710–91)' in Gibbons and O'Conor (eds), *Charles O'Conor of Ballinagare, 1710–91*, p. 27.   **109** C.F. Blake-Forster, *The Irish chieftains or a struggle for the Crown* (Dublin, 1872), appendix, p. 587.   **110** C.E. Lart, *Jacobite extracts, registers of Saint Germain-en-Laye*, 2 vols (London, 1910–12), i, p. 112.   **111** Ibid., pp 42, 74, 112.   **112** Edward Corp, pers. comm.   **113** A. MacDermott, 'The Irish regiments in the Spanish service', *Irish Genealogist*, 2:9 (July 1952), pp 259–68.   **114** M. O'Gara-O'Riordan, 'Charles O'Conor and the Annals of the Four Masters' in Gibbons and O'Conor (eds), *Charles O'Conor of Ballinagare, 1710–91*, pp 230–3; MacDermott, 'The Irish regiments in the Spanish service', p. 267.   **115** AHN, Madrid, Micros 112 NP/377 exp. 5854, MM Santiago, f. 9r.

second son,[116] enlisted in the Regiment of Hibernia in Spain. In his long military career he rose from the rank of captain in the 1720s to colonel by 1755.[117] Joseph, the youngest of the three military sons, also served in Spain. As a captain in the Irlanda Regiment in the 1740s, he was seriously wounded during the Italian campaign of that decade. He was knighted in 1761 and received his commission as brevet colonel the following year.[118]

COUNT O'GARA AND THE AUSTRIAN HABSBURGS

In contrast to the military careers followed by his father and three brothers, Charles O'Gara was employed in the household of the dukes of Lorraine for all of his working life. At his baptism in the chapel royal at St Germain in 1699, his godfather had been 'the very noble and powerful Prince, James II, King', who signed himself, 'Jacques Roi'.[119] At a young age, Charles was recommended for future service to Leopold Joseph, duke of Lorraine, by Count Francis Taaffe. Taaffe was a cousin of the O'Garas and had himself served in the regiment of the duke and of his father.[120]

Charles held positions as 'gentleman of the chamber and senior groom to the duke'.[121] After the death of the duke, he remained in the service of his son, Francis Stephen, who was elected Holy Roman emperor in 1745.[122] Later, Charles was a senior major-domo in the household of Princess Charlotte of Lorraine, a sister of the duke.[123] He was a member of the council of state in Vienna, and by 1761 had been knighted and awarded the Order of the Golden Fleece by the emperor.[124]

As a younger man, Charles had supported his mother when she wished to return to Ireland to pursue her legal rights arising from her first marriage. Although Mary

---

116 Lart, *Jacobite extracts*, i, p. 112; M. O'Gara-O'Riordan, 'Births, baptisms and deaths in the exiled O'Gara family after the Jacobite defeat', *Corran Herald*, 42 (2009–10), p. 26. **117** M. Walsh, 'A Galway officer of the Spanish Navy', *JGAHS*, 26 (1954–5), p. 32. **118** AHN, Madrid, Microfilm exp. 1085, Alcántara, f. 53r; H. Gallwey, 'Irish officers in the Spanish service', *Irish Genealogist*, 6:2 (1981), p. 207. **119** Lart, *Jacobite extracts*, i, p. 74. **120** J.C. O'Callaghan, *History of the Irish brigades in the service of France* (Dublin, 1869), p. 88; *Mémoire de M. Mac Donagh* (1792), Halliday Pamphlets, no. 619, Royal Irish Academy Library, Dublin, fn 1, p. 35. **121** AHN, Madrid, Microfilm exp. 1085, Alcántara, f. 50v. **122** AHN, Madrid, Microfilm exp. 1085, Alcántara, f. 35v. Father Friar Domingo O'Conor of the Order of St Dominic, provincial vicar and solicitor general for the province of Ireland at the court of Madrid as a sponsor for Don Joseph O'Gara to be awarded the knighthood of Alcántara in Spain, in 1761, was questioned under oath about the relatives of Joseph. Fr O'Conor stated 'Don Carlos O Gara, who currently serves the Emperor and his sister princess Carlota of Lorena with great honour and distinction …'. **123** AHN, Madrid, Microfilm exp. 1085, Alcántara, ff 49r–50r. Pedro Tyrry, member of the Council of His Majesty and honorary minister of the Tribunal of the Great Chancellry of Accounts Chiefs of this Court of Madrid, sponsor for Don Joseph O'Gara to be awarded the knighthood of Alcántara in Spain, in 1761. **124** Archives Generales Du Royaume, Brussels, solicitors of Brabant, deed no. 51, 17 Apr. 1776. 'On this day, the 17 Apr. 1776 the very noble and powerful Lord, His Excellency Count Charles O'Gara, closest senior member of the Council of State to their Imperial and Royal Apostolic Majesties; Knight of the Golden Fleece: the greatest authority of the court of her late Royal Highness Princess Charlotte of Lorraine.' Permission was given by the Archives Generales Du Royaume to publish this reference on 4 Aug. 1998.

O'Gara's first husband, Richard Fleming, had died many years earlier, at the Siege of Derry in 1689, she petitioned for arrears of rental income in the 1720s that had been due to her as his widow. After several appeals,[125] an act of parliament was passed in England in 1726 that gave her the right to return to Ireland and sue for her entitlement to income from her jointure lands. With the expectation of winning her case, and recovering the rents due to her, Mary signed a deed in 1728 in Dublin, which stipulated that her son, Charles, who had supported her financially during the legal process, was to get the principal share of the arrears:

> Pay unto her beloved son Charles O'Gara out of ye sd Arrears ye sum of one thousand six hundred pounds in Discharge & Satisfaction for the money by him Advanced for sd Mary in obtaining sd Act of Parliamt.[126]

When Charles O'Gara died in 1777, royal associates, household staff, friends and family in Europe and in Ireland were to benefit from his substantial will. The principal beneficiaries were two members of the Plunkett family, grandchildren of Bridget Fleming Plunkett, who had married Lord Dunsany in 1711.[127] Bridget was Charles' half-sister, daughter of Mary O'Gara from her first marriage to Richard Fleming.[128]

Another to benefit was Charles O'Conor of Ballinagare, his second cousin.[129] O'Conor was at the time in financial difficulties and in danger of losing his property due to the hardships of the Penal Laws. In a letter to a relative, he described how 'the legacy of my cousin Count O'Gara came opportunely to my relief and eased me of a great part of my burden'.[130]

Charles O'Gara also remembered those who were living in poverty in the O'Gara ancestral lands in Sligo. He asked that any new items of clothing in his wardrobe be sold for their benefit: 'whatever is new be sold and the money be given to the poor in the Bishopric [district] of Coolavin in Ireland, where this donation will be placed in the hands of the Bishop of the Diocese [Achonry] to be distributed amongst the poor'.[131]

125 The National Archives, Kew, England, S.P. 63/379, scan 0066.tif. **126** Registry of Deeds, Dublin, O'Gara to Barnewall et al., no. 39572, book 57, p. 527. **127** J. Lodge, *The peerage of Ireland: or, a genealogical history of the present nobility of that kingdom* (Dublin, 1789), vi, p. 211. **128** R. Bligh, Reports of cases heard in the House of Lords upon appeals and writs of error and decided during the Session 1836, vol. X, 6th & 7th W. IV (London, 1838), 'Slane Peerage Case', 1835, p. 12. **129** Count Charles O'Gara's paternal grandmother was Mary O'Conor of Ballinagare, grand-aunt to Charles O'Conor, who explains his relationship with Colonel Oliver O'Gara's family in a letter to an O'Conor cousin c.1769. See C.C. Ward and R.E. Ward (eds), *The letters of Charles O'Conor of Belanagare*, 2 vols (Ann Arbor, MI, 1980), i, Letter 202, pp 271–2. **130** R.E. Ward, J.F. Wrynn and C. Coogan Ward (eds), *The letters of Charles O'Conor of Belanagare,* 2 vols (Washington, 1988), ii, Letter 353, pp 413–14. **131** Departemente des Imprimes, Bibliotheque Royale, Brussels, Will of Count Charles O'Gara, 1773, article 4. Permission was given to publish this translation of Count O'Gara's will on the 4 Aug. 1998 to Maura O'Gara-O'Riordan.

O'GARA MARRIAGE AND FAMILY CONNECTIONS

As has been shown, the O'Gara dynasty had connections with other families that extended over several generations, especially the O'Conors, the MacDermots, the Taaffes and the Dillons.

Ardconnell townland was the property of John, Viscount Taaffe, before the Confederate and Cromwellian wars and was inherited by his son and heir, Theobald, who had about 11,000 acres around Ballymote restored to him by Charles II. Given that Theobald's aunt or grand-aunt was married to 'Farrell' (Fergal) O'Gara, it is possible to speculate that Theobald made some of this land at Ardconnell available to him after he was dispossessed and this is why he seems to have been living here in 1663, as noted.

A strong reliance on a network of connections between these families is evident in the O'Gara references in the Annals of Loch Cé. For example, an entry from 1584 refers to a link between the ruling family of O'Gara and the much stronger MacDermot (Mac Diarmaida) family:

> The daughter of Mac Diarmada, i.e., Sadhbh, daughter of Eoghan, the wife of O'Gadhra, i.e. Diarmaid, son of Eoghan Ó'Gadhra, died.[132]

Other members of the O'Gara ruling family had marriage alliances with both the MacDermots of Moylurg and with O'Conor Sligo, and there was little change up to the sixteenth century in these influential links between noble Connacht families.[133]

Although living in France for much of his life, it is likely that Colonel Oliver O'Gara had some contact with his Irish clerical cousins, the brothers Bernard and Michael O'Gara, natives of Co. Mayo, who were described 'as very close relatives'.[134] It is generally held that their father, Charles, was another son of Fergal O'Gara, patron of the Annals of the Four Masters, as noted.[135] Both Bernard and Michael studied in France – the former at the Jesuit College in Douai and the latter at the Irish College in Paris. Bernard was appointed archbishop of Tuam in 1723 and served there until his death in 1740.[136] Prior to his death, Bernard signed the genealogy of Myles MacDermot of Coolavin, in 1738 as 'Ber. AB Tuam'.[137] The following year, Bernard had a stone altar erected in memory of his father at the Augustinian friary at Ballyhaunis, Co. Mayo, which reads:

---

132 *ALC* 1584.   **133** B. Cunningham, *Clanricard and Thomond, 1540–1640: provincial politics and society transformed* (Dublin, 2012), p. 29.   **134** AHN, Madrid, microfilm exp. 1085, Alcántara, f. 39r.   **135** N. Ó Muraíle, 'The townlands of Bekan' in M. Comer and N. Ó Muraíle (eds), *Béacán/Bekan: portrait of an east Mayo parish* (Ballinrobe, 1986), p. 41.   **136** RIA, MS 1220 (C iii 3) f. vr. RIA, isos.dias.ie.   **137** MS 50,536/66, catalogue.nli.ie/Record/vtls000752120.

PRAY FOR Y SOULS OF CHARLIS O GARA AND FAMILY FOR WHOM THIS
TOMB WAS MADE BY HIS SON BER. AR. OF TUAM AN. DM. 1739.

Michael lived in Spain for many years where he served as rector of the Irish College in
Alcalá de Henares from 1728 to 1740.[138] Michael was made archbishop of Tuam in
1740 following the death of his brother, Bernard. In 1742, he too endorsed the
pedigree of Myles MacDermot.[139]

BURIAL PLACE AT TEMPLERONAN

In Cuppanagh townland lies the ruin of an originally early medieval church called
Templeronan. Located on the east side of Loch Gara facing the castle there, it has been
the final resting place for some O'Gara families for centuries.[140] There are a number of
O'Gara plots with headstones within the church walls. This old church ruin was also
a burial place of the MacDermots of Coolavin.[141] From the early sixteenth century the
MacDermots of Moylurg had expanded northwards from their Roscommon base.[142]
The Annals of Loch Cé records that:

> Ruaidhri Mac Diarmada secured, and firmly established, many of the neigh-
> bouring and distant territories under his government and heavy tribute, for he
> exacted … sixty cows from O'Gadhra …[143]

In the surrounding churchyard at Templeronan, which continues to be used as a burial
ground, there are two enclosed square spaces with one adjoining wall. One of the
spaces, which has no marked stones, was the burial place of the MacDermots of
Coolavin.[144] The second square plot is the burial place of the O'Garas of
Derrymaquirk, formerly of Cuppanagh. There are a number of other O'Gara marked
graves, including one for the O'Gara family of Cuppanagh in whose name the
graveyard was registered in the nineteenth-century Griffith Valuation as tenants of
Viscount Lorton.[145] The viscount was a descendant of the Lord Kingston, who was
granted almost all of Fergal O'Gara's townlands in Coolavin following the Confederate
and Cromwellian wars in the mid-seventeenth century.

---

138 P. O'Connell, *The Irish College at Alcala De Henares 1649–1785* (Dublin, 1997), pp 40–1.   139 MS
50,536/66, catalogue.nli.ie/Record/vtls000752120.   140 RIA, MS 23 L 44, G. Petrie, *Diary of a tour of Longford
and Sligo* (1837), pp 13–14; see Egan, Byrne and Sleeman, *Archaeologial inventory of Co. Sligo*, p. 408.
141 Petrie, *Diary of a tour of Longford and Sligo*, pp 13–14; MacDermot, *MacDermot of Moylurg*, pp 245, 275,
279.   142 O'Dowd, *Power, politics and land*, pp 22–3.   143 *ALC* 1549.   144 Petrie, *Diary of a tour of Longford
and Sligo*, pp 13–14.   145 Griffith's Valuation, Boyle Union, Cuppanagh townland, parish of Killaraght, barony
of Coolavin, Co. Sligo, Catherine O'Gara, p. 30.

NINETEENTH-CENTURY PRESENCE IN SLIGO

Although the location and extent of O'Gara territory changed over time, in recent centuries they lived in the areas that cover parts of present-day counties Sligo, Roscommon and Mayo. Official records confirm the presence of O'Gara names in these locations in the nineteenth and into the twentieth centuries. The Tithe Applotment Books[146] list twenty-seven heads of households with the surname 'O'Gara' or 'Gara' in Co. Sligo. Griffith's Valuation[147] records 136 holdings in counties Roscommon, Mayo and Sligo with the surname 'O'Gara' or 'Gara'. In the 1901 census,[148] there are about 160 households of the name listed in counties Roscommon, Mayo and Sligo.

MODERN TECHNOLOGY AND O'GARA RESEARCH

Modern technology and scientific methods have provided additional tools for assessing traditional historical research with greater accuracy. The history of the O'Gara dynasty, as described in this chapter, has benefited from these new methods in two ways. The first relates to a genetic programme which confirmed the findings of centuries-old genealogical tables that indicated a common ancestry for the O'Garas and the O'Haras. The second, an online facility that allows ancient Irish manuscripts to be enlarged for greater scrutiny, has helped to identify an incorrect insertion that was added at a later time to the Annals of the Four Masters.

In 2002, twenty-seven O'Gara men were accepted as volunteers for a Y-chromosome project carried out in the population genetics laboratory in Trinity College Dublin.[149] All were descended from O'Gara families registered in the Griffith's Valuation books in the mid-nineteenth century but had no known relationship with one another. Of the 192 Gara/O'Gara heads of households registered in the thirty-two counties of Ireland in the nineteenth century, 59 were located in Roscommon, 53 in Donegal, 45 in Sligo, 32 in Mayo and a small number in Longford and Leitrim. The modern samples included 22 from the Connacht counties of Mayo, Roscommon and Sligo, and 5 from the Ulster county of Donegal.

The laboratory results showed that fifteen of those males of Connacht origin shared a common ancestor. Of the three other paternity groups, all the Ulster volunteers had

---

146 Compiled between 1823 and 1837 to determine the amount which occupiers of agricultural holdings over one acre should pay in tithes to the Church of Ireland. See National Archives of Ireland website, Tithe Applotment Books, titheapplotmentbooks.nationalarchives.ie/search/tab/home.jsp; see appendix 1.   **147** Assessment of holdings carried out between 1848 and 1864 to determine liability to pay a rate to support the Poor Law Union. See Ask About Ireland website, 'Griffith's Valuation', askaboutireland.ie/griffith-valuation.   **148** National Archives of Ireland, *Census of population, 1901*, census.nationalarchives.ie.   **149** The Y-chromosome is passed from father to son and is recognized as the paternally inherited male chromosome. No females inherit the Y-chromosome.

a common male ancestor; another group of five Connacht men also had a common ancestor, and the third group of two shared an ancestor.

The first phase of testing suggested that the fifteen volunteers of Connacht origin might have a common ancestor dating back at least six or seven hundred years. As the tenth-century genealogical tables clearly indicate a common (male) ancestor for the O'Gara and O'Hara lines, phase two of the project selected ten O'Hara volunteers. The tests confirmed that seven of the Connacht O'Hara participants did indeed share a common (male) ancestor with the group of fifteen Connacht O'Gara men, thus confirming the centuries-old connection between the two which is mentioned in the genealogies.

Dr Brian McEvoy explained the process in establishing the O'Gara/O'Hara common ancestry:

> We looked at Y-chromosome DNA as a new way to explore the history of Irish surnames. Like a surname, the Y-chromosome is passed from father to son and if one man started a surname in the past then all men of that surname today should (in theory) have the same Y-chromosome. We looked at over one thousand people and more than 40 surnames and found that on average people of the same surname are far more likely to be related to each other than people of different surnames.
>
> Y-chromosomes in the O'Gara and O'Hara surnames showed that there was one major founder for each surname. Even more remarkably, it was the same Y-chromosome in each, meaning that the founders of the two names were probably closely related, as traditional historical sources had indicated.[150]

The School of Celtic Studies at the Dublin Institute of Advanced Studies has made Irish manuscripts available in digitized form through its Irish Script on Screen (ISOS) project. Since the first years of this century, it has been possible to examine in detail the manuscript copies of both sets of the Annals of the Four Masters. Obscure and darkened handwriting can be enlarged to allow researchers greater ease in their interpretation of the documents.

As has been discussed, one set of the Annals of the Four Masters incorrectly refers to the O'Garas as lords of Luighne south (*deisc[eir]t*) in the tenth century. However, the second set of the Annals of the Four Masters correctly describes the O'Garas as being lords of Luighne at this period.

Although both sets of the annals were compiled in the 1630s and would have been carefully cross-checked by the compilers and scribes to maintain uniformity, the two

---

150 I am grateful to Dr Brian McEvoy for this information. Dr McEvoy collaborated on the programme while completing his PhD, entitled 'Genetic investigation of Irish ancestry and surname history', in 2004 at Trinity College, Dublin. See B. McEvoy and D. Bradley, 'Y-chromosomes and the extent of patrilineal ancestry in Irish surnames', *Human Genetics*, 119:1–2 (2006), pp 212–19.

sets had been separated by late 1636. The close supervision and revision that applied at the time of their compilation was at an end. Any changes or revisions to one set would no longer be reflected in the other.

After their separation, it is believed that one set was presented to Fergal O'Gara as patron of the work, while the other set was taken to Louvain with the intention of preparing the manuscript for printing. The two manuscripts that formed the O'Gara set were circulated among scholars and consequently were heavily annotated with many additions.[151] The whereabouts of the O'Gara manuscripts are documented for a number of years in the seventeenth century, but their location is not known between 1685 and 1724.[152]

When John O'Donovan was preparing his translation of the Annals of the Four Masters in the 1840s,[153] he did not have the benefit of viewing the original manuscripts. He had to rely instead on an eighteenth-century copy as his source, and so repeated the error that limited tenth-century O'Gara territory to '*south* Luigne'. From the second half of the nineteenth century, other historians consulted O'Donovan's work and the transcribed manuscripts and so the error continued. The original O'Gara manuscript was returned to the Royal Irish Academy library in 1883 from England, was catalogued as RIA, MS 1220 (C iii 3) and was later made available for viewing. However the opportunity to compare entries in that manuscript with entries in the Franciscan manuscript (the Louvain set) occurred shortly after that manuscript of the annals was transferred to University College Dublin in September 2000 as part of the Irish Franciscan archive, Killiney, Co. Dublin, where it was catalogued UCD–OFM, MS A 13. The two manuscripts were digitized for ISOS: RIA, MS 1220 (C iii 3) in 2002 and UCD–OFM, MS A 13 in 2004.

In the on-screen digitized and enlarged form of the original copy of the Annals of the Four Masters RIA, MS 1220 (C iii 3),[154] it is evident that the last word, *deisc*[*eir*]*t*, which follows the word '*luighne*' (in line three) 'is in a very different ink from all the rest' (fig. 6.1).[155]

The Annals of the Four Masters UCD–OFM, MS A 13 does not include the word *deisc*[*eir*]*t* (fig. 6.2). Its absence is in line with the fact that the corresponding annal entry in the *Chronicon Scotorum*, the likely source for the original Four Masters' entry, similarly refers to Úa Gadhra as the 'King of Luighne' rather than king of South Luighne.[156]

By adding the word *deisc*[*eirt*] to the Annals of the Four Masters, RIA, MS 1220 (C iii 3), this unknown person incorrectly limited O'Gara rule to *south* Luigne by the

151 See B. Cunningham, *The Annals of the Four Masters: Irish history, kingship and society in the early seventeenth century* (Dublin, 2010), p. 164, n. 72.   **152** N. Ó Muraíle, 'The manuscripts of the Annals of the Four Masters since 1636' in E. Bhreathnach and B. Cunningham (eds), *Writing Irish history: the Four Masters and their world* (Dublin, 2007), p. 61.   **153** J. O'Donovan (ed.), *The Annals of the Four Masters*, 7 vols (Dublin, 1848–51; 2nd ed., 1856; repr. 1990).   **154** isos.dias.ie, accessed 17 July 2014.   **155** Dr Bernadette Cunningham, 1 Feb. 2013, pers. comm.   **156** CS 964 [*recte* 966].

6.1 Extract from the O'Gara set of the Annals of the Four Masters under the year AD 964. See RIA, MS 1220 (C iii 3), f. 376r (reproduced by permission of the Royal Irish Academy © RIA).

6.2 Extract from the Louvain set of the Annals of the Four Masters under the year AD 964. See UCD–OFM, MS A 13, f. 389r (reproduced by permission of the UCD–OFM Partnership).

tenth century, whereas the reduction in their territory from Luigne to south Luigne did not occur until the division of the O'Gara-O'Hara areas of jurisdiction in the twelfth century.

The two sets of the Annals of the Four Masters separated in 1636, as noted. At an exhibition in Trinity College Dublin in 2007, the original manuscripts – the O'Gara set and the Louvain set – were reunited for the first time since their completion more than 370 years earlier.[157] The Gaelic scholar, Nollaig Ó Muraíle, commenting on Fergal O'Gara's historical role as sponsor of the Annals of the Four Masters, wrote at the time that 'without that patronage, the work would almost certainly not have been compiled in the first place'.[158]

CONCLUSIONS

As has been shown in this paper, the history of the O'Gara family can be dated back to the eighth century. The research gives an account of the historical developments attributed to members of the family over the centuries, including alliances with other

---

157 Bhreathnach and Cunningham (eds), *Writing Irish history*, p. 117.   **158** N. Ó Muraíle 'The manuscripts of the Annals of the Four Masters since 1636' in Bhreathnach and Cunningham (eds), *Writing Irish history*, p. 61.

prominent Gaelic families through marriage, and accounts of the rise and fall of the family fortunes as a result of political and strategic necessity.

The evidence shows that the main branch of the O'Garas successfully negotiated the change from Gaelic chief to English-style landowners. Fergal O'Gara, patron of the Annals of the Four Masters, was a wealthy, powerful man who was part of both Gaelic and Anglo-Irish/English milieus.[159] In a 1635 survey, his possessions included at least 4,000 acres of profitable land.[160] He was the largest landowner, along with Kean O'Hara, of Gaelic-Irish origin in Co. Sligo in 1641.[161] However, his lands were to be confiscated by the Cromwellians in the 1650s and this was confirmed by the Act of Settlement in 1662 and he appears to have died as a tenant of his Taaffe cousin at some time after 1664, when his name disappears from the historical records. While the fortunes of the O'Garas declined in Ireland in the seventeenth century, three of Fergal O'Gara's great-grandsons pursued military careers in Europe during the eighteenth century, and a fourth became a count of the Holy Roman Empire.[162]

159 O'Dowd, *Power, politics and land*, pp 82, 97.   **160** Ibid., p. 78; see appendix 1.   **161** Ibid., p. 75.
162 Registry of Deeds, Dublin, O'Gara to Barnewall et al., no. 39572, book 57, p. 527.   Lart, *Jacobite extracts,*
i, p. 74; Patrice (Patrick), but was listed as Juan (John, was a knight of Santiago – see AHN, Micros 112 NP/377,
exp. 5854, MM Santiago; Walsh (ed.), *Spanish knights of Irish origin*, p. 6). Oliver and Mary's second child,
Jacques Olivier (James Oliver), was baptized on 15 Dec. 1694 but was referred to as Oliver in military records
(see Lart, *Jacobite extracts*, i, p. 112). The third son who survived was Charles, baptized on the 6 July 1699, who
was later ennobled as a count and died in 1777 (Lart, *Jacobite extracts,* i, p. 74); the fourth son who survived was
Joseph Arthur (referred to as Joseph), baptized 5 July 1708, and who later became a knight of Alcántara – see
AHN, microfilm exp. 1085, Alcántara, f. 53r; see, also, H. Gallwey, 'Irish officers in the Spanish service', *Irish
Genealogist,* 6:2 (1981), p. 207; Lart, *Jacobite extracts,* ii, p. 110.

CHAPTER SEVEN

Moygara Castle: the topographical and geophysical surveys

KEVIN BARTON

INTRODUCTION

Geophysical survey can help to identify buried sub-surface features within many archaeological sites. Features such as walls, foundations, ditches, pits and hearths can be detected using these non-invasive, non-destructive methods.[1] Results from geophysical survey are regularly used by archaeologists to inform and guide subsequent targeted excavation and this was partly the case at Moygara Castle.[2] Furthermore, geophysical survey can also give archaeologists an insight into what occurs beneath the soil in parts of the site that are not excavated. If the results from geophysical survey are carefully analyzed, different phases of activity and functional areas can also be recognized at a site without recourse to expensive, invasive excavation.

Topographical and geophysical fieldwork at Moygara Castle was carried out in annual programmes between 2005 and May 2008. Topographical survey was used to create a simple, geo-referenced base map on which to display the geophysical survey results, to aid interpretation of the results and to investigate topographic variation in the survey area. The different geophysical methods used at Moygara Castle included: earth resistance survey; electrical resistivity tomography survey; magnetic gradiometer survey; and ground penetrating radar survey. This chapter draws together evidence from these annual topographical and geophysical surveys. Technical details of this work between 2005 and 2008 can be found in a series of unpublished reports.

1 A. Aspinall, C. Gaffney and A. Schmidt, *Magnetometry for archaeologists* (Lanham, 2011); K. Barton and J. Fenwick, 'Geophysical investigations at the ancient royal site of Rathcroghan, County Roscommon, Ireland', *Archaeological Prospection*, 12:1 (2005), pp 3–18; A. Clark, *Seeing beneath the soil: prospecting methods in archaeology* (London, 1996); L.B. Conyers, *Ground-penetrating radar for archaeology* (Lanham, 2004); C. Gaffney and J. Gater, *Revealing the buried past: geophysics for archaeologists* (Stroud, 2003); A. Schmidt, *Earth resistance for archaeologists* (Lanham, 2013); A. Witten, *Handbook of geophysics and archaeology* (London, 2006); G.N. Tsokas, P.I. Tsourlos and N. Papadopulos, 'Electrical resistivity tomography: a flexible technique in solving problems of archaeological research' in S. Campana and S. Piro (eds), *Seeing the unseen: geophysics and landscape archaeology* (London, 2008), pp 183–204. **2** See chapter 8.

OUTLINE CASTLE PLAN AND TOPOGRAPHICAL SURVEY

The base map, geo-referenced in Irish National Grid co-ordinates, consists of an outline castle plan with associated field walls and is shown in figure 7.1.[3] The mapped modern field walls are a by-product of the topographic mapping and are not complete. In the vicinity of the castle, the walls radiate outwards from the four corner towers and the northern platform. A gently curving field wall lies immediately to the west of the gatehouse, blocking the presumed entrance road to the castle.[4]

A number of loose and ground-fast stones are found within the bawn and outside it to the north of the northern platform (fig. 7.1). The stones range in size from cobbles up to 0.2m in diameter to boulders, with some of these having dimensions exceeding 1m. The stones appear to be randomly distributed within the bawn – the larger ones, however, tend to be in the northern half of the bawn. Those stones to the north, outside of the bawn, appear to mark out a shallow arc.

The topographic survey of the extant castle was carried out using a Total Station and extended outwards some 30m from the bawn walls. The survey was carried out on a 1m by 1m grid within the bawn and north of the bawn wall. Data were collected on a 2m by 2m grid in the rest of the survey area. A small area within the south-western corner of the bawn was not surveyed due to an accumulation of rubble or tumble. A map contoured at 0.25m intervals is shown in figure 7.2. The height datum is arbitrary and is based on a height of 100.0m being assigned to Control Station 1.[5] The overall contour pattern shows the castle to lie at the eastern end of a well-defined ridge that trends in an east-north-east direction.[6] The ridge is likely to be composed of clayey soils underlain by sands and gravels which form a number of glacial features in the area. The contours show the highest point on the site to be associated with the northern platform (fig. 7.2), with the steepest gradient lying to the north and north-west of the platform. The lowest gradient lies to the west of the gatehouse where a generally level area extends westwards in the direction of the presumed entrance road.[7] There are gentle topographic gradients to the south and east of the castle.

The apparent topographic focus associated with the northern platform is illustrated by the use of computer-processed, hill-shaded images derived from the topographic data. An image showing the data illuminated from the north-north-east at an angle of forty-five degrees above the horizon is shown in figure 7.3a. The illumination partially highlights an oval to circular area with the northern platform lying to the south-west of its inner margin. To the south and south-west of the platform, there is a distinct curving shadow cast that coincides with a small 'step' in the topographic data. This marks the southern extent of the oval area. The larger, loose and ground-fast stones

---

3 K. Barton, 'Control station layout and geo-referenced outline castle plan of Moygara Castle' (Landscape and Geophysical Services Report 06/76/01, 2006). **4** See chapter 3. **5** K. Barton, 'Control station layout and geo-referenced outline castle plan of Moygara Castle'. **6** See chapter 3. **7** Ibid.

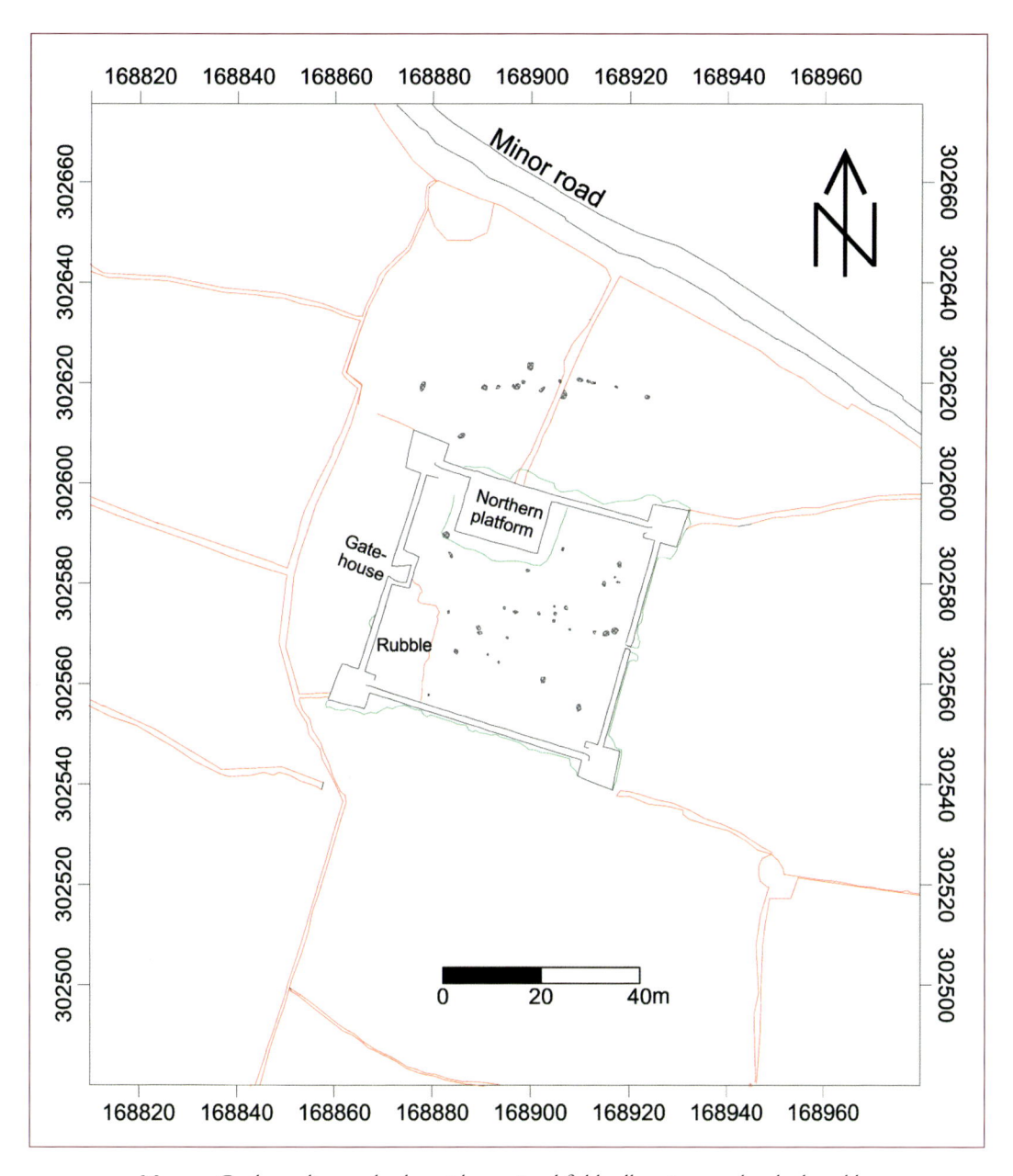

7.1 Moygara Castle: outline castle plan with associated fieldwalls, minor road and selected loose and ground-fast stones (© Kevin Barton).

(fig. 7.1) are apparent as shadows cast in the hill-shaded images (fig. 7.3). Those visible stones outside the bawn to the north of the northern platform do not precisely coincide or align with the northern edge of the oval area but lie just outside it. There

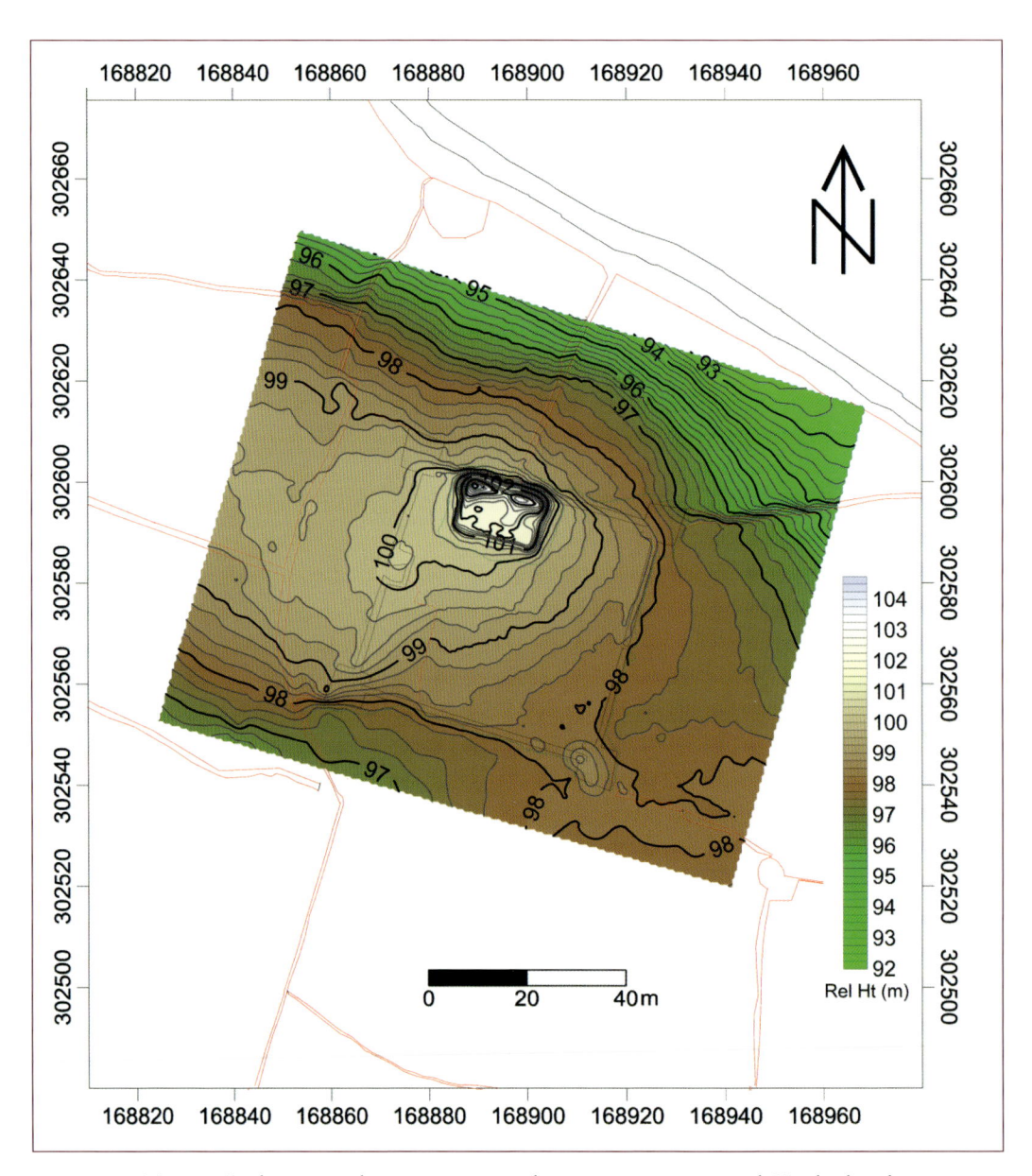

7.2 Moygara Castle: topographic contour map with a 0.25m contour interval. Heights based on an arbitrary datum of 100.0m (© Kevin Barton).

is a possible correlation of the visible stones inside the bawn with the hill-shaded image at the southern and south-western margins of the interpreted oval.

When the topographic data are illuminated from the south at forty-five degrees above the horizon (fig. 7.3b), the area to the north of the platform is better defined.

7.3 Moygara Castle: hill-shaded images of the topographic data: a) data illuminated from the north-north-east at forty five degrees above the horizon; b) data illuminated from the south at forty-five degrees above the horizon; and c) the estimated location of an oval feature (T1) superimposed on the image of 7.3a (© Kevin Barton).

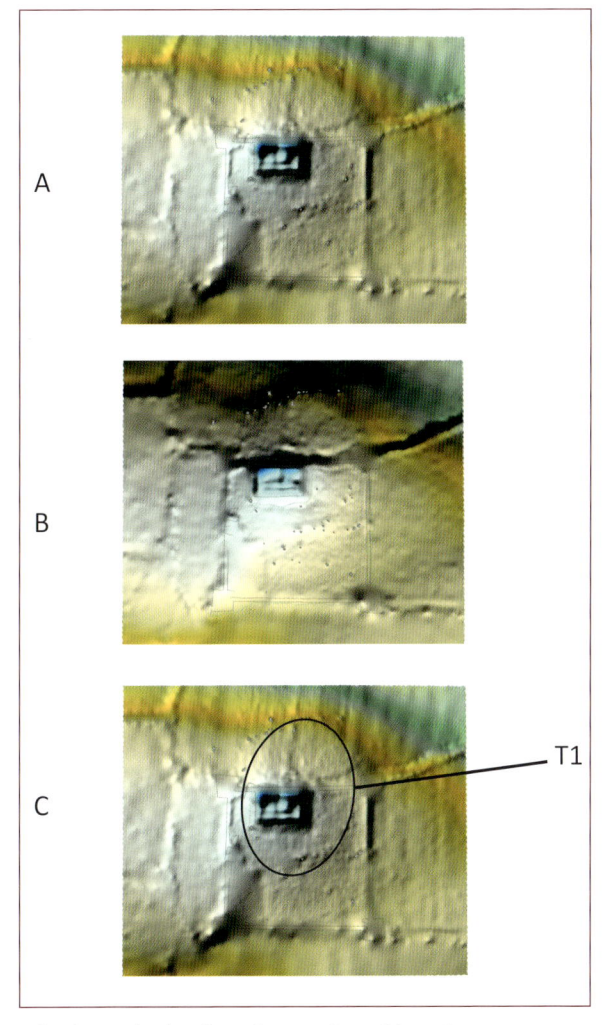

This area appears to jut out overlooking the land to the north and has the appearance of a small platform with a curving northern margin. The latter is the northern margin of the oval area described above. Within this platform lies a current field wall (figs 7.1, 7.3a), which is nearly perpendicular to the outer northern bawn wall. The shallow arc of the stones to the north of the bawn wall lies just outside the identified margin of the small platform, with perhaps some of the central ones just marking the edge of the platform.

Combining the features both visible and identified in figures 7.3a and 7.3b, it is possible to sketch the idealized form and location of an interpreted oval shape and this is indicated by T1 in figure 7.3c. The northern platform lies inside and near the margin of the south-west quadrant of the oval. The location and orientation of the platform may indicate that this feature and the oval are not contemporary. In this visualization, the long axis of the oval appears to be about 44m and the short axis measures about 33m.

EARTH RESISTANCE SURVEY[8]

Earth resistance survey essentially measures variations in the electrical resistance of the ground using an array of stainless steel electrodes. The pattern of resistance variation indicates variations in the sub-soil due to its moisture retention and/or mineral properties. This resistance variation can be interpreted to indicate the presence or absence of sub-surface archaeological features. Where there are solid buried walls, foundations or compacted ground with less or low moisture retention, compared to the soils in which they lie, the resistance measured would be high. Contrastingly, porous or permeable buried pits or ditches would retain more moisture than the more compact soils they were cut into and low resistance would be measured. The results from a systematic earth resistance survey are presented in the form of maps that show sub-surface resistance variation. The range and pattern of this variation is then interpreted or visualized to provide an indication of possible sub-surface archaeological features.

The earth resistance survey used a twin probe array with a constant 0.5m spacing between the electrodes. The survey on a 0.5m by 0.5m grid was carried out in two phases: the area in and to the west of the bawn was surveyed in the winter of 2006, and that to the north in the spring of 2008. The depth of investigation of this twin probe array was about 0.5m. Soil moisture conditions at the time of the two surveys were undoubtedly different. Weather conditions were very wet in 2006 but drier in 2008. The difference in conditions does not appear to have had a significant overall effect on the data (fig. 7.4) where the values recorded in the bawn are perhaps slightly lower than those to the north.

The data are presented as a graduated greyscale image with the lowest resistance values in black and the highest values in white. The scale has been adjusted to maximize the contrast between high and low resistances measured in different seasons in different years. There is a distinct resistance zonation within the bawn where higher values lie to the south and predominantly lower values to the north. Outside the bawn, to the north, there is a distinctive zonation with lower values lying closest to the bawn.

The main interpreted zonations and features recognized are indicated in figure 7.5. In the bawn, the southern zone can be further sub-divided into a number of areas. There is a distinct area of high resistance in the south-west corner that coincides with the extent of the stone rubble or tumble. To the east of the tumble lie two quite well defined zones of intermediate resistance values that appear quasi-circular in part

---

8 See footnote 1 for references to earth resistance survey.

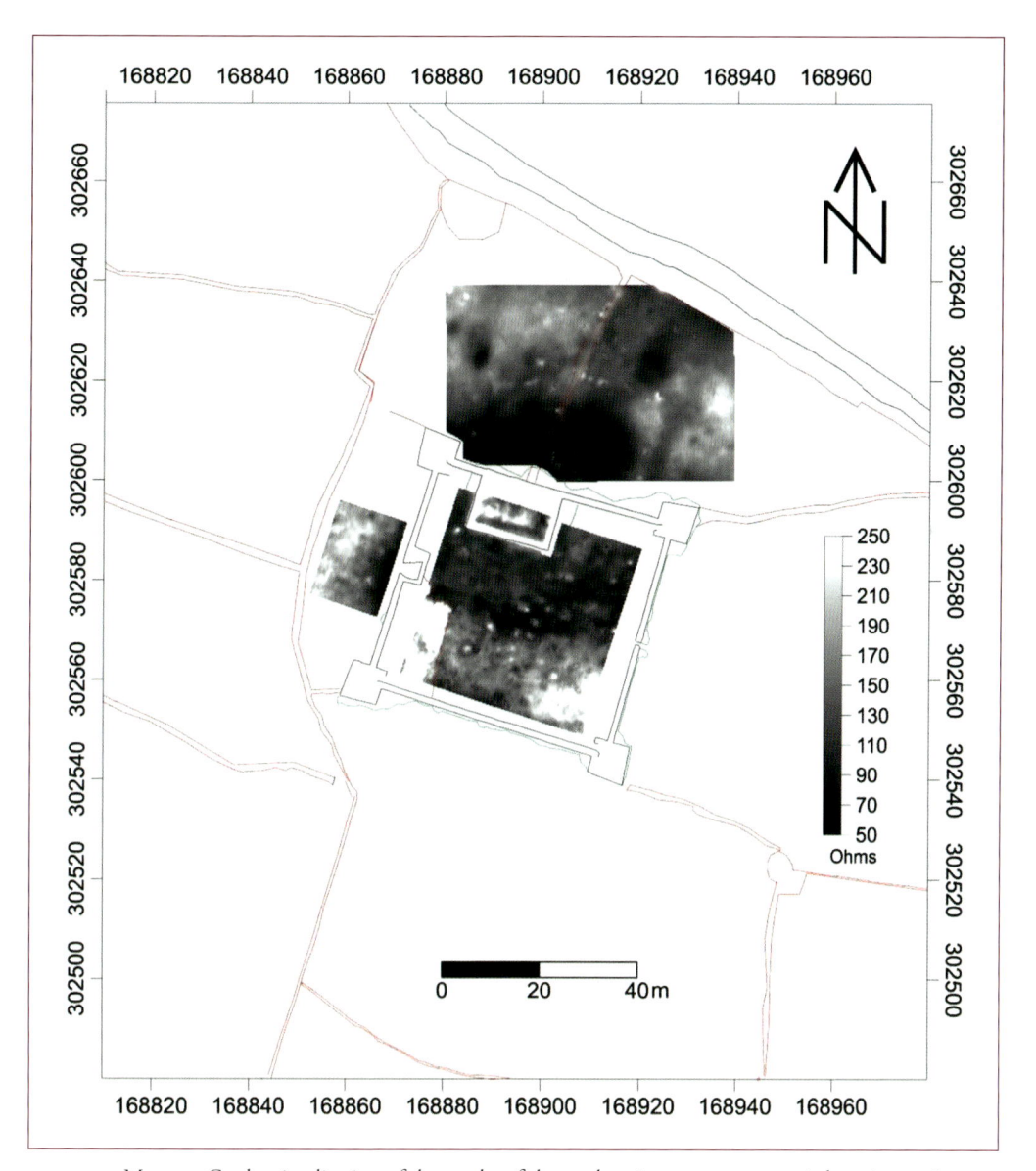

7.4 Moygara Castle: visualization of the results of the earth resistance surveys carried out in 2006 and 2008 (© Kevin Barton).

(R7 and R9). Within these two zones lie isolated high values that largely relate to the visible loose and ground-fast stones. Features R7 and R9 lie in, or appear to be connected by, an area of similar intermediate value resistance (R8). These zones of intermediate resistance could be due to underlying stone or cobbling or compacted ground indicating some functional use of the area such as a parade ground.

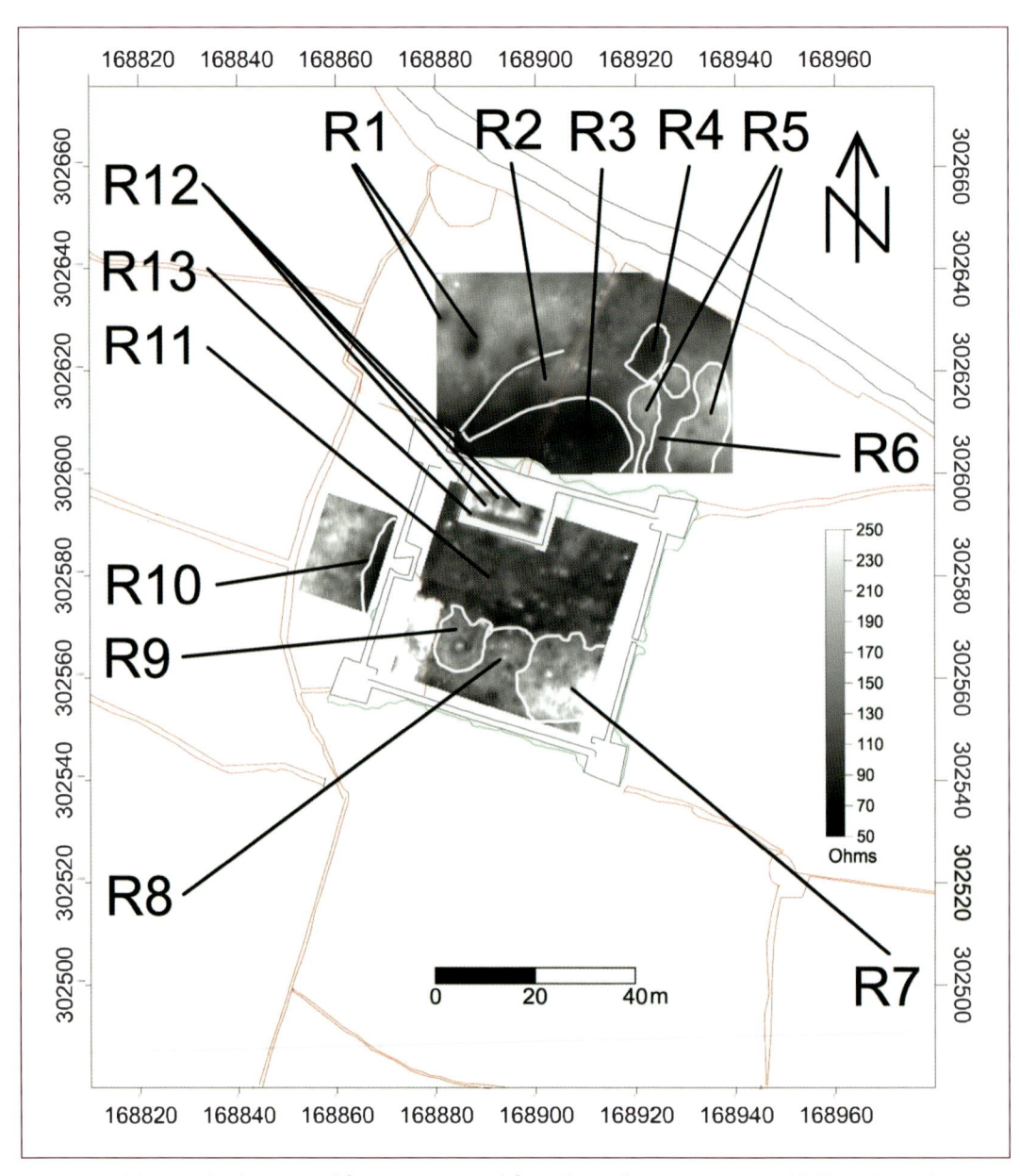

7.5 Moygara Castle: principal features interpreted from the earth resistance survey (© Kevin Barton).

The overall lower resistance zone in the north of the bawn (R11) surrounds a significantly higher resistance area associated with the northern platform. Internally the northern platform shows a very distinct rectangular zonation of alternating high and low values. At the centre are a series of narrow, linear, high resistance features perhaps indicating some segmentation, inner foundations, walls or rubble (R12). The latter features are surrounded by low resistance (R13), perhaps indicating silted ditches or areas composed of either clay or very wet soil. The soil-covered, visible outer stone wall is shown as a very well-defined high resistance feature.

The area outside the bawn to the north of the northern platform contains a number of quite well-defined features. The low resistance zone in the bawn surrounding the northern platform appears to continue outside (R3). The northern limit of the zone forms an irregular curve that lies against intermediate and then higher resistance to the north. The overall appearance is that there is a low resistance zone that surrounds the northern platform both inside and outside the bawn. The platform lies to the west of its approximate centre. The southern and northern margins of the low resistance zone inside and outside the bawn are well defined and extend to about 48m. The western and eastern margins of the zone inside the bawn are not defined. However, outside the bawn they may extend to about 35m.

The north-west margin of the low resistance zone to the west of the field wall (fig. 7.1) is not sharply defined but has a transition zone or band of intermediate higher resistance (R2), which passes into distinctly higher resistance. This intermediate zone could be due to drier/drying soils at a break in slope or, instead, be due to an in-filled ditch. It should be noted that a number of loose and ground-fast stones are found in or close to this area of intermediate resistance. In the higher resistance area to the north-west, there are two distinctive lower resistance features (R1). These could be natural sediment-filled depressions or constructed pits. To the east of the perpendicular field wall (fig. 7.1) and north of low resistance zone R3, there is an abrupt change in resistance where the zone of high resistance, seen to the west, does not immediately continue eastwards. In this area the resistance has intermediate values that enclose a number of features. R4 is a distinct zone of lower resistance that lies against a well-defined area of high resistance (R5). The latter area is cut by, or contains, a linear zone of lower resistance (R6). This could be a natural feature such a gully or be a silted, cut feature such as a ditch.

The area to the west of the gatehouse can perhaps be divided into three areas. Close to, and perhaps parallel with, the bawn wall is an area of low resistance (R10). This area could correlate with the low resistance found inside the bawn. Alternatively, it could be indicating an area of wetter soil due to runoff from the outer bawn wall or be the zone of a foundation trench for the bawn wall. Indeed, it may well be a combination of all three possibilities. To the west this low resistance area gradually passes into intermediate values that contain some irregular high resistance features. These features do not appear to be directly aligned with the gatehouse, although there is a small gap between them. The high resistance could be due to a change in soil type, ground compaction or buried stones. The high resistance may be evidence for an increase of activity or footfall at the entrance to the gatehouse. There is no evidence in the resistance data, albeit collected over a geographically limited area, for a perpendicular road, track or path leading to the gatehouse.

ELECTRICAL RESISTIVITY TOMOGRAPHY (ERT)[9] SURVEY

The ERT technique provides a two-dimensional (2D) depth section or modelled pseudo-section across a survey area or feature as opposed to a map that is the result of an earth resistance survey. The technique can be used to estimate the dimensions and nature of sub-surface targets such as the soil/bedrock interface and depth to and width of walls and ditches. The technique differs from the earth resistance method in that the depth of investigation is largely controlled by using a variable electrode spacing. The survey is controlled by a computer that sequentially increases the electrode spacing, thus allowing for successively deeper sub-surface levels to be investigated.

In order to investigate some of the possible sub-surface features indicated by the topographic and earth resistance surveys and the foundation conditions of the castle, a series of ERT survey transects were carried out. The location of these transects are given in figure 7.6a. The ERT surveys were carried out using an electrode spacing of 1m and the data was modelled to produce 2D sections to a depth of 3m beneath the ground surface. A Total Station was used to collect a topographic profile along each transect and this is draped on the 2D section. The heights shown on the left-hand axis of each section are relative to the arbitrary datum of 100.00m at Control Station 1.6. Each section has an x2 vertical exaggeration. The distance in metres along each section is shown above the draped topographic profile.

The modelled section for ERT Line 1 is shown in figure 7.6b with south being to the left of the section. This section was carried out to investigate the earth resistance response inside the bawn (fig. 7.4). The section shows high resistivity to the south, with a sharp change at 21m to low and intermediate values to the north. The majority of the section is underlain by low resistivity material, which perhaps may be due to a thick sequence of clays whose base is not seen in the section. The topography along the section rises from south to north.

The highest near-surface resistivity to the south correlates well with that found in the earth resistance data. The magnitude of the highest resistivity values found is of the order of 500 Ohm-m, which may not necessarily indicate that this is due to compact or competent bedrock but rather to drier sands, gravels and cobbles with perhaps some compaction. The zone is thickest at over 2m near the southern bawn wall, where there is perhaps more foundation material. It thins to just over 1m northwards, towards the centre of the bawn. Here the underlying low resistivity is likely to be due to wet, more clayey, soils.

---

9 See footnote 1 for references to the electrical resistivity tomography technique.

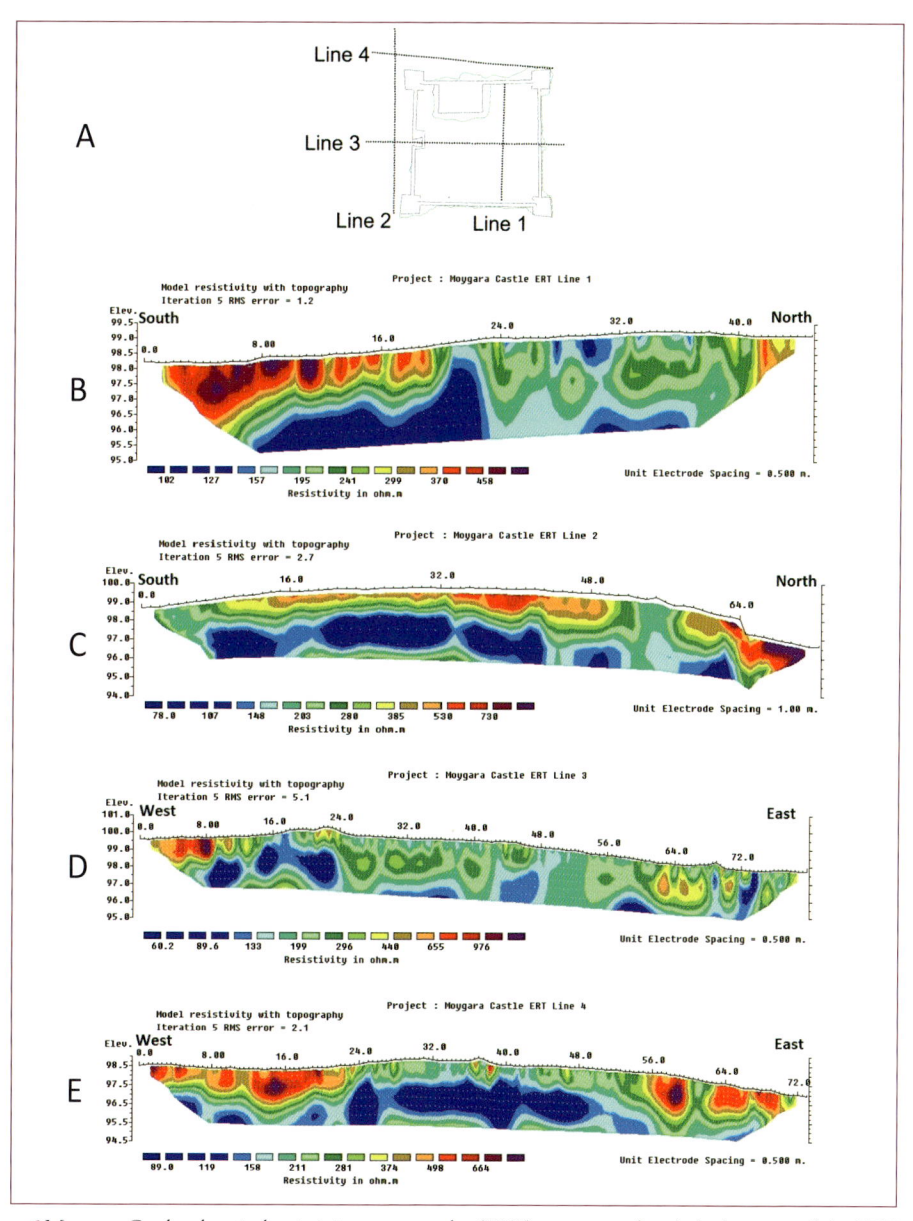

7.6 Moygara Castle: electrical resistivity tomography (ERT) survey results: a) the location of the ERT survey transects; b) Line 1, modelled ERT pseudosection; c) Line 2, modelled ERT pseudosection; d) Line 3, modelled ERT pseudosection; e) Line 4, modelled ERT pseudosection (© Kevin Barton).

The sharp change at 21m to overall lower and intermediate values indicates a distinct shift in the nature of the soil or fill within the bawn. There is no recognizable pattern of low and intermediate values, perhaps indicating a general mixture of soils, clays, sands, gravels and cobbles. The overall zone of low and intermediate resistivity correlates with that seen in the earth resistance data.

At 41m along the section there is a return to distinctive high resistivity, which likely marks the zone of the foundation of the bawn wall and rubble lying against it.

The modelled section for ERT Line 2 is shown in figure 7.6c with south being to the left of the section. The section runs from south to north outside, and parallel to, the gatehouse and western bawn wall. The section was carried out to investigate the area outside the gatehouse and foundation conditions associated with the south-west and north-west towers. The overall response is of a thin layer of higher resistivity material underlain by low-resistivity sediments, with a sharp break near the northern end. There is a very gentle rise in topography northwards towards the centre of the section and then this falls away gently further northwards until there a sharp drop at the edge of the ridge (fig. 7.2).

At the southern end of the section, in the vicinity of the south-west tower, there is a narrow zone of intermediate resistivity of 200–300 Ohm-m. There is no indication of high resistivity that might indicate a stone foundation to the tower. The section runs some 3m from the base of the tower and it may be that the foundation does not extend this far. The intermediate resistivity passes into a thin layer of high resistivity at 5m along the section. This layer is generally at least 1m thick until it thickens to nearly 2m from 32m to 51m along the section. This high resistivity could indicate a specific soil type, drier conditions or compacted ground. Almost the entire length of the section is underlain by low-resistivity material, perhaps indicating wet, more clayey soils. Another possibility for the high resistivity response is that there is a significantly wide stone foundation along the western wall needed to stabilize the wall on low-resistivity wet, clayey soils.

From 51m to about 58m, the section runs within 4m of the north-west tower. Here there is a distinct zone of intermediate resistivity similar to that seen near the south-west tower. Again it could be that the foundation does not extend as far as the line of the section. This finding of lower resistivity in the vicinity of each tower might indicate that there was a trench or area excavated prior to the construction of the towers, which was back-filled once the towers were built on an integral stone foundation. From 58m to the end of the section at 72m, there is a zone of high resistivity, which corresponds with the edge of the ridge and break in slope.

The modelled section for ERT Line 3 is shown in figure 7.6d with west being to the left of the section. The section runs from west to east, starting outside and passing through the gatehouse, and the bawn, ending to the east of the gap in the eastern bawn wall. The section was carried out to provide a complete section though the bawn to investigate its foundations. The overall section shows high resistivity at the start of the section, associated with the gatehouse, inside and at the eastern bawn wall with assorted intermediate values in the bawn area. There is a gentle rise in topography from the west towards the gatehouse, a levelling off to the centre of the bawn and a gradual fall across the remainder of the bawn and outside to the east.

Outside the castle, at the western end of the section there is a 2m thick zone of high resistivity that thins to less than 1m towards the east. This correlates with a similar high resistivity zone seen in ERT Line 2. At about 14m there is a change to an approximately 4m-wide zone of low resistivity, which lies immediately in front of the gatehouse. This correlates with the low earth resistance found in this area (fig. 7.4) and may indicate the presence of a back-filled or silted foundation trench, discussed above. The passage of the section through the gatehouse at about 19m is marked by a brief rise and fall in topography and a small zone of intermediate and high resistivity. The resistivity variation cannot be directly attributed to stone foundations, as there is a larger amount of stone rubble and tumble in the area of the gatehouse. From 26m onwards towards the centre of the bawn at about 48m, the topography levels out and there is a distinctive zone of intermediate resistivity. This may indicate a change in soil or sediment type. From 48m eastwards, the topography gently falls with a less variable zone of intermediate resistivity occurring until alternating intermediate and high values are intersected at 62m. Here a tentative correlation could be made with the most easterly quasi-circular zone of higher resistance seen in the earth resistance data (fig. 7.5, R7). A small rise in topography at 69m marks the route of the section through the gap in the eastern wall. The gap coincides with a narrow zone of low resistivity perhaps up to 2m in width. This may indicate a narrow wall foundation trench which cuts into the high resistivity zone seen from 62m eastwards that may continue immediately to the east of the gap.

The modelled section for ERT Line 4 is shown in figure 7.6e with west to the left of the section. The section runs from west to east starting to the north-west of the north-west tower and running outside the northern platform and northern bawn wall towards the north-east tower. The section was carried out to provide sub-surface information on the features seen in the topographic and earth resistance data and the foundation conditions associated with the nearby northern platform. The overall section shows high resistivity at the start and end of the section and a thin zone of intermediate resistivity in the central portion. Low resistivity underlies the central part of the section. There is a gentle fall and rise in topography from the west towards the field wall (fig. 7.1), which marks the approximate centre of the section at 36m. From the latter point eastwards, there is a gentle fall in topography.

The western end of the section is marked by a zone of high resistivity up to 2m thick, extending to 24m along the section. The central portion of the section, up to perhaps 55m, comprises a thin (up to 1m) layer of intermediate resistivity underlain by low resistivity to near the base of the section. The very thin zone of intermediate resistivity seen at the base of the section is likely to be an artefact of the modelling of the section. This marked zone of intermediate resistivity is some 32m in width and correlates with the zone of low resistance seen in figure 7.5 (R3). It also correlates in general terms with the shaded topographic relief images of figures 7.3a and 7.3b and the oval shown in figure 7.3c. It may be indicating drier soils with incorporated sands and gravels overlying a thick clayey or earthen base. The latter earthen base continues at least to the 3m depth or thickness of the section and possibly is of greater thickness. This poses the question as to whether this earthen feature, situated on a prominent location on the end of the ridge, is the remnant of a natural or built feature.

From 55m eastwards to the end of the section, there is an over 2m-thick zone of high resistivity which is cut by a narrow intermediate zone between about 60m and 62m. This intermediate zone coincides with the western wall of the north-east tower and may be indicating a foundation trench. This trench contains the tower which may have a stone foundation as indicated by the high resistivity.

MAGNETIC GRADIOMETER SURVEY[10]

Magnetic gradiometry is a commonly used geophysical technique allowing rapid mapping of magnetized archaeological objects and features contained within the sub-soil. Archaeological objects or features, if they contain certain types of iron minerals, can become magnetized by the Earth's magnetic field, due to them having an appreciable inherent magnetic susceptibility. The degree of magnetic susceptibility can therefore provide a measure of the ability of an object or feature to be magnetized when lying in the Earth's magnetic field. The magnetic susceptibility of an object or feature can be enhanced if it is subject to high-temperature burning. Buried objects or features with enhanced magnetic susceptibility can provide a detectable contrast with the normally low background magnetic susceptibility values found in host soils and sediments.

Small changes in the Earth's total magnetic field due to buried magnetized objects and features, having enhanced magnetic susceptibility, can be measured by a survey instrument such as a magnetic gradiometer. The magnetic gradiometry technique can be used in archaeological investigations to detect: soil and/or bedrock variation, silted ditches, in-filled pits, walls, hearths, burnt or fired remains and ferrous metals.

The gradiometer survey was carried out with a fluxgate gradiometer with sensors spaced 0.5m vertically apart. The depth of investigation of the instrument is about 1m. The processed data (fig. 7.7) is presented as a graduated greyscale image with positive gradient in white and negative gradient in black. Conventionally, positive magnetic gradient is interpreted as being a response due to cut features such as pits and ditches.

The data clearly indicates a number of elements that extend inside and outside the bawn. The main features recognized are indicated in figure 7.8. The largest element is

---

10 See frootnote 1 for references to the magnetic gradiometry technique.

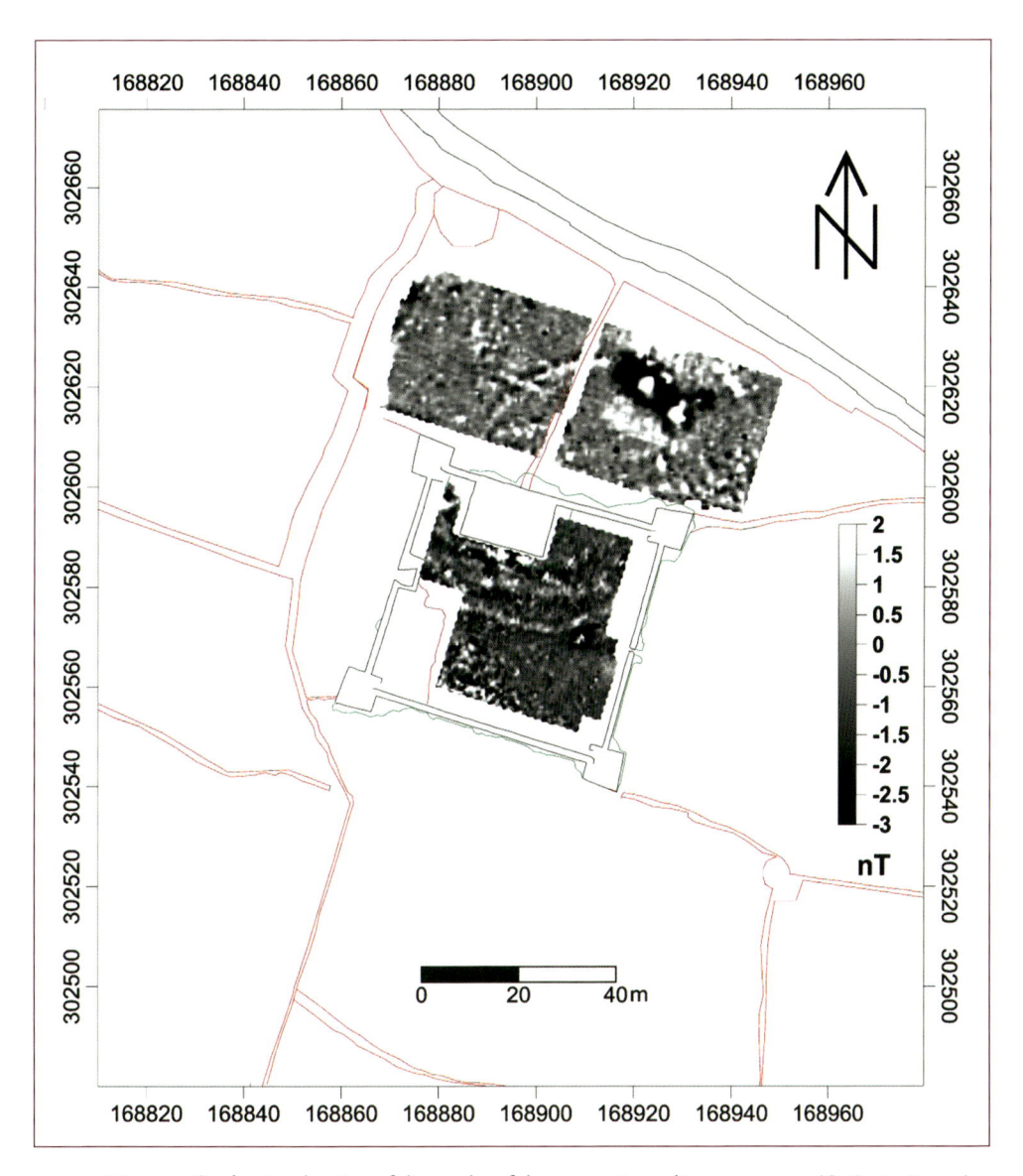

7.7 Moygara Castle: visualization of the results of the magnetic gradiometer survey (© Kevin Barton).

an oval-shaped ditch indicated by positive gradient (G1, possibly G8 and G12, G13). The northern platform lies to the south-west of the centre of this ditched oval area that measures a maximum of some 55m on its long axis and possibly 35m to 45m on its short axis in this visualization. The overall location, shape and dimensions of this large ditch correlate with the shaded topographic relief (figs 7.3a, 7.3b), the earth resistance (fig. 7.5, R3) and the ERT data (figs 7.6b, 7.6d). The oval-shaped ditch, as indicated

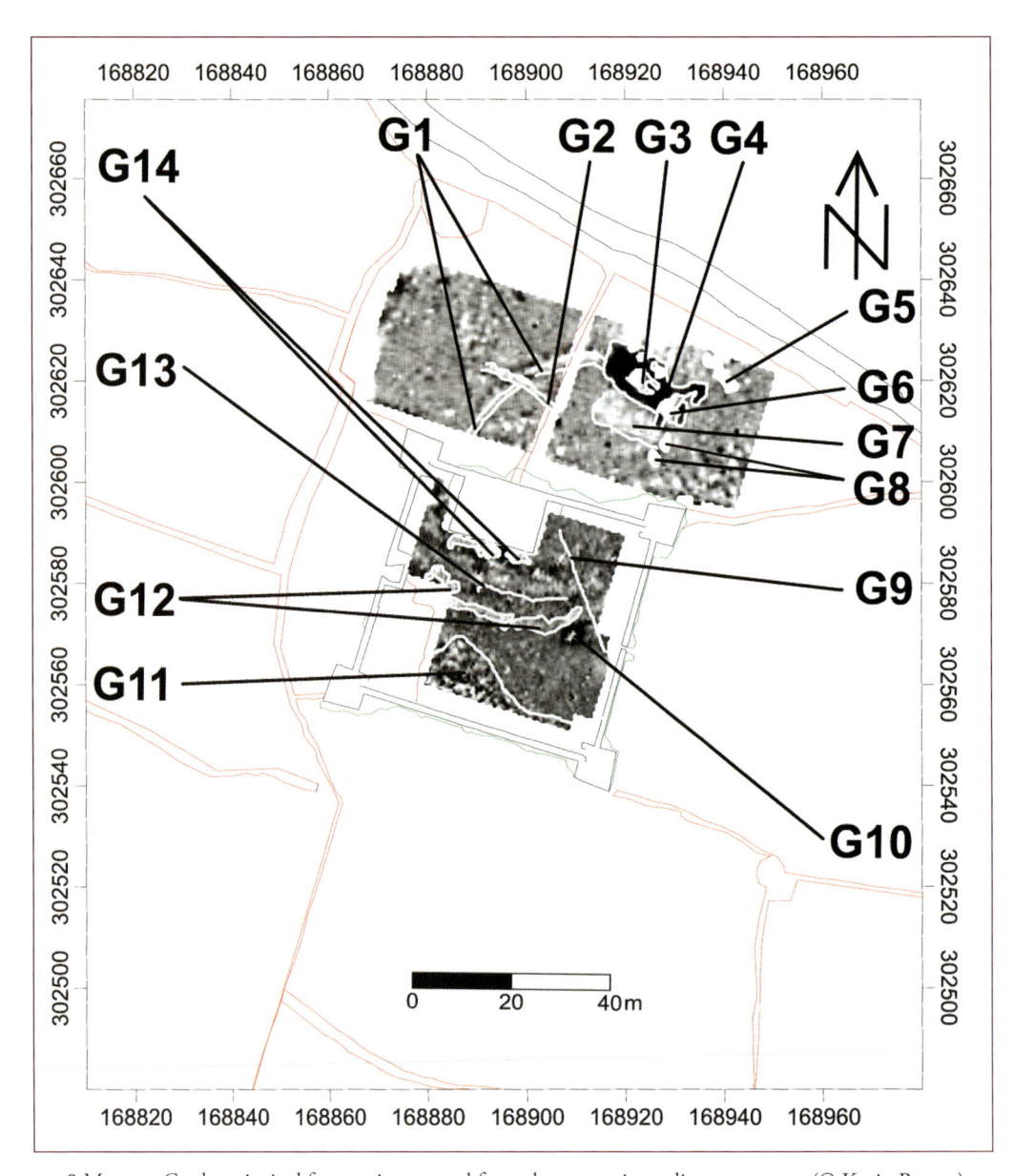

7.8 Moygara Castle: principal features interpreted from the magnetic gradiometer survey (© Kevin Barton).

in the magnetic data, is larger in its long and short axes than the comparable axes of the oval-shaped zones seen in the shaded relief, earth resistance and ERT data. This may indicate that the ditch encloses the other recognized features.

Outside the bawn, the ditch of this oval-shaped area is cut or overprinted in several places by other features. At the north-west it is cut by a short east-west curvilinear feature with a positive gradient (G2). At the north-east there is a strong magnetic overprint of two discrete 'blocks' of positive gradient (G3 and G6) surrounded by negative gradient (G4). The former (G2) could be a ditch and the latter could be very magnetic rocks, zones of intense burning or the foundations of a single or several burnt structures. There is a change in the 'texture' of the magnetic response (G7) lying immediately to the south of the 'blocks' of positive gradient. This may be indicating a change in the nature of the ground in this area. It could be a well-defined zone of cobbles or imported material. To the south-east of G7, there are two small zones of positive gradient (G8) which may be sediment-filled pits. To the north-east of G6, there is a small recognized response of positive gradient (G5) which may be a sediment-filled pit or hollow.

Within the northern half of the bawn, there are several curving features with a positive gradient which appear to partially enclose the northern platform (G12, G13 and G14). G12 and G13 have a similar, but weaker response to G1 and either can be interpreted to be the southern element of the ditch defining the oval area. Additionally, G13 and G14 could be short sections of ditch or cut features associated with the northern platform. In the south-western part of the bawn, there is an area which shows a distinctive texture compared with the rest of the bawn (G11). It is marked by a rapidly alternating pattern of positive and negative gradient. This indicates a change in soil type in this part of the site which could relate to a functional area. To the west of the gap in the eastern bawn wall, there is a strong, coherent positive magnetic anomaly (G10) which could be due to a filled pit, hearth or ferrous object. There is a weak linear feature (G9) extending from north-west to south-east in the north-eastern section of the bawn. The south-eastern end of the feature runs close to the gap in the eastern bawn wall and could be a modern path.

GROUND PENETRATING RADAR (GPR)[11] SURVEY

GPR is a very high spatial resolution survey technique, which allows 2D depth sections and depth slices to be produced. The technique transmits pulses of electromagnetic energy from an antenna into the ground and, using a second antenna, records their reflection or absorption by sub-surface features. Both transmitting and receiving antennas are mounted on a frame, cart or sled which is moved along survey lines or a grid set out over the survey area. It is a technique that can detect sub-surface features under tarmac and concrete as well as those buried in soils and sediments.

GPR surveys generate a large amount of data which sometimes makes it difficult to visualize the results for interpretation purposes. Modern data-processing techniques enable horizontal depth slices to be created from a series of evenly spaced, parallel survey lines. The software assembles the GPR response at a common depth from the

---

[11] See footnote 1 for references to the ground penetrating radar (GPR) technique.

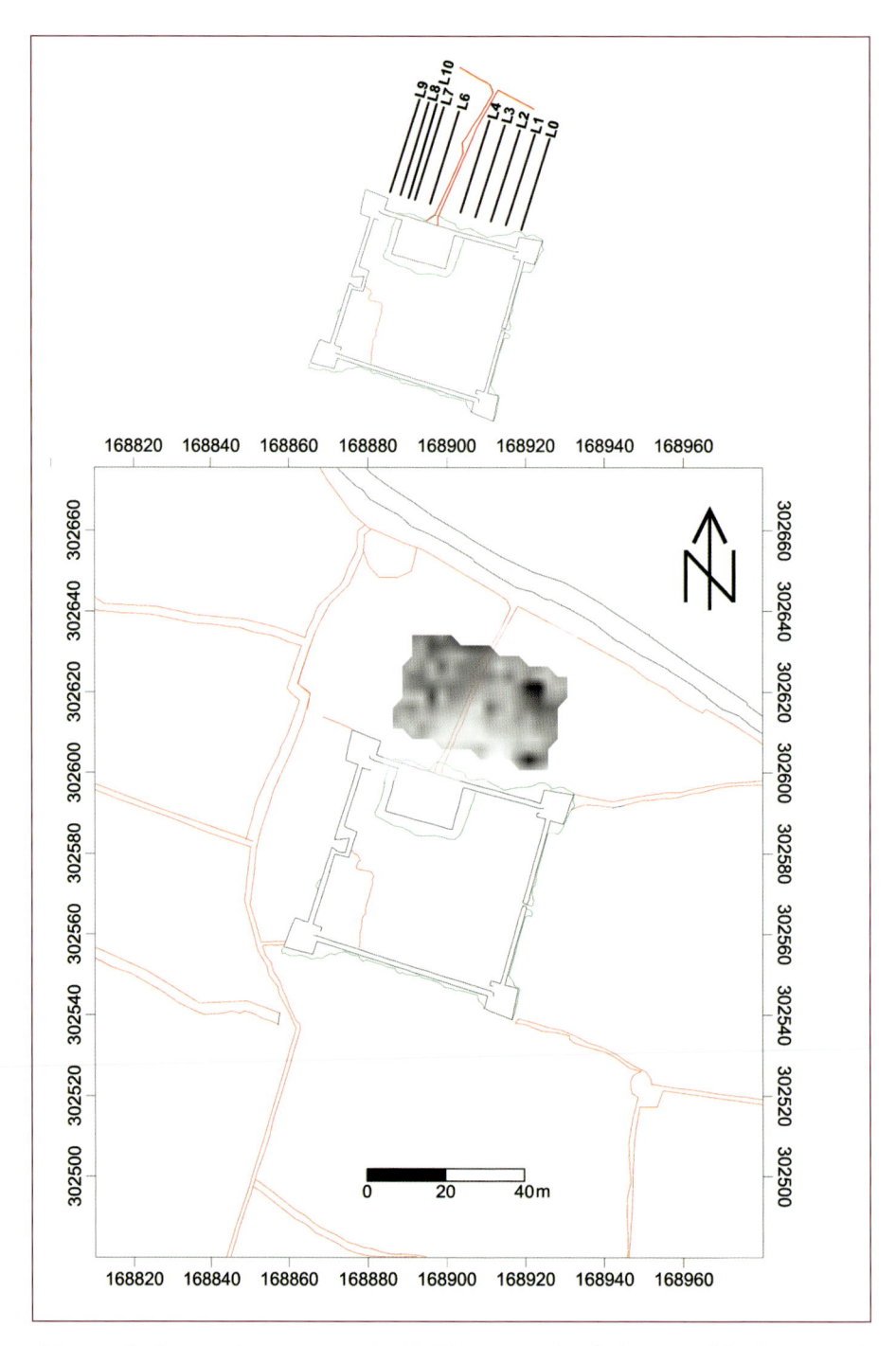

7.9 Moygara Castle: ground penetrating radar (GPR) survey results: the location of the GPR survey lines (above); visualization of a horizontal depth slice at an estimated depth of 1m (below) (© Kevin Barton).

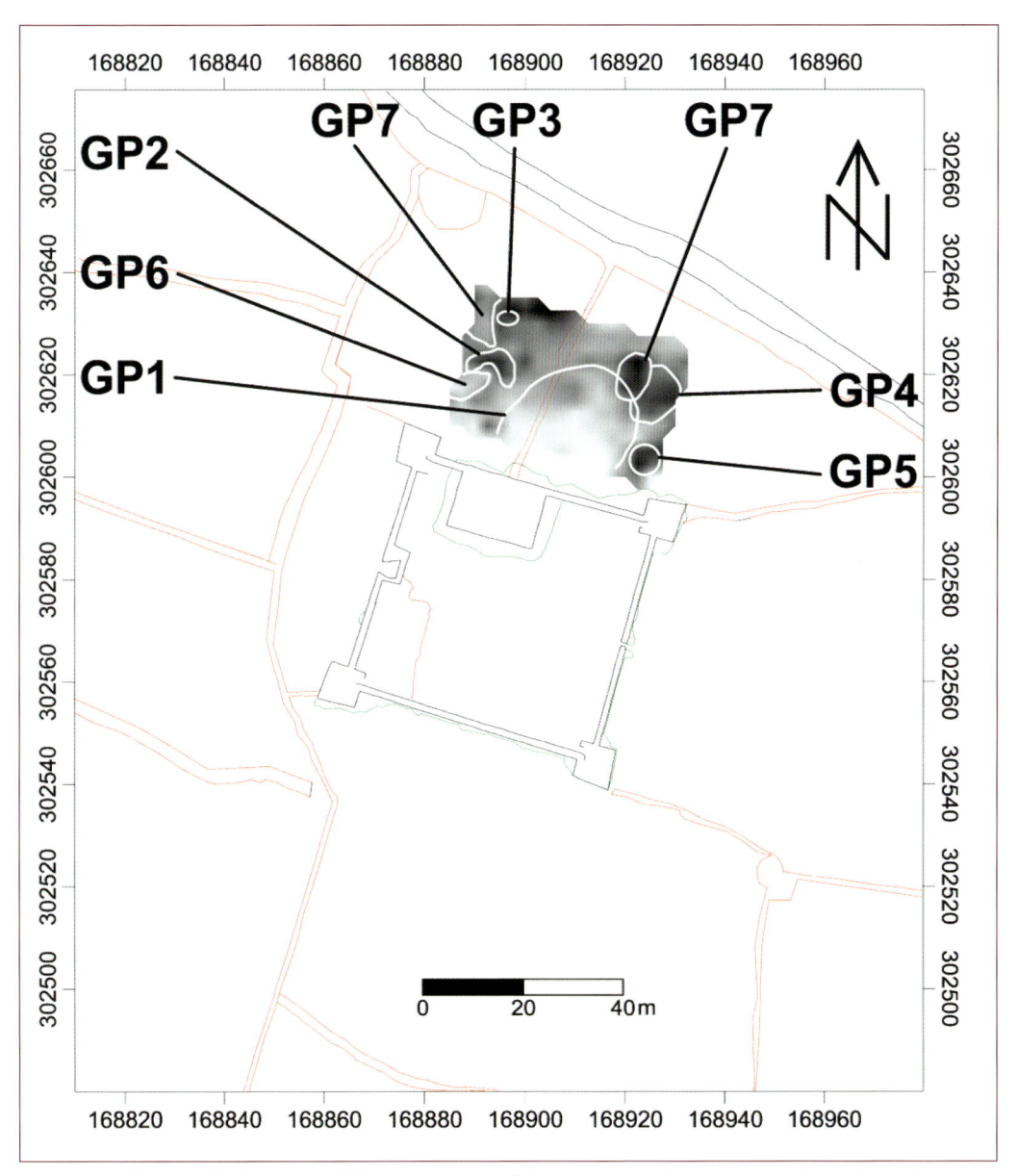

7.10 Moygara Castle: principal features interpreted from the ground penetrating radar horizontal depth slice at an estimated depth of 1m (© Kevin Barton).

GPR depth section along each survey line. It then creates a horizontal slice or a map by interpolating data values between the lines. Multiple horizontal slices can be created for specified depth intervals, which, when viewed from shallow to deeper levels, simulate the effect of carrying out an excavation.

Depending on the targets sought, choice of antenna frequency, sampling interval and suitable ground conditions, GPR can detect sub-surface features in the range of a few centimetres to about 10m. Typical GPR applications in archaeology are in detecting buried caves, crypts, voids, souterrains, floors, masonry, ditches and walls.

The GPR survey was carried out on a reconnaissance basis to further investigate the features to the north of the northern platform and bawn wall identified from the topographic, earth resistance and magnetic gradiometry surveys. Eleven south to north GPR survey lines 28–29m in length were planned to be surveyed (fig. 7.9) with a 250 MHz system which would provide an estimated depth of investigation of up to 2m or 3m. The line spacing was 5m with a measurement interval of 0.05m. Ten lines were completed as a field wall impeded the path of Line 5.

In order to consolidate and interpret the radar dataset, a series of fifty successively horizontal deeper depth slices were created down to an estimated 2m and reviewed. The response in the shallower slices, down to an estimated 1m, was quite noisy, likely due to a near-surface accumulation of stones and cobbles. The interpolation between the lines, needed to create each slice, could not produce images with a recognizable coherent pattern. At an estimated depth of 1m, features of possible archaeological significance became recognizable. A slice in this depth range shows a coherent zone of response (in white) straddling the field wall (fig. 7.9).

The features recognized in the slice are indicated in figure 7.10. The edge of the main coherent response is indicated by GP1. This denotes a curving margin similar to those seen in the other topographic and geophysical datasets where it is referred to as being the northern part of an oval-shaped feature. The slice contains more discrete features but they are based on interpolation between the GPR survey lines some 5m apart and may not be a true representation of sub-surface features and zones. A number of tentative correlations can, however, be made with features seen in the magnetic dataset. GP4 and GP7 appear to correlate with the intense magnetic responses (fig. 7.8, G3, G4, G6). GP2 broadly correlates with the magnetic response of the short, linear ditch (fig. 7.8, G2). There is a correlation between GP5 and the southern pit of figure 7.8, G8. GP3 and GP5 indicate isolated, small zones of response that may be artefacts of the interpolation or reflect localized changes in soil structure.

CONCLUSIONS AND RECOMMENDATIONS

Even prior to excavation, it was clear from both the topographical, geophysical and architectural surveys carried out beforehand that the site at Moygara has undergone a long period of occupation culminating in the visible remains of the castle that we see today. The main interpreted features from the topographic and principal geophysical mapping surveys have been summarized in figure 7.11. Arguably, the main result of the various geophysical surveys carried out at Moygara between 2005 and 2008 was

7.11 Moygara Castle: summary of the results of the topographic and principal geophysical surveys draped on 3D models of the topographic data viewed from the north-east at seventy degrees above the horizon: a) topographic data illuminated from the south at forty five degrees above the horizon; b) earth resistance results draped on topographic data illuminated from the north-east at seventy degrees above the horizon; c) magnetic gradiometry results draped on topographic data illuminated from the north-east at seventy degrees above the horizon (© Kevin Barton).

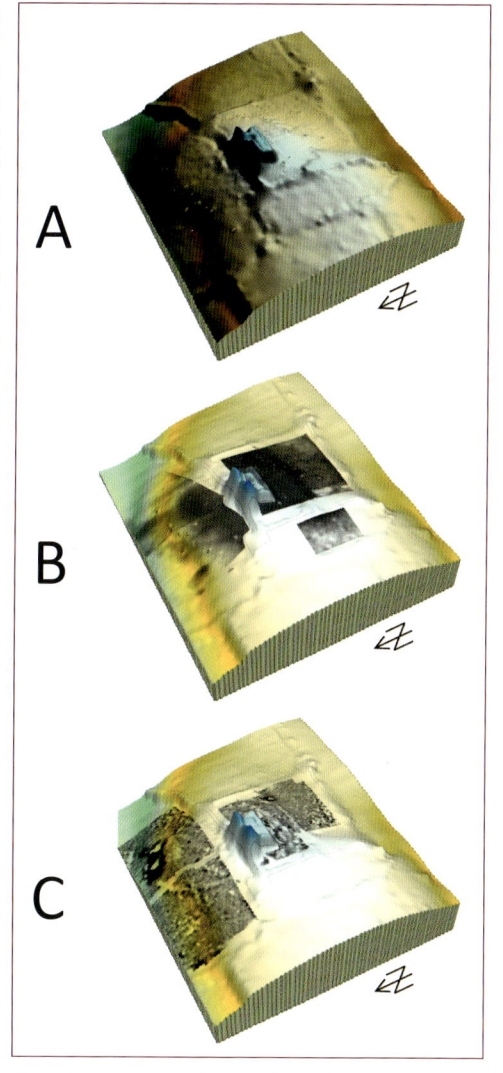

and is the recognition that a ditched oval enclosure underlies and predates the multi-phase masonry castle.

All the topographic and geophysical datasets show good correlation of responses at the north of the interpreted oval enclosure. The magnetic gradiometry alone defines the edge of the oval enclosure as being an enclosing ditch. The magnetic response is stronger in the north compared to that to the south in the bawn where the southern edge could be denoted by either one of two curvilinear responses to the south of the northern platform. Associated with the ditch are features lying at and immediately to its north-west and north-east. To the north-west lies a linear cross-cutting ditch which may post-date the ditch of the oval enclosure. To the north-east, on the perimeter of the ditch, lie a series of intriguing features which have a very strong magnetic response whose pattern may indicate burnt features. The response could be related to settlement or industrial activity.

The northern platform within the bawn has some inner features which are likely to be foundations of a masonry building.[12] To the south of this feature lie a series of curvilinear features, likely to be ditches which may or may not be contemporary with it. One of these ditches may be the southern part of the oval enclosure. The southern sector of the bawn has a number of quasi-circular features which may be related to functional areas. There is a possibility that some of this area has compacted or cobbled ground.

Based on the limited geophysical data, there is no evidence as yet for a westerly access road to the gatehouse. There appears to be a possible ditch dug immediately outside the gatehouse. This could be associated with the construction of the gatehouse or it could possibly be a defensive feature. There is evidence from the ERT survey that there were ditches or trenches dug to facilitate the construction of the towers and possibly the bawn wall.

Prior to excavation, therefore, it was clear that the evidence from the topographical and geophysical surveys and the architectural analysis[13] of what remains of the castle above ground that a numbers of phases of activity could be seen at Moygara Castle. These were tentatively interpreted by the present writer as:

Phase 1 – a ditched oval enclosure.
Phase 2 – a building within the northern platform.
Phase 3 – the bawn, gatehouse and flankers.
Phase 4 – a later rectangular building constructed on the south-western side of the
       bawn.[14]

---

12 These foundations were shown by subsequent excavation to be the basal walls of a deliberately collapsed tower house: see chapter 8. **13** See chapter 4. **14** Ibid.

CHAPTER EIGHT

Excavations at Moygara Castle, 2013–17: preliminary results

CHRISTOPHER READ

INTRODUCTION

Over four short field seasons, from 2013 to 2015 and, again, in 2017, I was privileged to lead the excavation of Moygara Castle. Each field season comprised only two weeks and was staffed by first-year archaeology students from the Institute of Technology Sligo.[1] Due to the limited timeframe and resources, this work was done under a remit of archaeological testing. This meant that sub-surface archaeological features could be exposed and recorded, but not fully excavated. Certain features were further explored through partial excavation to assess their nature and depth, and retrieve datable materials, if possible.

The purpose of this test excavation was twofold: firstly, to assess the overall levels of archaeology at Moygara in advance of a larger-scale excavation project; secondly, to further elucidate the chronology and relationships between the different elements of the site's above and below ground remains, if possible. To this end, six cuttings of various sizes and shapes were excavated, comprising a total of 124m² (fig. 8.1). These cuttings were specifically located to examine both extant architectural elements of the castle and potential below-ground features identified through topographical and geophysical survey.[2] A number of key areas of likely archaeological potential at Moygara were not targeted in the test excavation process, namely the corner towers and gatehouse, as they were either too substantial to tackle in a two-week period and/or presented health-and-safety concerns because of the dangers of collapse. These concerns need to be addressed before a larger-scale excavation can be undertaken at the site.

Of the six cuttings, two (cuttings 1 and 2) were situated outside the north wall of the bawn to investigate geophysical anomalies and a possible pre-bawn oval ditched enclosure (fig. 8.1).[3] The remaining four cuttings were located inside the bawn. Of these, one cutting (cutting 5) was focused on the remains of a large stone building in the south-west corner of the castle and a further two (cuttings 3 and 4) on geophysical anomalies within it. The remaining cutting (cutting 6) within the bawn was situated to explore the platform on its northern side. The size of the area investigated during

---

1 IT Sligo is now part of the Atlantic Technological University.   2 See chapter 7.   3 See chapter 7.

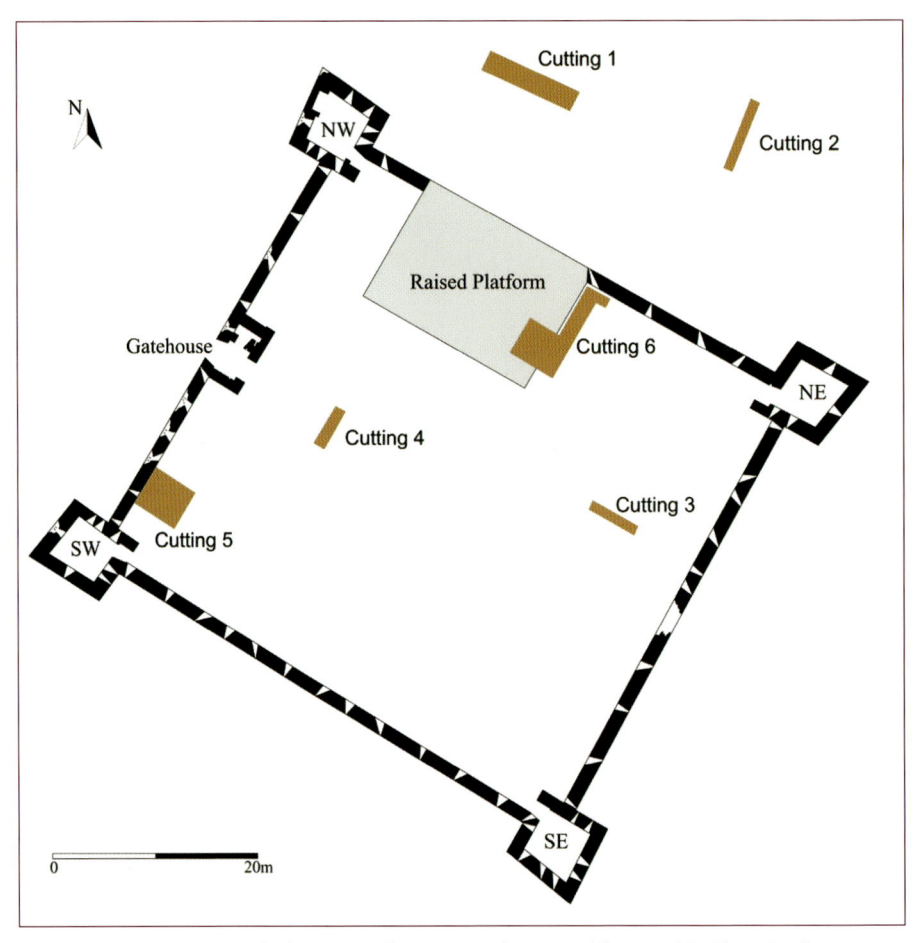

8.1 Moygara Castle: locations of cuttings and principal features (© Chris Read).

the test excavation was small relative to Moygara Castle's large footprint and the distances between individual cuttings prohibited the possibility of making solid stratigraphic linkages between areas. However, the nature of the archaeology itself, some of the artefacts recovered and a single radiocarbon date have added substantially to our understanding the site's use and chronology. It might be added that, in general, stratigraphy across the site was relatively shallow, especially within the bawn, reaching subsoil in many places within the first 0.1m or so.

TEST EXCAVATION RESULTS

The description of the archaeology revealed at Moygara is organized under the following headings: the oval-ditched enclosure (cuttings 1 and 3); the platform (cutting 6); burning outside the north wall (cutting 2); and the castle interior (cuttings 3, 4 and 5). As the post-excavation portion of the project is still on-going, the following descriptions and interpretations can only be considered preliminary.

THE OVAL-DITCHED ENCLOSURE

An oval ditched enclosure, identified during the site geophysical survey and interpreted as being the earliest visible phase of activity at Moygara,[4] as it predates the masonry castle, was a principal target of the test excavation programme. Topographical and geophysical survey identified an oval-shaped enclosure measuring approximately 50m north–south by 35m east–west, seemingly partially lying under the platform/early tower house and surviving as sub-surface remains both inside the bawn wall and outside it to the north. It was initially investigated in 2013 by cutting 3 inside the north-eastern corner of the bawn and cutting 1 outside the castle. The full width of the ditch in cutting 1 was revealed and a small, 0.30m-wide sondage was excavated (0.40m) to the base of this feature. While the ditch was also partially revealed in cutting 3, time constraints did not allow its further assessment in 2013. Cutting 1 was re-opened in 2014 and was enlarged by opening a total area of 30m². The full width of the ditch was again revealed and further assessed with the excavation of a 1m-wide sondage to a depth of 0.60m.

Appearing somewhat differently inside and outside the bawn, the geophysics suggests that they form part of the same enclosure. In cutting 3, the ditch was revealed as being 1.5m wide and 0.40m deep. The ditch had straight to gently tapering sides on the west and was more irregular on the east. Its base was flat. The fill of the ditch in this location had three distinct layers, two deposits of heavy clay separated by a layer of medium-sized stones. No finds or ecofacts were recovered from any of the ditch fills in this cutting.

The ditch, as revealed in cutting 1, is substantially larger, with a width of 2.40m and a depth of 0.60m. It was assessed through the excavation of a 1m-wide sondage that revealed irregular to gently sloping sides and a rounded base. This ditch had two separate fills. The lower layer was only 0.10m thick and contained small amounts of charcoal and a single large bone, a cattle ulna that has produced a radiocarbon date of AD 1445–1524 (2 sigma 95.4 per cent). The upper fill was of mixed friable clay and small stones. This upper fill also produced a small amount of animal bone and a single piece of what may be late medieval/post-medieval pottery (figs 8.2 and 8.3). The observed differences in the size and depth of the ditch inside and outside the bawn wall is likely to be due to the removal of its upper layers through the levelling of the site in advance of the construction of the tower house and/or the later bawn walls.

---

4 See chapter 7.

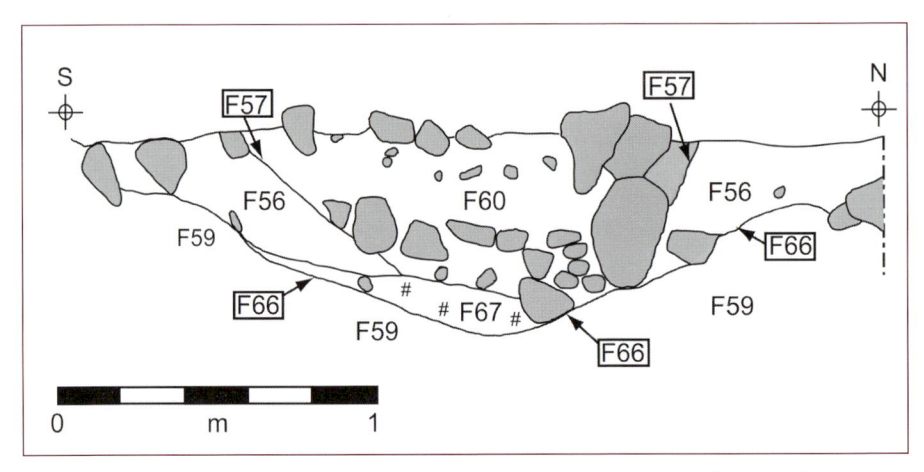

8.2 East-facing section of the Oval Enclosure's ditch, cutting 1 (© Chris Read).

8.3 Section through the Oval Enclosure's ditch in cutting 1, looking west (© Chris Read).

The only other features of note revealed in these two cuttings that targeted the ditched enclosure were a large pit (measuring at least 1.60m by 1.00m), partially revealed in cutting 3 and not assessed, and a rough arc of six shallow postholes revealed in cutting 1. It was not possible to link these features with the ditch stratigraphically beyond the fact they all cut the natural subsoil and were sealed with similar deposits. The pit would have been located inside the oval enclosure, as were the six postholes. The postholes ranged from sub-circular to oval in shape and in width from 0.15m to

0.25m. They were all half sectioned, revealing a range of fills and shapes and depths varying between 0.07m and 0.22m. The postholes may represent the truncated remains of a simple circular or semi-circular structure with an approximate diameter of 3–4m. No finds or ecofacts were recovered from the six postholes.

The enclosure ditch, as revealed in cutting 1, was cut by a later, shallow linear ditch. This ditch was 1.40m wide and 0.44m deep. The size of this later ditch is more comparable to that revealed in cutting 3 based upon size. It, like the ditch in cutting 3, was filled with a substantial amount of stone, although seemingly more organized in this location. The fill of this ditch also yielded animal bone, glass, a single glass bead, slag and charcoal. The presence of bottle glass in the fill of this feature indicates it was likely in-filled in the seventeenth or eighteenth century, making it substantially later than the larger ditch it cut.

The ditches, in cuttings 1 and 3, were sealed by similar deposits of heavy clay and small to medium stones. These deposits, particularly those revealed outside the castle in cutting 1, had a large amount of animal bone, charcoal and post-medieval finds in them, including iron, glass, ceramic (including clay pipes), possible lithics and small amounts of slag. These deposits in cutting 1 outside the bawn wall may indicate a formal dump.

THE PLATFORM/TOWER HOUSE

The platform dominates the northern portion of the castle interior and what lies within it is clearly earlier than the spear-shaped bastioned towers and associated bawn wall.[5] It had been suggested prior to the excavation that this platform may represent the ruined and later modified remains of an earlier tower house, a theory now confirmed by the results of the 2017 field season. The platform was first investigated in 2015 with the excavation of cutting 6, which was positioned along its eastern wall and thus situated to examine both the platform's foundations and its relationship with the existing bawn wall (fig. 8.4). The clearance of rubble piled against the eastern wall of the platform prior to excavation revealed a blocked ground-floor entrance defined by cut-stone door jambs and located 4.20m south of the platform/bawn wall juncture. This revelation led to cutting 6 being enlarged in 2017, the excavation in that year being focussed on top of the platform on its south-eastern corner, in line with the opening revealed earlier in 2015.

The excavation of cutting 6 (figs 8.5 and 8.6) revealed all the elements of a typical tower house ground-floor entrance, buried under over 1.5m of rubble. The excavation of this cutting has added enormously to our understanding of the platform and its potential role in the later bawn castle. The full architectural description of the tower

5 See chapter 4.

8.4 Cutting 6: eastern wall and entrance of the tower house, looking west (© Chris Read).

house features is not yet complete. What follows includes a basic description and measurements.

The easternmost feature of the tower house is the east-facing entrance revealed during the 2015 excavation season. This entrance is defined by cut-stone jambs, 1.02m apart, and two large flat, flagstones that span the full width of the doorway. The main external wall of the tower house was exposed on the northern side of the entrance only in this cutting. This wall is battered, 1.31m wide and survives to a height of 0.70m in section. It is also clear from this south-facing section that the much rougher masonry that makes up the visible revetment wall of the platform sits directly on a foundation comprising the base of the original tower house wall. The quality of the stonework is vastly different, with the tower house wall consisting of much larger stones, many of which exhibit rough shaping. There is also evidence of lime-bedding mortar used in the tower house construction, which is not apparent in the later, clay-bonded stonework of either the building in the south-west corner of the bawn or the platform itself.

There is a gap of 1m between the inner face of the external wall and a substantial internal north–south orientated wall with a second entrance aligned directly with the first. This wall is 0.75m wide and survived to a height of between 1.30m and 1.40m. The inner entrance, defined by large flat sill stones (0.30m to 0.35m wide) and a surviving jamb on the southern side, was 1.45m wide. The small amount of floor revealed in the cutting inside the inner entrance consisted of roughly laid medium-sized stones. Found lying directly on this floor was a nearly intact circular quern-stone.

8.5 Cutting 6: looking south, showing the entranceway lobby and the remains of the stone stairs ascending to the upper floors of the tower house (© Chris Read).

8.6 Cutting 6: south-facing section showing the external and internal walls of the tower house. The base of the small doorway from the entrance lobby into the small northern room or 'guard chamber' can also be seen (© Chris Read).

0   5m

8.7 Ground-floor plan of Clara tower house Co. Kilkenny (courtesy of Dundalgan Press). The original plan of the ground floor of the tower house at Moygara Castle looked similar to this.

In this respect, it may be worth noting that a number of medieval and post-medieval houses have quern-stones deliberately placed for such things as to prevent ill-health or bad luck on or near significant parts of houses, such as thresholds, entranceways and doorways.[6]

Between the internal and external walls, to the south of the entrance, were two large flat stones, seemingly tied into the internal wall and stepped, indicating a likely staircase in this location to upper floors (as tower houses were normally four to five floors in height). These stones extend 0.95 m in length (disappearing into the eastern

6 See, in particular, K. Dempsey, '"Making a House a Home": odd deposits in ordinary households in later medieval Ireland 1200–1600 AD' in C. Tente and C. Theune (eds), *Household goods in the European medieval and early modern countryside*, Ruralia, 14 (Leiden, forthcoming).

8.8 Clara tower house, Co. Kilkenny. The tower of the original Moygara Castle probably looked something like this (photograph courtesy of Con Manning).

baulk) and are 0.20m and 0.45m wide respectively. There also appears to be another entranceway from the lobby to the right of the main entranceway, presumably leading into a small room. The interior of this potential room was outside the limits of excavation.

In all, therefore, the excavated evidence suggests that the original tower house at Moygara was entered by a ground-floor doorway, located in its eastern wall. This doorway led into a small lobby, which had a stairway leading up to the tower house's upper floors on its left-hand, southern side, a doorway straight ahead into what appears to be the main ground-floor room of the building (which, as elsewhere, was probably used for storage), and, lastly, a doorway leading into what can only have been a small room on its northern side. This entranceway arrangement is a common one for tower houses across Ireland.[7] For example, such an entranceway arrangement can be seen in the ground floor of the very well preserved, five-storey, late fifteenth-/early sixteenth-century tower house that stands today at Clara, Co. Kilkenny (figs 8.7 and 8.8).[8]

\7 H.G. Leask, *Irish castles and castellated houses* (Dundalk, 1941), pp 79–80; T.E. McNeill, *Castles in Ireland: feudal power in a Gaelic world* (London, 1997), p. 218.   **8** Leask, *Irish castles and castellated houses*, p. 80.

Apart from a few animal bones and one clay pipe fragment, the material in cutting 6 that sealed the tower house features, described above, had no finds. The vast majority of the material excavated from this cutting, over 1.5m deep in places, consisted of rubble and small amounts of clay. This rubble consisted of small, medium and large stones with bits of lime mortar, suggesting much of this material came from the upper portions of the original tower house. The homogeneity of these deposits and lack of finds indicates it was likely the result of a singular event, with the majority of the material having fallen or, more likely, being deliberately demolished from a north–south direction.

The northern wall of the tower house was left intact to a height of *c.*3m above ground level and was then incorporated into the later bawn wall. The eastern, southern and western sides of the tower house were reduced to a height of 1.3m–1.4m. A dry-stone wall was then built on top of these walls to a height of 1.3m to 1.6m to revet the collapsed material, deliberately turning it into the platform that is still visible today.

The excavation of cutting 6 revealed that the foundation course of the tower house/platform rested on natural subsoil and on an earth-fast boulder at the juncture of the platform's east wall and the bawn wall, only 0.25m below the current ground level. There was no evidence of a foundation trench for either wall.

BURNING OUTSIDE THE NORTH WALL

The geophysical survey of the area north of the castle identified a significant magnetic anomaly outside and to the east of the early ditched enclosure approximately 20m from the bawn wall.[9] This was investigated in both 2013 and 2014 with the excavation of cutting 2. This portion of the site is quite steeply sloped, with the ground descending northwards from the castle walls.

Cutting 2, first excavated in 2013, revealed very little beyond a small patch of fire-reddened clay, medium stones and charcoal at the southern, castle end, of this north–south orientated trench. This seemed to indicate that the cutting just clipped some potentially structured archaeological deposits and the likely source of the magnetic anomaly. In 2014 this area was further investigated with an extension of the excavated area southwards towards the castle to further reveal the burnt deposits uncovered in 2013.

The features uncovered in this 2014 extension of cutting 2 included a single, shallow posthole (0.20m-0.25m in diameter) and an irregular north–south-orientated linear cut, 1.50m long and 0.20m to 0.40m wide. A small sondage through this linear feature revealed that this cut had a depth of 0.10m to 0.12m. It was flat with straight

9 See chapter 7.

sides and filled with friable clay/stone fill. This linear feature extended southwards from the extensive area of fire-reddened clay, the same as that revealed earlier at the northern, adjoining end of the cutting. This spread of fire-reddened clay, charcoal flecking and loose small- to medium-sized stones covered a total area that measured 3m north/south and extended beyond the limits of the 1.5m wide cuttings to the east and west. A small sondage was excavated across this deposit, revealing it was only 0.03m to 0.12m deep, thinning as it extended southwards. A considerable amount of iron slag was recovered from this and covering deposits, indicating these features may constitute a badly preserved iron-smelting furnace with the remnants of a flue and no evidence of a bowl.

It is unknown how this burning/potential iron-smelting furnace relates chronologically to either the early oval-shaped ditched enclosure, the tower house or the later bawn. A total of four pieces of stone, white in colour with some type of greenish glassy glaze on it were recovered from cutting 2. A large number of clay-pipe fragments were retrieved from the layers that sealed the burnt deposits observed in this cutting.

THE CASTLE INTERIOR

Cuttings 3 and 4, excavated in 2013, contribute to our knowledge of the types of archaeological deposits and features to be found within the castle's bawn wall. Cutting 4 was positioned on a north–south orientation 10m east from the gatehouse located in the castle's western wall to investigate evidence of east–west-orientated features identified during the geophysical survey. The cutting did in fact reveal three features, orientated east–west. A narrow slot trench was uncovered that was between 0.25m and 0.4m wide and 0.25m deep. It had a flat base with relatively flat sides. Situated approximately 1m and 2m to the north of this feature were two linear stone arrangements on the same orientation. The closest of these stones to the slot trench was relatively unorganized and consisted of medium to large stones sitting on the natural subsoil. The furthest, and extending north beyond the limits of the cutting, appeared more organized and could have been the bottom course of a narrow wall, *c*.0.4m in width. Cutting 4 contained quite a lot of archaeological material including pottery, clay-pipe fragments, slag, glass and a single bead found among the northern-most linear stone arrangement.

Cutting 3 was positioned further east to investigate, as noted, a section of the early, pre-castle oval ditched enclosure inside the bawn wall but it also revealed a portion of a large pit cutting the natural subsoil and a thin deposit of charcoal-enriched soil sitting on the subsoil. There is no indication of what date these features may be as they were not further excavated and they yielded no datable finds. As in other cuttings, most of the finds come from upper, clearly later deposits.

8.9 Cutting 5: external wall, cobbling and drain of the later rectangular building on the southern part of the western side of the bawn, looking west (© Chris Read).

8.10 Cutting 5: fireplace inside the later rectangular western building, looking north (© Chris Read).

Identified during the architectural survey of Moygara Castle,[10] there is clear evidence at ground level for the survival of a large rectangular building built parallel to the bawn's western wall, south of the gate, measuring approximately 15m north–south by 8m

10 See chapter 4.

east–west. This building was investigated through the excavation of cutting 5 (see figs 8.1 and 8.9), comprising a total excavated area of 5.5m by 7.75m. Despite the exposure of the wall, a door, a fireplace/chimney, external cobbling and a drain, all of the excavated material consisted of rubble mixed with soil. The rubble likely consists of both the remains of the building itself in addition to other stone from across the interior of the castle, which in living memory was cleared from east to west and mounded against the interior of the castle's western wall and over the building.[11]

Sherlock and O'Conor show in chapter 4 that this rectangular structure appears to be later in date than the bawn because it blocks a gun loop in its western wall. It is likely to have been a one- or two-storey domestic structure. It probably dates to the seventeenth or eighteenth centuries but it is not clearly indicated on the first-edition six-inch Ordnance Survey map, which dates to the late 1830s. It appears to have been built across the access route to the ground-floor doorway of the south-western tower of the bawn and it remains unclear if it was built to extend the accommodation available in the tower or if it functioned as an independent entity after the abandonment of this building.[12]

It should be noted, however, that while the eastern (north–south orientated) wall of this rectangular structure appears to extend in an unbroken line northwards from the southern bawn wall of the castle (thus preventing direct access to the south-west corner tower), the break in the wall identified in the 2015 season excavations marking an entrance doorway into the interior of the structure was not evident prior to excavation. Thus the possibility exists that a similar break may exist in another portion of this wall, which may have provided a separate access to the south-west corner tower through the north-south wall during its use. Alternatively, the southern wall of this rectangular structure may yet be proven through excavation to return westwards just north of the entrance to the south-west corner tower. While part of its walls butt against the inside face of the curtain wall and one end partially blocks a gun loop, as stated, suggesting it is a later addition, the exact dating of this rectangular building still remains somewhat unclear (other than having been constructed later than the bawn wall and towers).

The principal features revealed in cutting 5 were the component parts of the rectangular building: the north–south-oriented eastern clay-bonded wall of the structure;[13] its 1m-wide entrance doorway and stone threshold; a south-facing, stone-built enclosed wall fireplace and hearth within the building; cobbling exterior to the building, which had an associated stone-lined gully/drain within it. It might be added that evidence for an original distinctive white lime mortar render are found on both the internal and external faces of this building's walls.

---

11 P.J. O'Neill, pers. comm. **12** See chapter 4. **13** For clay-bonded buildings in Ireland, see S. Markley, 'Unearthing a forgotten medieval-building technique: an examination of earth-mortared stone construction in later medieval Ireland, 1100–1600AD' (PhD, TCD, 2018).

The stone-built wall fireplace is located 2m directly west of the entrance doorway within the interior of the building (fig. 8.10). The fireplace and hearth face south, strongly suggesting a room lay to the south of it within the interior of the building. This suggests that there was another room to the north. Put simply, this evidence suggests that this rectangular building had at least two rooms at ground-floor level when in use.

DISCUSSION

The programme of test excavation at Moygara Castle has revealed the site's significant archaeological potential and revealed a number of key features identified during the geophysical and architectural surveys. The excavation of the platform in 2017, properly identifying it as a tower house, and the exposure of its ground-floor entrance, in addition to the single radiocarbon date from the infilling of the earlier ditched enclosure, allows the present writer to propose what he considers to be a fairly secure chronology for the main elements of the site.

The earliest definitive element of the site was the oval enclosure, the lowest fill of which has produced a date from a cattle bone of AD 1445–1524 (2 sigma 95.4 per cent). With this ditched enclosure sealed by the platform, it is clear the next phase was the construction of what is clearly a tower house, based on the ground plan exposed by the excavation. The evidence from the aforementioned radiocarbon date suggests that the construction of this tower house took place sometime between *c.*1450 and the earliest historical reference to there being a castle at Moygara, which was in 1538.[14] The excavation did not date the construction of the bawn with its towers but the architectural evidence clearly shows it to be later than the tower house.[15] The excavation does indicate or suggest that the tower house was re-used, with most of its upper portions levelled and incorporated into the defences of the north wall, possibly as a firing platform for artillery.[16] Sometime afterwards, in the later seventeenth or perhaps even early in the eighteenth century, the internal building adjacent the west wall was constructed. It is argued that this building was substantial, evidenced not only by its overall size but also the width of its entrance, in addition to the size and quality of the fireplace. The building, which seems to have had at least two rooms in it, could be a later residence added after the castle fell out of use or, more probably, related to the use of the castle when it functioned as a barracks.[17] The quality of the fireplace may suggest that at least the room which it heated functioned as an officer's or officers' quarters. The only mollusc shells recovered during the excavation came from this building, namely oyster, and may be indicative of food eaten within the building.

---

14 For historical references to Moygara Castle, see chapter 2.   **15** See chapter 4.   **16** See chapter 10.   **17** See chapter 2. However, see chapter 10 for an alternative function for this building.

The function of the earlier oval enclosure can only be hypothesized. The depth and width of the ditch does not suggest a feature constructed with defence as a primary concern. Its position on the highest part of the site indicates that visibility was important. The date of the infilling of this ditch was during the later fifteenth or early sixteenth centuries and this event was likely associated with the preparation of the ground for the construction of the tower house. This could suggest that this oval enclosure may originally have been more substantial, once having had an earthen bank and deeper ditch. These latter features may have been erased, along with the upper part of the ditch, during the levelling and preparation of ground for the later stone structure.

The area of potential burning to the north of the castle, identified through geophysics and revealed in cutting 2, has the appearance of a badly damaged iron-smelting furnace, with an abundance of fire-reddened clay, a potential flue and a few postholes. It is also possible that this concentration of burnt material represents a dump, given its location on a fairly steep north-facing slope. It is unclear as to how this burning relates chronologically with the other features of the site, namely the ditched enclosure, the tower house and the later bawn. The finds recovered from this area were mostly late in date but were recovered predominantly from topsoil contexts. A small amount of iron slag was found in this cutting, but not nearly as much as was recovered from cuttings inside the castle. Three stones with some sort of greenish glassy glaze were also retrieved from this area and may provide an indication of the nature of the burning in the area, or may be a by-product of heating other materials.

Inside the castle walls, the four trenches excavated have revealed various elements of the site's archaeological potential. These include the continuation of the oval-ditched enclosure into and under the north-east quadrant of the bawn, as revealed in cutting 3.

Other features revealed inside the bawn wall in cuttings 3 and 4 include an assortment of pits, linear cut features and spreads of burnt material. The depth of archaeological deposits within these cuttings is quite shallow and consists mainly of features cutting into or lying on the natural subsoil, at depths of 0.15m to 0.2m. Most of the finds recovered inside the bawn come from topsoil layers and are mostly post-medieval in date.

The artefacts recovered from throughout the site from the four field seasons of excavation include post-medieval crockery and bottle glass mixed with animal bone (cattle, sheep and pig). A few sherds of post-medieval pottery, a copper alloy button (possibly from a uniform) and two lead musket balls were also recovered. A small selection of definite and possible lithics of flint and chert were recovered across the site, indicating the presence of prehistoric activity in the vicinity, which, given its vantage point over Lough Gara to the north, is not at all surprising.[18]

---

18 For the rich prehistory of the Lough Gara area, see C. Fredengren, *Crannogs* (Dublin, 2002), pp 112–201.

The substantial building seen in the south-western quadrant of the castle, with its fireplace, is clearly later than the bawn, as stated. The architectural remains are consistent with a building from the later seventeenth or eighteenth centuries and given its size and features, may be related to the role of the castle as a barracks during this period, as implied by the site's history.[19] Based upon the large size of the building, it could be a high-status residence, although as the only stone building identified within the bawn at this stage and its likely use as a military barracks/fortification at the time that it was built, it is deemed plausible that it is most likely related to a more functional use, in keeping with the very practical architecture of the castle. Very little other archaeological material was recovered from this area, with a substantial amount of rubble, likely the result of both the collapse of the south-east corner tower and later clearance, comprising the majority of the excavated material. The only mollusc shells recovered during the excavation came from this area, namely oyster, and may be indicative of food eaten within the building. Given Moygara's distance from the sea, which lies over 40km away to the north, they are an interesting find.

CONCLUSIONS

In conclusion, the eight weeks spent in total excavating over four years at Moygara Castle have provided a tantalizing glimpse of the site's archaeological potential. The most important conclusion from the excavation is that the platform consists of the remains of a levelled earlier tower house, seemingly built sometime after the mid-fifteenth century.

Over the course of the project, more than fifty archaeology students got their very first taste of working on an excavation. Many of these students have also contributed to the on-going post-excavation programme, focusing on the recording and analysis of the artefacts and ecofacts recovered from the Moygara excavation.

---

19 See chapter 2. As stated, see chapter 10 for an alternative argument as to the original function of this building.

CHAPTER NINE

Dating the mortars of Moygara Castle

JASON BOLTON

INTRODUCTION

Building materials offer physical evidence of how archaeological structures were built and how they changed over time. Studies on the characterization of archaeological building materials provide information on the origin and transportation of raw materials, and the level of technology and craftsmanship at the time of construction. In addition, differentiation between mortars found at a site can provide insights into the phasing of complex monuments through relative dating, and certain components in lime mortars offer material suitable for radiocarbon dating.

The building mortars of Moygara Castle were first examined in 2008 and 2009. A radiocarbon-dating project was commissioned by Maura O'Gara-O'Riordan of the O'Gara Clan Association in 2008 to identify and extract material suitable for radiocarbon dating from the different structures at the site to gain a view on when the castle was first constructed, and when it was modified and/or rebuilt. The work was undertaken with the permission of the then landowner, Mr Frank O'Neill. Samples were taken under licence from the National Monuments Service, then in the Department of the Environment, Heritage and Local Government, and the National Museum of Ireland.

In 2009, a conservation report was commissioned by P.J. O'Neill on behalf of the Moygara Castle Research and Conservation Project, with the assistance of the Heritage Council, to determine the vulnerability and conservation needs of the castle. This allowed further investigation of the different structures during 2009, and the opportunity to analyze mortars using polarized light microscopy (PLM) to characterize and understand the nature and performance of the historic lime mortar to guide materials proposed for conservation. In 2015, additional radiocarbon dating was made possible through the Royal Irish Academy's Radiocarbon Date Schemes to compare dates obtained from different components of mortars previously sampled from Moygara.

SAMPLING

Samples of mortar were taken from seven locations at Moygara Castle (fig. 9.1) representing mortars from the tower house, the later bawn's gatehouse and its defensive

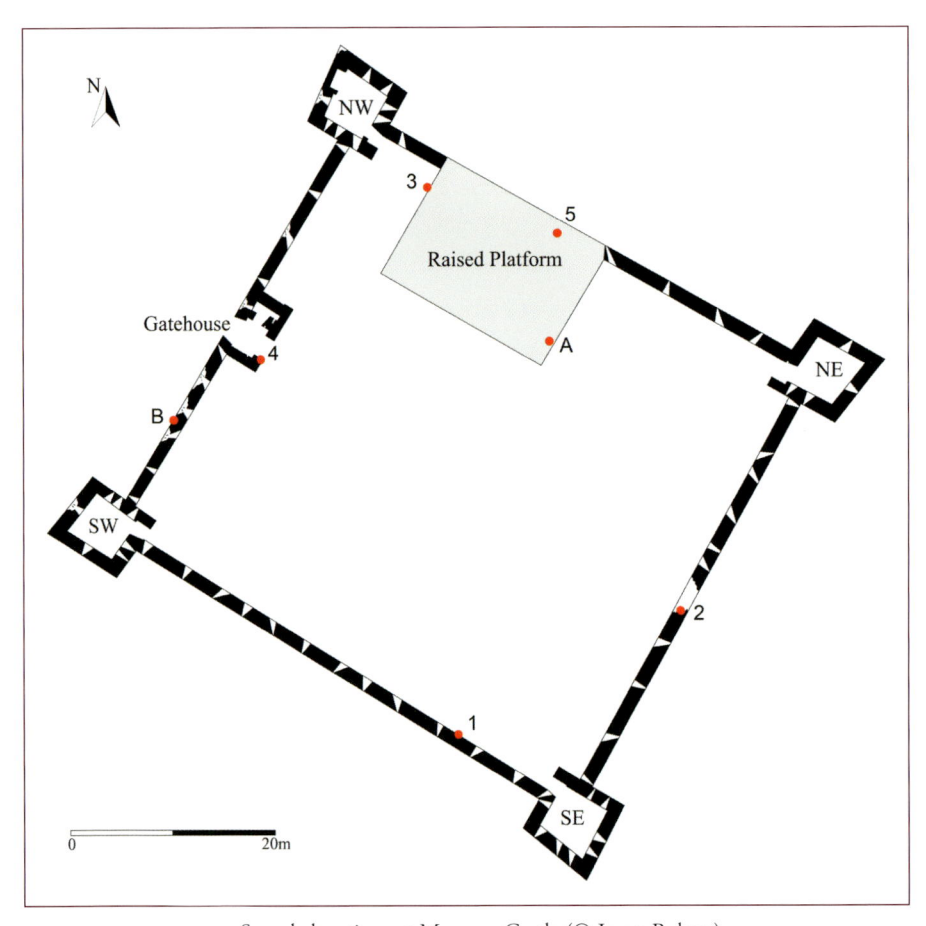

9.1 Sample locations at Moygara Castle (© Jason Bolton).

Table 9.1 Lime mortars sampled from Moygara Castle in 2008.

No.	Sample Location	Type
1	South bawn wall, north (inner) elevation at collapsed outer leaf	Wall core
2	East bawn wall at breach in centre of wall	Wall core
3	Tower house, west elevation	Bedding mortar
4	Gatehouse, east elevation, south of arched entrance	Bedding mortar
5	Tower house, north elevation, at collapsed outer leaf	Wall core
A	Tower house, east elevation	Bedding mortar
B	West bawn wall, west (outer) elevation at collapsed outer leaf	Wall core

circuit of curtain walls (table 9.1). Collapsed areas of inner and outer masonry leaves and breaches in the walls allowed a wide range of mortar surfaces to be examined prior to sampling. All samples chosen contained three types of component with potential for radiocarbon dating: relict fuel fragments entrapped in the mortar; 'lime lumps' (rounded particles of unslaked lime); and areas of lime binder relatively free of fine limestone aggregate. The samples were initially examined with visual microscopy, with representative fragments selected for thin sectioning for PLM; and with fragments containing dateable components selected for AMS radiocarbon dating.

BUILDING STONE OF MOYGARA CASTLE

The upstanding masonry of Moygara Castle consists of rectangular and flaggy stone blocks laid as uncoursed rubble masonry with the outer faces roughly hewn. This masonry treatment is found throughout the tower house, the gatehouse, the bawn wall and the corner towers. The largest stones are found at the base of the wall. Where large stones occur higher up, they function as quoins, squinches and other architectural elements. Large boulders were used to form the foundation of the north-west tower, and other large boulders are found scattered around the circuit. The vast majority of the building stone of Moygara Castle is a red-brown pebbly sandstone/conglomerate from the local Moygara Formation. The quarry source is unclear but there are abundant sources in the surrounding landscape, including boulders which lie in the immediate vicinity. Conglomerate sandstone is exposed immediately east of the south-east tower, and there are significant outcrops in the forested areas 0.3km–2km south of the castle.

A relatively small amount of limestone is found scattered among the towers and defensive circuit. These include two limestone keystones with carved detail found lying in the passageway of the gatehouse (mon. nos. SL044-052002, SL044-052003)[1] and dressed corbels, for example, in the south-east tower. A few roughly hewn limestone blocks are found indiscriminately placed among the sandstone rubble, but these are relatively scarce. Occasional punch-dressed limestone stones are also found scattered among the rubble masonry. Inside the north-west tower, two grey punch-dressed limestone blocks lie incongruously with the red-brown sandstone (fig. 9.2) and these may have been re-used from an earlier building. Sandstone blocks showing thermal shock covered with biofilm are seen on the south and west elevations of the tower house. While it is tempting to associate this with fire damage from a historical reference to the burning of Moygara Castle in 1581,[2] the damage could equally have occurred at a later date. However, it is plausible that the dressed limestone found in the north-west tower and elsewhere was salvaged for re-use from the tower house.

---

1 See fig. 4.15, chapter 4.   **2** *ALC* 1581.18.

9.2 Dressed limestone re-used among the sandstone rubble inside the north-west tower (© Jason Bolton).

9.3 Render basecoat on the external face of the south-west tower (© Jason Bolton).

LIME MORTARS AT MOYGARA CASTLE

The masonry walls at Moygara were built using the classical two-leaf-and-masonry core method of inner and outer leaves of rubble masonry enclosing a solid lime-concrete core. Strength was clearly a concern in the construction of the defensive circuit as the masonry walls were built entirely with lime mortar, without the use of easy-to-obtain clay and lime-clay mortars sometimes used as inert filler in masonry wall cores. A significant amount of quicklime was required to construct the massive lime-concrete wall-core, the bedding mortars and the rendering and plastering mortars which coated the inner and outer masonry walls of the castle. Surviving traces of the base coat of an external rendering mortar survive on the exterior of the north-east, south-east and south-west towers (fig. 9.3). Traces of a lime plaster base coat can also be seen along the interior walls of the south-east tower at current ground level below the level of the corbels, and at all levels of the south-west and north-east towers. A notable feature of the masonry of Moygara is the absence of any significant difference in composition or observable discontinuities between the external render, bedding and internal plaster. This integration indicates that the walls were rendered and plastered as they were raised and not afterwards. This differs from later construction practice from the eighteenth century onwards when thinner brick and stone masonry walls were erected, and subsequently finished with internal plaster and external render as a separate operation. The integrated technique is far superior for massive stone masonry walls as it allows thorough carbonation; but it also suggests that stone selectivity and the manner of coursing was not an aesthetic factor, as there was a presumption that the wall surfaces would be covered inside and out as building progressed to protect the stone and the joints. Despite weathering, ruination and biofilm, remnants of external renders and plasters survive throughout the defensive circuit of Moygara Castle. These lime coatings change our perception of how the masonry at Moygara Castle appeared when first built. The spearhead-shaped towers and walls would have appeared off-white throughout, with the mortars offering a number of practical benefits: insulating and protecting the towers from weather and temperature extremes; preventing early colonization by plants, insects and vermin; and making a small contribution to the defensibility of the castle by presenting a textured unclimbable surface.

The building renders, plasters and bedding mortars at Moygara consist of a range of sand- to pebble-sized aggregate 'floating' in a lime binder matrix. None of the mortar samples showed any evidence of intentional additions such as straw, hair, brick dust, wood ash or other additives historically put into mortars to improve their properties, workability or durability. The mortars from all the buildings contained relict fuel fragments and lime lumps indicating that there was no screening of the lime mortar prior to use. All mortar samples showed a broadly similar range of poorly sorted sub-rounded to sub-angular natural stones including fossiliferous and other limestones, polycrystalline and monocrystalline quartz and a range of other lithics[3] 'floating' in a lime-rich mix. The key distinction between the mortars of the tower house and the bawn walls was that charcoal and lime lumps in the tower house tend to be much smaller than those found in the defensive circuit. The wall core mortars of the bawn wall had the coarsest aggregate and the largest underburnt limestone fragments.

SOURCE OF THE LIME

Moygara Castle was built in a sandstone area, requiring a substantial amount of building lime to be brought to the site. From the tenth century to the mid-twentieth century, lime was produced all over Ireland, wherever limestone, marble, dolomite or other calcareous stones or seashells occurred. Surviving kilns and historical maps bear testament to a landscape bestrewn with small lime kilns producing lime for construction, agriculture or the preparation of leather. The quality of lime produced could vary substantially depending on the knowledge and skill of the lime burner, and the properties of the local limestone. The term limestone refers to a family of related stones which contain over 50 per cent calcium carbonate ($CaCO_3$) in the form of a lime mud or crystalline matrix and/or calcareous particles such as fossils and ooids. Firing very 'pure' limestone of >94 per cent calcium carbonate would produce a non-hydraulic lime which sets slowly through carbonation. However, even a 'pure' limestone contains a percentage of other materials such as quartz, feldspar, pyrite, chert and silica and alumina clay minerals. Some of these other components are reactive impurities which, when the limestone is fired, impart hydraulic qualities allowing it to set faster, harder and even underwater. There are three types of limestone found in the landscape surrounding Moygara Castle, and each of them, when fired, would have produced hydraulic lime mortars.

The closest limestone to Moygara is the Oakport pale grey limestone found *c*.0.27km north-west of the castle. This was a lime mud, with some beds of fossils and argillaceous (clay-rich) wackestones that would have probably impacted a weak hydraulic set. A better building lime would have been produced from the dark grey calcareous shales and fine-grained limestones of the Lisgannon Shale *c*.0.7km also to the north-west of Moygara, or the fossiliferous shales and strongly argillaceous Kilbryan limestone from the shoreline of Lough Gara to the south-east. Partially burnt limestone fragments were found in mortars from the tower house and the later bawn wall (table 9.1, samples A and B). These were a fossiliferous biomicritic limestone of

---

[3] These were probably obtained from a local gravel pit, a number of which are marked on historic Ordnance Survey maps of the area. A modern pit is found 100m north of Moygara and the aggregate was broadly similar to that found in the castle.

9.4 Sample B from the bawn wall contains a range of components including relict fuel fragments entrapped in the mortar and lime lumps formed during lime production. The mortar also contains underburnt limestone fragments, in this case a fossiliferous limestone wackestone biomicrite (© Jason Bolton).

wackestone/packstone texture and a lime mud (fig. 9.4), and probably sourced from the Oakport limestone north-west of the castle. This suggests that the builders of both the tower house and the bawn wall obtained limestone for burning from the closest possible source, rather than the better-performing limestone slightly further away. Historic practice was to transport limestone to burn at the building site to allow immediate use of quicklime for general construction, and slaking on site for any lime which required storage for later use. Any kilns associated with the construction of Moygara were probably located between the construction site and the source of the limestone, but placed downwind as the fumes from lime burning were noxious. The kiln was probably erected north-west of, but reasonably close to, the castle.

DATING THE MORTARS

Mortar dating relies on radiocarbon dating of carbonate material in the mortar. This can be charcoal or wood trapped in the mortar, particles of unslaked lime known as 'lime lumps' which are a by-product of lime production (fig. 9.5), or carbonates that formed with the hardening of a lime binder through the carbonation process. There are challenges in achieving accurate date ranges with each type of material. Charcoal

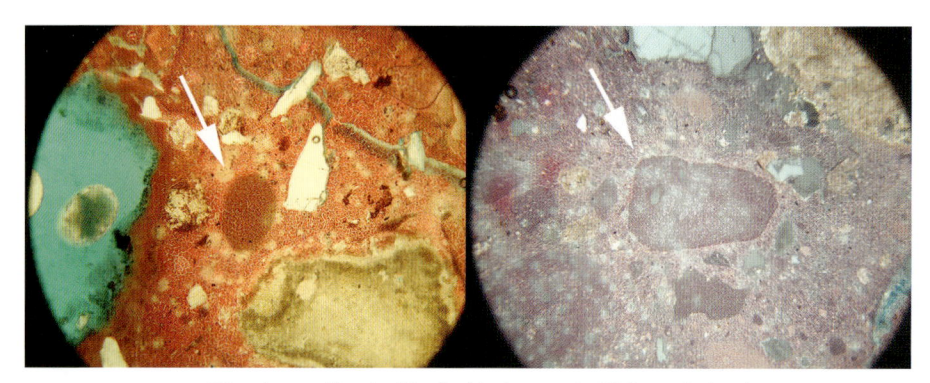

9.5 Lime lumps 'floating' in the binder matrix (© Jason Bolton).

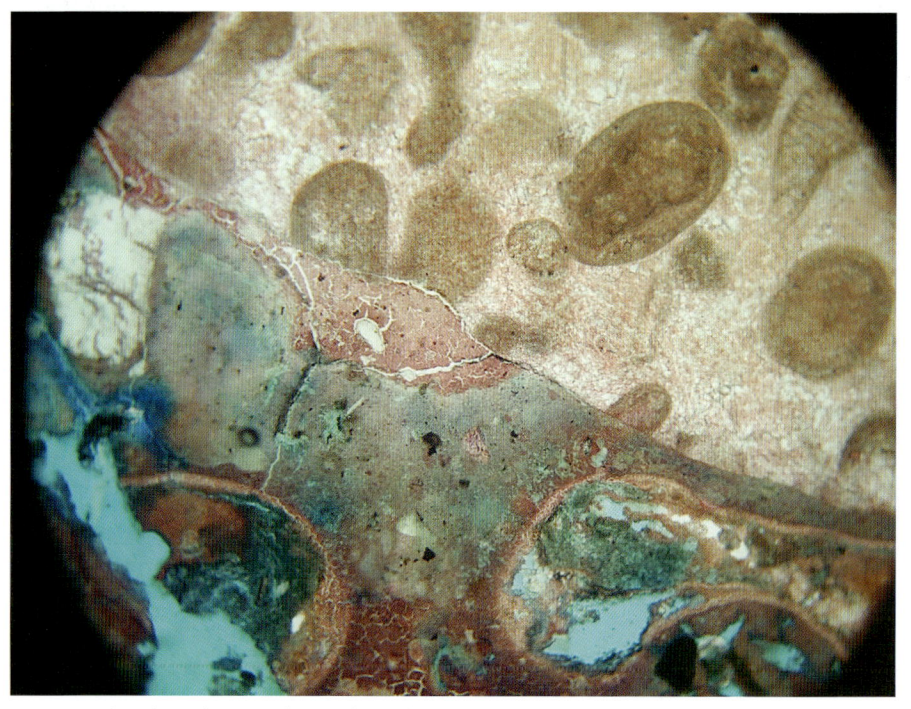

9.6 Sample 5 from the tower house showed abundant recrystallization of the lime binder due to weathering processes and inhomogeneity of the lime binder. The stone is a fossiliferous wackestone, probably Oakport limestone (© Jason Bolton).

and wood are open to arguments of the 'old wood' effect, i.e. that the wood used in firing was 'old' because it came from the older rings of a tree of considerable age, or was timber salvaged from an older building. Charcoal and wood dates may therefore give much older dates than the construction of the building.[4] A lime binder achieves

4 These problems with dating charcoal fragments in mortar have been recognized for at least thirty-six years. See,

Table 9.2 Results of lime mortar dating

No.	Radiocarbon dates obtained	Material
Tower house: Moygara A	(Beta 252783): BP date: 680 +/- 40 BP Cal. date (2 Sigma): Cal. AD 1270 to 1320 (Cal. BP 680 to 630)	Charcoal
Tower house: Moygara A	(QUB UBA-29920) BP date: 333 +/- 22 Cal. date (2 sigma): Cal. AD 1485 to 1640	Lime lump
Tower house: Moygara 3	(Beta 250444): BP date: 640 +/- 40 BP Cal. date (2 sigma): Cal. 1280 to 1400 (Cal. BP 670 to 550)	Charcoal
Bawn wall: Moygara B	(Beta 252784): BP date: 340 +/- 40 BP Cal. date (2 sigma): Cal. AD 1450 to 1650 (Cal. BP 500 to 300)	Charcoal
Bawn wall: Moygara B	(QUB UBA-29921) BP date: 332 +/- 23 Cal. date (2 sigma): Cal. AD 1484 to 1640	Charcoal
Bawn wall: Moygara 2	(Beta 250443): BP date: 450 +/- 40 BP Cal. date (2 sigma): Cal. AD 1420 to 1480 (Cal. BP 540 to 470)	Charcoal
Gatehouse: Moygara 4	(Beta 250445): BP date: 490 +/- 40 BP Cal. date (2 sigma): Cal. AD 1400 to 1450 (Cal. BP 550 to 500)	Charcoal

Note: Samples 1–5 dated at Beta Analytic. Samples A and B dated at QUB.

full carbonation over time, so the date of carbonation would be 'younger' than the date of construction. Weathering processes and fire damage can also result in a 'younger' date if there has been partial recrystallization of the binder matrix (fig. 9.6). Lime lumps are formed at the time of lime burning, and should be reasonably contemporaneous with construction. However, partially burnt lime lumps can return ancient dates of the raw limestone. To further complicate matters, there is also the possibility that mortar was re-used from an earlier building, thus giving an 'older' date, and not the construction date of the new building. Regardless of these challenges and limitations, absolute dating of mortars from buildings can be very useful, especially where written sources are vague, dendrochronology is not possible and where archaeological strata are difficult to read or open to different interpretations.

At Moygara, two components were selected for radiocarbon dating: charcoal in the form of relict fuel fragments entrapped in the mortar matrix, and 'lime lumps'; both of which are by-products of the lime production process. Samples of charcoal were initially radiocarbon dated in 2008 by Beta Analytic (table 9.2). Fragments from two samples were dated again in 2015 at Queen's University Belfast (QUB). Moygara A was one of two samples from the tower house which returned a very early date, and a lime lump from the same sample was submitted to QUB for dating as a comparison. Another charcoal fragment of Moygara B from the western bawn wall was submitted to QUB as a control.

for example, M.B. Schiffer, 'Radiocarbon dating and the "old wood" problem: the case of the Hohokam chronology', *Journal of Archaeological Science*, 13 (1986), pp 13–30; en.wikipedia.org/wiki/Old_wood. See, also, chapter 10.

DISCUSSION

Without wishing to place undue emphasis on such raw data and small sample numbers, there is an important aspect to these results which requires consideration. The two calibrated charcoal results from the tower house are much earlier than the date range provided by the 'lime lump' from the same building. There are a number of possible reasons for early charcoal dates (including use of standing dead wood). However, if these mortar-entrapped relict limekiln fuel fragments are from 'old wood', this would suggest that the lime burners may have harvested a variety of different diameter tree trunks and/or timbers from standing buildings for inclusion within the limekiln charge. If this is a case of the 'old wood effect' and that the data suggests that the wood formed significantly earlier than the construction event in question, then this has implications for relict kiln fuel studies as traditional craft practice has assumed young branches and scrub were often used for kiln firing. It also emphasizes the potential of dating lime lumps as comparative dating material.

Petrographic study of the mortars uncovered a number of important findings. Firstly, the builders of the tower house and later gatehouse and bawn all drew from the same source of limestone for lime burning to produce the mortars used for construction. Underburnt limestone fragments from mortars in both the tower house and bawn wall indicate that limestone fired for lime was sourced from the Oakport Formation 0.270km north-west of Moygara. This produced a weakly hydraulic lime. There is therefore continuity in obtaining limestone for lime burning from the closest available source in both instances. The mortar samples obtained from Moygara are remarkably similar in composition: lime-rich, with locally obtained poorly sorted sand, and with no attempt to modify or improve the mix using clay, ash, wood, hair or any one of a number of additives used in medieval buildings.[5] Finally, the use of integrated mortars in construction where the external render and internal plasters were applied as the walls were raised changes our perception of Moygara Castle when first built from red-brown sandstone structures, to a complex finished with textured off-white lime mortars.[6]

---

5 Unfortunately the lack of traditional additives such as wood ash to the weak hydraulic lime mortar used at Moygara has left it vulnerable to weathering, and is an underlying factor in the deep dry joints and masonry collapses seen today.   6 The initial work at Moygara Castle was funded by Maura O'Gara-O'Riordan in 2008; with a conservation report for the building prepared for P.J. O'Neill in 2009. Samples taken under license from National Monuments Service in 2008 were dated by Beta Analytic; with further dating in 2015 at Queen's University Belfast courtesy of the Royal Irish Academy's Radiocarbon Date Scheme. I am very grateful to Kevin Barton for his assistance during sampling.

CHAPTER TEN

Moygara Castle through time

KIERAN O'CONOR

INTRODUCTION

It was stated in the introduction to this book that Moygara Castle is one of the most impressive archaeological monuments standing today in north Connacht and yet, when the Moygara Castle Research and Conservation Project began in 2005, virtually nothing was known about this dramatic-looking site. In the years since then, the project, under the able chairmanship of P.J. O'Neill, brought together a number of scholars from different disciplines in an attempt to understand the development and role of the castle through time. These scholars included an architectural historian, archaeologists, historians, local historians, a geo-physicist and a built-heritage conservator, and thus the research carried out over the years at the castle has been truly inter-disciplinary in its scope. In terms of understanding a complex medieval building like Moygara Castle, this collaborative approach has been invariably found to be the best. No one discipline or method usually has the full answer to understanding the way, say, an abbey, friary or castle, occupied for centuries, looked like when first built and then how such sites were altered in subsequent centuries. In the case of Moygara Castle, combining evidence from a range of disciplines and methods has proved fruitful in interpreting and understanding the remains there.

It is the aim of this concluding chapter to bring together the main findings of this inter-disciplinary research that has taken place at the castle over the years. In this regard, a number of research questions were postulated at the beginning of the Moygara Castle Research and Conservation Project in 2005 and an attempt will be made to answer at least some of these in the following pages.

PHASING MOYGARA CASTLE

One question asked in 2005 was how many phases of construction and occupation could be seen in the castle?[1] In this respect, very often local communities and heritage groups, while understanding that these sites were inhabited for generations, make the understandable mistake of seeing castles in their areas as being of one building phase only. Such local groups regularly believe that the standing visible remains at these

---

[1] See foreword.

places date exclusively to the time of the earliest historical references to them. However, research on castles carried out by professional scholars, often archaeologists and architectural historians, has clearly shown that many, even most, castles built across medieval Europe were rebuilt and modified on a number of occasions.[2] It must always be remembered that many castles were inhabited for centuries and so structural changes were made to them at quite regular intervals due to the evolving fashion, defensive and living requirements of their occupants, particularly their lords. Castles could be so physically transformed at times that they would have been unrecognizable in their final forms to their original builders.[3] For example, a relatively recently published survey of Rindoon Castle in Co. Roscommon, which lies an hour's drive to the south-east of Moygara Castle, is interesting in this regard. The castle, whose first masonry phase dates to the period 1227–35, was modified at least three times after the latter date, with the last large-scale modification dating to the very late sixteenth century. However, hints from the surviving historical sources and an analysis of the curving ground plan of the masonry castle suggest that it was built on a pre-Norman timber fortification, possibly erected by either Turlough or Rory O'Conor in the twelfth century. Furthermore, local folklore and analysis of the castle's interior indicate that a herd's house, with outbuildings, was built within it during the nineteenth century. In all, this analysis of Rindoon Castle indicates that there were at least six phases of building activity at this site.[4] Again, Roscommon Castle was constructed as a royal castle by the Dublin government in the late thirteenth century but was later massively transformed into a large fortified house and garden by Sir Nicholas Malby, a New English government official and soldier, in the late sixteenth century.[5] Staying in modern Co. Roscommon, Ballintober Castle was built by Richard de Burgh, earl of Ulster and lord of Connacht, in the first decade of the fourteenth century. In the early seventeenth century the north-western angle tower of the castle was effectively turned into a seven-room (or so) fortified house by the insertion of mullioned-and-transomed windows, fireplaces and a chimney. Arguably, this modification and modernization of this part of the castle is linked to the fact that its Gaelic-Irish owner, Sir Hugh O'Conor, the O'Conor Don, had by then become an English-style landlord, holding his lands by primogeniture and under common law, rather than by Brehon Law with its strong emphasis on partible inheritance. Parts of the south-western angle tower at Ballintober were also rebuilt at this stage and gun loops were inserted in places into the

---

2 For example, see W. Meyer, 'Castle archaeology: an introduction' in M. Carver and J. Klapste (eds), *The archaeology of medieval Europe*, ii: *twelfth to sixteenth centuries AD* (Aarhus, 2011), p. 234. **3** Ibid. **4** K. O'Conor, P. Naessens and R. Sherlock, 'Rindoon Castle, Co. Roscommon: a border castle on the Irish frontier' in P. Ettel. A.-M. Flambard-Hericher and K. O'Conor (eds), *Château Gaillard, 26: château et commerce* (Caen, 2014), pp 313–23; K. O'Conor, P. Naessens and R. Sherlock, 'Rindoon Castle, Co. Roscommon: an Anglo-Norman castle on the western shores of Lough Ree' in B. Cunningham and H. Murtagh (eds), *Lough Ree: historic lakeland settlement* (Dublin, 2016), pp 83–109. **5** M. Murphy and K. O'Conor, *Roscommon Castle: a visitor's guide* (Roscommon, 2008).

curtain wall of the castle at this time, if not somewhat earlier.[6] It might also be added that timber castles of twelfth- and thirteenth-century date were also subject to massive re-buildings and transformations. For example, excavation has shown that the timber-and-cob buildings and defences in the motte-and-bailey castle at Hen Domen, Powys, Wales, were constantly being upgraded and replaced over the course of its 200-year occupation.[7] Again, the primary motte at Rathmullan, Co. Down, seems to date to the very late twelfth century, being built on top of an earlier still-occupied ringfort. This motte was heightened at some later stage, with a new summit being created as a result.[8] The basic message from this short review is that castles of all types, including timber ones, were often re-built and transformed to meet changing lordly needs.

It should come as no surprise, therefore, to learn that at least four phases of activity have been recognized at Moygara. Three masonry phases are visible in the architecture of the castle there. Furthermore, geophysical survey and excavation has indicated at least one phase of activity at the site that pre-dates the erection of the first masonry castle at Moygara.[9] These will now be discussed in order.

THE FIRST PHASE OF ACTIVITY AT MOYGARA: THE OVAL ENCLOSURE

The geophysical survey carried out in stages by Barton between 2005 and 2008 suggested that the masonry castle at Moygara was built on top of a pre-existing oval enclosure. This enclosure, at a rough guess, seems to have measured *c.*55m north-east/south-west and *c.*35–*c.*38m north-west/south-east internally.[10] Read's later excavation at the site over two-week periods in both 2013 and 2014 confirmed this finding, showing that the enclosure was defined by a quite shallow fosse. It appears that this ditch is 1.5–2.4m in width and between 0.4m and 0.6m in depth.[11] The evidence from the excavation suggests, at present at least, that this enclosure was not defensive or domestic in nature.[12] It may have functioned as a field, stock enclosure or garden of some sort. However, saying all of that, it must be said that Read's investigation of this enclosure and its ditch was quite short and not intensive, due to time restraints. A more extensive excavation of this enclosure in the future may well change the current interpretation of this feature as being a non-residential site, without

6 K. O'Conor, 'English settlement and change in Roscommon during the late sixteenth and and seventeenth centuries' in A. Horning, R. Ó Baoill, C. Donnelly and P. Logue (eds), *The post-medieval archaeology of Ireland, 1550–1850* (Dublin, 2007), pp 199–200. See, also, J. Lyttleton, *The Jacobean plantations in seventeenth-century Offaly* (Dublin, 2013), pp 266–8 for a similar phenomenon in west and south Offaly of members of the Gaelic elite changing into English-style landlords. Seemingly, one manifestation of this change was to build and live in fortified houses. **7** R. Higham and P. Barker, *Hen Domen, Montgomery: a timber castle on the English-Welsh border: a final report* (Exeter, 2000). **8** C.J. Lynn, 'The excavation of Rathmullan, a raised rath and motte in Co. Down', *Ulster Journal of Archaeology*, 44–5 (1981–2), pp 65–171. **9** See chapter 7; see, also, chapter 8. **10** See chapter 7. **11** See chapter 8. **12** Ibid.

much in the way of defences, although it is a bit large in size to have been a ringfort.[13] In fact, little can be said about this enclosure at present, other than that it surely indicates that the later masonry castle was built on open, farmed ground. If truth be told, the exact function of this earlier enclosure remains a conundrum and this is clearly a major question for future research at the site.

THE SECOND PHASE OF ACTIVITY AT MOYGARA: THE TOWER HOUSE

One question asked at the start of the Moygara Castle Research and Conservation Project in 2005 was who built the castle at Moygara? However, in light of the fact that there seems to be three major construction phases visible in the masonry at Moygara, this question quickly changed somewhat to who built the first masonry castle at the site, when did this happen and what form did it take?

The detailed architectural survey of the standing remains at Moygara Castle undertaken in 2005 and 2006 suggested that the externally visible north wall of the rectangular platform on the northern side of the bawn was clearly the earliest masonry phase of building on the site.[14] In turn, this indicated that the remains of the earliest stone castle at Moygara lay within this rectangular platform. The later excavation at the site, which took place over short periods between 2013 and 2017, clearly indicated that this early castle was in fact a tower house – one that had been deliberately demolished at a much later date to form the rectangular platform, which, as stated, can be seen today as a prominent feature on the northern side of the later bawn.[15]

The tower house was clearly the most common form of castle built across late medieval Ireland, with at least three thousand constructed across the country, mainly in rural areas but also in towns, starting in the second half of the fourteenth century with the last ones being built in the 1640s. However, the consensus is that most tower houses in Ireland date to the fifteenth and sixteenth centuries. They were mainly constructed by the Gaelic and gaelicized elite, who ranged in rank from noblemen to minor gentry, but were also erected and occupied by the gentry of the Pale around Dublin, urban merchants and, from the later sixteenth century onwards, some New English settlers and officials. The principal element of this type of castle was a tall, defensible, rectangular tower, which was anything up to five storeys in height and, so, dominated its local landscape. Tower houses often stood within stone-walled, defended enclosures known as bawns. Some bawns, however, were defined by wooden palisades or even thick hedges, presumably of prickly blackthorn or hawthorn. Agricultural, residential, public and administrative buildings, mostly built of timber (including

---

13 Ibid. Read does briefly wonder in his chapter if this enclosure is the truncated remains of what was once a more substantial earthwork, largely levelled during the building of the later stone castle, albeit at the time of writing the available evidence does not really support this view.   **14** See chapter 4.   **15** See chapter 8.

post-and-wattle) or possibly cob, lay within these bawns. It would appear, however, that some tower houses never had bawns and this meant that their adjacent ancillary buildings did not lie within a defended enclosure. Tower houses were primarily the defended homes (and, in rural areas where they were the most common, estate centres) of the upper echelons of society in late medieval Ireland, but it must be emphasized that they were not designed to withstand full-scale attack and siege by large bodies of men. Instead, tower houses and their bawns provided adequate defence, if needed, for their occupants against the low intensity warfare of feuding, succession disputes and cattle raiding that was quite common in late medieval Ireland and which mostly involved relatively few combatants.[16]

The fact that the original masonry castle built at Moygara, in this second phase of activity at the site, was a tower house is interesting. The orthodox view that has emerged over the years, as just stated, is that anything up to three thousand tower houses were built across late medieval Ireland.[17] The tower house, then, looking at this figure alone, was clearly the most popular type of castle built in Ireland during the whole of the later medieval period. However, using evidence from surviving historical and cartographic sources for castles for which there is little or no surviving visible surface remains today, Barry has even argued that anything up to seven thousand tower houses were built in Ireland by *c.*1600.[18] This is a very large number indeed and is, at first glance, open to question. In this regard, however, research over the last decade in Co. Roscommon, including fieldwork in areas of that county that are literally visible from Moygara, has shown that upon detailed investigation, the sites of historically attested castles, for which little or no evidence exists above ground today, have invariably turned out to be tower houses.[19] The importance of this evidence from Co. Roscommon and the fact that a hitherto-unrecognized tower house has been identified

---

16 For general information on tower houses in Ireland, see, for example, C. Cairns, *Irish tower houses: a Co. Tipperary case study* (Athlone, 1987); T.E. McNeill, *Castles in Ireland: feudal power in a Gaelic world* (London, 1997), pp 201–3; P.D. Sweetman, *The medieval castles of Ireland* (Cork, 1999), pp 137–74; K. O'Conor, 'Castles' in R. Moss (ed.), *Art and architecture of Ireland*, i: *medieval, c.400–c.1600* (Dublin and New Haven, 2014), pp 341–5; R. Sherlock, 'Tower houses' in R. Moss (ed.), *Art and architecture of Ireland*, i: *medieval, c.400–c.1600* (Dublin and New Haven, 2014), pp 354–6; idem, 'The evolution of the Irish tower house, 1400–1650' in R. Oram (ed.), *Tower studies, 1 & 2: 'A house that thieves might knock at'* (Donington, 2015), pp 258–69; O'Keeffe, *Medieval Irish buildings, 1100–1600*, Maynooth Research Guides for Irish Local History, 18 (Dublin, 2015), pp 255–301; idem, *Ireland encastellated*, AD 950–1550: *insular castle-building in its European context* (Dublin, 2021), pp 189–209. For a really detailed study of tower houses, however, see V. McAlister, *The Irish tower house: society, economy and environment, c.1300–1650* (Manchester, 2019). **17** For example, see H. Leask, *Irish castles and castellated houses* (Dundalk, 1941), pp 73, 153; Cairns, *Irish tower houses*, pp 3, 21; T. McNeill, *Castles in Ireland*, p. 210; K. O'Conor, *The archaeology of medieval rural settlement in Ireland* (Dublin, 1998), p. 25. **18** T.B. Barry, 'Rural settlement in Ireland in the Middle Ages: an overview', *Ruralia*, 1 (1996), p. 140. **19** K. O'Conor, 'Castle studies in Ireland: the way forward' in P. Ettel, A.-M. Flambard Héricher and T.E. McNeill (eds), *Château Gaillard*, 23: *bilan desecherches en castellogie* (Caen, 2008), pp 329–32; K. O'Conor and J. Williams, 'Ballinagare Castle, Co. Roscommon' in L. Gibbons and K. O'Conor (eds), *Charles O'Conor of Ballinagare, 1710–91: life and works* (Dublin, 2015), pp 63–4; D. Curley, 'A multi-disciplinary study of lordly centres in the later medieval Uí Chellaig lordship of Uí Maine, *c.*1100–1600 AD' (PhD, NUI Galway, 2022), pp 383–6.

at Moygara is that it adds greater credence to Barry's belief that much larger numbers of tower houses were constructed in late medieval Ireland than was once thought. Certainly, at the very least, this evidence suggests that the traditional estimate of three thousand tower houses being built across the landscape of late medieval Ireland is too low by far.[20] Of course, whatever the exact number of tower houses originally built, be it well over three thousand or even as much as seven thousand, Ireland was clearly one of the most castellated parts of Europe by the late sixteenth century. Furthermore, within the lordship of Coolavin, this evidence may suggest that the two other historically attested O'Gara castles at Cuppanagh and on Derrymore Island out on Lough Gara were, in all probability, originally tower houses. The tower house at Moygara was, of course, the primary castle and centre (*ceann aitt*) of the O'Gara lordship. The fact that the New English governor of Connacht stayed at Moygara in 1586 suggests that the tower house and its ancillary buildings provided at the very least adequate, but probably comfortable, accommodation by the standards of the time.

What do such numbers tell us about the nature of society in late medieval Ireland, particularly during the fifteenth and sixteenth centuries, when most tower houses were built across the island? Traditionally scholarship has viewed the widespread building of tower houses across Ireland in these two centuries as primarily a reaction to endemic raiding, feuding and lawlessness. Yet the building of a tower house was costly and it has been suggested that perhaps the level of threat to the occupants of tower houses has been exaggerated and that, in fact, the erection of large numbers of these towers during this period is a clear indication of wealth, prosperity and social mobility on the island at this time.[21] Certainly, prior to the wars of the Tudor Reconquest, there is evidence for prosperity across Ireland during the fifteenth century and in the first half of the next century, although sometimes this is not evident in the surviving documentary sources, particularly those pertaining to Gaelic and gaelicized Ireland during these 150 or so years. Magnificent new friaries were built in large numbers across the country. Older friaries, monasteries and parish churches were rebuilt on a grand scale too.[22] The interiors of these buildings were filled with wall paintings, carvings, wooden sculptures and elaborate mural tombs. Great literary works were written during this period and intellectual life thrived too. These are all indications of prosperity and a resurgence of confidence, particularly in Gaelic and gaelicized parts of the country, which covered most of the island at this time. We can imagine that the tall tower house at Moygara, surrounded by wooden agricultural and public buildings, with its own watermill about 0.5km to its west, set within mixed farmland (which produced cattle in abundance and at least some grain),[23] would have been a picture of

---

20 McAlister, *The Irish tower house*, p. 12.   21 McNeill, *Castles in Ireland*, pp 225–7; O'Keeffe, *Ireland encastellated, AD950–1550*, p. 209; see, also, McAlister, *The Irish tower house*, passim.   22 See, for example, H. Leask, *Irish churches and monastic buildings* (Dundalk, 1960), vol. 3.   23 See appendix 1, especially the entries for the quarters of Carrowcaslan, Kilnaskorny (these two quarters are incorporated into the modern townland of Moygara), Mahanagh and Mullaghroe, for the agricultural potential of the demesne lands associated with

prosperity in its heyday. The castle was also visible for kilometres around in certain directions and lay beside a locally important road and was close to a significant regional one. Lough Gara and the Boyle River, which emits from the lake and is a tributary of the great Shannon, occurred just to the east of the tower house and so the castle was seemingly also well connected by water to much of Ireland. A small village seems to have existed to the south-east of the tower house and this nucleated settlement would have housed some of the O'Garas' retainers, which would have included servants and labourers to work lands held in demesne by the castle. A visitor to the tower house at Moygara in ordinary times of peace would have encountered a castle set within a prosperous, ordered and productive landscape. Following on from this, castles during the whole medieval period could also be seen as centres of learning and high culture, at least at a local level. The pardons in 1604 at the end of the bloody Nine Years War give a good indication of the type of men employed and patronized by a middle-ranking late medieval Gaelic or gaelicized lord, such as Irriel O'Gara. Leaving aside labourers, servants and fighting men, the latter's household included at least four or five 'gentlemen' (presumably Irriel's sons and relatives), two harpers, a poet, a friar and a doctor.[24] Musical performances on the harp, bardic poetry recitations and presumably at least some intellectual discussion took place on a regular basis within the hall of the tower house at Moygara – table talk there must have been stimulating. Perhaps such cultural influences played a role in Fergal O'Gara's formation, making him appreciative from childhood of the value of native learning in its widest sense, and, so, may partly explain why he became a patron of the Annals of the Four Masters in the 1630s.[25]

It has been fashionable since the 1990s to dwell on the more peaceful functions of castles, partly as a reaction to the purely military interpretations of castle architecture and function taken by most prominent scholars over the course of the twentieth century (many of whom had served in uniform over two world wars and had experiences which, to be fair, may have pre-disposed them to hold such views). In turn, this has led to a much greater understanding of the various roles played by castles across medieval Europe. Nevertheless, it is possible that at times this has led to a tendency to downplay the fact that on occasion, even regularly in some frontier areas, castles were actually attacked and that the defensive features seen on them were needed at times.[26] The various surviving documentary sources, in particular the annals, do show relatively continuous unrest in north or Lower Connacht during the fifteenth and sixteenth centuries, prior to the bloody Nine Years War (1593–1603) and wars of the seventeenth century, which could be described as almost genocidal in the 1640s and early 1650s. Again, in most cases during the fifteenth and sixteenth centuries,

Moygara Castle.   **24** See chapter 2.   **25** See B. Cunningham, *The Annals of the Four Masters: Irish history, kingship and society in the early seventeenth century* (Dublin, 2010), pp 295–8, concerning Fergal O'Gara's role as a patron of these annals.   **26** See O'Conor, 'Castle studies in Ireland: the way forward', pp 333–5.

prior to the last decades of the latter century, this unrest was not outright war involving large bodies of troops. Indeed, if attacked by a clearly superior force during this period, one option for their owners was to abandon their tower houses. These lords then used the wilder parts of their lordships' landscape to hide their precious cattle and non-combatants. This left them free to use the natural landscape itself as a tool in territorial defence against superior forces.[27] The other option was, of course, for lords to surrender on terms. As stated, tower houses were really only a protection against attacks by relatively small bodies of men involved in raiding and feuding. At times tower houses were attacked, even taken, in such low-intensity warfare. The first actual mention of Moygara Castle occurs during an O'Donnell raid in 1538 and the tower house seems to have been taken at this time, albeit temporarily. The next surviving reference to Moygara comes in 1581 when the castle was taken and burnt by Scots mercenaries.[28] The stones on the external face of the tower house bear evidence to this day of having been exposed to extreme heat.[29] This may have been caused either by the historically attested sackings of the castle in 1538 or 1581, or by an unrecorded attack. This discussion shows that at times the defences of tower houses were needed and on occasion tested. The defences of tower houses in late medieval Ireland were not just there for show but at times were very necessary.

How do we reconcile this evidence for raiding, sackings and burnings of tower houses like Moygara and the obvious prosperity (evidenced more by archaeological remains than by surviving documentary sources) and even high culture seen in late medieval Gaelic and gaelicized Ireland? In order to do this, perhaps, we may have to leave behind our early twenty-first-century Western sensibilities and core beliefs, which see peace and the rule of law applied by centralized democratic governments as absolutely necessary and a prerequisite for prosperity, societal development and cultural achievement. We must remember, to quote the English novelist L.P. Hartley, that 'the past is a foreign country: they do things differently there'. The evidence from places like Moygara and the lifeways of septs like the O'Garas indicate that prosperity and cultural achievement did exist within a society where there was persistent relatively low-level violence at both local and national levels.

By the fifteenth century, if not even earlier, it is very clear over most of Ireland that the Gaelic Irish elite and a majority of the descendants of Anglo-Norman lords, who had first arrived in the late twelfth century, had merged culturally, due to close proximity to one another in many areas and, of course, intermarriage, since 1169. This is traditionally seen as men of Anglo-Norman descent adopting Gaelic culture and becoming 'more Irish than the Irish themselves'. However, the adoption of tower houses as defended residences by many (but by no means all) members of the Gaelic elite from, say, *c.*1400 onwards, perhaps a bit earlier, is a reminder that cultural change

27 O'Conor, *The archaeology of medieval rural settlement in Ireland*, pp 97–103.   **28** See chapter 2.   **29** See chapter 9.

also affected the native Irish themselves.[30] Tower houses were really the first time the Gaelic elite started to build in large numbers what modern scholars accept as masonry castles. While there are some examples of Gaelic-built stone castles erected prior to *c.*1400, they were never particularly common.[31] The historical and architectural evidence really does suggest that most masonry castles, particularly the larger and more complex ones of late twelfth- to early fourteenth-century date, were built by Anglo-Norman lords. The relatively widespread building of tower houses in Gaelic lordships like Coolavin after 1400 or so, therefore, was really the first major physical reflection in a secular context of the cultural uniformity that prevailed across most of Ireland by the fifteenth century.[32] The tower house is really the first secular settlement form to show clearly and in a major way this fusion of cultures and ideas in late medieval Ireland. It should be emphasized that this process of cultural mingling was extremely important for the development of society on this island and the formation of the modern Irish nation. Arguably, however, the importance of this phenomenon of widespread tower house building can be blurred somewhat by an over-emphasis at times on finding individual examples of earlier Gaelic-built masonry castles or even timber castles. It is important, therefore, to recognize and keep in mind that this shift to widespread masonry castle building by members of the Gaelic elite after *c.*1400 was very significant.

The precise spur to this relatively widespread adoption of the tower house by many members of the Gaelic elite is not fully understood as yet. Intermarriage between groups has been a reason for cross-cultural exchange since time immemorial. In this respect, while Gaelic women married Anglo-Norman men right from the late twelfth century onwards, it is noticeable, for example, from the O'Conor, MacDermot and O'Kelly genealogies that women of ultimately Anglo-Norman lineage, particularly Burkes, only began to marry Irish lords from around the mid-fourteenth century onwards.[33] The progeny of these unions were perhaps a bit more open than their patrilineal forebears, even their fathers, to adopting ideas such as the widespread (rather than the occasional) building of and living in masonry castles, which had been popular in Anglo-Norman-dominated parts of Ireland from the late twelfth century onwards. Such men may have been among the first Gaelic lords to build tower houses.

---

30 For example, see McNeill, *Castles in Ireland*, p. 227; O'Conor, *The archaeology of medieval rural settlement in Ireland*, pp 102–4; Colin Breen, *The Gaelic lordship of the O'Sullivan Beare: a landscape cultural history* (Dublin, 2005), p. 84.   31 For example, McNeill, *Castles in Ireland*, pp 157–64: See, also, O'Keeffe, *Ireland encastellated*, pp 17–20 for the *possible* identification of a pre-Norman masonry castle at Lotteragh, Co. Limerick. However, this pre-1169 date for the primary masonry phase at this site still needs to be proved, possibly by excavation or, more cheaply and quickly, by getting radiocarbon dates from 'lime lumps' or bits of charcoal trapped within the mortar of this rather simple enclosure. The former material might be better for dating the period when this fortification was first built – see chapter 9. See, also, the discussion on pre-tower house Gaelic elite settlement in K. O'Conor, 'Gaelic lordly settlement in 13th- and 14th-century Ireland' in I. Holm, S. Innselet and I. Øye (eds), '*Utmark': the outfield as industry and ideology in the Iron Age and the Middle Ages* (Bergen, 2005), pp 209–21; K.O'Conor, 'Settlement in Gaelic Ireland, 1100–1350', *Eolas: the Journal of the American Society of Irish Medieval Studies*, 13 (2021), pp 43–71.   32 Cairns, *Irish tower houses*, p. 9; O'Conor, *The archaeology of medieval rural*

This leads to the question of when the tower house at Moygara was actually built. Unlike history, archaeology rarely gives exact dates in terms of calendar years. However, using a combination of evidence gleaned from radiocarbon dating, the excavation of the site and the historical sources, it is possible to come up with a general date for the erection of this tower house, despite the fact that there is no surviving direct reference to when the castle was first constructed.

At a very early stage in the research, it was realized that the first reference to the existence of a castle at Moygara occurs in 1538, as has been noted in this volume on a number of occasions already.[34] Looking at the overall evidence from the site this was taken to mean, right from the start of the research project, that a masonry castle existed at the site by the late 1530s, having been built at some earlier unknown date. Although Read's later excavation at the site was small in scale, its results were very important. As stated, one of its major conclusions was that this 'first' masonry castle at Moygara was, in fact, a tower house. This evidence was important as, a few years prior to the excavation, one of the calibrated radiocarbon dates taken from a sample of charcoal from within this building (then unidentified) produced a remarkably early date, suggesting, if it was taken at face value, that this structure could have been built in either the late thirteenth or early fourteenth century. The other calibrated radiocarbon date from another sample of charcoal in the mortar from the tower house, produced a slightly later but still very early date.[35] Given the dimensions of the rectangular platform on the northern side of the site, within which this clearly earlier building lies, and given these two early radiocarbon dates, it was wondered initially if this 'first castle' was, in fact, a hall house of later thirteenth- or early fourteenth-century date, similar to the mid-thirteenth century example seen today at Temple House, Co. Sligo, which lies about 15km to the north-west of Moygara.[36] Read's excavation, however, clearly and importantly indicated that this hypothesis from the early years of the project was incorrect and that the first castle at the site was, in fact, a tower house and not a hall house.

It was shown above that Irish scholarship sees the great majority of tower houses, particularly those found in a Gaelic context, as being either fifteenth or sixteenth century in construction date. However, it is also clear that some tower houses date to the fourteenth century. It has even been suggested that the earliest tower houses in

settlement in Ireland, p 103.   **33** C.O. O'Conor (O'Conor Don), *The O'Conors of Connaught* (Dublin, 1891), p. 146; D. Mac Dermot, *Mac Dermot of Moylurg: the story of a Connacht family* (Manorhamilton, 1996), p. 90; Curley, 'A multi-disciplinary study of lordly centres in the later medieval Uí Chellaig lordship of Uí Maine, *c.*1100–1600 AD', p. 382.   **34** See, for example, chapter 2.   **35** See chapter 9, table 9.2.   **36** For the thirteenth-century hall house/chamber-tower at Temple House, see K. O'Conor and P. Naessens, 'Temple House; from Templar castle to New English mansion', in M. Browne and C. Ó Clabaigh (eds), *Soldiers of Christ: the Knights Hospitallers and the Knights Templar in medieval Ireland* (Dublin, 2016), pp 124–50. Another example of this castle type seems to exist at Castlemore/Glebe, near Ballaghaderreen, in modern Co. Roscommon, approximately 12km south-east of Moygara. The existence of these two sites does show that hall houses (or chamber towers, as they are often called) do occur in the general Moygara area.

Ireland date to the early fourteenth century, albeit always in Anglo-Norman contexts.[37] Therefore, these early radiocarbon dates from two charcoal samples in the mortar from the tower-house phase at Moygara Castle beg the obvious question of whether it is possibly an early example of this type of castle, dating to the earlier years of the fourteenth century? Again, the overall evidence suggests that this is not the case and that this structure was erected at a much later date. Why is this so? Firstly, a calibrated radiocarbon date from a cattle ulna found in the ditch fill of the oval enclosure, which, as stated, predates and underlies both the tower house and even later bawn, produced a date in years between *c*.1450 and *c*.1525.[38] Secondly, another radiocarbon date from a 'lime lump' (a particle of unslaked lime) trapped in the mortar of the tower house's basal wall suggested that this structure could date, in terms of its construction, to somewhere between the late fifteenth and early seventeenth century.[39] Looking at the overall evidence, therefore, keeping in mind that a castle was in existence at Moygara by 1538, the tower house at the site was built sometime between the mid-fifteenth century and the 1530s, which is a period that ties in with the evidence for when the construction of tower houses occurred throughout Ireland, but especially in many Gaelic lordships.[40] In fact, a more detailed examination of the calibrated radiocarbon dates from the 'lime lump' in the mortar of the tower house and, perhaps, the cattle ulna in the fill of the oval enclosure's ditch may further suggest a more specific construction date for this primary castle at Moygara in the very last years of the fifteenth century and the early years of the next. In saying this, the general date for the construction of the tower house at Moygara at some stage between the mid-fifteenth century and the late 1530s accords exactly with the accepted dating for the vast majority of tower houses across Ireland. This general date suggests that it was either Eogan O'Gara, lord of Coolavin, who died in 1469, his son Diarmait, who is known to have been alive in 1495 (as he was captured in an O'Donnell raid) or his grandson, another Eogan who died in 1537, who built the tower house at Moygara.[41]

How, then, if the tower house at Moygara dates in terms of its construction to the later fifteenth or early sixteenth century, do we explain the fact that two very early calibrated radiocarbon dates come from charcoal preserved in the mortar taken from the remains of this castle? Bolton, in chapter 9, acknowledges that radiocarbon dating of charcoal and wood fragments trapped in lime mortars used in the construction of medieval buildings of all types can provide accurate dates for the construction of these places, but only if the method is used carefully. This is because there are problems associated with this form of dating and so this method is not without controversy. For example, as Bolton explains, wood may have been used in the firing process for

37 Cairns, *Irish tower houses*, pp 8–10; see, also, T.B. Barry, *The archaeology of medieval Ireland* (London and New York, 1987), pp 186–7. **38** See chapter 8. **39** See chapter 9, table 9.2. **40** In terms of tower house dating, also see R. Sherlock, 'Using new techniques to date old castles', *Archaeology Ireland*, 27 (2013), pp 19–23. **41** See *AConn* under the years 1469, 1495 and 1537; see, also, chapter 6. See MacDermot, *MacDermot of*

making lime mortar that came from the heartwood of an ancient tree, such as a mature oak. In such cases, the charcoal from such wood dates the early years of the much older tree rather than the building that the mortar sample was taken from. Basically, the charcoal from such a tree could give a 'false' date for the construction of the latter building, suggesting wrongly that it was built at a far earlier date than was the actual case. Alternatively, the wood used in the lime mortar-making process could have been salvaged from a much older building than the one in which the mortar was used. Again, the charcoal from such salvaged wood would give a false, inaccurate, too-early date for the latter building. This problem with charcoal-sourced radiocarbon dates from lime mortars is known to scholarship as 'the old wood effect' or, alternatively, 'the old oak effect'.[42] Furthermore, Werner Meyer, the Swiss archaeologist and internationally renowned castle expert, has criticized this dating method of using charcoal or wood fragments trapped in mortars preserved within the walls of medieval stone-built buildings. He has noted the widespread tendency of medieval masons to re-use mortar material from demolished earlier stone buildings in new mortar mixes for later ones. This means that, again, radiocarbon determinations from charcoal found in the mortars of many medieval masonry buildings can give inaccurate, earlier dates than the actual periods in which these sites were erected.[43]

This discussion shows that the dating of medieval buildings solely using radiocarbon dates from charcoal found within the mortar of their walls is fraught with danger. While at times this method provides excellent results,[44] it cannot always be assumed that the charcoal derives from freshly cut wood or that the mortar mix does not contain re-used mortar material from a much earlier building. It suggests that gaining an understanding of the general construction dates of medieval masonry buildings, such as tower houses like Moygara, can only be achieved by weighing up all the available evidence, which includes not only the results from radiocarbon dates but also the information derived from the available historical, archaeological, architectural and cartographic evidence.[45] Caution needs to be taken when solely using radiocarbon dates of charcoal from mortar mixes to date the initial erection of a medieval masonry building or, indeed, subsequent large-scale modifications to the site in question. The overall message is that all the combined evidence for dating needs to be taken into account before assigning a date to the building in question.[46] As noted in this regard,

---

Moylurg, pp 411–15 for a detailed O'Gara genealogy.   **42** See chapter 9.   **43** Meyer, 'Castle archaeology: an introduction', p. 233.   **44** For an example of where this method was used successfully, see F. Beglane, 'Theatre of power: the Anglo-Norman park at Earlspark, Co. Galway, Ireland', *Medieval Archaeology*, 58 (2014), p. 309. **45** See C. Manning, 'The date of the round tower at Clonmacnoise', *Archaeology Ireland*, 11:2 (1997), pp 12–13. **46** I would like to thank Dr Rory Sherlock and Sam Moore for helping me with this critique of the radiocarbon dating of charcoal found in mortar mixes. For the potential problems associated with the radiocarbon dating of charcoal from all archaeological contexts, see P.J. Ashmore, 'Radiocarbon dating: avoiding errors by avoiding mixed samples', *Antiquity*, 73 (1999), pp 124–30; T.S. Daubjerg et al., 'A field guide to mortar sampling for radiocarbon dating', *Archaeometry*, 63:5 (2021), pp 1121–40.

the overall evidence, when pieced together, suggests that the O'Gara tower house at Moygara was built at some stage in the later fifteenth or early sixteenth century. This suggests, therefore, these two charcoal samples taken from the remains of the tower house came from either the heartwood of a mature tree cut down (or which had fallen) at the time of the latter building's erection or from re-used wood or mortar from a much earlier masonry building.

It is unlikely that these charcoal samples come from re-used mortar mixes from an earlier stone building, as prior to the construction of tower houses, few masonry secular buildings existed in Gaelic-dominated parts of later medieval Ireland like Coolavin – houses and fortifications were predominantly made of wood, post-and-wattle or dry-stone walling.[47] It is, of course, possible that these charcoal fragments derived from re-used wood from an earlier timber building taken down at the time it was decided by the O'Garas to erect a tower house at Moygara. However, early cartographic evidence from a late sixteenth-century map and the historical sources suggest that large stands of mature deciduous woodland existed just to the south, east and north-east of the castle.[48] Arguably, it is likely that the two charcoal samples came from the heartwood of a great tree from these woods.[49]

One last question needs to be posed about this phase of activity at the site. Did the tower house have an associated bawn and is there any evidence for it today? It is noteworthy, in this regard, that while the north-western external wall of the tower house does not bond with stonework of the later bawn's curtain wall, this is not the case on this earlier tower's south-eastern edge, as here its stonework seems to blend seamlessly with the latter wall.[50] This may be a hint, no more, that the northern wall of a bawn associated with the tower house, or part of one, was incorporated into the later seventeenth-century bawn wall.[51] However, this is unclear.

THE THIRD PHASE OF ACTIVITY AT MOYGARA: THE HEAVILY FORTIFIED BAWN

The remains of the third episode of activity at Moygara, which saw the second phase of masonry construction at the castle, which is the period of building activity at the site most visible today and the one most visitors to the place associate with it, consists of a square bawn with four substantial, spearhead-shaped flanking towers, one at each corner, and a gateway that originally had a box machicolation over it and a portcullis in its entrance passageway. A myriad of gun loops can be seen today in the curtain

---

47 See, for example, K. O'Conor, 'Housing in later medieval Gaelic Ireland', *Ruralia*, 4 (2002), pp 197–206. 48 See chapter 3, fig. 3.3; see, also, appendix 1. 49 For example, a great storm with extremely high winds hit Ireland in 1477, causing much damage. See *AConn* 1477. 50 I am grateful to Martin Timoney of Keash for pointing this out to me, at a late stage in the research. 51 Future research at Moygara should try to answer the question of whether or not the tower house originally was associated with a bawn – be it constructed of earth-

walls and towers and it is presumed that more existed in the merlons of the now-
destroyed crenellations at battlement level. While this will be discussed further below,
it can be said that the defences of this second phase of building were extremely strong
and up-to-date for the time, making Moygara Castle during this period defensible
against a sustained infantry attack in a way that the earlier tower house was not.[52]

Much energy was expended in this volume on dating this dominant and dramatic
second phase of masonry construction at Moygara Castle. While it was admitted that
this phase of building at the site could have occurred sometime between *c.*1580 and
the mid-seventeenth century, it is felt that the best architectural parallels for it were
bawns erected by New English and Lowland Scots settlers, along with some Gaelic
gentry, across Ulster and north Connacht between *c.*1610 and the very late 1630s.[53]
This all also suggests that the bawn at Moygara could have been built in the 1640s, as
well. For example, it was noted that the stairs' alcoves in the towers at Moygara were
architecturally similar to those seen in the main residential block at Ardtarmon Castle
in north Sligo, which dates to *c.*1640.[54] One initial problem with the dating of this
second phase of masonry building at the site to the period between *c.*1610 and *c.*1640
lay in the fact that, again, early radiocarbon dates came from samples of charcoal
preserved in the mortar of the bawn wall and gatehouse belonging to this period of
construction at Moygara. In fact, two of these calibrated radiocarbon dates, if taken at
face value, suggest that this second phase of mortared stone building could date to the
fifteenth century – far too early a date for the architectural style and features seen in
this phase.[55] Here again, it seems, is evidence of the 'old wood effect'. It would appear
that either heartwood from a mature tree or wooden beams or an old mortar mix from
an older building were used in the mortar-making process for this second phase of
masonry construction at Moygara.

These radiocarbon dates, nonetheless, are interesting because they might be
pointing at evidence for elements of the economy in the Moygara area during the first
half of the seventeenth century. It is just possible that the charcoal that was used to
obtain these dates came from an older building. Read's excavation noted that the tower
house at the site was seemingly taken down in one levelling action to create the
rectangular platform visible today on the northern side of the bawn.[56] It will be
suggested below that this event took place as part of this second phase of construction
at the site. Perhaps the wooden beams or even the old mortar mix from this tower
house were used in the firing process to help create the mortar for this second phase of
masonry building at the site. However, other evidence suggests that this was not the
case. There was a massive expansion of the timber trade in Ireland right from the first
years of the seventeenth century. Woodland throughout the island was cut down for

and-timber or stonework.   **52** See chapters 4 and 5. Visitors to Moygara Castle regularly comment on the strong
defences of this second phase of building at the site.   **53** See chapter 5.   **54** Ibid.   **55** See chapter 9, table 9.2.
56 See chapter 8.

profit. Some of this wood was used in the expanding native iron, leather and barrel-making industries. Timber was exported to Britain and the Continent throughout the seventeenth century on a massive scale to act as the raw material for shipbuilding, house-framing and, again, barrel-making industries.[57] It was said in the 1620s that all French and Spanish wine was placed in casks made of Irish wood.[58] It is quite clear, for example, that Fergal O'Gara, lord of Coolavin, from the 1620s onwards was exploiting the extensive woodlands in the Coolavin area. The profit from this industry added to his significant wealth.[59] In the present context, this must have meant that many mature deciduous trees were cut down in the vicinity of Moygara Castle and it is quite possible that heartwood from some of these old trees was used in the firing for the mortar-making process and that this helps explain the early radiocarbon dates for what is clearly a seventeenth-century phase of stone construction at Moygara Castle.

A more specific date can be postulated for the construction of this dramatic-looking second phase of mortared masonry fortification at Moygara Castle (seen as the third phase of recognizable activity at the site). The 1635 reference to Moygara Castle refers to it as an 'ould' castle.[60] It is highly improbable that this massive and very dramatic second phase of stone building at Moygara Castle, with its up-to-date architectural features and defences, would have been described as old in that year. This reference must be referring to the earlier tower house.[61] Furthermore, at this date, it would appear that the castle had lost its position as the main residence of the O'Garas within Coolavin, as Fergal O'Gara was residing at that time – and apparently had been doing so since at least 1623 or 1624 – in Cuppanagh townland, where there was some form of castle (possibly a tower house) sited within an earlier moated site.[62] The replacement of Moygara Castle by Cuppanagh as the main O'Gara residence at this time is interesting. In terms of its siting, the castle and moated site at Cuppanagh occur right beside the point where the Boyle River exits Lough Gara and then flows past Boyle to join the Shannon. Boats of different sizes and trading activity were common along the whole Shannon system during the sixteenth and seventeenth centuries, as well as during earlier periods.[63] In this regard, rivers were regularly used during the seventeenth century to transport and float timber downstream to markets, industrial sites such as ironworks and seaports.[64] Perhaps the reason why Fergal O'Gara was living at Cuppanagh in the 1620s and 1630s was linked to the movement of commercial timber down the Boyle River.

---

57 E. McCracken, 'The Irish timber trade in the seventeenth-century', *Irish Forestry Journal*, 21:1 (1964), pp 7–20; idem, *The Irish woods since Tudor times* (Dublin, 1971), pp 57–121. **58** McCracken, 'The Irish timber trade in the seventeenth-century', p. 8. **59** See chapter 2; M. O'Dowd, 'Landownership in the Sligo area, 1585–1616' (PhD, UCD, 1978), p. 439. **60** See chapter 2; BL, Harleian MS 2048, Coolavin barony, p. 3. **61** See chapter 2; see, also, chapter 5. **62** See chapter 6; see, also, chapter 2. **63** See K. O'Conor and P. Naessens, 'The medieval harbour beside Rindoon Castle, Co. Roscommon' in P. Ettel, A.-M. Flambard-Héricher and K. O'Conor (eds), *Château Gaillard*, 27: *château et commerce* (Caen, 2016), pp 237–42; H. Murtagh, 'Boating on Lough Ree' in B. Cunningham and H. Murtagh (eds), *Lough Ree: historic lakeland settlement* (Dublin, 2016), pp 200–1. **64** McCracken, 'The Irish timber trade in the seventeenth-century', pp 7–8. The archaeology and

The impression from this discussion is that the tower house at Moygara had lost its primary position as the principal castle within Coolavin by 1635 – it may even have been somewhat dilapidated at this stage. The evidence, therefore, when examining both the historical and architectural evidence, strongly indicates that the bawn in this major second phase of masonry building at Moygara Castle was constructed at some stage after 1635, either in the late 1630s or even into the 1640s. In turn, as argued, this suggests that Fergal O'Gara, as the last lord of Coolavin, was the person who ordered the construction of this massive rebuilding of Moygara, changing its appearance and size so dramatically that the original builders of the tower house there would not have recognized the site.

All visitors to the castle comment on the impressiveness of the bawn's defences, which are extremely strong.[65] A full sixty-seven gun loops can be seen at ground level within the bawn today. These occur in the ground floors of all four flanking towers and along the four sides of the curtain wall.[66] These gun loops covered all approaches to the bawn, as many of them are angled, while others point straight outwards. A close analysis of them indicates that while many occur at chest-height externally, musketeers firing out through them would have had to have been kneeling to fire out at targets that were no more than 3m or 4m away.[67] This was because the interior of the bawn was somewhat higher than the external ground level. Furthermore, the south-western tower stands to its full height today. An analysis of its architecture indicates that the remains of thirty-seven gun loops (or narrow lights that could serve as such) can be seen within it, at ground-, first-, second-floor and battlement levels.[68] It is unclear as yet whether the other towers were built to their full heights.[69] Nevertheless, whatever their original height, these three towers are replete with gun loops at both ground- and first-floor levels.[70] Furthermore, the fact that gun loops can still be seen at battlement level in the south-western tower has other implications.[71] It suggests the strong possibility that the now-destroyed battlements of the bawn's curtain wall, if ever finished, also had gun loops within their merlons, like, for example, the enclosure which surrounds the tower house and later fortified house at Pallas, Co. Galway (Mon. No. GA117-078). Following on, the gatehouse of the bawn at Moygara (while apparently not originally planned for) is also very well defended.[72] Geophysical survey suggests some sort of defensive ditch may have occurred in front of this gatehouse, although this needs to be confirmed by future excavation at the site.[73] The entrance passageway through the gatehouse was defended by a portcullis.[74] Furthermore, like

---

history of riverine trade in Ireland needs to be more fully researched.   **65** See chapter 4.   **66** See chapter 4, fig. 4.1.   **67** Pádraig Lenihan, University of Galway, pers. comm.   **68** See chapter 4, figs 4.1, 4.4–4.6, 4.11. **69** One cheap way to find out whether these three towers were built to the same height as the south-western tower would be to remove, under licence, the build-up of rubble in the ground floors of these buildings and see if architectural fragments that one would expect from battlement levels turn up, such as drip stones.   **70** See chapter 4, figs 4.1, 4.8–4.10.   **71** See chapter 4, figs 4.6, 4.11.   **72** See chapter 4; see, also, chapter 2, fig. 2.10. **73** See chapter 7.   **74** See chapter 4, fig. 4.14.   **75** See chapter 9.

the tower house before it, the bawn walls' external and internal render, apart from weatherproofing the whole structure and protecting the mortar bonding its stones from erosion, added to the site's defensibility by making the walls smooth and unclimbable.[75]

This all clearly indicates that this second phase of mortared masonry building at Moygara Castle was very strongly defended and capable of defence against sustained attack. In fact it was much more of a fortress, primarily built for a military purpose, than an ordinary residential castle. Indeed, a more in-depth analysis of the remains within the castle suggests that it was actually even more defensive than it first appears. The centre of the top of the rectangular platform on the northern edge of the bawn corresponds to a V-shaped notch in the curtain wall (i.e. the part of the bawn's wall that incorporated the northern base of the old tower house's wall). This notch was clearly visible in 1791 and, again, in 1878.[76] It gives the impression of being an original feature and its existence seems to be linked to the creation of the rectangular platform. Read's excavation, as has been partly discussed already, indicated that this platform was seemingly created in a singular event, which saw the tower house deliberately collapsed to its ground-floor level to form this feature. In all, the best way to interpret this evidence is that the platform was formed to carry a cannon, possibly a demi-culverin, or a slightly smaller saker, which fired out through the notch towards the north and north-east of the site. A demi-culverin was capable of firing a ten- to twelve-pound iron shot accurately over 700 yards (*c.*650m), either in a horizontal line or, perhaps a bit more, at elevation. The fact that the cannon sat on a 1.5m high platform may have given it a longer range than normal, particularly if elevated. Demi-culverins and sakers were highly regarded by military commanders from the late sixteenth century onwards for their accuracy and range.[77] The low foundations of a small building, *c.*5.5m by *c.*4m in measurement internally and open to the north and north-east (towards the field, so to speak), can be just about seen on top of the platform today. This indicates that the cannon placed here was protected from the elements, suggesting that it was permanently located on this feature. The cannon's function seems to have been to prevent men forming up for attack in the fields to the north and north-east of the castle. In turn, this suggests that the main threat to Moygara Castle at the time of this great rebuilding during this second phase of masonry construction at the site was seen as coming from this general northerly direction. In all, the platform and the cannon on it must have substantially added to the defensibility of an already militarily strong fortification.

It is worth stressing again that Moygara Castle, after this complete rebuilding of the site at some stage after 1635, having well in excess of a hundred gun loops originally,

---

76 See chapter 1, fig. 1.4, and chapter 2, fig. 2.10.   **77** R. Norton, *The gunner shewing the whole practice of artillery* (London, 1628); Anon., *The compleat gunner in three parts* (London, 1672), p. 4; see, also, C. Henry and B. Delf, *English Civil War artillery, 1642–51* (Oxford, 2005), pp 9–13, 31. I would like to thank Dr Pádraig

a strong gatehouse and evidence for an emplacement for a cannon, was built for war in a way that the earlier tower house was not. So, given this fact, when is the best time between 1635 and, say, the late 1640s for Fergal O'Gara, as the last O'Gara lord of Coolavin, to have ordered the construction of this major re-building of Moygara Castle? What was the reason why he turned an old, perhaps neglected, tower house into a heavily defended fortress? It could be argued that the twenty or so years after 1635, which saw the Confederate Wars, which started with the 1641 rebellion and ended with the Cromwellian conquest in 1653 (low-level guerrilla war, however, was to continue for the rest of the 1650s), were among the most traumatic ever experienced by the Irish people. It has been suggested that anything between 15 per cent and 25 per cent of the population on the island of Ireland had died of disease, starvation and war by 1653.[78]

In 1635 the lord deputy of Ireland, Thomas Wentworth, began legal processes and land evaluations (known as the Strafford Survey) whose aim was to facilitate a plantation of most of Connacht. If such a plantation had gone ahead, this would have meant that Catholic gentry of both Gaelic and Old English stock in the province would have lost at least some of their lands. Indeed, due to legal weaknesses with the titles of Connacht gentry and aristocracy to their estates, a plantation was proposed there by New English officials as early as the 1620s.[79] Quite obviously, this proposed plantation would have caused much disquiet among members of the Connacht gentry, like Fergal O'Gara. The latter was aware of these plans and the fact that his lands had been included in the 1635 survey. Connon, in chapter 2, suggested one possible reason for the transformation of Moygara into a first-rate fortress by O'Gara at this time was worry over the fact that he could lose his lands, or at least some of them.[80] In this scenario, the creation of such a fortification could be viewed as a statement by O'Gara that he was willing to fight to keep his lands and position if confiscations associated with the proposed plantation went ahead. However, this explanation for the major repurposing and remodelling of Moygara Castle, while possible, is somewhat unlikely. Firstly, there is no other evidence in 1635 or the late 1630s for Connacht gentry fortifying their lands to prevent Wentworth's proposed plantation. Secondly, during the 1630s, Fergal O'Gara was very much an establishment figure loyal to Charles I, like most other Gaelic gentry at the time.[81] His survival as one of the richest landowners of Gaelic-Irish stock in Sligo owed much to his cautious and conservative

Lenihan, University of Galway, for providing me with these references.   **78** P. Lenihan, 'War and population, 1649–52', *Irish Economic and Social History*, 24 (1997), pp 1–21; idem, '"That most wasted country"; wartime Roscommon 1641–47' in R. Farrell, K. O'Conor and M. Potter (eds), *Roscommon history and society: interdisciplinary essays on the history of an Irish county* (Dublin, 2018), p. 260; W. Smyth, *Map-making, landscapes and memory: a geography of colonial and early modern Ireland, c.1530–1750* (Cork, 2006), pp 158–61. For an outline of this bloody period in Sligo between the outbreak of the 1641 Rebellion there in December of that year and the end of the Cromwellian War in 1652–3, see M. O'Dowd, *Power, politics and land: early modern Sligo, 1568–1688* (Belfast, 1991), pp 117–30.   **79** For example, see R. Gillespie, *Seventeenth-century Ireland: making Ireland modern* (Dublin, 2006), pp 100–2.   **80** See chapter 2.   **81** For example, see Cunningham, *The Annals*

nature, along with his close conections to the Old English gentry of the county.[82] It is unlikely that Fergal would have made a unilateral decision to build such a well-defended fortress, as it would have been seen by the authorities as a provocation and an act of disloyalty, which could, in turn, have been used against him. Thirdly and most importantly, Connacht's Old English families, in particular the Clanricarde Burkes, successfully resisted Wentworth's proposed plantation by directly lobbying the king and not by incendiary acts like building strong fortifications, such as the one at Moygara. By 1640, when Wentworth was recalled to England, the idea for a plantation of Connacht had evaporated.[83] This evidence strongly suggests, therefore, that this major rebuilding of Moygara by Fergal O'Gara did not take place in the second half of the 1630s, as it would have appeared disloyal. Arguably, it would have been counter-productive and not in his best interests at the time. Indeed, to have done such a thing would have been out of character.

Connon's second suggestion, however, that Fergal O'Gara carried out this major rebuilding at Moygara after 1641 to counter the instability created by the Confederate and Cromwellian Wars, which ended in 1653, has much merit to it.[84] Most of Sligo and Roscommon suffered heavily during these wars, particularly during the period 1641–7. The whole region during the latter years was effectively a violent no-man's land between Protestant settler garrisons in west Ulster (with one also located at Manorhamilton, Co. Leitrim, commanded by the notorious Sir Frederick Hamilton) and the southern two-thirds of the island, which was mostly under the control of the Confederate Irish Catholic forces, whose headquarters lay in Kilkenny city. Small armies, marauders and famine ravaged much of these two counties in particular during these years.[85] Leitrim also saw much fighting during the 1640s.[86] This all gives the impression that what is now north-east Connacht was an extremely unstable place during much of the 1640s and into the 1650s. In these difficult circumstances, it is easy to see why Fergal O'Gara would have quite quickly turned an old, possibly dilapidated tower house at Moygara into a markedly defensive fortification to protect his family, retainers and at least some of his possessions against attacks by Protestant English and Lowland Scots settlers and, later, Parliamentary forces, as well as perhaps by bands of opportunistic freebooters belonging to no side.

Arguably, however, if Fergal O'Gara had just wanted to protect his family and retainers against the instability of the 1640s, he could have upgraded the defences of his by-then main residence at Cuppanagh, where he appears to have been living at the

---

*of the Four Master*s, p. 296.   **82** O'Dowd, *Power, politics and land*, p. 124.   **83** Gillespie, *Seventeenth-century Ireland*, p. 102.   **84** See chapter 2.   **85** Lenihan, '"That much wasted country": wartime Roscommon 1641–47', p. 260; idem, 'War in the Gap, Sligo 1641–91' in K. O'Conor (ed.), *Sligo history and society: interdisciplinary essays on the history of an Irish county* (Dublin, forthcoming). See, also, D. Rooney, 'Sir Frederick Hamilton (1590–1647), Leitrim planter' in L. Kelly and B. Scott (eds), *Leitrim history and society: interdisciplinary essays on the history of an Irish county* (Dublin, 2019), pp 259–78.   **86** B. Scott, 'Seventeenth-century Leitrim: plantation to rebellion' in L. Kelly and B. Scott (eds), *Leitrim history and society: interdisciplinary essays on the history of an Irish*

start of the 1641 rebellion, which seems to have begun in the Sligo area in December of that year. The fact that he did not do this suggests that there were other reasons, other than just personal security, as to why Moygara Castle was substantially rebuilt and turned into a heavily defended fortress by him at this time. Fergal O'Gara, clearly a man of ability, appears to have been a reluctant rebel in 1641 but one nevertheless.[87] The platform on the northern side of the bawn seems to have been created to act as a heightened and protected position for a cannon, which could fire in a general northerly direction. As stated already, this may suggest that the main threat to Moygara at the time came from the north. This seems a reasonable conclusion as, for example, the formidable Sir Frederick Hamilton's garrison in Manorhamilton lay to the north-east in modern Leitrim and he and his men spent much the 1640s raiding and campaigning in the north and mid-Sligo areas, to the north-east of Moygara.[88] The nearest proximate military threat, however, to Fergal O'Gara and Moygara Castle in the early to mid-1640s was the settler garrison at Boyle, which lies about 13km to the east. This garrison, billeted in the old Cistercian abbey there, which had been fortified since the late sixteenth century, was under the command of Robert King and seems to have included mounted men who had the ability to range farther distances than infantrymen.[89] As noted, an important medieval and post-medieval routeway into the whole Sligo area, which branched off in Boyle from another major road, lay just to the north of Moygara Castle.[90] It is possible, therefore, that another reason why Fergal O'Gara converted and transformed Moygara Castle into a strong fortress at this time was to allow it and its garrison to block or harass any movement of enemy troops advancing from Boyle along this important road. Furthermore, patrols from Moygara would have been in a good position to stop mounted foraging and raiding parties from Boyle, and other settler garrisons like Knockvicar or even Manorhamilton, from ravaging the countryside around the castle, thus protecting the lands directly owned by O'Gara. Indeed, Moygara may also have been a secure base from which the rebels themselves could harass and attack Boyle, as there is some evidence that the garrison there was under constant threat from local Irish forces in the early 1640s.[91] It might be added that Boyle and a number of other Protestant settler garrisons in the Roscommon

---

county (Dublin, 2019), pp 284–93.   **87** See chapters 2 and 6. Exactly when Fergal O'Gara became an active rebel is open to question. He does not appear to have taken part in the initial stages of the rebellion but seems to have joined their ranks at some stage in early to mid-1642, as the Catholic Confederation took gradual control of the revolt and the forces involved in it. In early 1643, however, Fergal was named as one of the sixteen prominent Co. Sligo men accused of atrocities and robberies at various stages since the start of the rebellion – O'Dowd, *Power, politics and land*, pp 124–6. See, also, B. Jennings, *Michael Ó Cleirigh, chief of the Four Masters and his associates* (Dublin, 1936), pp 143–4. Despite these accusations, there is also strong evidence that Fergal sheltered and protected Protestant non-combatants during these terrible years – TCD, MS 831, f. 68v.   **88** Lenihan, 'War in the Gap, Sligo 1641–91', passim.   **89** Lenihan, '"That much wasted country": wartime Roscommon 1641–47', pp 260, 266.   **90** See chapter 3.   **91** J. D'Alton, *The history of Ireland, from the earliest period to the year 1245, when the Annals of Boyle, which are adopted and embodied as the running text authority terminate: with a brief essay on the native annalists, and other sources for illustrating Ireland, and full historical notices of the barony of Boyle*

area, including Tulsk, Elphin, Castle Coote and Jamestown, were captured in August 1645 by a combined Royalist-Catholic Confederate army under the command of Theobald, Viscount Taaffe.[92] This may have eliminated the immediate and nearest threat to Moygara. Nevertheless, the whole region to the north of the castle was still very much disputed territory and was to remain so, as Protestant garrisons loyal to Parliament were by then dotted throughout Co. Sligo.[93] Taaffe's force was itself heavily defeated outside Sligo in October 1645.[94]

We can never be fully certain of the exact motives behind the decision by Fergal O'Gara to completely rebuild Moygara Castle and turn it into a heavily defended fortress. As argued, fears for personal security and, perhaps more importantly, strategic reasons may well have influenced him to do this. The main point, however, is that the historical and architectural evidence suggests that the best time to see the construction of this dramatic second phase of masonry construction at Moygara by O'Gara is quite quickly in the aftermath of the start of the 1641 rebellion in the Sligo/Roscommon area, sometime in the early 1640s.

Sculptural evidence from this second phase of mortared masonry building at Moygara Castle is also interesting and informative but has received little academic attention in recent decades. As noted in chapter 2, Canon O'Rorke stated in 1889 that the coat of arms and motto of the O'Garas of Coolavin could be seen broken into pieces, apparently within the main gatehouse of the castle.[95] As stated, as no vestiges of these arms can be seen today, it is possible (but not certain) that O'Rorke mistook the carving of what seems to be a copulating couple extant today on a stone in the passageway of the gatehouse for the arms of the O'Garas.[96] It might be added that O'Rorke made another statement about the architecture of Moygara Castle that also seems to be erroneous. He states quite categorically that there was a tower in the centre of the bawn's eastern wall.[97] There is absolutely no indication of this tower today in the eastern wall of the bawn, nor on the external ground surface in front of it. Most importantly, the plan of the site on the first-edition six-inch Ordnance Survey map for the area, which dates to the late 1830s, depicts the bawn's corner towers, the gatehouse and the northern platform. There is no indication on this map of a central, mural

(Dublin, 1845), p. 249.   **92** Ó Donnchadha, Tadhg (ed.), 'Cin Lae Uí Mhealláin', *Analecta Hibernica*, 3 (1931), p. 35; Lenihan, '"That much wasted country": wartime Roscommon 1641–47', pp 272–3.   **93** Lenihan, '"That much wasted country": wartime Roscommon 1641–47', p. 273.   **94** O Donnchadha (ed), 'Cin Lae Uí Mhealláin', p. 35.   **95** T. O'Rorke, *The history of Sligo*, 2 vols (Dublin, 1889), ii, p. 365.   **96** See chapter 2. **97** O'Rorke, *The history of Sligo*, ii, p. 365. However, in his brief account of Moygara Castle, O'Rorke outlined the local folklore concerning the castle. He stated that a tree in the bawn's south-eastern tower grew from the shoot of another tree from which the O'Garas hanged criminals and that the north-western tower had once housed a nun or nuns, presumably in Penal times or just after the closure of the monasteries in the area during the later sixteenth or seventeenth century. It might be added that evidence within O'Rorke's account of Moygara Castle hints that at least some, if not many, locals in the vicinity were Irish-speaking in the 1880s (ibid., p. 366). Obviously the area is firmly English-speaking today but it is clear that the folklore concerning the castle outlined by him in his 1889 book is still very much extant locally at present.

tower in the eastern curtain wall of the site.[98] This suggests that one never existed. Why, then, did O'Rorke state there was a central tower along this side of the bawn wall? Today a 2m-wide gap occurs in the centre of the wall here[99] – presumably this was knocked out at some stage in the past to allow cattle and sheep graze within the interior of the bawn, long after it was deserted. It is possible that the reason why this part of the wall was chosen to knock through was due to the fact that an opening in the form of a postern gate existed here originally. A postern is a door or small gate, secondary to the main gatehouse, within a fortification such as a castle. Such a door or gate often acted as a sally port during a siege, allowing the besieged to launch a surprise attack on the besiegers.[100] For example, a small postern gate (possibly no larger than a doorway) with a box machicolation over and covering it can be seen in the bawn of Kilcolgan More Castle, Co. Offaly, which apparently dates to the late 1640s.[101] Perhaps something similar occurred at Moygara Castle and O'Rorke, during his visit to the site in the late 1880s, misinterpreted the postern and machicolation over it at battlement level for a mural tower. This interpretation certainly helps explain the divergence between O'Rorke's description of this part of the bawn and the very different evidence from the first-edition six-inch Ordnance Survey map for the area and what can be seen on the ground today.

The rough carving of a copulating couple that can be seen today on the ground right beside the gatehouse occurs on a stone that possibly functioned as one of the corbels that supported the now-collapsed machicolation over the bawn's gate.[102] The main point in assessing the function and importance of this carving is that it was originally located in the gatehouse facing outwards. This feature (copulating couples such as this are referred to as being in the X-position) has previously been recorded as an exhibitionist sculpture in relief and put in the same category as the mostly late medieval figurative carvings known as Sheela-na-Gigs.[103] Carvings like this are invariably located at entranceways to buildings, such as churches or castles, beside doorways or windows, at corners or, often, on gatehouses, such as the one on the western side of the bawn at Moygara.[104] Indeed, the nearest analogy to the Moygara carving is the relatively famous 'evil eye' stone, built on its side, which is to be seen in the late fifteenth- or early sixteenth-century gatehouse at Kilkea Castle, Co. Kildare. This carving depicts a man copulating in an X-position with a semi-human creature, who has the head of a dog or wolf, among other things (fig. 10.1).[105]

98 See chapter 3.   **99** See chapter 4, fig. 4.1.   **100** For example, see J.R. Kenyon, *Medieval fortifications* (Leicester and London, 1990), pp 71, 211.   **101** J. Lyttleton, *The Jacobean Plantations in seventeenth-century Offaly* (Dublin, 2013), p. 143.   **102** See chapter 2, fig. 2.9 and chapter 4, fig. 4.15.   **103** W.F. Wakeman, 'The church on White Island, Lough Erne, parish of Magherculmoney, county of Fermanagh', *JRSAI*, 15 (1879–82), p. 282; E. Guest, 'Irish Sheela-na-Gigs in 1935', *JRSAI*, 66 (1936), pp 111, 124.   **104** R. Moss, 'Exhibitionist figures' in Rachel Moss (ed.), *Art and architecture of Ireland*, i: *medieval, c.400–c.1600* (Dublin and New Haven, 2014), p. 77. For a comprehensive review of the whole phenomenon of Sheela-na-Gig sculpture in Ireland, see E.P. Kelly, *Sheela-na-Gigs: origins and functions* (Dublin, 1996).   **105** I would like to thank Dr Rachel Moss for bringing this carving at Kilkea Castle to my attention and for giving me her valued opinion on the Moygara Castle carving.

10.1 The carving in the gatehouse at Kilkea Castle, Co. Kildare (photograph by Rachel Moss).

The mainstream consensus about Sheela-na-Gigs and variants of this sculptural genre, such as the carvings at Kilkea Castle and Moygara Castle, is that they had a talismanic purpose. They were created to avert evil influences and bad luck from entering the buildings or fortifications in which they were placed.[106] They were, in effect, a form of defence but of the supernatural kind. The fact that this carving at Moygara had an apotropaic function is interesting, given that a quernstone may have been deposited in the entrance area of the earlier tower house at the site for a similar reason.[107] Both the carving of the copulating couple and the quernstone perhaps provide an insight into the folk beliefs of the O'Garas from late medieval times into the middle years of the seventeenth century. In fact, most Sheela-na-Gigs in Ireland date to the fifteenth and sixteenth centuries, being mainly associated with tower houses when found in a secular context.[108] This evidence may suggest that the carving was originally created for and placed in the earlier tower house at Moygara, before being moved to the gatehouse in the early 1640s when the former building was largely levelled to create a platform for some form of cannon.

It is clear that by *c.*1630 the Catholic Church in Ireland was beginning to disapprove of these carvings, as an order went out from the Synod of Tuam in 1631 to

106 Moss, 'Exhibitionist figures', p. 77.   **107** See chapter 8.   **108** Moss, 'Exhibitionist figures', p. 77.

take down and then bury these images.[109] The fact that Fergal O'Gara chose in the first years of the 1640s to place one of these traditional carvings in the gatehouse of a state-of-the-art fortification at Moygara is arguably a metaphor for his life and career. This action is perhaps further proof of Connon's point that O'Gara was more than able to straddle and operate in both the Gaelic and New English worlds.[110] He comes across today, almost four centuries later, as a man aware and proud of his ancient heritage but, also, well able to operate within an English milieu. As a cultured man, educated in both Gaelic and New English fashions, he was capable of adopting new ideas but maintained a respect for older ways too.

THE FOURTH PHASE OF ACTIVITY AT MOYGARA CASTLE: THE RECTANGULAR HOUSE IN THE SOUTH-WESTERN CORNER OF THE BAWN

Fergal O'Gara, as a Catholic landowner and participant in the wars of the 1641–53 period, had his lands in Coolavin presumably confiscated by the Cromwellian authorities during the 1650s. Attempts by him and other Catholic landowners in 1664 during the Restoration period to have their lands restored failed abjectly. The available evidence, such as it is, suggests he became a tenant of his wife's Taaffe relatives and resided in Ardconnell townland, near Ballymote, which lay about 14km north of Moygara Castle.[111] O'Gara appears to have lived there until his death, which may have occurred in the late 1660s (he was about 68 in 1664) or just possibly the early to mid-1670s. O'Gara must have been devastated by the loss of his ancestral lands in Coolavin. The territory had been controlled by his family since the early medieval period and the O'Garas had actually resided there since at least the thirteenth century.[112] While O'Gara lost much of his status, wealth and power due to the Cromwellian confiscations, it must not be presumed that he and his family sunk into abject poverty after this event. It is probably safe to presume that his wife's Taaffe relatives gave O'Gara a good tenancy. Men like O'Gara and his son John were educated men of ability with strong contacts, including ones of blood, across the agricultural, business and trading world of north-west Ireland. It is highly possible that after the Restoration, in the period of peace that followed, a level of prosperity was achieved by the O'Garas at Ardconnell, despite the loss of their Coolavin lands. For example, Fergal O'Gara's grandson, Colonel Oliver O'Gara (whose mother was an O'Conor of Ballinagare), commanded a regiment of infantry in the Jacobite army during the Williamite War of 1689–91.[113] Oliver's relatively high rank in James I's army suggests he had originally received a proficient military education, arguably paid for by profits made from the rented Ardconnell lands and perhaps other financial supports given to him by his close Taaffe and O'Conor relatives.

---

109 Ibid.   **110** See chapter 2.   **111** See chapter 6.   **112** See chapter 2.   **113** See chapter 6.

Three of Colonel O'Gara's sons had successful military careers as officers in the armies of France and Spain – something denied them at home in Ireland or Britain because of their Catholic religion and the discriminatory Penal Laws.[114] His fourth son, Count Charles O'Gara, reached high office in the service of the dukes of Lorraine and the Hapsburgs.[115] He was clearly a very capable man, even more successful than his soldier brothers. Catholic emigres of ability, like the O'Gara brothers, were an immense loss to Ireland from 1691 onwards and throughout much of the eighteenth century. The energy and drive of thousands of such men were lost to the island and benefitted other countries instead during these long years. This was a great pity – even a tragedy – for Ireland.

Count O'Gara died as late as 1777, a very wealthy man, and despite his family having lost control of Coolavin about 120 or so years beforehand, he left money from the sale of his clothes to be distributed among the poor of that half-barony.[116] There is something poignant and generous about this act. Despite being born at St Germain in France (his godfather being no less than the deposed James II), O'Gara still felt a sense of duty to the poorer inhabitants of his ancestral lands – perhaps an example of *noblesse oblige*. Many others in Ireland and Europe were to benefit from his will, including the antiquarian Charles O'Conor, his second cousin and one of the founders of the Catholic Committee in 1757, who used the money to help save his estate at Ballinagare, Co. Roscommon, from an avaricious younger brother,[117] who tried to claim it by converting to Protestantism and using clauses in the Penal Laws.[118]

What of Moygara Castle during this whole period? The historical evidence clearly implies that the castle had been deserted by the very late 1650s, presumably either abandoned or its garrison forced out at some stage during the course of the Confederate War or, perhaps more likely, as it was not one of the Sligo fortresses mentioned as being in Parliamentary hands in 1646, Fergal O'Gara was forced to leave Moygara because it was taken during the subsequent even bloodier Cromwellian conquest of 1649–53.[119] For example, the 1659 census of Ireland lists no garrison of any sort in Moygara Castle in that year, be it English or Irish, and no gentlemen living within it or anywhere else within the townland. Only ordinary Irish people lived in the townland, presumably working the land, apparently outside the castle.[120] Boyle, by contrast, clearly had a military garrison within it in 1659. The actual town of Boyle in that year had a population of 53 English, including Sir John King and one other gentleman, and 251 Irish. Apart from these townspeople, however, an infantry

114 For example, see É. Ó Ciardha, *Ireland and the Jacobite cause, 1685–1766* (Dublin, 2004) for the experiences of Irish Catholic gentry like the O'Garas in Europe during this whole period. See, also, M. O'Conor, *Military history of the Irish nation; comprising memoirs of the Irish Brigade in the service of France, with an appendix of official papers relative to the Brigade from the archives at Paris* (Dublin, 1845).   **115** See chapter 6.   **116** Ibid.   **117** Ibid.
118 D. Ó Catháin, 'Some account of Charles O'Conor and literacy in Irish in his time' in Luke Gibbons and Kieran O'Conor (eds), *Charles O'Conor of Ballinagare, 1710–91: life and works* (Dublin, 2015), p. 35.   **119** See chapter 2.   **120** *Census of Ireland, 1659*, p. 603; see chapter 2.

company commanded by one Captain Francis King is separately listed as being stationed in the town in that year. Including wives, this garrison consisted of 89 English and, interestingly, five Irish. Two junior officers, both English, belonging to this company, are actually named in the census too.[121] The absence of any record or figures like this for Moygara, along with the fact, mentioned above, that Fergal O'Gara's lands in Coolavin had been confiscated by 1659, with the country well under the control of the English at the time, suggests that Moygara Castle no longer functioned as a military fortress or even a gentleman's residence by the later 1650s.

One interpretation is that the castle lay deserted until the start of the Williamite War in 1689, when a Jacobite garrison was installed there for the war, which lasted until 1691. It was called at this time a place of 'considerable strength', which it surely was, even at this stage when its defences may have been in a decayed state.[122] Presumably its defences and existing buildings were repaired at this time. There are even hints from the historical sources that after the war, a Williamite garrison commanded by an Irish Catholic ex-Jacobite officer was installed for a time at Moygara Castle, with the place being abandoned as a government fortress in the early eighteenth century, if not earlier around 1700, as the country became more peaceful.[123] It was shown that the foundations of a one- or possibly two-storey rectangular building, which has a large ground-floor fireplace within it, can be seen on the south-western interior of the castle, abutting the flanking tower there. One interpretation of this building, whose masonry is not bonded into the curtain wall of the bawn and blocks at least one gun loop, meaning that it is later in date than the main architectural remains at the site, is that it was erected to provide extra accommodation for the garrison that was stationed here from 1689 onwards.[124] This rectangular building, therefore, while indicating a fourth phase of activity at the site, represents a third phase of masonry construction visible in the remains of Moygara Castle today.

There is another interpretation to explain this third phase of masonry building at Moygara. With its clay-bonded walls and large fireplace, there is nothing distinctly military about this later rectangular building in the bawn's south-west corner. Indeed, one of its walls blocks a gun loop, meaning that its construction took away from the defensive strength of the bawn, if only slightly. In this respect, at the start of the Williamite War in 1689, we hear that the Jacobites expelled the pro-Williamite Lord Kingston's tenants from the castle. The latter had been granted most of the old O'Gara holdings in Coolavin in the 1650s after they had been confiscated from Fergal O'Gara.[125] This can, of course, be taken as meaning that the mainly Irish Catholic Jacobites threw out some of Kingston's tenantry who had taken refuge in the deserted Moygara Castle as a protection against the instability and chaos seen at the beginning

---

121 *Census of Ireland, 1659*, p. 585.   **122** See chapter 2.   **123** Ibid.   **124** See chapter 4; see, also, chapter 8.
125 M. Ó Duigeannáin, 'Three seventeenth-century Connacht documents', *JGAHS*, 17 (1936–7), p. 154; see chapter 2.

of the war. However, alternatively, the original reference can also be better interpreted, when viewed, as meaning that these tenants of Lord Kingston, whether Catholic Irish or Protestant English (but probably the latter), had been put out of their own house within the castle. This may suggest that the later rectangular house in the south-west corner of the bawn, the third identifiable phase of masonry construction at Moygara Castle, was, in fact, a dwelling house erected by a relatively well-to-do tenant of Kingston at some stage prior to 1689, in the relatively peaceful Restoration period of the 1660s to 1680s. In which case, while its defences may have been allowed to decay, simply because they were not needed, Moygara Castle was perhaps not deserted for very long after the end of the Cromwellian War and the later 1650s. Of course, if this interpretation is correct, this existing house would also have greatly added to the accommodation available to the garrisons (both a Jacobite one and, apparently, a Williamite one) that were stationed and billeted in Moygara from 1689 onwards, until the fortification was deserted.

SUMMARY AND CONCLUSIONS

It is hoped that this volume has gone at least some way towards explaining the development through time of the dramatic phenomenon that is Moygara Castle today and that the site gains the prominent place in castle studies that it so richly deserves and, so, is rescued from the obscurity that its relatively remote location has given it in recent times. In summary, the research has indicated four identifiable periods of activity at the Moygara Castle site, with three construction phases visible today in the masonry of the castle. Firstly, a geophysical survey and, then, the later excavation have shown that the later castle was built on top of an oval enclosure, whose edges are defined by a shallow ditch. This primary pre-masonry castle phase represents the first known period of activity at the site. The present writer is hesitant to call this an occupation phase, as the available evidence at this point does not suggest that this enclosure had a defensive or even residential function – it may have been nothing more than a small field, garden or stock enclosure. Nevertheless, only a small proportion of this enclosure was excavated over a short period of time and, perhaps, future excavation at the site may change this interpretation. The second major phase of activity at Moygara saw the construction of a tower house at some stage in the later fifteenth or early sixteenth century. This first castle was the one mentioned in the historical sources in 1538. This tower house functioned as the centre of the middle-ranking O'Gara lordship of Coolavin and, so, was one of the most important places in the landscape of late medieval north or Lower Connacht. Any future excavation at the site should attempt to find evidence for the ancillary, presumably mostly wooden or post-and-wattle, agricultural and administrative buildings that must have existed beside this tall masonry tower. This tower house seems to have lost its importance by the 1620s, as Fergal O'Gara, lord of Coolavin, was living at nearby Cuppanagh, possibly because this latter site was a better location from which to oversee the burgeoning timber industry in the Coolavin area. Indeed, the archaeological complex at the latter site is also worthy of investigation in the future by those interested in continuing research into the O'Gara clan and, in particular, Fergal O'Gara. At some stage after 1635, most likely in the early 1640s, in the chaos created by the 1641 rebellion and the early years of the Confederate Wars, it was argued that Fergal O'Gara completely rebuilt and remodelled Moygara Castle, turning it into a markedly defensive fortification for strategic purposes and, perhaps, for reasons of personal security in this time of war. This third phase of activity at the site saw Moygara transformed into the castle that dominates the site today and so impresses visitors to this part of rural south Sligo. Lastly, the fourth phase of recognizable activity at Moygara Castle saw the building of a rectangular house on the south-western side of the bawn. This house was either built by a tenant of Lord Kingston (the King family of Boyle had been granted most of Fergal O'Gara's lands in the 1650s) during the period from the Restoration of Charles II and the outbreak of the Williamite War in 1689 or by the garrisons who occupied Moygara Castle after the latter year. The best guess is that the castle was abandoned *c.*1700, although this has yet to be fully confirmed by future excavation at the site. After its abandonment, the castle transitioned into the romantic ruin that can be seen today at the site and which lies within farmland owned by the O'Neill family.

What of the future for the splendid ruins that comprise Moygara Castle today? Does it still have a role to play in the attractive countryside along the borderlands between modern Sligo and Roscommon? In this respect, the ongoing conservation works at the castle should soon be finished and the site made safe for visitors. This is important as it is felt by all the contributors to this volume that such a dramatic-looking and beautifully sited castle, with its rich links to the proud O'Gara clan, should play a prominent part in the cultural-tourism product offered in counties Sligo and Roscommon to visitors. Evidence from throughout Europe demonstrates that castles have the highest visitor numbers in comparison to other archaeological monuments, if properly presented to the public. Properly illustrated, well researched information plaques and guidebooks are clearly important in this regard. Furthermore, it is hoped that the greater understanding of Moygara Castle brought about by the inter-disciplinary research carried out at the site since 2005 will be of interest to local people in south Sligo, as well as those living in adjacent areas of north Roscommon, and add to their already strong sense of place and community. Above all, it is wished that children and young people living in the immediate vicinity of the site realize and appreciate the importance of Moygara Castle and, so, help safeguard it during their lifetimes and pass it on intact to future generations.

A listing and description of the land denominations of the half-barony of Coolavin on a parish-by-parish basis as found in sixteenth- to nineteenth-century sources

ANNE CONNON

ABBREVIATIONS

Abbreviations for sources

Inq. 1614 (a)	An inquisition, taken in 1614, into the lands held by Irriel O'Gara at his death in 1613.[1]
Inq. 1614 (b)	Second part of an inquisition, taken in 1614, into the lands held by Irriel O'Gara at his death in 1613; this part enumerates the lands he rented to Sir William Taaffe.[2]
Inq. 1615	A second inquisition, taken in 1615, into the lands held by Irriel O'Gara at his death in 1613, now in the possession of his heir, Fergal O'Gara.[3]
TCD Survey 1617	A seventeenth-century transcript of the 1616 surrender and regrant inquisition of lands in Connacht, organized on a barony-by-barony basis.[4]
Cal. Ir. Pat. Rolls Jas. I	The 1616 surrender and regrant inquisition of lands in Sligo is also found in the *Calendar of Irish patent rolls of James I*, enrolled under the year 1617, pat. 14, Jas I, pp 321–2.[5] This document is very similar to TCD, MS 570 above, but organized according to owner, rather than barony.
1635 Strafford Survey	Notes for the Strafford Survey of Connacht, undertaken between 1633 and 1635, in preparation for a planned plantation of the latter province. The survey is now lost, but detailed notes survive for Co. Sligo in BL, MS Harleian 2048.[6]
BSD pre-1641	The Books of Survey and Distribution (BSD) record landownership before and after the Cromwellian confiscations of the 1650s. They also note the amount of profitable and unprofitable land, as well as the

---

1 NAI, MS R.C. 9/15, Inquisition 17, pp 511–12.   2 NAI, MS R.C. 9/15, Inquisition 17, pp 513–15.   3 NAI, MS R.C. 9/15, Inquisition 19, pp 517–20.   4 TCD, MS 570, folios 34–6. Sir John King's lands are listed at folio 36v; Brian McDonogh's at folio 37r; and Fergal O'Gara's, Brian McDermott's, and the bishop of Achonry's at folio 45v.   5 M.C. Griffiths (ed.), *Calendar of the Irish patent rolls of James I* (Dublin, 1965). The Coolavin lands are mainly recorded on p. 321 (lands belonging to Brian McDonogh and Sir John King) and p. 322 (lands belonging to Fergal O'Gara). References to any other pages in the *Calendar* will be specifically footnoted as such. 6 BL, MS Harleian 2048. See, also, W.G. Wood-Martin, *History of Sligo, county and town, from the earliest ages to*

land type. Occasionally, other details are included as well. Here, 'pre-1641' refers to the owner of the land before the Cromwellian confiscations of the 1650s. The Books are edited and published for Roscommon, Galway, Mayo, and Clare, but the Sligo text exists only in manuscript form.[7]

BSD post-Cromwellian   As above, but recording the landowners after the Cromwellian confiscations in the 1650s.

Petty's map   William Petty's county map of Sligo from his *Hiberniae delineatio: atlas of Ireland* (London, 1685; repr. Newcastle upon Tyne, 1968). This is the most detailed seventeenth-century map available for Coolavin as none of the detailed parish maps Petty drew up are extant for the half-barony.[8] The county map includes many of the townland names seen today.

Census 1659   The 'census' of Ireland undertaken in 1659, listing the number of inhabitants within the country on a parish-by-parish, barony-by-barony, county-by-county basis. A distinction is made between Irish and English, but only the 'titulados' of an area are named.[9]

Hearth Roll 1665   For the purpose of enabling the collection of a tax based on the number of fireplaces owned, this source details the names, townland addresses, and number of hearths of individuals – of both Irish and English extraction – throughout Sligo.[10]

ASE 1678   The Acts of Settlement and Explanation (*ASE*) officially enrolled the lands confiscated during the Cromwellian period into the hands of their new landowners. They correspond very closely to the post-Cromwellian section of the Books of Survey and Distribution.[11]

TFE 1688   After the Williamite War of 1688–91, some further lands were confiscated and sold.[12]

Larkin map 1819   A map of the county of Sligo, by William Larkin: 6 sheets (engraved by S.J. Neele, London, 1819).[13]

TAB 1834   For the purposes of recording tithes owed on each division of land, the *Tithe Applotment Books* (*TAB*) record, on a parish-by-parish basis, the name of each division of land and its acreage. Although compiled in the first half of the nineteenth century, the *Tithe Applotment Books* retain many of the old townland names, frequently giving their modern aliases. They are thus a valuable source for determining modern-day equivalents of now obsolete land divisions.[14]

the close of the reign of Queen Elizabeth (Dublin, 1882), pp 402–5.   **7** NAI, Books of Survey and Distribution: Sligo (microfilm). Killaraght townlands are listed on pp 129–31; Kilcolman townlands on p. 131; and Kilfree townlands on pp 131–2.   **8** See chapter 3, fig. 3.4.   **9** S. Pender (ed.), *A census of Ireland circa 1659, with supplementary material from the poll money ordinances, 1660–1661* (Dublin, 1939), pp 602–3.   **10** E. MacLysaght (ed.), 'Seventeenth century hearth money rolls with full transcript relating to County Sligo', *AH*, 24 (1967), pp 1–89.   **11** See 'Abstracts of grants of lands and other hereditaments, under the Acts of Settlement and Explanation, A.D. 1666–1684', *Record Commissioners Report*, 15 (London, 1825). Sir John King's lands are listed on p. 130, and Bryan Magrath's lands on p. 258.   **12** The records of their new owners are recorded in: 'Abstracts of the conveyances from the trustees of the forfeited estates and interests in Ireland in 1688', *Record Commissioners Report*, 15 (London, 1825), p. 370.   **13** This map in six sheets is available online at logainm.ie under the 'Toponymy Resources' section of the 'Resources' menu.   **14** NAI, Tithe Applotment Books 1834 (microfilm); they are also available to search online at titheapplotmentbooks.nationalarchives.ie.

Other abbreviations

a.	acre
li.	libra (pound)
prof.	profitable land
unprof.	unprofitable land

NOTES ON ORTHOGRAPHICAL CONVENTIONS

Square brackets are used in the appendix to indicate a land denomination which is referred to by a different name by the source in question. This name is sometimes an alias, and sometimes a larger unit within which the land denomination is subsumed.

Round brackets are used to indicate authorial comments.

Boldface type is used to help highlight the name of a land denomination when it occurs within a passage listing multiple denominations.

LAND DENOMINATIONS IN THE PARISH OF KILLARAGHT

Although the *Books of Survey and Distribution* allocate Killaraght to the barony of Coolavin, Petty's maps place it in the barony of Boyle, Co. Roscommon. Its changing jurisdiction between Sligo and Roscommon likely accounts for its omission from many of the early modern sources such as the Strafford Survey and the Sligo Hearth Money Roll.[15]

Annagh

MODERN EQUIVALENT:	Cuppanagh (most likely)
CIVIL PARISH:	Killaraght
TAB 1834	?Annagh: 24 a.
COMMENT:	While there is a townland in Killaraght now known as 'Annagh' (directly east of Portnacrinnaght), that quarter appears to correspond to the townland referred to by early modern sources as 'Annagh-vicknarine' (see below). Since the TAB have separate entries for 'Annaghvicknarine' and 'Annagh', they would appear to be distinct entities. The suggestion that the TAB's 'Annagh' was in Cuppanagh derives from the labelling of the peninsula section of Cuppanagh as 'Annagh' in a map of the townland dating to 1823. Furthermore, the listing for 'Annagh' in TAB directly precedes that of Cuppanagh.

---

15 The Inquisition entries for the Killaraght land denominations in this appendix are limited to lands owned by the O'Gara family at the time the Inquisitions were undertaken. The initial aim of the appendix was to collate information relating specifically to O'Gara lands, rather than to Coolavin lands as a whole. By the time the decision was made to extend the appendix to the entire half-barony, circumstances did not allow for further

Annaghvickanarine

MODERN EQUIVALENT:	Annagh
CIVIL PARISH:	Killaraght
TCD Survey 1617	the cartron of Annaghvickanarine: Bishop of Achonry
BSD pre-1641	Annaghmcannaroe 1 cartron: ffarrell O'Gara
	22 a. prof.
	wast mosse & bog belonging to the same: 19 a. unprof.
BSD post-Cromwellian	Lord Kingston (listed as part of a larger group of lands that included 120 profitable acres)
Petty's map	Anagh (Petty's baronial map of Boyle shows Anagh as part of the Boyle parish of Kilnamanagh rather than of Killaraght)
Acts of Settlement and Explanation 1667	
	Annaghnarrow or Aghnanarrow, 22 a. prof. 19 a. unprof.: John Lord Kingston.
	(Listed within a group of lands collectively worth 17*l* 12s. 1¼d. rent *per annum*.)
TAB 1834	Annaghvicnarow: no acreage given; composition rent: 1.5.11
COMMENT:	The 'vicknanarine' element in the place-name suggests that this land was originally associated with the Augustinian monastery of Inchmacnerin on Church Island, Loch Cé.[16] It does not appear as part of the sixteenth-century possessions of the monastery and, thus, probably came into the possession of the O'Gara family before the dissolution of the monasteries (see note on Carrovickryny in the parish of Kilfree).

Ardgallin

MODERN EQUIVALENT:	Ardgallin
CIVIL PARISH:	Killaraght
BSD pre-1641	Ardgallin 1 qr: Sir Robert King
	199 a. prof. collectively with other 3 qrs (see 'comment' section below)[17]
BSD post-Cromwellian	Lord Kingston
Hearth Roll 1667	Oagly?, William, Ardgallin, Killaraght.[18]
TAB 1834	Ardgallen: 66.1.15 a.
COMMENT:	BSD groups together: 'Carrowenerlare 1 qr; Ardmoile 1 qr; Ardgallin 1 qr and the qr of Lisserlagh'.

Ardgrillin

MODERN EQUIVALENT:	Emlagh (south-east corner)
CIVIL PARISH:	Killaraght
TCD Survey 1617	the qrter of Ardgrillin: Sir John King
Cal. Pat. Rolls Jas. I	Ardgrillin ... 1 qr each: Sir John Kinge
BSD pre-1641	Ardgrilline 1 qr: Sir Robert King

archival work involving the Inquisitions. **16** Gwynn and Hadcock, *Medieval religious houses: Ireland*, p. 179. **17** Ibid. **18** MacLysaght (ed.), 'Seventeenth century hearth money rolls with full transcript relating to County Sligo', p. 77.

47 a. prof.

?Mosse & bogg in common between Ratany and Ardgilline and Lisherlagh: 47 a. unprof.; Sir Robert King/Lord Kingston (this note occurs in BSD after the entry for Ratany (Rathtinaun))

BSD post-Cromwellian	Lord Kingston
Petty's map	Ardgrelin (Boyle baronial map)
TAB 1834	[Emlagh: 52.2.10 a.]
COMMENT:	The Kingston estate map of 1770 locates Ardgrillin in the south-east corner of Emlagh townland. This map was copied from a map dating to 1724.[19]

Ardleg

MODERN EQUIVALENT:	Probably Killaraght
CIVIL PARISH:	Killaraght
BSD pre-1641	Ardleg 1 qr: Sir Robert King
	162 a. prof.
Petty's map	Ardleac (Boyle baronial map)
BSD post-Cromwellian	Lord Kingston
COMMENT:	The position of Ardleg in Petty's map would appear to locate it in the modern townland of Killaraght.

Ardlona

MODERN EQUIVALENT:	Ardlona
CIVIL PARISH:	Killaraght
TCD Survey 1617	the qrter of Ardlona: Sir John King
Cal. Pat. Rolls Jas. I	Ardloana … 1 qr each: Sir John Kinge
BSD pre-1641	Ardlone 1 qr: Sir Robert King
	32 a. unprof.
	Bog between Ardlona & Rossnegree: 22 a. unprof.
	Turffe bogg in common between Lismerane & Ardlone: 30 a. unprof., p. 129
BSD post-Cromwellian	Lord Kingston
Petty's map	Ardlone (Boyle baronial map)
TAB 1834	Ardlona: 79.2 a.

Ardmoyle

MODERN EQUIVALENT:	Ardmoyle
CIVIL PARISH:	Killaraght
TCD Survey 1617	the qrter of Ardmoyle: Sir John King
Cal. Pat. Rolls Jas. I	Ardmoile … 1 qr each: Sir John Kinge
BSD pre-1641	Ardmoile 1 qr: Sir Robert King
	199 a. prof. (collectively with other 3 qrs)
BSD post-Cromwellian	Lord Kingston
Petty's map	Ardmoyle (Boyle baronial map)

19 NLI, MS 21 F 13, no. 39.

TAB 1834	Ardmile: 002.0.26 a.
COMMENT:	BSD groups together: 'Carrowenerlare 1 qr; Ardmoile 1 qr; Ardgallin 1 qr and the qr of Lisserlagh'.

Ardmunekin

MODERN EQUIVALENT:	Probably Ross
CIVIL PARISH:	Killaraght
TCD Survey 1617	the towne and lands of Ardmunneshin, the qrter of Ardmunekin: Brian McDermott
Cal. Pat. Rolls Jas. I	To Bryan McDermott of Carrigg, esq … The town, lands, and qr of Ardmunnechin; the town and lands of Ardsorine or Ardsornie; saving to Owen Grana McRorie, Dermott McRory, and Hugh McQuyn, and their heirs a yearly rent of 10s. 6d. Eng. out of the two qrs of Runepoll.[20]
BSD pre-1641	[Ardsorin & Ardmony 2 qrs: Bryne mcDermott 24 a. unprof., 120 a. prof. Moss in common between Ardmoglis & Rossmale: 33 a. unprof.]
BSD post-Cromwellian	Lord Kingston
TAB 1834	[?Ardsoreen East: 70 a. Ardsoreen West: 122.3 a.]
COMMENT:	The Kingston estate map which is copied in 1770 from a 1724 map shows Ardsoreen as 'Ardmonkin',[21] but the fact that several sources include both Ardmunekin and Ardsoreen indicates that they were originally distinct entities and not aliases for one another. Larkin's nineteenth-century map shows 'Ardmichan' and 'Ardsoran' as two distinct denominations. The grouping of Ardmunekin and Ardsoreen together suggests that the now obsolete denomination of Ardmunekin was absorbed into Ardsoreen; however, the placement of 'Ardmichan' on Larkin's map indicates that the present-day townland of Ross may be the most likely location.

Ardsallagh

MODERN EQUIVALENT:	Probably Reask (or possibly western part of Killaraght?)
CIVIL PARISH:	Killaraght
TCD Survey 1617	the towne and lande of Ardsallagh, the qrter of Ardsallagh: Sir John King
Cal. Pat. Rolls Jas. I	Ardsallagh: Sir John Kinge
BSD pre-1641	Ardsallagh 1 qr: Sir Robert King 82 a. prof. (After the entry for Lismerrane) Bogg in common with Ardsallagh 26 a. unprof.
BSD post-Cromwellian	Lord Kingston
Petty's map	Ardsalla (Boyle baronial map)
TAB 1834	(Not in TAB as 'Ardsallagh' *per se*) [Reesk: 101.2.25 a.]

---

20 Griffiths (ed.), *Calendar of the Irish patent rolls of James I*, p. 332.   **21** NLI, MS 21 F 13, no. 39.

COMMENT: The placement of 'Ardsalla' in Petty's map suggests that it corresponds either to Reask or to the north-west section of Killaraght. Since BSD notes that Ardsallagh was said to have shared a bog with Lismerraun, Reask seems the most likely of the two.

Ardsorin

MODERN EQUIVALENT: Ardsoreen
CIVIL PARISH: Killaraght
TCD Survey 1617   the towne and lands of Ardsorin, and the qrter of Ardsorin
Cal. Pat. Rolls Jas. I   To Bryan McDermott of Carrigg, esq … The town, lands, and qr of Ardmunnechin; the town and lands of Ardsorine or Ardsornie; saving to Owen Grana McRorie, Dermott McRory, and Hugh McQuyn, and their heirs a yearly rent of 10s. 6d. Eng. out of the two qrs of Runepoll.
BSD pre-1641   Ardsorin & Ardmony 2 qrs: Bryne McDermott
                    24 a. unprof., 120 a. prof.
                    Moss in com*m*on between Ardmoglis & Rossmale: 33 a. unprof.
BSD post-Cromwellian Lord Kingston
Petty's map   Ardsorin (Boyle baronial map)
Census 1659   Ardsorine: 7 Irish[22]
Hearth Roll 1665 McDermott, Bryne, Ardsorine, Killaraght
                    Grana, Owen, Ardsorrine, Killaraght
                    O Money, Rory, Ardsorrine, Killaraght
                    Roirke, Edmond, Ardsorrine, Killaraght[23]
TAB 1834   [?Ardsoreen West: 122.3 a. Ardsoreen East: 70 a.]
COMMENT: See note for Ardmunekin.

Ardtubbart

MODERN EQUIVALENT: ? Reask
CIVIL PARISH: Killaraght
BSD pre-1641   Ardtubbart & Cloonesessa 2 qrs: Bishop of Achonry
                    230 a. prof.
                    A small parcell of Gleab belonging to the Church of Killaraght: 3 a. prof.
                    Bishop of Achonry
                    (After entry for Liserlagh)
                    Turffe bogg in com*m*on between Lishmerane, Ardtubrett & Carrowennerlare: 15 a. unprof.; Sir Robert King/Lord Kingston
BSD post-Cromwellian Bishop of Achonry
Petty's map   Ardtubber (Boyle baronial map)
Hearth Roll 1665 Quyn, Edmond, Artubrud & Kerrownurlare, Killaraght[24] (p. 79)
TAB 1834   ?Kilaraght: 415 a.

22 Pender (ed.), *A census of Ireland circa 1659*, p. 603.   **23** MacLysaght (ed.), 'Seventeenth century hearth money rolls with full transcript relating to County Sligo', pp 34, 53, 72, 80.   **24** Ibid., p. 79.

COMMENT: BSD notes that there was bog in common between Ardtubbert, Lismerraun and Carrownurlar, which suggests that the modern townland of Reask – between Lismerraun and Carrownurlar – likely corresponds to Ardtubbert. This identification is in line with Petty's placement of Ardtubbert below Ardmoyle on his map (which does not include Reask). As Ardtubbert and Cloonesessa belonged to the bishop of Achonry both before and after the Cromwellian confiscations, they were likely part of the parish lands (as opposed to the larger monastic estate) of Killaraght.

Ballybane

MODERN EQUIVALENT: Ardmoyle
CIVIL PARISH: Killaraght
TAB 1834   Ballybane: 12.2.35 a.
COMMENT: Ballybane is marked as the easternmost section of Ardmoyle on the Kingston estate map of 1770, copied from a map dating to 1724.[25]

Carrowbrackane

MODERN EQUIVALENT: Derrinoghran
CIVIL PARISH: Killaraght
BSD pre-1641   Parcel of mount: belonging to qrs in Culliaghbegg Culliaghmore Carrowbrackane & Skehane Derrenecrome Castleline & Keg. Great woods and Bogg with 2 or 3 small parcells of arrable in pssn. of ffarrell O'Gara but Sr. Robt. King doth challenge the wood at Calliagh & som other woods adjoyning.
                    200 a. unprof. 127 a. prof.: fferrall O'Gara
BSD post-Cromwellian Lord Kingston
ASE 1667   The woods of Cullaghbeg, Cullaghmore, Carrowbrackane, Skehane Rey or Key, and Donenerance, 127 a.; in or near the ½ bar. of Coolavin, co. Sligo: John Lord Kingston
                    (Listed within a group of lands collectively worth 17*l* 12s. 1¼d. rent *per annum*.)
TAB 1834   [Derrynaghrine: no acreage given; composition rent: 5.2.10]
COMMENT: Larkin's nineteenth-century map locates 'Carrowbrickan' in the northern tip of modern-day Derrinoghran.

Carrowgarve

MODERN EQUIVALENT: Killaraght?
CIVIL PARISH: Killaraght
BSD pre-1641   Carrowgarve 1 qr; Bishop of Achonry
                    128 a. prof.
BSD post-Cromwellian Bishop of Achonry
Petty's map   Carrogarry (Boyle baronial map)
TAB 1834   [? Kilaraght: 415 a.]

---

25 NLI, MS 21 F 13, no. 39.

COMMENT:	Petty places 'Carrogarry' on the most south-easterly end of the parish in a position that suggests it is now part of modern Killaraght townland. This identification would be in line with its possession in BSD by the bishop of Achonry.

Carrownane

MODERN EQUIVALENT:	Carrownaun
CIVIL PARISH:	Killaraght
TCD Survey 1617	the towne and lands of Carrowaanane, the qrter called Carrowanane: Sir John King
Cal. Pat. Rolls Jas. I	The towns, lands, and qrs of Carrowannain … : Sir John Kinge
BSD pre-1641	Carrownane 1 qr: Sir Robert King
	50 a. prof.
BSD post-Cromwellian	Lord Kingston
Petty's map	Caronany (Boyle baronial map)
Hearth Roll 1665	Dingwell, Robert, Carrownane, Killaraght[26]
TAB 1834	Caranane: 47 a.

Carrownurlar

MODERN EQUIVALENT:	Carrownurlar
CIVIL PARISH:	Killaraght
TCD Survey 1617	the qrter called Carroanurlare: Sir John King
Cal. Pat. Rolls Jas. I	Carrowanurlane: Sir John Kinge
BSD pre-1641	Carrowenerlare 1 qr: Sir Robert King
	199 a. prof. collectively with other 3 qrs (see 'comment' section below)
BSD post-Cromwellian	Lord Kingston
Census 1659	Carownorclare: 5 Irish
Hearth Roll 1665	Quyn, Edmond, Artubrud & Kerrownurlare, Killaraght[27]
TAB 1834	Caranurlar: 79.3.20 a.
COMMENT:	BSD groups together: 'Carrowenerlare 1 qr; Ardmoile 1 qr; Ardgallin 1 qr and the qr of Lisserlagh'.

Cashel

MODERN EQUIVALENT:	Cashel
CIVIL PARISH:	Killaraght
TAB 1834	Cashel: 100.2.24 a.
COMMENT:	Cashel is called 'Baralack' in Larkin's nineteenth-century map. See comment below for Castleline.

Castleline

MODERN EQUIVALENT:	?Cashel or possibly Derrinoghran
CIVIL PARISH:	Killaraght
BSD pre-1641	Parcel of mount: belonging to qrs in Culliaghbegg Culliaghmore Carrowbrackane & Skehane Derrenecrome Castleline & Keg great

---

26 MacLysaght (ed.), 'Seventeenth century hearth money rolls with full transcript relating to County Sligo', p. 35.
27 Ibid., p. 79.

woods and Bogg with 2 or 3 small parcells of arrable in pssn. of ffarrell O'Gara but Sr. Robt. King doth challenge the wood at Calliagh & som other woods adjoyning.

200 a. unprof. 127 a. prof.: fferrall O'Gara

BSD post-Cromwellian	Lord Kingston
ASE 1667	The woods of Cullaghbeg, Cullaghmore, Carrowbrackane, Skehane Rey or Key, and Donenerance, 127 a.; in or near the ½ bar. of Coolavin, co. Sligo: John Lord Kingston
	(Listed within a group of lands collectively worth 17*l* 12s. 1¼d. rent *per annum*.)
TAB 1834	[?Derrynaghrine: no acreage given; composition rent: 5.2.10]
COMMENT:	Given the association of Castleline with other townlands known to be in the vicinity of Derrinoghran, it is possible that it corresponds to the modern townland of Cashel; however, given its explicit association with mountainous land, it might be in Derrinoghran itself.

Clonaghbane

MODERN EQUIVALENT:	Ardmoyle
CIVIL PARISH:	Killaraght
TAB 1834	Clonaghbane: 27 a.
COMMENT:	Clonaghbane is the middle of the eastern section of Ardmoyle (Ballybane is the easternmost section of Ardmoyle), according to the Kingston estate map of 1770, which was copied from a map dating to 1724.[28]

Cloncuny

MODERN EQUIVALENT:	Clooncunny
CIVIL PARISH:	Killaraght
Inq. 1614 (a)	[?2 qr de Ball … : Irriel O'Gara]
Inq. 1614 (b)	Carrow Clomcoonnii: Irriel O'Gara let to Taaffe
Inq. 1615	2 qr voc. Carrowloomcloonagh et Carrowclooncunny alias Leghballi-spellane: Irriel O'Gara
TCD Survey 1617	the towne and lande of Cloncuny, the qrter of Cloncuny: Brian MacDonagh
Cal. Pat. Rolls Jas. I	The towns, lands, and qrs of Cloncunny, Lumclunagh, and of Carrowntihannacoilmore; Rinnasharragh, 1 qr … : Brian McDonagh
1635 Strafford Survey	[Levalleispallan .2. qrs
	The inheritance of ffarrill o Gara whoe setts it to undertenn.for 30. li. it is like tawnanomucklogh altogether in qualities, it will grase .300. cowes, et it is worth .30. li. *per* Annu*m*.]
BSD pre-1641	Clonconie 1 qr: ffarrell O'Gara
	39 prof. acres
	Inchmore island belongs to it.
BSD post-Cromwellian	Lord Kingston

28 NLI, MS 21 F 13, no. 39.

Petty's map	Cloncoin
ASE 1667	Clonecunny, 1 qr 51 a. : John Lord Kingston
	In first group of lands worth 17*l* 12s. 1¼d.
TFE 1688	Ballyspillane, 2 qrs: George Gore
TAB 1834	Cloncunny: 2.14.01
COMMENT:	Together with Carrow Lumclonnagh, Clooncunny comprises Leighvallii I Spellan. See entry for Lomcloon.

Cloonloogh

MODERN EQUIVALENT:	Cloonloogh
CIVIL PARISH:	Killaraght
TAB 1834	Clonloo: no acreage given; composition rent: 3.4.5

Clonloo Stonepark

MODERN EQUIVALENT:	Stonepark
CIVIL PARISH:	Killaraght
TAB 1834	Clonloo Stonepark: no acreage given; composition rent: 1.7.6

Cloonesessa

MODERN EQUIVALENT:	Reask?
CIVIL PARISH:	Killaraght
BSD pre-1641	Ardtubbart & Clonesessa 2 qrs: Bishop of Achonry
	230 a. prof.
	(entry below, found after Lisherlagh entry in BSD)
	Turffe bogg in common between Lishmerane, Ardtubbrett & Carrowennerlare: 15 a. unprof.; Sir Robert King/Lord Kingston
BSD post-Cromwellian	Archbishop of Achonry
COMMENT:	The suggestion that Cloonessa may have been in Reask derives from the fact that it is linked to Ardtubbart in BSD. The most likely location for the now obsolete denomination of Ardtubbart is Reask (see entry for 'Ardtubbart'). Clonessa would very likely have been one of the original 4 quarters of Killaraght.

Cornementane

MODERN EQUIVALENT:	Ross?
CIVIL PARISH:	Killaraght
TCD Survey 1617	the towne and lande of Cornementane, the qrter of Cornementane: Sir John King
Cal. Pat. Rolls Jas. I	The towns, lands, and qrs of … Cornementane … 1 qr each: Sir John Kinge[29]
BSD pre-1641	Rossmoyle & Carnementon 2 qrs: Sir Robert King
	163 a. prof.
	Moss in common with Rosnagree: 9 a. unprof.
BSD post-Cromwellian	Lord Kingston

---

29 Griffiths (ed.), *Calendar of the Irish patent rolls of James I*, p. 321.

TAB 1834	[?Ross: 130]
COMMENT:	The suggestion that Cornementane might be in Ross is based on its association with 'Rossmoyle', which Petty's map locates in the modern-day townland of Ross. BSD groups together: Rossmoyle and Carnementan; Lishgallon; Ratermmon and Rosnagree; Derrybeg als. Lissiniskie; and Ardlone.

Cullaghbeg

MODERN EQUIVALENT:	?Cuppanagh, Cashel, Tawran or Derrinoghran
CIVIL PARISH:	Killaraght
BSD pre-1641	Parcel of mount: belonging to qrs in Culliaghbegg Culliaghmore Carrowbrackane & Skehane Derrenecrome Castleline & Keg great woods and Bogg with 2 or 3 small *par*cells of arrable in pssn. of ffarrell O'Gara but Sr. Robt. King doth challenge the wood at Calliagh & som other woods adjoyning.
	200 a. unprof. 127 a. prof.: fferrall O'Gara
Petty's map	Cullinagh (Boyle baronial map)
BSD post-Cromwellian	Lord Kingston
ASE 1667	the woods of Cullaghbeg, Cullaghmore, Carrowbrackane, Skehane Rey or Key, and Donenerance, 127 a.; in or near the ½ bar. of Coolavin, co. Sligo: John Lord Kingston
	(Listed within a group of lands collectively worth 17*l* 12s. 1¼d. rent *per annum*.)
TFE 1688	Colloghbegg and Colloghmore, 2 qrs: George Gore

Cullaghmore ?

	Cuppanagh, Cashel, Tawran, or Derrinoghran.
	See entry for Cullaghbeg above.

Cuppanagh

MODERN EQUIVALENT:	Cuppanagh
CIVIL PARISH:	Killaraght
Inq. 1614 (b)	Coppaanagh: Irriel O'Gara let to Taaffe
Inq. 1615	qr de Copnagh: Irriel O'Gara
Cal. Pat. Rolls Jas. I	Deed from Oriell O'Garye alias O'Gariye of Moyghygarye in the county of Sligo, to Donogh O'Connor Sligo, of Sligo, in said county, granting to the said O'Connor Sligo for ever, all his interest in the town and castle of Moyghygarye, **the castle of Copnaghe**, the castle of Derrymore in the half barony of Cullovin in said county, with all the lands, tenements, lordships, mill, territories, &c. to the same belonging; with covenants against all other persons. – 21 May, 1st, 1603.
1635 Strafford Survey	Coppenegh .1. quar.
	The inheritance of ffarrell o Gara whoe keepes it in his own lands; it is good arr. lande et heathey grounde, it hath some shelter et good turffe, 10 dayes mowinge, it will grase .200. cowes, et it is worth .20. li. p*er* Annu*m*.

BSD pre-1641	Copenagh 1 qr: ffarrell O'Gara
	44 a. prof.
	Carownevimelly(?) *par*cell of Copenagh: Sir Robert King; 16 a. prof.
	(Following entry for Emlagh)
	Emlogh another *par*cell of Copenagh: ffarrell O'Gara
	13 a. prof.
	Another *par*cell of rocky pasture: 17 a. prof.
	A *par*cell of waste mosse: 11 a. unprof.
	Another *par*cell of mosse of Copenagh: 29 a. unprof.
	Heath pasture of Copenagh: 12 a. unprof.; 11 a. prof.
	Tall thick woods of Copenagh: 64 a. unprof.; 63 a. prof.
	more mosse of Copenagh: 22 a. unprof.
	All owned by ffarrell O'Gara
Petty's map	Coppenagh (Boyle baronial map)
Hearth Roll 1665	O Bryne, Brien, Copunagh, Killaraght
	Mc Kee, Donnagh, Copunagh, Killaraght
	Mc Kee, Mullronny, Copunagh, Killaraght
BSD post-Cromwellian	Lord Kingston
ASE 1667	Cappenagh, 1 qr 164 a. prof. 155 unprof.: John Lord Kingston
	(Listed within a group of lands collectively worth 17*l* 12s. 1¼d. *per annum*.)
TFE 1688	Cauponagh, 1 qr: George Gore
TAB 1834	Cuppanagh: 150.1.30
COMMENT:	The modern-day townland of Cuppanagh contains the sub-denomination of 'Annagh' and possibly the now obsolete denominations of Cullaghbeg and Cullaghmore (see entries for the respective townlands above).

Derrinoghran – see entries for Carrowbrackane, Cullaghbeg and Cullaghmore, Donerance and Skehane Rey.

Derrybeg	(alias Lisiniskie)
MODERN EQUIVALENT:	Derrybeg
CIVIL PARISH:	Killaraght
TCD Survey 1617	the qrter of Deribbiggs: Sir John King
Cal. Pat. Rolls Jas. I	Derribeg: Sir John King
BSD pre-1641	Derybegg als. Lisiniskie 1 qr: Sir Robert King
	43 a. prof.
	Turffe bogg Lisiniske: 2 a. unprof.
	parcell of Lishiniskie: 4 a. prof.
	more Turffe mosse: 3 a. unprof.
	more by the Distribution: 94 a. prof.
Petty's map	Derebeg (Boyle baronial map)
TAB 1834	Doory beg Island 16.3.36

Derrymore Island

MODERN EQUIVALENT:	Derrymore Island
CIVIL PARISH:	Killaraght
Cal. Pat. Rolls Jas. I	To sir John Kinge, knt, privy councillor. – In Coolavin Half Bar. The towns, lands, and qrs of Carrowannain, of Ardsallagh, of Cornementane, of Rossmile, of Rathtermon, and of Ross-Ininmickdonagh otherwise Rosstorpan; Lishmeran, Ardmoile, Carrowanurlane, Lisherlaga, Argrillin, Rossdillan, Ardloana, Derribegg, 1 ar each; Liss-Igallane, ½ qr ... (goes on to list the names of very many other Sligo landowners and their holdings before finishing by referring to the manors of several of the biggest landowners, including King) ... the lands granted to sir John Kinge, knt, are created the **manor of Derrimore**, with 500 a. in demesne; power to create tenures, and to hold courts leet and baron[30]
	Deed from Oriell O'Garye alias O'Gariye of Moyghygarye in the county of Sligo, to Donogh O'Connor Sligo, of Sligo, in said county, granting to the said O'Connor Sligo for ever, all his interest in the town and castle of Moyghygarye, the castle of Copnaghe, **the castle of Derrymore** in the half barony of Cullovin in said county, with all the lands, tenements, lordships, mill, territories, &c. to the same belonging; with covenants against all other persons. – 21 May, 1st, 1603.[31]
BSD pre-1641	Derrimore Island on the Lough with an old Castle and chappell wall within it: Sir Robert King
	19 a. unprof.
Petty's map	Derynure (Boyle baronial map)
BSD post-Cromwellian	Lord Kingston
TAB 1834	Doorymore Island: 31.2.17 a.
COMMENT:	The Annals of Loch Cé record the following entries under the year 1586: Caislen mor Meic g-Coisdealb, ocus leath thigernuis in tíre, do thabhairt do Thaboid Diluin do Mac Goisdealb .i. Sean mac inGilla Dhuibh meic Hoiberd (The great castle of Mac Goisdelbh Costello, and half the lordship of the country, were given to Tibbot Dillon by Mac Goisdelbh, i.e., John, son of the Gilla-dubh, son of Hubert).[32]
	O Gadhra do thabhairt cuig m-baile na rand, ocus **caislen Doire Mhoir**, don fir cedna. Oillilin O Gadhra tug sin uadha (O'Gadhra gave five towns in his division, and the castle of Daire-mór, to the same man. Oilillin O'Gadhra that gave those away.)[33]
	The *Elizabethan Fiants* record a pardon given to a McDermott associated with Derrymore: 'Pardon to Dualtagh m'Shane oge O Gary m'Brian m'Dermot, of **Dirremore**, Kedo M'Dermotte roe, of same ... '[34]

---

30 Griffiths (ed.), *Calendar of the Irish patent rolls of James I*, pp 321–2.   **31** Ibid., p. 475.   **32** *ALC* 1586.34.
33 *ALC* 1586.35.   **34** K.W. Nicholls (ed.), *The Irish fiants of the Tudor sovereigns: during the reigns of Henry VIII, Edward VI, Philip and Mary and Elizabeth I*, vol. 3 (Dublin, 1994), 5848 (6652), p. 229.

Donenerance

MODERN EQUIVALENT:	Probably Derrinoghran
CIVIL PARISH:	Killaraght
BSD pre-1641	Parcel of mount: belonging to qrs in Culliaghbegg Culliaghmore Carrowbrackane & Skehane Derrenecrome Castleline & Keg great woods and Bogg with 2 or 3 small parcels of arrable in pssn. of ffarrell O'Gara but Sr. Robt. King doth challenge the wood at Calliagh & som other woods adjoyning.
	200 a. unprof. 127 a. prof.: fferrall O'Gara
BSD post-Cromwellian	Lord Kingston
Hearth Roll 1665	O Conilaun, Rory boy, Deeyhumughuirne (Derrinoghran), Killaraght
ASE 1667	the woods of Cullaghbeg, Cullaghmore, Carrowbrackane, Skehane Rey or Key, and Donenerance, 127 a.; in or near the ½ bar. of Coolavin, co. Sligo: John Lord Kingston
	(Listed within a group of lands collectively worth 17*l* 12s. 1¼d. rent *per annum*.)
TAB 1834	Derrynaghrine: no acreage given; composition rent 5.2.10

Dooseen(?) Island

MODERN EQUIVALENT:	Uncertain
CIVIL PARISH:	Killarght?
TAB 1834	[Dooseen Island: no acreage given; composition rent: 0.1.4]

Emlagh

MODERN EQUIVALENT:	Emlagh
CIVIL PARISH:	Killaraght
BSD pre-1641	(First mention immediately follows entry for Lisherlagh)
	Dry mosse in common with Lisherlagh ½ qr and Emlagh: 9 a. unprof.
	Sir Robert King/Lord Kingston
	(Second set of mentions specifically related to Emlagh)
	Emlogh another parcell of Copenagh: ffarrell O'Gara
	13 a. prof.
	Another parcell of rocky pasture: 17 a. prof.
	A parcell of waste mosse: 11 a. unprof.
	Another parcell of mosse of Copenagh: 29 a. unprof.
	Heath pasture of Copenagh: 12 a. unprof.; 11 a. prof.
	Tall thick woods of Copenagh: 64 a. unprof.; 63 a. prof.
	more mosse of Copenagh: 22 a. unprof.
BSD post-Cromwellian	Lord Kingston
COMMENT:	See also entry for Ardgrillin

Killaraght

	alias Artubbrett, Clonesessa, Carrowgarve and Ardgrilline?
MODERN EQUIVALENT:	Killaraght
CIVIL PARISH:	Killaraght
Inq. 1615	4 qr de Killaragh: Irriel O'Gara

35 TCD, MS 570, f. 56r.

TCD Survey 1617	And that the said Lord Bishopp of Aghconrie in right of his see of Aghconrie is seized in his demeasne as of ffee of the fower quarters o Killaghrath …[35]
	(Later, in a section of the same survey devoted to confiscated crown lands, the survey notes that Thomas Wood assigned to 'Johannes Kinge' all of the hospital or religious house of 'Termonkilraght' lying in Co. Sligo, along with its four quarters, at a rent of 13 shillings 4 d.)[36]
1635 Strafford Survey	(?see entries for Carrowgarve, Ardtubbart, Cloonesessa and Ardeog)
BSD pre-1641	A small parcel of glebe belonging to the church of Killaraght: Bishop of Achonry.
	(See also entries for Ardleac, Ardsallagh, Carrowgarve, Ardtubbart & Cloonesessa).
BSD post-Cromwellian	Bishop of Achonry
Census 1659	Killaragh: 9 Irish; Henry Tifford gent: Titulado[37]
Hearth Roll 1665	Dowane, Richard, Killaraght, Killaraght
TAB 1834	Kilaraght: 415 a.
COMMENT:	The modern townland of Killaraght is located in the far south-east of the parish; however there is no early modern denomination of land actually called 'Killaraght', which complicates the attempt to delineate the four quarters of Killaraght. A further complication is that the original monastic termon of Killaraght would seem to have been far more extensive than just the four quarters associated with the parish church.[38] The latter seem likely to have corresponded to the modern townlands of Killaraght and Reask (Carrowgarve, Ardtubbart and Cloonesessa and possibly Ardleag and Ardsallagh).
	An Elizabethan fiant (dated to 1593) grants to Tirlagh O Byrne a number of monastic lands that had been hidden from the crown during the Dissolution and then re-discovered. They included 'three quarters of land by the water called Lorgbella, viz., two carucates beyond the water towards the north, and another quarter on this side the water towards the west, co. Roscommon, possessions of the religious house of Killarighta, in said co. (30s.)'.[39] Since modern Killaraght or Reask are not on the lake, these lands probably refer to some of the lands in Killaraght in the possession of the King family. The reference to the denomination of 'Bello West' in the TAB listing of lands in Killaraght is likely linked to the 'Lorgbella' of the Fiants.

Lishgallon

MODERN EQUIVALENT:	Lisgullaun
CIVIL PARISH:	Killaraght
TCD Survey 1617	the halfe qrter of Lisshgallan: Sir John King
BSD pre-1641	Lishgallon 1 qr: Sir Robert King
	48 a. prof.
BSD post-Cromwellian	Lord Kingston

---

36 Ibid., f. 284r.   **37** Pender (ed.), *A census of Ireland circa 1659*, p. 603.   **38** P. MacCotter, 'Diocese of Achonry: church, land, and history', *Peritia*, 24–5 (2013–14), p. 250.   **39** Nicholls (ed.), *The Irish fiants of the Tudor*

Petty's map	Lisgallen (Boyle baronial map)
Census 1659	Lesgalan: 31 Irish
TAB 1834	Liscullane: 170.2.10 a.

Lisserlagh

MODERN EQUIVALENT:	Lisserlough
CIVIL PARISH:	Killaraght
TCD Survey 1617	the qrter of Lisserlagh: Sir John King
Cal. Pat. Rolls Jas. I	Lisherlagha … 1 qr each: Sir John Kinge
BSD pre-1641	(Lisserlagh is mentioned in 3 separate entries in BSD; the first treats it within a group of lands collectively encompassing 199 profitable acres)
	Carrowenerlare 1 qr; Ardmoile 1 qr; Ardgallin 1 qr and **the qr of Lisserlagh**: Sir Robert King
	199 a. prof. collectively with other 3 qrs
	(The second mention, following shortly afterwards, treats Lisserlagh individually)
	Lisherlagh ½ qr: Sir Robert King
	24 a. prof.
	A parcel of pasture mosse cont. 2 a. unprof.; 2 a. unprof.
	Dry mosse in common with Emlogh 9 a unprof.[40]
	(The third mention occurs after the Ratany entry)
	Mosse & bogg in common between Ratany and Ardgilline and Lisherlagh: 47 a. unprof.; Sir Robert King
Petty's map	Liserlagh (Boyle baronial map)
BSD post-Cromwellian	Lord Kingston
Hearth roll 1665	Mc Edury, Thomas, Lisserlagh, Killaraght Gormully, Hugh, Lisserlagh, Killaraght[41]
TAB 1834	Liserlogh: 61 a.
COMMENT:	BSD groups: 'Carrowenerlare 1 qr; Ardmoile 1 qr; Ardgallin 1 qr and the qr of Lisserlagh', collectively encompassing 199 acres of profitable land.

Lissmeran

MODERN EQUIVALENT:	Lissmeran
CIVIL PARISH:	Killaraght
TCD Survey 1617	the qrter of Lissmeran: Sir John King
Cal. Pat. Rolls Jas. I	Lishmeran … 1 qr each: Sir John Kinge
BSD pre-1641	(There are two separate mentions of Lissmeran in BSD)
	Lishmerrane 1 qr: Sir Robert King
	93 a. prof.
	Bogg in common with Ardsallagh 26 a. unprof.
	(Second mention)
	Turffe bogg in common between Lishmerane, Ardtubrett & Carrowenerlare: 15 a. unprof.: Sir Robert King/Lord Kingston

sovereigns, vol. 3, p. 223. **40** Ibid. **41** MacLysaght (ed.), 'Seventeenth century hearth money rolls with full transcript relating to County Sligo', pp 40, 52.

BSD post-Cromwellian	Lord Kingston
Petty's map	Lismeran (Boyle baronial map)
TAB 1834	Lismurrane: 99 a.
COMMENT:	Grouped in BSD with Ardsallagh and Ardeog.

Lumcloonagh

MODERN EQUIVALENT:	Lomcloon
CIVIL PARISH:	Killaraght
Inq. 1614 (b)	Carrow Lumclonnagh: Irriel O'Gara let to Taaffe
Inq. 1615	2 qr voc. Carrowloomcloonagh (Lomcloon, Killaraght) et Carrow-clooncunny alas Leghballispellane: Irriel O'Gara
TCD Survey 1617	the towne and lande of Lumclunagh, the qrter of Lumclunagh: Brian McDonogh
Cal. Pat. Rolls Jas. I	towns, lands, and qrs of … Lumclunagh … : Brian McDonagh
1635 Strafford Survey	[Levalleispallan .2. qrs
	The inheritance of ffarrill o Gara whoe setts it to undertenn.
	for 30. li. it is like tawnanomucklogh altogether in qualities, it will grase .300. cowes, et it is worth .30. li. *per* Annu*m*.]
BSD pre-1641	Lumclone 1 qr: ffarrell O'Gara
	12 acres (prof.)
	Two parcells of pasturable woods part of the said Lumclone 8 a. unprof.; 9 a. prof.
	A parcell of bog whereof ¾ wast belonging to the aforesd 2 qrs (Clooncunny and Lomcloon) in common; 212 a. unprof.; 70 a. prof.
BSD post-Cromwellian	Lord Kingston
Petty's map	Lamlone
ASE 1667	Lumcloune, 1 qr 118 a. prof. 220 a. unprof.: John Lord Kingston
	In first group of lands worth 17*l* 12s. 1¼d.
TAB 1834	Lumcloon: no acreage given; composition rent 3.5.2
COMMENT:	Lomcloon and Clooncunny – the two modern townlands that form the land 'bridge' across Lough Gara connecting the civil parish of Killaraght to the civil parish of Kilcolman – together comprised the 2 quarters of 'Levalleispallan', the *leth bhaile* (half baile) of the Uí Spelláin family.

Rathtermon

MODERN EQUIVALENT:	Rathtermon
CIVIL PARISH:	Killaraght
TCD Survey 1617	the towne and lande of Rathtermon, the qrter of Rathtermone: Sir John King
Cal. Pat. Rolls Jas. I	The towns, lands, and qrs of … Rathtermon … 1 qr each: Sir John Kinge
BSD pre-1641	Ratermon 1 qr & Rossnagree: Sir Robert King
Petty's map	Ratternan (Boyle baronial map)
BSD post-Cromwellian	Lord Kingston

---

42 MacLysaght (ed.), 'Seventeenth century hearth money rolls with full transcript relating to County Sligo', pp 22, 83.

Census 1659	Ratharmon: 15 Irish
Hearth Roll 1665	O Drenane, Mortagh, Rathermon, Killaraght
	O Sercoide, Owen, Rathtermon, Killaraght
	Sercoyde, Edmond, Rathtermon, Killaraght[42]
TAB 1834	Ratarmon: 100 a.
COMMENT:	The name indicates that it was almost certainly part of the original termon lands of Killaraght.[43]
	BSD groups together: Rossmoyle and Carnementan; Lishgallon; Ratermmon & Rosnagree; Derrybeg als. Lissiniskie; and Ardlone.

Ratany

MODERN EQUIVALENT:	Rathtinanun
CIVIL PARISH:	Killaraght
BSD pre-1641	Ratany 1 qr: Sir Robert King
	66 a. prof. Mosse & bogg in common between Ratany and Ardgilline and Lisherlagh: 47 a. unprof.
Petty's map	Rattany (Boyle baronial map)
BSD post-Cromwellian	Archbishop of Achonry
TAB 1834	Ratina: 41.3 a.

Rossdillon

MODERN EQUIVALENT	Ross?
CIVIL PARISH:	Killaraght
TCD Survey 1617	the qrter of Rossdillan: Sir John King
Cal. Pat. Rolls Jas. I	The towns, lands, and qrs of … Rossdillan: Sir John Kinge
TAB 1834	?Ross: 130 a.

Ross Inin MicDonagh

MODERN EQUIVALENT:	Ross?
CIVIL PARISH:	Killaraght
TCD Survey 1617	the towne and lande of RosseIninmickDonagh, the qrter of Rossinin-mickdonagh, als. Ross tarpane: Sir John King
Cal. Pat. Rolls Jas. I	The towns, lands, and qrs of … Ross-Ininmickdonagh otherwise Rosstorpan: Sir John Kinge
TAB 1834	?Ross: 130 a.
COMMENT:	'Ininmickdonagh' is an anglicization of 'Ingen Meic Donnchadha', 'The daughter of Mac Donnchadha'. Fergal O'Gara's mother was a MacDonagh. Was she, or an earlier Mac Donagh bride, the 'Ingen' in question?

Rossmoyle

MODERN EQUIVALENT:	Ross?
CIVIL PARISH:	Killaraght
TCD Survey 1617	the towne and lande of Rosmoyle, the qrter of Rosmoyle: Sir John King

---

43 MacCotter, 'Diocese of Achonry: church, land, and history', p. 250.

Cal. Pat. Rolls Jas. I	Rossmile: Sir John King
BSD pre-1641	Rossmoyle & Carnementon 2 qrs: Sir Robert King
	163 a. prof.
	Moss in common with Rosnagree: 9 a. unprof.
BSD post-Cromwellian	Lord Kingston
Census 1659	Rossmoyle: 19 Irish
Hearth Roll 1665	Conry, Augustine, Rossemoyle, Killaraght
	Conry, Oyne, Rossemoyle, Killaraght
	Mc Dermott, Brian, Rossmoyle, Killaraght[44]
TAB 1834	?Ross: 130 a.
COMMENT:	BSD groups together: Rossmoyle and Carnementan; Lishgallon; Ratermmon & Rosnagree; Derrybeg als. Lissiniskie; and Ardlone.

Rossnagree

MODERN EQUIVALENT:	Rathtermon
CIVIL PARISH:	Killaraght
BSD pre-1641	Ratermon 1 qr & Rosnagree: Sir Robert King
	94 a. prof.
	Mosse in comon with Rossmoyle & Carnementon 2 qrs and Rosnagree 9 a. unprof.
BSD post-Cromwellian	Lord Kingston
Petty's map	Rosgree (Boyle baronial map)
TAB 1834	Ratarmon: 100 a.[45]
COMMENT:	BSD groups together: Rossmoyle and Carnementan; Lishgallon; Ratermmon & Rosnagree; Derrybeg als. Lissiniskie; and Ardlone. The now obsolete denomination of Rossnagree is very likely situated within modern-day Rathtermon.

Stonepark – see entry for Clonloo Stonepark

Skehane Rey or Key

MODERN EQUIVALENT:	?Derrinoghran
CIVIL PARISH:	Killaraght
BSD pre-1641	Parcel of mount: belonging to qrs in Culliaghbegg Culliaghmore Carrowbrackane & Skehane Derrenecrome Castleline & Keg great woods and Bogg with 2 or 3 small parcells of arrable in pssn. of ffarrell O'Gara but Sr. Robt. King doth challenge the wood at Calliagh & som other woods adjoyning.
	200 a. unprof. 127 a. prof.: fferrall O'Gara
BSD post-Cromwellian	Lord Kingston
ASE 1667	the woods of Cullaghbeg, Cullaghmore, Carrowbrackane, Skehane Rey or Key, and Donenerance, 127 a.; in or near the ½ bar. of Coolavin, co. Sligo: John Lord Kingston

44 MacLysaght (ed.), 'Seventeenth century hearth money rolls with full transcript relating to County Sligo', pp 30, 34.   **45** NAI, Tithe Applotment Books 1834 (microfilm), p. 35.

(Listed within a group of lands collectively worth 17*l* 12s. 1¼d. rent *per annum.*)

TAB 1834	[Derrynaghrine: no acreage given; composition rent: 5.2.10]

Tawron

MODERN EQUIVALENT:	Tawran
CIVIL PARISH:	Killaraght
1635 Strafford Survey	Tawron .1. quar. The inheritance of ffarrell O Gara whoe setts it to undertenn*a*nts.
	for .10. li. p*er* Annu*m*. it is all woode et mounteyne, it will grase .100. cowes et it is worth .10. li. p*er* Annu*m*.
Hearth Roll 1665	Mc Neile, Laurence, Dawrane Tauraw?, Killaraght
	Mc Neile, Neile, Dawrane, Killaraght[46]
TAB 1834	Tawrawn: no acreage given; composition rent: 6.3.9

LAND DENOMINATIONS IN THE PART OF KILCOLMAN PARISH THAT BELONGED TO THE HALF-BARONY OF COOLAVIN

Carrowna Corhawny

MODERN EQUIVALENT:	Sroove
CIVIL PARISH:	Kilcolman
Inq. 1614 (a)	qr de Carrowna Corhawny: Irriel O'Gara
Inq. 1614 (b)	Carrona Corhawnii: Irriel O'Gara let to Taaffe
Inq. 1615	qr vocat. Cahrownecorhawny: Irriel O'Gara
TCD Survey 1617	the towne and lands of Corhawny, the quarter of Corhawnay: Fergal O'Gara
Cal. Pat. Rolls Jas. I	the town, lands, and qrs of … Corhawny: Ferrall O'Gara of Moygara
BSD pre-1641	Shruive & Carhownagh 2 qrs: fferrall O'Gara
	353 a. prof.
	p*ar*cell of waste bog belonging to the same: fferrall O'Gara
	26 a. unprof.
	(Comments below occur after entry for 'ffalyn').
	A great p*ar*cell of Mount: to the qr of ffalyn Shruive & Carhownagh
	2 qrs ¼ p*ar*t wast: fferrall O'Gara
	167.2 a. unprof. 502.2 a. prof.[47]
BSD post-Cromwellian	332 a.: Philip Ormsby
COMMENT:	The pairing of Corhawny with Sroove in BSD suggests that the now obsolete denomination is part of modern-day Sroove.

46 MacLysaght (ed.), 'Seventeenth century hearth money rolls with full transcript relating to County Sligo', p. 76.
47 Ibid.

Carrownasrowie

MODERN EQUIVALENT:	Sroove
CIVIL PARISH:	Kilcolman
Inq. 1614 (a)	qr de Carrownasrowie: Irriel O'Gara
Inq. 1614 (b)	Carrona Shrovii: Irriel O'Gara let to Taaffe
Inq. 1615	qr. vocat. Carrownesravy: Irriel O'Gara
TCD Survey 1617	the towne and lands of Carrownesrwowy, the quarter of Carrownescowvy: Fergal O'Gara
Cal. Pat. Rolls Jas. I	The town, lands, and qrs of … Carownesrowvy: Ferral O'Gara
1635 Strafford Survey	Corownesrue 1. quar.
	The inheritance of fferrill o Gara whoe setts it to undertenn.
	for .18. li. it hath a good *pa*rcell of arr. lande, et a greate scope w*t*hwoode, et heathey grounde, it hath good turff, 8 dayes mowinge it will grase .70. cowes, et it is worth .18. li. *per* annu*m*.
BSD pre-1641	Shruive & Carhownagh 2 qrs: fferrall O'Gara
	353 a. prof.
	*pa*rcell of waste bog belonging to the same: fferrall O'Gara
	26 a. unprof.
	(Comments below occur after entry for 'ffalyn').
	A great *pa*rcell of Mount: to the qr of ffalyn Shruive & Carhownagh 2 qrs ¼ *pa*rt wast: fferrall O'Gara
	167.2 a. unprof. 502.2 a. prof.
BSD post-Cromwellian	332 a.: Philip Ormsby
Petty's map	Srivin
Hearth Roll 1665	Cullane, Phellim, Sruiffe, Kilcolman
	Gara, Dudley, Sruiffe, Kilcolman[48]
COMMENT:	May contain the now obsolete denomination of Corhawny.

Carrownawalim

MODERN EQUIVALENT:	Falleens
CIVIL PARISH:	Kilcolman
Inq. 1614 (a)	qr de Carrownawalim: Irriel O'Gara
Inq. 1614 (b)	Carrona=wallnii: Irriel O'Gara let to Taafe
Inq. 1615	qr voc. Karrownewallynie: Irriel O'Gara
TCD Survey 1617	the towne and lands of carrownavalleyny, the qrter called carrownavalleyny: Fergal O'Gara
Cal. Pat. Rolls Jas. I	the town, lands, and qr of Carownavaleyny: Ferral O'Gara
1635 Strafford Survey	Carownevallenew .1. qr
	The inheritance of fferrill o Garra whoe setts it for 8 li. *per* Annu*m*
	it is all tymber woode et mounteyne, it will grase .40. cowes et it is worth 8 li. *per* Annu*m*.
BSD pre-1641	ffalyn 1 qr: fferrall O'Gara
	53 a. prof.
	*pa*rcell of *pro*fitable mount: & stony pasture: fferrall O'Gara
	160 a. unprof. 50 (or is it 60?) a. prof.

---

48 MacLysaght (ed.), 'Seventeenth century hearth money rolls with full transcript relating to County Sligo',

p*ar*cell of unp*ro*fitable Bogg p*ar*t of ffalyn: fferall O'Gara
23 a. unprof.
A great p*ar*cell of Mount: to the qr of ffalyn Shruive & Carhownagh
2 qrs ¼ p*ar*t wast: fferrall O'Gara
167.2 a. unprof. 502.2 a. prof.

BSD post-Cromwellian	113 a. prof.: Lord Kingston
Petty's map	Fallin
ASE 1667	Fallin, 1 qr 113 a. prof. 203 a. unprof.: John Lord Kingston
	In first group of lands worth 17*l* 12s. 1¼d.
TFE 1688	Falline, 1 qr: George Gore
BSD post-1688	Trustees of the Barracks

Cashellmore

MODERN EQUIVALENT:	Clogher
CIVIL PARISH:	Kilcolman
Inq. 1614 (b)	Cashellmore: Irriel O'Gara let to Taaffe
Inq. 1615	qr voc. Cashellmore: Irriel O'Gara
TCD Survey 1617	the towne and lands of casselmore, the qrter of cassellmore: Fergal O'Gara
Cal. Pat. Rolls Jas. I	Cashellmore … 1 qr each: Ferral O'Gara
COMMENT:	The Ordnance Survey Name Books for Sligo identify Cashelmore as the south side of Clogher, near the road from Gurteen to Ballagha-derreen.[49] This placement fits with the grouping of it in the *Calendar of Irish patent rolls* as 'the town, lands, and qr of Carownavaleyny, of Cashellmore, of Clogher, and of Tawnaghnamucklagh'. It might be added that a large cashel can still be seen in this part of Clogher townland today (Mon. No. SL046-034).[50]

Clogher

MODERN EQUIVALENT:	Clogher
CIVIL PARISH:	Kilcolman
Inq. 1615	qr vocat. Curronclogher: Irriel O'Gara
TCD Survey 1617	the towne and lands of Clogher, the qrter of Clogher: Fergal O'Gara
Cal. Pat. Rolls Jas. I	Clogher: Fergal O'Gara
1635 Strafford Survey	Lavalleinclogher .2. qr
	The inheritance of ffarrell o Gara whoe setts it to underten*n*.
	for 30 li. it is a p*ar*te good tymber wood, it hath good turffe .5. – dayes mowinge, it will grase .100. et 50 cowes, et is worth .30. li. *per Annum.*
BSD pre-1641	ffogher 2 qrs: ffarrell O'Gara
	43 a. unprof.; 129 a. prof.
	A p*ar*cell of graseable mount: & some pasture woods belonging the 2 qrs of Clogher: ffarrell O'Gara

240 a. unprof.; 79 a. prof.

BSD post-Cromwellian	Lord Kingston: 129 a. of ffogher & 32 a. graseable mountain
Petty's map	Clogher
Census 1659	Clogher: 8 Irish
Hearth roll 1665	Cahussy, Thomas, Clogher, Kilcolman
	O'Hara, Keyne, Clogher, Kilcolman
ASE 1667	Clogher, 2 qrs 161 a. prof. 330 a. unprof.: John Lord Kingston (Listed within a group of lands collectively worth 11*l* 8s. 7¾d. rent *per annum*.)
COMMENT:	Modern Clogher also contains the now obsolete denomination of Cashelmore (see entry above).

Dromuckoo

MODERN EQUIVALENT:	Drumacoo
CIVIL PARISH:	Kilcolman (Roscommon part)
Inq. 1614 (b)	Carrow Dromuckoo: Irriel O'Gara let to Taaffe
Inq. 1615	qr voc. Droomuckoo: Irriel O'Gara
1635 Strafford Survey	Drommackow .1. qr.
	The inheritance of my Lo: Dillon or ffarrill o Gara, it is indifferent betwixt them, my Lo: Dillo says it is of the county of Mayo et his owen inheritance, et mr. fferrell o Gara sayes the controrarey but it is his owne inheritance in the countey of Sligoe et halfe Baroney of Coolevin, it is all wood et mounteyn it will grase .100. cowes, et it is worth .10.£ per Annum.
BSD pre-1641	BSD Mayo, Kilcolman parish, barony of Costello: Dromokoe als Dromocke 1 QR, 243 acres profitable, 75 acres profitable: Lord Dillon
BSD post-Cromwellian	Lord Dillon
COMMENT:	Drumacoo now lies in the Roscommon portion of the civil parish of Kilcolman rather than the Sligo portion. Formerly, the Roscommon section of Kilcolman belonged to Mayo, which is why it is included in the Mayo BSD.

Monasteredan

MODERN EQUIVALENT:	Monasterredan
CIVIL PARISH:	Kilcolman
Inq. 1614 (b)	Carrowmannister Bydan: Irriel O'Gara let to Taafe
Inq. 1615	qr vocat. Monasterdoan: Irriel O'Gara
TCD Survey 1617	the qrter of Manisserraddane: Fergal O'Gara
Cal. Pat. Rolls Jas. I	Manisteridan … 1 qr each: Ferral O'Gara
1635 Strafford Survey	Manestedan .1. quar.: Fergal O'Gara
	The inheritance of ffarrill o Gara whoe setts it to undertenn.
	for .7. li. it is all wood et mounteyne, it will grase .25. cowes, et it is worth .7. li. per Annum.
BSD pre-1641	Monestradon 1 qr: ffarrell O'Gara
	25 a. unprof. 68 a. prof.

parcell of mount: with some pasture: fferrell O'Gara

58 a. unprof. 116 a. prof.

parcell of unprofitable stony wood in the same: ffarrell O'Gara

26 a. unprof. 5 a. prof.

BSD post-Cromwellian	82 a. of Monestradon & parcell of mountain: Bryan Magrath 29 a.
	" " " : Lord Kingston
ASE 1667ASE 1678	Monesterdame, 29 a. prof. 181 a. uprof..: John Lord Kingston

(Listed within a group of lands collectively worth 17*l* 12s. 1¼d. *per annum*.)

Munesteradan, 1 qr 82 a. 16s 7¼d.: Bryan Magrath

Group of lands worth 8*l*. 6s. 7½d.; rent *per annum*

Tawnii Mucklagh

MODERN EQUIVALENT:	Tawnymucklagh
CIVIL PARISH:	Kilcolman
Inq. 1614 (b)	Carrow Tawnii Mucklagh: Irriel O'Gara let to Taafe
Inq. 1615	qr vocat Carrowtawnymucklagh: Irriel O'Gara
TCD Survey 1617	the towne and lands of Tawnamucklagh, the qrter of Tawnaghne-mucklagh: Fergal O'Gara
Cal. Pat. Rolls Jas. I	Tawnaghnamucklagh … 1 qr each: Ferrall O'Gara
1635 Strafford Survey	Levalletawnaemucklagh .2. qrs

The inheritance of ffarrell o Gara whoe setts it to under=tenan*n*ts for 30. li. it is some p*ar*te good arr. lande, it hath good timberwood, et 8 dayes mowinge if it were keepte, it hath good turffe, it will grase .200. cowes, et it is worth .20. li. p*er* Annu*m*.

BSD pre-1641	Tenemucklone 1 qr: ffarrell O'Gara
	23 a. unprof.; 67 a. prof.

A p*ar*cell of Bog belonging to the same: ffarrell O'Gara

268 a. unprof.

BSD post-Cromwellian	61 a. Tenemucklone: Lord Kingston
	6 a. Tenemucklone: Bryan Magrath
Petty's map	Tonemuklo
Census 1659	Fawnymuckelagh: 23 Irish
ASE 1667	Tonemucklagh, 1 qr. 61 a. prof. 291 a. unprof.: John Lord Kingston
	In first group of lands worth 17*l* 12s. 1¼d.
ASE 1678	in Tuonemucklon, 1 qr, 6 a. 1s. 2.5d: Bryan Magrath.
	Group of lands worth 8*l*. 6s. 7½d. rent *per annum*
BSD post-1688	Trustees for the Barracks
TFE 1703	Tawnamucklagh, 1 qr: George Gore

LAND DENOMINATIONS IN THE PARISH OF KILFREE

Annaghmore

MODERN EQUIVALENT:	Annaghmore
CIVIL PARISH:	Kilfree

Inq. 1614 (a)	qr de Carrowannaghmore: Irriel O'Gara
Ing. 1614 (b)	Carro Annaghmore: Irriel O'Gara let to Taaffe
Inq. 1615	qr vocat. Annaghmore: Irriel O'Gara
TCD Survey 1617	the qrter of Annaghmore: Fergal O'Gara
Cal. Pat. Rolls Jas. I	Annaghmore: Ferrall O'Gara of Moygara
1635 Strafford Survey	Annaghmore .1. quar
	The inheritance of ffarrell o Gara whoe setts it for 4 li. *per* An.
	it is all tymber wood; it will grase [—-] cowes; it is worth 5 li. per
	annum
BSD pre-1641	Annaghmore 1 qr: 49 a. profitable land: ffarrell O'Gara
BSD post-Cromwellian	Bryan Magrath: 49 a
Petty's Map	Anaghmore
ASE 1678	Annaghmore 1 qr 49 a. 9s. 11d.: Bryan Magrath
TAB 1834	Anaghmow: 293 a.

Ardcullenan (part of 2 qrs of Gortygara)

MODERN EQUIVALENT:	South-east section of Mountirvine townland
CIVIL PARISH:	Kilfree
Inq. 1614 (a)	qr de Arcullenane: Irriel O'Gara
Inq. 1614 (b)	Carro Ardcullenan: Irriel O'Gara let to Taaffe
Inq. 1615	qr voc. Ardcullenan: Irriel O'Gara
TCD Survey 1617	the quarter of Ardcullenan: Fergal O'Gara
Cal. Pat. Rolls Jas. I	Ardcullanan … 1 qr each: Ferral O'Gara of Moygara
1635 Strafford Survey	[Levallegortigara .2. qrs
	The inheritance of ffarill o Gara whoe setts it to undertenna*n*ts for
	.12.£ it is good arr. land, it hath good turffe et some heathy ground,
	et good wood, it will grase .60. cowes et it is worth .12.£ p*er* Annu*m*.]
BSD pre-1641	(Occurs twice in BSD)
	Gortigarra als. Ardcolman als. Cloonhigles 1 qr: 147 a. prof.
	p*ar*cell of Bogg to the Same the most Grazeable:
	58 a. unprof.; 28 a. prof.: ffarell O'Gara
	Gortivara als. Gurtigara Ardullman and Lishoshina als Lishierovine
	2 qrs: 139 a. prof.; Two severall p*ar*cells of Bogg belonging to the sd
	2 qrs: 85 a. unprof.; An other p*ar*cell of pasturable Bogg: 3 a. unprof.;
	3 a. prof.: fferrall O'Gara
BSD post-Cromwellian	First entry: 175 a.: Lord Kingston
	Second entry: 142 a: Lord Kingston
Petty's map	Killonon
ASE 1667	[Gortmorra alias Gortegorra, 1 qr: John Lord Kingston
	(Gortegorra is part of a group of Kingston's lands in Coolavin
	collectively valued at an annual rent of 11 *l* 8 s. 7 ¾ d.)]
TAB 1834	[Gurtigara 175 a]
COMMENT:	Larkin's 1819 map of Sligo locates Ardcullenan in the south-east
	quadrant of Mountirvine townland, just north of Knockmore Abbey.
	The '-igles' element of 'Cloonhigles' – the alias given for Ardcullenane

51 M. Timoney, 'Where are they now, the Knockmore Early Christian slabs', *The Corran Herald*, 30 (1997), p. 3;
see also, A. Gwynn and R.N. Hadcock, *Medieval religious houses: Ireland* (London, 1970), p. 290.

in the BSD – suggests the presence of a church (*eclais*) at the site. Larkin's map of Sligo locates Ardcullenane just north-east of Knockmore Abbey, a fourteenth-century Carmelite friary, said to have been founded by the O'Gara family *c.*1320.[51] It is not impossible that Knockmore was the *eclais* in question, although the name 'Ardcolman' suggests that there may have been an ecclesiastical site predating the abbey which was dedicated to Colmán, the local patron saint.

Grouped in pat. 14, Jas. I as 'Coilstraghlan, Rathmadder, Knockneshamore, Caltenan, Lishosyny, Ardcullanan, Annaghmore, 1 qr each'

Calteraun	see entry for Cultenane

Carro Knocknahooa

MODERN EQUIVALENT:	Knocknahoo
CIVIL PARISH:	Kilfree
Inq. 1614 (b)	Carro knocknahooa: Irriel O'Gara let to Taaffe.
Inq. 1615	qr vocat. Carrowknonehoowa: Irriel O'Gara
TCD Survey 1617	the qrter of knocknahowna: Fergal O'Gara
Cal. Pat. Rolls Jas. I	Knocknahowa … 1 qr each: Ferrall O'Gara
1635 Strafford Survey	Knocknehua .1. qu.
	The inheritance of fferrill o Gara whoe setts it to underte for 7.£ it hath good turffe noe wood it is good arr. lande, it hath 5. dayes mowinge of some meddowe, it will grase .35. cowes, et it is worth 7 li. p*er* annum.
BSD pre-1641	Knocknehew 1 qr: fferrall O'Gara 141 a. prof.
BSD post-Cromwellian	141 a: Bryan Magrath
ASE 1678	Knocknehow, 1 qr. 141 a. 1*l* 8s. 6.5d.: Bryan Magrath
	(Listed within a group of lands collectively worth 8*l*. 6s. 7½d. rent *per annum*.)
TAB 1834	Knocknehoo: 112 a.

Carrontemple

	(alias Kilfry in many of the early modern sources)
MODERN EQUIVALENT:	Carrowntemple
CIVIL PARISH:	Kilfree
Inq. 1614 (b)	Carro enteample: Irriel O'Gara let to Taaffe
Inq. 1615	qr voc. Carrontample: Irriel O'Gara
1635 Strafford Survey	(The Strafford Survey 'Kilfrey' probably refers to the quarters of Carrownewer and Carrowentobber (see below for entries), which constitute the modern townland of Kilfree, rather than to the modern townland of Carrowntemple)
	[?Killfrey .2. quar: The inheritance of ffarrell o Gara whoe setts it to undertennante for 12 libra per annum. Not duties, it hath but a little partch of arr. land it hath good turffe, et fir-wood, it hath a greater scope of heathey grounde not meddowe, it will grase 60. cowes, et it is worth 12 libra per annum].

BSD pre-1641	Kilfree als Carrowtemple 1 qr whereon the old Church of Kilfrey standeth: Bishop of Achonry
	39 a. prof.
	A great parcell of Grazeable Mount: belonging to the same: Bishop of Achonry 400 a. unprof.; 197 a. prof.
BSD post-Cromwellian	236 a.: Bishop of Achonry
Petty's map	Kilfrie
Census 1659	[Killfry: 16 Irish] (Unsure which denomination of the early modern Kilfree this represents)
Hearth Roll 1665	[Mc Dermott, Teige, Kilfree, Kilfree
	O Gara, Owen, Killfree, Kilfree
	O Gara, Phellim, Killfree, Kilfree
	O Gara, Teige, Killfree, Kilfree
	Mc Morish, Teige, Killfree, Kilfree
	Mc Shaneboy, Teige, Killfree, Kilfree][52]
	(Uncertain if referring to Carrownewer and Carrowntobber here or to Carrowntemple)
TAB 1834	Carantampul: 320 a.
COMMENT:	The modern townland of Carrowntemple corresponds to the early modern quarter of Kilfree. Conversely, the modern townland of Kilfree rather confusingly corresponds to the early modern quarters of Carrownewer and Carrowentobber (see above).

Carrowblaagh   (alias Clonloughin)

MODERN EQUIVALENT:	Cloonlaheen
CIVIL PARISH:	Kilfree
Inq. 1614 (a)	qr de Carrowlagh: Irriel O'Gara
Inq. 1614 (b)	Carroan Lagha: Irriel O'Gara let to Taaffe
Inq. 1615	Carrowblaagh: Irriel O'Gara
TCD Survey 1617	the towne and lands of Carrowbleagh, the qrter called carrowbleagh: Fergal O'Gara[53]
Cal. Pat. Rolls Jas. I	Carowvleagh: Fergal O'Gara
1635 Strafford Survey	[?Carownetona .1. quar
	The inheritance of ffarrell o Garra whoe setts it to undertennante for 4 li. per annum. it is all tymberwood et heathy ground, et it (will graze) 25 cowes, et it is worth .5. li. per Annum]
BSD pre-1641	Clonloughin als. Carrowbleagh 1 qr; 60 a. prof.: ?ffarrell O'Gara[54]
	[?Knockneshamer 1 qr: ?fferrall O'Gara; 87 a. prof.][55]
BSD post-Cromwellian	60 a.: Bryan Magrath
	[Knockeshamer: 87 a: Bryan Magrath]

---

52 MacLysaght (ed.), 'Seventeenth century hearth money rolls with full transcript relating to County Sligo', pp 34, 47, 73, 83. 53 TCD MS 570, folio 45v. 54 It is uncertain from the layout of the text who owned the land, but it was likely owned by Fergal O'Gara, or possibly jointly owned by Fergal O'Gara & Owen O'Gara. NAI, Books of Survey and Distribution: Sligo (microfilm), p. 132. 55 It is uncertain from the layout of the text who owned the land, but it was likely owned by Fergal O'Gara, or possibly jointly owned by Fergal O'Gara & Owen O'Gara. NAI, Books of Survey and Distribution: Sligo (microfilm), p. 132.

Petty's map	Clonlaghin
Census 1659	[Cloonlehkeene: 31 Irish]
ASE 1678	[Clooneleaghim, 1 qr 60 a. 12s. 1¾d.: Bryan Magrath]
TAB 1834	Knockneshamur & Carnabilada: 145 a.
	[Cloonlaheen & Curiaghnetona: 230 a.]
COMMENT:	BSD says Carrowbleagh is an alias for Cloonloughin (Cloonlaheen). The nineteenth-century Tithe Applotment Books group Cloonlaheen with Curiaghnetona, which is why the Strafford Survey entry for Carownetona is included here; however, the Applotment books also group Carnabilada (Carrowblaagh) with Knocknashamur, which is why the latter entry is included here under the pre-1641 BSD slot. That said, Knockneshamore and Carrowblaagh appear as separate entities in the *Calendar of Irish patent rolls of James I.*

Carrowcaslan   (the quarter of the castle)

MODERN EQUIVALENT:	Moygara
CIVIL PARISH:	Kilfree
Inq. 1614 (a)	'de castro de Moygarra cum 3 qr. viz: qr de Mullaghroy, qr de Kyleskorny, qr de Carronmahowny': Irreil O'Gara
Inq. 1614 (b)	the 3 qr of Moagh Igara, viz the qr of the Castle, Carrownakylly-skornii, Carrowna Mahanii, Carroan Mullaghroy: Irriel O'Gara let to Taaffe
Inq. 1615	de castro et vill. de Moygara. ac de 3 qr. viz. qr de Mullaghroy. qr de Carrownemahawny, qr de Killeskarny: Irriel O'Gara held by knight's service
TCD Survey 1617	the mannor, castle, towne, and lands of Moygarra, the quarter called Carrcaslane, the qrter called Carrownakilskorny, the quarter called Carrowanmullagh roe als killmcruohe: Fergal O'Gara
Cal. Pat. Rolls Jas. I	To Ferral O'Gara of Moygara … The castle, manor, town, and lands of Moygara; Carowcaslane, Carownakilskorny, Carrownamullaghroe or Kilmacruahy, Carownameahany, 1 qr each.
1635 Strafford Survey	[Moygara .1. quar. The inheritance of ffarrill o Gara, whoe sets it to undertennants for .21.£ it is some parte good arr. lande, it hath good shelter et firewood, et a greate scope of mounteyne, 7. dayes mowinge it will grase .205. cowes, et is worth .21.£ per Annum. ther is an ould castle uppon this quar.]
BSD pre-1641	[Moggarra 2 qrs: fferrall O'Gara 35 a. unprof. 230 a. prof. Stonie wood belonging to the same: fferrall O'Gara 46 a. unprof.; 46 a. prof.]
BSD post-Cromwellian	[Moggarra: 276 a. prof.: Lord Kingston]
Petty's map	[Moygara]
Census 1659	[Moygara: 38 Irish]
Hearth Roll 1665	(See entry for Moygara)
ASE 1667	Carrowlassan, Moygarrow, and Lisornagh or Killscornagh, 2 qrs 276 a. prof. 81 a. unprof.: John Lord Kingston

(Listed within a group of lands collectively worth 17*l* 12s. 1¼d. rent
per annum.)

TAB 1834   [Moygara: 710 a.]

Carrowenewer

MODERN EQUIVALENT: Kilfree
CIVIL PARISH: Kilfree

Inq. 1614 (a)   qr de Carrowenewer: Irriel O'Gara
Inq. 1614 (b)   Carroennoier: Irriel O'Gara let to Taafe
Inq. 1615   qr voc. Carrownwire: Irriel O'Gara
TCD Survey 1617   the town and lands of triananire, the qrter a third parte of a quarter
                            called triananire: Ferrall O'Gara
Cal. Pat. Rolls Jas. I   the town, lands, qr, and 1/3 qr of Triananinre, and of Triancloon-
                            sillagh: Fergal O'Gara
1635 Strafford Survey   (The two quarters of 'Killfrey' in the possession of Fergal O'Gara in
                            the Strafford Survey were likely Carrowenewer and Carrowentober).
                            [Killfrey .2. quar:
                            The inheritance of ffarrell o Gara whoe setts it to undertenna*n*te for
                            12 li*bra* p*er* annu*m* not vutsoe, it hath but a little patch of arr. land it
                            hath good turffe, et fir-wood, it hath a greater scope of heathey
                            grounde not meddowe, it will grase 60. cowes, et it is worth 12 li*bra*
                            p*er* annu*m*.]
BSD pre-1641   Carrowtubber als. Treentober & Carrowewer als. Treenenewer 2 qrs:
                            ffarrell O'Gara
                            54 a. prof.
                            A great p*a*rcell of Grazeable Mount. in Summer pastureable woods
                            belonging to ffarrell O'Gara's 2 qrs of Killfrey: ffarrell O'Gara
                            1291 a. unprof.; 300 a. prof.
Petty's map   Caronever
Census 1659   [Killfry: 16 Irish[56] (Unsure which denomination of Kilfree this
                            mention represents.)]
Hearth Roll 1665   [Mc Dermott, Teige, Kilfree, Kilfree
                            O Gara, Owen, Killfree, Kilfree
                            O Gara, Phellim, Killfree, Kilfree
                            O Gara, Teige, Killfree, Kilfree
                            Mc Morish, Teige, Killfree, Kilfree
                            Mc Shaneboy, Teige, Killfree, Kilfree][57]
                            (Uncertain if Kilfree here refers to Carrownewer and Carrowntobber
                            or to Carrowntemple.)
BSD post-Cromwellian   54 a.: Bryan Magrath
ASE 1678   Carrownetoler and Carrownea 2 qrs 54 a. 10s 11¼d: Bryan Magrath
                            (Listed as part of group of lands collectively worth 8*l*. 6s. 7½d. rent
                            per annum)
TAB 1834   Carantubber or Kilfree: 563 a.

---

56 Pender (ed.), *A census of Ireland circa 1659*, p. 602.   **57** MacLysaght (ed.), 'Seventeenth century hearth money
rolls with full transcript relating to County Sligo', pp 3, 4, 47, 73, 83.

COMMENT:	Based on the identification made in the *TAB*, the now obsolete quarters of Carrowentobber and Carrownewer were likely located in the modern-day townland of Kilfree. Together they probably comprised the two quarters of Kilfree belonging to Fergal O'Gara. Somewhat confusingly, the denomination of land (and the actual church site) referred to as Kilfree in the early modern sources is not the modern-day Kilfree but rather the modern-day Carrowntemple. Carrowentobber and Carrownewer are referred to in several sources as 'trians' (thirds) rather than quarters, a division often associated with ecclesiastical lands. The remaining third appears to have been the trian of Cloonsillagh to the immediate east.

Carrowentyhane

MODERN EQUIVALENT:	Cuilmore
CIVIL PARISH:	Kilfree
Inq. 1614(b)	Laghvuline Killemore viz Carro Rugnnesharragh, Carron Tyan – : Irriel O'Gara let to Taaffe.
Inq. 1615	2 qr. de Koylmore vocat Carrowrummesharragh et Carrowentyhane: Irriel O'Gara
TCD Survey 1617	The towne and lande of Carrowantighane warcoilmore the qrter called carroneantihannacuillmore: Brian McDonagh
Cal. Pat. Rolls Jas. I	[Grant from the King to sir Arthur Savage, knt, privy councillor… SLIGO Co'. In Coilmore, Shean, and Rinsharragh, 1 qr; the estate of Teig O'Gary otherwise Teig ne Gann, slain in rebellion; rent, 5s. – To hold for ever, as of the castle of Dublin, in common soccage. (This entry appears 3 years before the reference below to Carrowntihan-nacuilmore within the general lists of Sligo landownership, p. 265)] towns, lands, and qrs of … Carrowantihannacoilmore; Rinnasharragh, 1 qr: Bryan McDonogh
1635 Strafford Survey	[Collemore .2. qrs The inheritance of Mr Dodwell whoe lett this (?) for .30. li. p*er* Annu*m*. it is some p*ar*te good arr. lande, it hath good wood, et turffe, some 8. dayes mowinge, it will grase .300. cowes et are worth .30. li.per Annu*m*.]
BSD pre-1641	Killmore als Carrowintihan 2 qrs: ?fferrall O'Gara 228 a. prof. p*ar*cell of mountaine graseable in summer belonging to Kilmore etc.: ?fferall O'Gara[58] 102 a. prof.; 35 a. unprof. An other p*ar*cell of Boggy mount: belonging to Killmore 259 a. unprof.
BSD post-Cromwellian	263 a.: Lord Kingston

---

58 It is uncertain from the layout of the text who owned the land, but it was likely owned by Fergal O'Gara, or possibly jointly owned by Fergal O'Gara & Owen O'Gara. NAI, Books of Survey and Distribution: Sligo (microfilm), p. 132.

Petty's map	[Killmore]
TAB 1834	[Kelmore: 596 a.]
COMMENT:	A Crown Rental says the lands of Coilemore Risharragh et Shean were confiscated from Teige O'Gary als Teige ne Gannie, who was attainted for rebellion, and assigned to Arthur Savage at 5 shillings per year rent.[59] This statement is in line with the first entry for Coilmore in the *Calendar of Irish patent rolls* noted above.

Carrowgortinenearny (?another name for Clooneheglishe)

MODERN EQUIVALENT:	Probably Gorteen
CIVIL PARISH:	Kilfree
Inq. 1614 (a)	qr de Carrogortinenearny: Irriel O'Gara gets annual return from
Inq. 1614 (b)	Carro Gortinerearagh: Irriel O'Gara let to Taaffe
Inq. 1615	[qr voc. Clonehagglishe: Irriel O'Gara]
Cal. Pat. Rolls Jas. I	[Cloonehagglis of Lisballilie: Fergal O'Gara]
BSD pre-1641	[Killprocklis a *parcell* of mount. did belong to the qr. of Caltinane: ffarrell & Owen O'Gara
	72 a. unprof.; 35 a. prof.
	parcell of unprofitable Bogg *part* of Killprocklis: ffarrell & Owen O'Gara45 a. unprof.]
BSD post-Cromwellian	[Presumably Lord Kingston, but no name actually given.]
ASE 1667	Clonehalasse alias Gortnegory 175 a. prof. 58 a. unprof.: John Lord Kingston
	(Listed within a group of lands collectively worth 17*l.* 12s. 1¼d. rent *per annum.*)
TAB 1834	Gurteen: 229 a.
	[Caltrane & Kelpruclish: 236 a.]
COMMENT:	*ASE* say that Carrowgortinenearny is an alias for Clooneheghlishe (Cuilpruiglish); *BSD* links Clooneheghlishe to Calteraun and Lisbaleely. TAB similarly links Cuilpruighlish to Calteraun.
	Inq. 1614 (a) groups Carrogortinenearny together with Carrowcowlskeaghan, Carrontobbber, Clonsellagh as lands from which O'Gara got an annual return.

Carrowkeile

MODERN EQUIVALENT:	Doon, Kilfree (west side)
CIVIL PARISH:	Kilfree
Inq. 1614 (a)	?qr de Carrom—k—— (occurs right after 3 qrs associated with castle): Irriel O'Gara
Inq. 1614 (b)	Carro Keile: Irriel O'Gara let to Taaffe
TCD Survey 1617	the qrter called Carrowkeile: Fergal O'Gara
Cal. Pat. Rolls Jas. I	Carowkeile … 1 qr each: Ferral O'Gara
BSD pre-1641	Carrowkeele 1 qr: ffarrell O Gara
	58 a.
BSD post-Cromwellian	58 a.: Bryan Magrath

59 TCD, MS 570, f. 285v.

Petty's map	Carokill
ASE 1678	Currowhill 1 qr. 58 a. 11s. 9¼d.: Bryan Magrath
	(Listed within a group of Magrath's lands collectively valued at an annual rent of 8 *l*. 6s. 7 ½ d. rent *per annum*)
TAB 1834	Carakeel or Wst Doon: 292 a.
COMMENT:	The now obsolete denomination of Carrowkeile is subsumed into the modern-day townland of Doon.

Carrowndowne

MODERN EQUIVALENT:	Doon
CIVIL PARISH:	Kilfree
Inq. 1614 (b)	Carro endoveene: Irriel O'Gara let to Taaffe
Inq. 1615	de castro et vill. de Moygara, ac de 3 qr, viz. qr de Mullaghroy, qr de Carrownemahawny, qr de Killeskarny ac **de qr de Carrowndowne**, et de qr de Carroreogh quod praemiss. tenentur de Rege in capite per servic. militare: Irriel O'Gara held by knight's service.
	(Mentioned a second time in the Inquisition)
	qr voc. Corrondweene: Irriel O'Gara
TCD Survey 1617	the qrter called Carrowanduan: Fergal O'Gara
Cal. Pat. Rolls Jas.	Carowanduan … 1 qr each: Ferrall O'Gara
1635 Strafford Survey	Levalle-dun-killefroy .2. qrt.:
	The inheritance of ffarrell o Garra whoe setts it to under tennannte for 12 li. *per* annu*m*. it is all wood et mounteyne, but a little it hath good fir-woode et turffe, noe meddowe it will grase .60. cowes et it is worth .12. li. *per* annu*m*
BSD pre-1641	Downe 1 qr: ffarrell O'Gara
	35 a. prof.
BSD post-Cromwellian	35 a.: Bryan Magrath
Petty's map	[Carokill]
Census 1659	[Kilfree 16 Irish]
ASE 1678	Downe 1 qr 35 a., 7s 1d: Bryan Magrath
	(Listed within group of lands collectively worth 8*l*. 6s. 7½d. rent *per annum*.)
TAB 1834	Doon East: 312 a.; Carakeele or wst Doon 292 a.[60]
COMMENT:	The modern townland of Doon represents the medieval quarter of Doon and the medieval quarter of Carrowkeel.

Carrownemahawny

MODERN EQUIVALENT:	Mahanagh
CIVIL PARISH:	Kilfree
Inq. 1614(a)	de castro (etc.) de Moygarra cum 3 qr. viz qr de Mullaghroy, qr de Kyleskorny, qr de **Carronamahowny**: Irriel O'Gara
Inq. 1614(b)	the 3 qr of Moagh Igara viz. the qr of the Castle, Carrownakylly-skornii, **Carrowna Mahanii**: Irriel O'Gara let to Taaffe

---

60 NAI, Tithe Applotment Books 1834 (microfilm), p. 33.

Inq. 1615	de castro et vill. de Moygara, ac de 3 qr, viz. qr de Mullaghroy, **qr de Carrownemahawny**, qr de Killeskarny ac de qr de Carrowndowne, et de qr de Carroreogh quod praemiss. tenentur de Rege in capite per servic. militare: Irriel O'Gara held by knight's service.
TCD Survey 1617	Carownameahany, 1 qr: Fergal O'Gara
Cal. Pat. Rolls Jas. I	To Ferrall O'Gara of Moygara. –In Coolavin Half Bar. The castle, manor, town, and lands of Moygara; Carowcaslane, Carownakilsorny, Carrownamollaghroe or Kilmacruahy, Carownameahany, 1 qr each
BSD pre-1641	Mehana 1 qr: ffarrell O'Gara
	62 a. prof.
	Pasturable Bogg to the same: ffarrell O'Gara
	9 a. unprof; 12 a. prof.
	Parcell of unprof. Bogg belonging to Maggarra & Mahanna lying to the Lough Side: ffarrell O'Gara
	106 a. unprof.
	A small parcell of good pasturable wood pt. of Mahana lying on the lough side: ffarrell O'Gara
	7 a. prof.
	A great parcell of Grazeable Mount. & pasture wood which anciently belonged to the qrs. before Expressed.
	1240 a. unprof.; 430 a. prof.
BSD post-Cromwellian	81 a.: Sir John King
	130 a.: Bryan Magrath
ASE 1678	Meaghana, 1 qr 81 ac prof. 115 unprof.: John Lord Kingston
	In first group of lands worth 17*l* 12s. 1¼d. rent *per annum*
TFE 1688	[Moygarra, 4 qrs: George Gore]
TAB 1834	Mahanagh, Graffy & Doobala: 527 a.
COMMENT:	Mahanagh appears to have been part of the demesne lands of Moygara Castle. Larkin's map shows several subdivisions of Mahanagh, including Meelick, Doballa, and Currynery.

Carownetona   (?alias Cloonlaheen (Tithe Applotment Books) alias Carrowbleagh?)
                           See entry for Carrowblaagh (modern Cloonlaheen)

Carrowntobber

MODERN EQUIVALENT:	Kilfree
CIVIL PARISH:	Kilfree
Inq. 1614 (a)	qr de Carrontobber: Irriel O'Gara gets annual return from
Inq. 1614(b)	Carro Tobbir: Irriel O'Gara let to Taaffe
Inq. 1615	qr vocat. Carrowntobber: Irriel O'Gara
TCD Survey 1617	the qrter and third parte of a qrter called triantobber: Fergal O'Gara
Cal. Pat. Rolls Jas. I	Triantobber, 1⅓ qr: Fergal O'Gara
1635 Strafford Survey	(The two quarters of Kilfree in the possession of Fergal O'Gara appear to have been Carrowenewer and Carrowentober.)
	[Killfrey .2. quar:
	The inheritance of ffarrell o Gara whoe sets it to undertennante for 12 li*bra* per annu*m* not vutsoe, it hath but a little patch of arr. land it

hath good turffe, et fir-wood, it hath a greater scope of heathey grounde not meddowe, it will grase 60. cowes, et it is worth 12 li*bra* p*er* annu*m*.]

BSD pre-1641	Carrowtubber als. Treentober & Carrowewer als. Treenenewer 2 qrs: ffarrell O'Gara
	54 a. prof.
	A great p*ar*cell of Grazeable Mount. in Summer pastureable woods belonging to ffarrell O'Gara's 2 qrs of Killfrey: ffarrell O'Gara
	1291 a. unprof.; 300 a. prof.
BSD post-Cromwellian	54 a.: Bryan Magrath
Petty's map	Carotober
Census 1659	[Killfry: 16 Irish (Unsure which denomination of Kilfree this represents.)]
Hearth Roll 1665	(See entry for Carrowenewer above)
ASE 1678	Carrownetoler and Carrownea 2 qrs 54 a. 10s. 11¼d: Bryan Magrath (Listed within a group of lands collectively worth 8*l*. 6s. 7½d. rent *per annum*)
TAB 1834	Carantubber or Kilfree: 563 a.
COMMENT:	See comment for Carrownewer above.
	Grouped with Carrogortinenearny, Carrowcowlskeaghan, and Clonsellagh as lands that O'Gara got an annual return from in Inq. 1614a.

Carrowreogh

MODERN EQUIVALENT:	Greyfield
CIVIL PARISH:	Kilfree
Inq. 1614 (b)	Carro Reogh: Irriel O'Gara let to Taafe.
Inq. 1615	de castro et vill. de Moygara, ac de 3 qr, viz. qr de Mullaghroy, qr de Carrownemahawny, qr de Killeskarny ac de qr de Carrowndowne, et **de qr de Carroreogh** quod praemiss. tenentur de Rege in capite per servic. militare (held by knight's service): Irriel O'Gara.
TCD Survey 1617	The towne and lands of carrrowreagh: Fergal O'Gara
Cal. Pat. Rolls Jas. I	The town, lands, and qrs of … Carowreogh: Ferrall O'Gara
1635 Strafford Survey	Carrowreagh .1. quar.
	The inheritance of fferrill o Garra whoe setts it to under tennants for .21.li it is good arr. lande, it hath good wood and turffe, et a greate scope of mounteyne, it will grase .205 cowes et it is worth .21. li. p*er* Annu*m*.
BSD pre-1641	Carrowreagh 1 qr: ffarroll O'Garra 1/3 cartron; Owen O'Garra 2/3 cartron 112 a. prof.
	p*ar*cel of Bog belonging to Sephin Moydow & Carrowreagh 157 a. unprof.
BSD post-Cromwellian	112 a.: Lord Kingston
Petty's map	Caroreigh
Hearth Roll 1665	McDonnagh, Brian, Carrowreagh, Kilfree
	Mc Tanist … Carrowreagh, Kilfree[61]

61 MacLysaght (ed.), 'Seventeenth century hearth money rolls with full transcript relating to County Sligo', pp 36, 86.

ASE 1667	Carrowreagh, 1 qr 112 a.: John Lord Kingston
	(Listed within a group of lands collectively worth 17*l* 12s. 1¼d. rent *per annum*.)
TFE 1688	Carrowneagh, 1 qr: George Gore
TAB 1834	Greyfield, Derilahan & Shraigh: 253 a.
COMMENT:	The modern name Greyfield seems to be a literal translation of *Ceathrar riabhach* ('Grey quarter'), from which the name 'Carrowreogh' was derived. Larkin's map gives both names.
	Sragh, which the Tithe Applotment books group with Greyfield, was possibly a detached upland portion of Carrowreagh. In line with this theory is the fact the Strafford Survey reports that it has a great scope of mountain, yet Greyfield itself doesn't have any mountain.

Carrowvickryny

MODERN EQUIVALENT:	Uncertain
CIVIL PARISH:	Kilfree
Inq. 1614 (b)	Carrovick-ryny: Irriel O'Gara let to Taaffe
Inq. 1615	qr voc. Carrowvickreny: Irriel O'Gara
TCD Survey 1617	the towne and lands of carrowvickreny, the quarter called carro-vickreny: Fergal O'Gara
Cal. Pat. Rolls Jas. I	the town, lands, and qrs of Cloonehaggliss, of Lisballilie, Carowreogh, Carowclooneihe, Cloonetecarna, **Carowvickreny**, Carowvleagh, Carownesrowvy, Corhawny: Ferrall O'Gara
BSD pre-1641	Carowcrinane als Carrowmicreene 1 qr: ?fferrall O'Gara 82 a.[62]
BSD post-Cromwellian	Lord Kingston: 82 a.
ASE 1667	?Carrowcrine 1 qr 82 a.: John Lord Kingston
	(Listed within a group of lands collectively worth 11*l* 8s. 7¾d. rent *per annum*)
COMMENT:	Based on the name 'Carrowvickryny', most likely, this land denomination originally belonged to the Augustinian monastery of Inchmacnerin, on Church Island in Loch Cé. The monastery was referred to in English sources as 'Inchvickrynye', so 'Carrowvickryny' probably means the quarter (carrow) of Inchmacnerin. The quarter was not listed as one of the possessions of Inchmacnerin at the dissolution of the monasteries, so would likely have been acquired by O'Gara at an earlier date.
	The location of Carrowvickryny is very uncertain. Given that Chacefield, Mweelroe, and Sragh are all absent from the early modern sources, it might be one of these. Its placement in the lists of land units in several of the early modern sources may lend further support to this theory since its name appears close to land units in the general Chacefield area. In BSD, however, it appears next to Cuilmore and it is possibly subsumed within that modern townland.

---

62 It is uncertain from the layout of the text who owned the land, but it was likely owned by Fergal O'Gara, or possibly jointly owned by Fergal O'Gara & Owen O'Gara. NAI, Books of Survey and Distribution: Sligo (microfilm), p. 132.

Cloneagh

MODERN EQUIVALENT:	Clooneagh
CIVIL PARISH:	Kilfree
Inq. 1614 (b)	Carro Cloneagh: Irriel O'Gara let to Taaffe
Inq. 1615	qr voc Cloneagh: Irriel O'Gara
TCD Survey 1617	The town and lands of carroclooneihe, the quarter called carrowsloonih: Fergal O'Gara
Cal. Pat. Rolls Jas. I	The town, lands, and qrs of … Carowclooneihe: Ferrall O'Gara
1635 Strafford Survey	Soyfin*n* & Cloneagh (2 .qrs.)
	The inherit. of ffarrell o Gara whoe setts them towe qr for .16. li it is all wood et mounteyns as aforsd. it will grase .30. cowes, et is worth .16. li. p*er* Annu*m*.
BSD pre-1641	Cloneigh 1 qr: ffarrell & Owen O'Gara
	62 a. unprof.; 110 a. prof.
BSD post-Cromwellian	Lord Kingston
Petty's map	Clouigh
Census 1659	[Sexifind: 71 Irish]
Hearth Roll 1665	[Colnire, Richard, Seefin, Kilfree
	Crirny', Collo, Seefyn, Kilfree
	McDonnaght, Brian, Seefin, Kilfree
	Fitzwilliams, Ross, Seefyn, Kilfree
	Koane, …, Seefyn, Kilfree][63]
ASE 1667	Cloneigh, 1 qr 110 a. prof. 62 a. unprof.: John Lord Kingston
	(Listed within a group of lands collectively worth 11/8s. 7¾d. rent *per annum*.)
TAB 1834	Clooneh & Drimhillock: 151 a.
COMMENT:	The 1635 Strafford Survey suggests that Clooneagh was grouped with Seefin.

Cloonehagglishe   (alias Gortnegory? alias Caltima/Caltnane?)

MODERN EQUIVALENT:	Cuilprughlish & probably Gorteen
CIVIL PARISH:	Kilfree
Inq. 1614 (a)	[qr de Carrogortinenearny: Irriel O'Gara gets annual return from]
Inq. 1614 (b)	[Carro Gortinerearagh: Irriel O'Gara let to Taaffe.]
Inq. 1615	qr voc. Clonehagglishe: Irriel O'Gara
Cal. Pat. Rolls Jas. I	The towns, lands, and qrs of Cloonehagglis … : Ferrall O'Gara
1635 Strafford Survey	Claneheglise .1. qr.
	The inheritance of fferrill o Gara whoe setts it to undertenne*n*ts for .7. li. it is some p*ar*te good arr. lande, et there is a church uppo*n* this quar. wherin they burey the dead of this halfe Barrony it hath good turffe 4. dayes of mowinge, it will grase .35. cowes et it is worth .7. li. p*er* Annu*m*.
BSD pre-1641	Killprocklis a p*ar*cell of mount. did belong to the qr. of Caltinane: ffarrell & Owen O'Gara
	72 a. unprof.; 35 a. prof.

---

63 MacLysaght (ed.), 'Seventeenth century hearth money rolls with full transcript relating to County Sligo', pp 27, 30, 36, 44, 67.

	parcell of unprofitable Bogg p*ar*t of Killprocklis: ffarrell & Owen O'Gara
	45 a. unprof.
BSD post-Cromwellian	(Presumably Lord Kingston, but no name actually given.)
Petty's map	[?Caltima]
ASE 1667	Clonehalasse alias Gortnegory 175 a. prof. 58 a. unprof.: John Lord Kingston
	(Listed within a group of lands collectively worth 17*l* 12s. 1¼d. rent *per annum*.)
TAB 1834	[?Gurteen: 229 a.] Caltrane and Kelpruclish: 236 a.
COMMENT:	Cloonehaghlishe is grouped with Lisbaleely by *Cal. Pat. Rolls of Jas. 1*, and with Caltinane by BSD; 'Caltinane' here seems to be the Caltima marked on Petty's map beside Mullaghroe and not Calteraun beside Greyfield. TAB also associates it with 'Caltrane', but doesn't provide a separate listing for the northern Calteraun. Does this omission imply that the TAB 'Calrane' is the one beside Greyfield? *ASE* says Cloonehaglishe is an alias for Gortnegory (probably Gorteen).

Cloonlaheen – see the entry for Carrowblaagh

Clonsellagh

MODERN EQUIVALENT:	Cloonsillagh
CIVIL PARISH:	Kilfree
Inq. 1614 (a)	Clonsellagh: Irriel O'Gara gets annual return from.
Inq. 1614 (b)	Clonsullagh: Irriel O'Gara let to Taaffe.
Inq. 1615	qr voc. Clonsullagh: Irriel O'Gara
TCD Survey 1617	The towne and lands of triancloonsillagh, the qrter of a third p*ar*te of the qrter of triansillagh: Fergal O'Gara
Cal. Pat. Rolls Jas. I	The town, lands, qr, and ¹/₃ qr of Triananinre, and of Triancloonsillagh: Ferrall O'Gara
1635 Strafford Survey	Clonselagh .2. quart.
	The inheritance of fferrell o Garra whoe setts it to undertenn*an*te for .19. li. it is some p*ar*te good arr. lande, et greater woods for tymber it hath good turffe, 5 dayes mowinge, it will grase .100. cowes, et it is worth .18. li. p*er* Annu*m*.
BSD pre-1641	Clonshenog als. Clonselagh 1 qr: ffarrell O'Gara
	106 a. prof.
	p*ar*cell of mount. belonging to Moggarra: ffarrell O'Gara
	69.2.0 a. unprof.; 139.2.0 a. unprof.
BSD post-Cromwellian	176 a.: Lord Kingston
ASE 1667	Cloonesallagh 1 qr and ¹/₃ d, 176 a. prof. 70 a. unprof.: John Lord Kingston
	(Listed within a group of lands collectively worth 17*l* 12s. 1¼d. rent *per annum*.)
BSD post-1688	69 a. of the 276 a. of Moygara and the 176 a. of Cloonsillagh went to Trustees of the Barracks.

TSE 1703	Clonsellagh, 1 qr: George Gore
TAB 1834	Cloonsillagh & Kelard: 224 a.
COMMENT:	Inq. 1614 (a) groups Clonsellagh with Carrogortinenearny, Carrow-cowlskeaghan, and Carrontobber as lands from which O'Gara got an annual return.

The reference to Cloonsillagh in the *Calendar of the Irish patent rolls of James I* as 'Triancloonsillagh' suggests that it may originally have been church land: typically, the division of a *baile* into thirds instead of quarters tends to be associated with ecclesiastical lands. The remaining two-thirds would appear to have been Triananire (Carrownewer) and Treentober (Carrowentober), which constitute the modern townland of Kilfree to the immediate west of Cloonsillagh.

Clontecarna

MODERN EQUIVALENT:	Cloontycarn
CIVIL PARISH:	Kilfree
Inq. 1614 (a)	qr de Clontecarna: Irriel O'Gara
Inq. 1614 (b)	Carroclontecarna: Irriel O'Gara let to Taaffe
Inq. 1615	Carrowclontecar— (word cut off): Irriel O'Gara
TCD Survey 1617	The towne and lands of Cloontecarna, the quarter of Cloontegarne: Fergal O'Gara
Cal. Pat. Rolls Jas. I	The town, lands, and qrs of … Cloontecarna … : Ferrall O'Gara
1635 Strafford Survey	Clointecarne .1. quar.
	The inheritance of fferrill o Gara whoe setts it to underte [*text obscured*] for 16.£ p*er* Annu*m* it hath some arr. lande, et woode for timber it hath good turffe, 5. dayes mowinge, if it weare kept, et it will grase .80. cowes, et it is worth .16. li. p*er* Annu*m*.
BSD pre-1641	Clontecarne 1 qr: fferrall & Owen O'Gara
	104 a. prof.
	p*ar*cell of unprofitable Bogg: fferrall & Owen O'Gara
	57 a. unprof.
BSD post-Cromwellian	Lord Kingston
Petty's map	Clontecarna
ASE 1667	Clonetecarne, 1 qr 104 a. prof. 57 a. unprof.: John Lord Kingston
	(Listed within a group of lands collectively worth 17*l* 12s. 1¼d. rent *per annum*.)
TAB 1834	Clonticarne and Drumlasta: 454.3.31 a.

Cuilmore – see entry for Killemore; also see entries for Carron Tyan and Rinnasharragh

Cuilprughlish – see entry for Cloonehagglishe

Cultenane

MODERN EQUIVALENT:	Calteraun
CIVIL PARISH:	Kilfree
Inq. 1614 (a)	qr de Cultenane: Irriel O'Gara

Inq. 1614 (b)	Carro Cultenan: Irriel O'Gara let to Taaffe
Inq. 1615	Carrowkaltrenan: Irriel O'Gara
TCD Survey 1617	The quarter of Caltenan: Fergal O'Gara
Cal. Pat. Rolls Jas. I	Caltenan … 1 qr each: Ferrall O'Gara
1635 Strafford Survey	Caltnan .1. quar.
	The inheritance of fferrill o Gara whoe setts it for .21.£ it is parte good arr. lande, it hath some wood et turffe, 8. dayes mowg it will grase .205. cowes, et it is worth .21. li. per Annum.
BSD pre-1641	Lisballiha and Cultinan 2 qrs: ?fferrall & Owen O'Gara
	262 a. prof.
	A parcell of Bogg to them
	49 a. unprof.
	(Entry for Killprockliss)
	Killprocklis a parcell of mount. did belong to the qr. of Caltinane: ffarrell & Owen O'Gara
	72 a. unprof.; 35 a. prof.
	parcell of unprofitable Bogg part of Killprocklis: ffarrell & Owen O'Gara
	45 a. unprof.
BSD post-Cromwellian	262 a.: Lord Kingston
ASE 1667	Lisballilee and Colternan, 2 qrs, 262 a. prof. 49 a. unprof.
TAB 1834	Caltrane & Kelpruclish: 236 a. Lisballilee & Chasefield: 223 a.
COMMENT:	There appears to be two townlands called Cultinan, as indicated by Petty's map: one called 'Caltima' south of Cloontycarn and Mullaghroe, perhaps located somewhere in present-day Mahanagh, and one called 'Caltiman' on the northern border of Kilfree just west of the Owenmore River (the present-day Calteraun). The first 'Caltima' is linked with Cuilpruighlish.

Doon – see entries for Carrondownne and Carrowkeile

Gorteen – see entries for Carrowgortinenearny, Ardcullenan and Lissoshinagh

Gortigara

MODERN EQUIVALENT:	Gortygara
CIVIL PARISH:	Kilfree
1635 Strafford Survey	Levallegortigara .2. qrs
	The inheritance of ffarill o Gara whoe setts it to undertennants for .12.£ it is good arr. land, it hath good turffe et some heathy ground, et good wood, it will grase .60. cowes et it is worth .12.£ per Annum.
	Lissosina .1. quar.
	The inheritance of ffarill o Gara whoe setts it to undertennants for .7.£ it is good arr. lande, it hath good turffe, noe wood- 4. dayes mowinge, it will grase .35. cowes et it is worth 7£ per Annum.
BSD pre-1641	(There are two separate mentions of Gortygara in *BSD*)
	a) Gortigarra als. Ardcolman als. Cloonhigles 1 qr: ffarrell O'Gara

147 a. prof.

p*ar*cell of Bogg to the Same the most Grazeable: ffarrell O'Gara

58 a. unprof.; 28 a. prof.

b) Gortivara als. Gurtigara Ardullman(?) and Lishoshina als Lishierovine 2 qrs: fferrall O'Gara

139 a. prof.

Two severall p*ar*cells of Bogg belonging to the sd 2 qrs: ?fferrall O'Gara (owner not explicitly stated)

85 a. unprof.

An other p*ar*cell of pasturable Bogg

3 a. unprof.; 3 a. prof.

BSD post-Cromwellian	a) 175 a.: Lord Kingston
	b) 142 a.: Lord Kingston
ASE 1667	Gortmorra alias Gortegorra, 1 qr: John Lord Kingston
	(Listed within a group of lands collectively worth 11*l* 8s. 7¾d. rent *per annum*.)
TAB 1834	Gurtigara: 175 a.
COMMENT:	The name 'Gortygara' appears to cover the 3 quarters of Lissoshinagh, Ardcullenan, and Gortygara itself. See the individual entries for these denominations for further references.

Greyfield – see entry for Carrowreogh

Kilfree (modern townland of Kilfree) – For the denominations of land corresponding to the modern townland of Kilfree, see the entries for Carrownewer and Carrowentober.

Kilfree	(The early modern denomination of Kilfree, not the modern one.)
MODERN EQUIVALENT:	Carrowntemple
CIVIL PARISH:	Kilfree
Inq. 1614 (b)	Kilfry: Irriel O'Gara let to Taaffe.
Inq. 1615	Killfreeh: Irriel O'Gara
1635 Strafford Survey	(Below likely refers to Carrowntobber and Carrownenewer)
	Killfrey .2. quar:
	The inheritance of ffarrell o Gara whoe setts it to undertenna*n*te for 12 li*bra* per annu*m* not vutsoe, it hath but a little patch of arr. land it hath good turffe, et fir-wood, it hath a greater scope of heathey grounde not meddowe, it will grase 60. cowes, et it is worth 12 li*bra* p*er* annu*m*.
BSD pre-1641	Kilfree als Carrowtemple 1 qr whereon the old Church of Kilfrey standeth: Bishop of Achonry
	39 a. prof.
	A great p*ar*cell of Grazeable Mount: belonging to the same: Bishop of Achonry
	400 a. unprof.; 197 a. prof.
BSD post-Cromwellian	236 a.: Bishop of Achonry
Petty's map	Kilfrie
Census 1659	Killfry: 16 Irish

Hearth Roll 1665	(Kilfree may refer here to the modern Kilfree, rather than Carrowna-temple, as Larkin's nineteenth-century map indicates a village at Kilfree.)
	Mc Dermott, Teige, Kilfree, Kilfree
	O Gara, Owen, Killfree, Kilfree
	O Gara, Phellim, Killfree, Kilfree
	O Gara, Teige, Killfree, Kilfree
	Mc Morish, Teige, Killfree, Kilfree
	Mc Shaneboy, Teige, Killfree, Kilfree[64]
TAB 1834	Carantubber or Kilfree: 563 a.
COMMENT:	The two early modern quarters comprising the modern townland of Kilfree are Carrowentobber and Carrowenewer (see above). The modern townland of Carrowntemple (which contains the church) corresponds to the early modern denomination of Kilfree.

Killemore	(alias Rinnasharragh and Carrowantyhane)
MODERN EQUIVALENT:	Cuilmore
CIVIL PARISH:	Kilfree
Inq. 1614 (b)	Laghvuline Killemore viz Carro Rugnnesharragh, Carron Tyan: Irriel O'Gara let to Taaffe
Inq. 1615	2 qr. de Koylmore vocat Carrowrummesharragh et Carrowentyhane: Irriel O'Gara let to Taaffe.
TCD Survey 1617	The towne and lande of Carrowantighane warcoilmore the qrter called carroneantihannacuillmore: Brian McDonagh
	the qrter of Rinnasharagh: Bryan MacDonagh
Cal. Pat. Rolls Jas. I	The towns, lands, and qrs of Cloncuny, Lumclunagh, and of Carrowantihannacoilmore; Rinnasharragh, 1 qr: Bryan McDonogh
1635 Strafford Survey	Collemore .2. qrs
	The inheritance of Mr Dodwell whoe sett this(?) for .30. li. p*er* Annu*m*. it is some p*ar*te good arr. lande, it hath good wood, et turffe, some 8. dayes mowinge, it will grase .300. cowes et are worth .30. li. per Annu*m*.
BSD pre-1641	Killmore als Carrowintihan 2 qrs: ?fferrall O'Gara[65]
	228 a. prof.
	p*ar*cell of mountaine graseable in summer belonging to Kilmore etc.: ?fferall O'Gara[66]
	102 a. prof.; 35 a. unprof.
	An other p*ar*cell of Boggy mount: belonging to Killmore
	259 a. unprof.
BSD post-Cromwellian	263 a.: Lord Kingston
Petty's map	Killmore

64 MacLysaght (ed.), 'Seventeenth century hearth money rolls with full transcript relating to County Sligo', pp 34, 47, 73, 83.   **65** It is uncertain from the layout of the text who owned the land, but it was likely owned by Fergal O'Gara, or possibly jointly owned by Fergal O'Gara & Owen O'Gara. NAI, Books of Survey and Distribution: Sligo (microfilm), p. 132.   **66** It is uncertain from the layout of the text who owned the land, but it was likely owned by Fergal O'Gara, or possibly jointly owned by Fergal O'Gara & Owen O'Gara. NAI, Books of Survey and Distribution: Sligo (microfilm), p. 132.

ASE 1667	Kealmore, 2 qrs 263 a. prof. 361 a. unprof.: Lord Kingston(Listed within a group of lands collectively worth 11*l* 8s. 7¾d. rent *per annum*.)
TAB 1834	Kilmore: 596 a.
COMMENT:	The two quarters of Rugnasharragh and Carrowantyhane are not specifically called Cuilmore in the TCD Survey of 1617.

Killeskorny

MODERN EQUIVALENT:	Moygara
CIVIL PARISH:	Kilfree
Inq. 1614 (a)	de castro (etc.) de Moygarra cum 3 qr. viz qr de Mullaghroy, qr de **Kyleskorny**, qr de Carronamahowny, ac de qr de Carrom—k—…: Irriel O'Gara
Inq. 1614 (b)	the 3 qr of Moagh Igara, viz. the qr of the Castle, **Carrownakylly-skornii**, Carrowna Mahanii: Irriel O'Gara let to Taaffe
Inq. 1615	de castro et vill. de Moygara, ac de 3 qr, viz. qr de Mullaghroy, qr de Carrownemahawny, **qr de Killeskarny** ac de qr de Carrowndowne, et de qr de Carroreogh quod praemiss. tenentur de Rege in capite per servic. militare': Irriel O'Gara held by knight's service
TCD Survey 1617	The mannor, castle, towne, and lands of Moygarra, the quarter called Carrcaslane, the qrter called Carrownakilskorny, the qurter called Carrowanmullagh roe als Killmcruohe, the qrter called car … : ffarell O'Gara
Cal. Pat. Rolls Jas. I	The castle, manor, town, and lands of Moygara; Carowcaslane, **Caronakilskorny**, Carrownamollaghroe or Kilmacruahy, Corwna-meahany, 1 qr each : Ferrall O'Gara
1635 Strafford Survey	Carrownekillscorny .1. qr. The inheritance of fferrill o Gara whoe setts it to undertennte for 21 li. *per* Annu*m*. it is some p*ar*te good arr. lande it hath good wood et turffe, 8. dayes mowinge, it will grase .200. et 5. cowes et it is worth 21 li. *per* Annu*m*.
BSD pre-1641	[Moggarra 2 qrs: fferrall O'Gara 35 a. unprof. 230 a. prof. Stonie wood belonging to the same: fferrall O'Gara 46 a. unprof.; 46 a. prof.]
BSD post-Cromwellian	[Moggarra: 276 a. prof.: Lord Kingston]
Petty's map	Moygara
Census 1659	[Moygara: 38 Irish]
Hearth Roll 1665	(See entry for Moygara)
ASE 1667	Carrowlassan, Moygarrow, and Lisornagh or Killscornagh, 2 qrs 276 a. prof. 81 a. unprof.: John Lord Kingston In first group of lands worth 17*l* 12s. 1¼d. rent *per annum*
BSD post-1688	[69 a. of the 276 a. of Moygara and the 176 a. of Cloonsillagh went to Trustees of the Barracks.]
TFE 1703	Moygarra, 4 qrs: George Gore
TAB 1834	[Moygara: 710 a.]

COMMENT: The now obsolete quarter of Killeskorny was one of two quarters that made up the modern townland of Moygara. The other was 'Carrowcaslane', the 'Quarter of the Castle'.

Kilstraghlane

MODERN EQUIVALENT:	Kilstraghlan or Ragwood
CIVIL PARISH:	Kilfree
Inq. 1614 (b)	Carro Coylstraghlane: Irriel O'Gara let to Taaffe
Inq. 1615	qr voc. Cowlestraghlane: Irriel O'Gara
TCD Survey 1617	the qrter of Coilsraghlane: ffarell O'Gara
Cal. Pat. Rolls Jas. I	Coilstraghlan … 1 qr each: Ferrall O'Gara
BSD pre-1641	Coilestradand 1 qr: ffarrell O'Gara
	96 a. prof.
	parcell of Bog belonging to the Same: ffarrell O'Gara
	42 a. unprof.; 4 a. prof.
BSD post-Cromwellian	100 a. Lord Kingston
ASE 1667	Coylestrackland or lane, 1 qr. 100 a. prof. 42 a. unprof.: John Lord Kingston
	(Listed within a group of lands collectively worth 17*l* 12s. 1¼d. rent *per annum*.)
TFE 1703	?Tuine-Coylehagan, 1 qr: George Gore
TAB 1834	[Ragwood: 170 a.]

Knockmore

MODERN EQUIVALENT:	Mountirvine
CIVIL PARISH:	Kilfree
Inq. 1614 (b)	Carro Knockmore: Irriel O'Gara let to Taaffe
Inq. 1615	qr voc. Knomore: Irriel O'Gara
BSD pre-1641	Knockmore 1 qr, abbey lande: Earl of Corke
	103 a.
	parcell of pastureable heath etc.: Earl of Corke
	10 a. unprof.; 11 a. prof.
	parcell of Bogg belonging to Knockmore: Earl of Corke
	31 a. unprof.;
	A great parcell of wast Bogg etc.: Earl of Cork
	600 a. unprof.; 83 a. prof.
BSD post-Cromwellian	196 a.: Earl of Strafford
Petty's map	Knockmore
Hearth Roll 1665	Mc Mullrooinfyn, Laughlin, Knockmore, Kilfree
TAB 1834	[Mount Irwin: 164 a.]
COMMENT:	The Elizabethan Fiants note a 'Grant to John Rawson and Henry Deane … the site, circuit, and precinct of the cell or house of friars, called Knockor, with a quarter of land, and the tithes to the house

---

67 J. Morrin (ed.), *Calendar of patent and close rolls of chancery in Ireland; from the 18th year to 45th of Queen Elizabeth*, vol. 2 (Dublin and London, 1862), p. 273.   **68** A. Gwynn and R. N. Hadcock, *Medieval religious houses: Ireland* (London, 1970), p. 290.

belonging, in the country of O'Garye, a parcel of land, called Knocknor'[67]

This was the site of a fourteenth-century Carmelite abbey founded by the O'Gara family.[68] See entry for Ardcullenane.

Knocknashammer: see entry for Carrowknockneshamer

Knockneskagh

MODERN EQUIVALENT:	Knockneskeagh
CIVIL PARISH:	Kilfree
Inq. 1614(b)	Carro Knockneskragh: Irriel O'Gara let to Taaffe
Inq. 1615	qr voc. Carrowknockneskagh: Irriel O'Gara
1635 Strafford Survey	Knocknoscagh .1. qr
	The inheritance of o Connor. which is some of my ladey Cresseyes dowrey from o Connor whoe setts it to undertennants for .8. li. it is good arr. lande, it hath good shelter. et good turffe. 6. dayes, mowinge, it will grase 40. cowes et is worth 8 li. p*er* Annu*m*.
BSD pre-1641	Knockneskeagh 1 qr: Sir Robert King
	6 a. unprof.; 138 [a]. prof.
BSD post-Cromwellian	138 a.: Earl of Strafford
Petty's map	K:neskea
ASE 1678	William Earl of Strafford and Thomas Radcliffe Esq … out of the ½ bar. of Cooleavin, 4 *l*. … which were settled on them by another decree, dated 17 August 1663, were created into the manor of Sligoe … Dated 12 March 1674 and Inrolled 9 April 1675.
TAB 1834	Knockneska & Urlar: 170 a.

Lissballile

MODERN EQUIVALENT:	Lisbaleely
CIVIL PARISH:	Kilfree
Inq. 1614 (b)	Carro Lissbullilln: Irriel O'Gara let to Taaffe
Inq. 1615	qr voc. Lisballis(?)y: Irriel O'Gara
TCD Survey 1617	Lissballylee, the qrter of Lisbalilee: ffarell O'Gara
Cal. Pat. Rolls Jas. I	The town, lands, and qrs … of Lisballilie … : Fergall O'Gara
1635 Strafford Survey	Lissballile .1. quar.
	The inheritance of fferril o Gara whoe setts it for .21. li it is good arr. lande a p*ar*te, it hath good wood et turffe, et 8. dayes mowinge, it will grase 205 cowes, et it is worth 21 li. p*er* Annu*m*.
	Caltnan .1. quar.
	The inheritance of fferrill o Gara whoe setts it for .21.£ it is p*ar*te good arr. lande, it hath some wood et turffe, 8. dayes mowg it will grase .205. cowes, et it is worth .21. li. p*er* Annu*m*.
BSD pre-1641	Lisballiha & Cultinan 2 qrs: ?fferrall & Owen O'Gara[69]
	262 a. prof.

---

69 It is uncertain from the layout of the text who owned the land, but likely it was jointly owned by Fergal O'Gara and Owen O'Gara. NAI, Books of Survey and Distribution: Sligo (microfilm), p. 132.

	A parcell of Bogg to them
	49 a. unprof.
BSD post-Cromwellian	262 a.: Lord Kingston
ASE 1667	Lisballilee and Colternan, 2 qrs, 262 a. prof. 49 a. unprof.: John Lord Kingston
	(Listed within a group of lands collectively worth 11*l* 8s. 7¾d. rent *per annum*)
TAB 1834	Lisballilee & Chasefield: 223 a.
	[Caltrane & Kilpruclish: 236 a.]
COMMENT:	There appears to be two townlands called Cultinan, as indicated by Petty's map: one called 'Caltima' south of Cloontycarn and Mullaghroe, perhaps located somewhere in present-day Mahanagh, and one called 'Caltiman' on the northern border of Kilfree just west of the Owenmore River (the present-day Calteraun).

Lissoshinagh

MODERN EQUIVALENT:	Gortygara
CIVIL PARISH:	Kilfree
Inq. 1614 (a)	qr de Licloshiny: Irriel O'Gara
Inq. 1614 (b)	Carro Lissoshimii: Irriel O'Gara let to Taaffe
Inq. 1615	qr voc. Carrowlissesheny: Irriel O'Gara
TCD Survey 1617	the qrter of Lisshesiny: Fergal O'Gara
Cal. Pat. Rolls Jas. I	Lishosyny … 1 qr each: Ferrall O'Gara
1635 Strafford Survey	Lissosina .1. quar.
	The inheritance of ffarill o Gara whoe setts it to undertennants for .7.£ it is good arr. lande, it hath good turffe, noe wood- 4. dayes mowinge, it will grase .35. cowes et it is worth 7£ *per* Annum.
BSD pre-1641	Gortivara als. Gurtigara Ardullman(?) and Lishoshina als Lishierovine 2 qrs: fferrall O'Gara
	139 a. prof.
	Two severall parcells of Bogg belonging to the sd 2 qrs: ?fferrall O'Gara (owner not explicitly stated)
	85 a. unprof.
	An other parcell of pasturable Bogg
	3 a. unprof.; 3 a. prof.
	[Gortigarra als. Ardcolman als. Cloonkigles 1 qr: ffarrell O'Gara
	147 a. prof.
	parcell of Bogg to the Same the most Grazeable: ffarrell O'Gara
	58 a. unprof.; 28 a. prof.]
BSD post-Cromwellian	142 a.: Lord Kingston
Petty's map	Lisconan
ASE	Lishin als Ruine, 1 qr 142 a. prof. 88 a. unprof.: John Lord Kingston
	(Listed within a group of lands collectively worth 11*l* 8s. 7¾d. rent *per annum*).
TAB 1834	[Gurtigara: 175 a.]

---

70 O'Flanagan (ed.), *Ordnance Survey Name Books, Sligo, Volume 1, from Achonry to Killaraght*, p. 424.

| COMMENT: | In the Ordnance Survey Name Books, Sligo, John O'Donovan says that 'Lissashonagh' is the name of the old fort near the east side of Gortygara.[70] |

Mahanagh – see entry for Carronamahowny

Mount Irvine – see entry for Knockmore

Moyduagh

MODERN EQUIVALENT:	Moydough
CIVIL PARISH:	Kilfree
Inq. 1614 (b)	?Carronii droagh: Irriel O'Gara let to Taaffe
Inq. 1615	Carrowmoydowe: Irriel O'Gara
TCD Survey 1617	the qrter of Moyduan: Fergal O'Gara
Cal. Pat. Rolls Jas. I	Moydowagh … 1 qr each: Ferrall O'Gara
1635 Strafford Survey	Moyduagh .1. quar.
	The inheritance of fferrill o Gara whoe setts it for 16£ *per* An. it is some p*ar*te good arr. lande, it hath some shelter, *et* some heathey grounde, it hath good turffe, 6. dayes mowinge, it will grase .80. cowes *et* it is worth 16 li. p*er* Annu*m*. (A second mention occurs after the entry for Carrowreagh) p*ar*cel of Bog belonging to Sephin Moydow & Carrowreagh
	157 a. unprof.
BSD pre-1641	Moydow 1 qr: ffarrell & Owen O'Gara
	55 a. prof.
BSD post-Cromwellian	Lord Kingston
Petty's map	Moydan
ASE 1667	Moydough, 1 qr. 55 a.: John Lord Kingston
	(Listed within a group of lands collectively worth 11*l* 8s. 7¾d. rent *per annum*.)
TAB 1834	Moydoo, Milroe, & Keldun: 187 a.
COMMENT:	The name 'Carronii droagh' listed in *Inq. 1614 (b)* is likely to be Moydough since it is listed between Cloonanure and Greyfield (Carrowreagh), the townlands directly to the north of Moydough. The minims at the end of 'Carronii' should perhaps be interpreted as 'Carromi'. TAB lists Moydough together with 'Milroe', which is presumably 'Mweelroe', the townland at the eastern border of Kilfree, and Keldun (unidentified). Perhaps Mweelroe, which is not at all contiguous to Moydough, was a detached upland portion of Moydow?

Moygara

	(See entries for Carrowcaslan and Killeskorny above)
MODERN EQUIVALENT:	Moygara
CIVIL PARISH:	Kilfree
TCD Survey 1617	The mannor, castle, towne, and lands of Moygarra: Fergal O'Gara

71 Griffiths (ed.), *Calendar of the Irish patent rolls of James I*, p. 322.

Cal. Pat. Rolls Jas. I	The **castle, manor, town, and lands of Moygara**; Carowcaslane, Caronakilskorny, Carrownamollaghroe or Kilmacruahy, Carowna-meahany, 1 qr each: Ferrall O'Gara[71] (Later separate entry below) Deed from Oriell O'Garye alias O'Gariye of Moyghygarye in the county of Sligo, to Donogh O'Connor Sligo, of Sligo, in said county, granting to the said O'Connor Sligo for ever, all his interest in **the town and castle of Moyghygarye**, the castle of Copnaghe, the castle of Derrymore in the half barony of Cullovin in said county, with all the lands, tenements, lordships, mill, territories, &c. to the same belonging; with covenants against all other persons. – 21 May, 1st, 1603.[72]
1635 Strafford Survey	Moygara .1. quar. The inheritance of ffarrill o Gara, whoe sets it to undertennants for .21.£ it is some parte good arr. lande, it hath good shelter et fir=wood, et a greate scope of mounteyne, 7. dayes mowinge it will grase .205. cowes, et is worth .21.£ per Annum. ther is an ould castle uppon this quar.
BSD pre-1641	Moggarra 2 qrs: fferrall O'Gara 35 a. unprof. 230 a. prof. Stonie wood belonging to the same: fferrall O'Gara 46 a. unprof.; 46 a. prof. (Second mention below after entry for Mahana) Parcell of unprof. Bogg belonging to Maggarra & Mahanna lying to the Lough Side: ffarrell O'Gara 106 a. unprof. A small parcell of good pasturable wood pt. of Mahana lying on the lough side: ffarrell O'Gara 7 a. prof. A great parcell of Grazeable Mount. & pasture wood which anciently belonged to the qrs. before Expressed. 1240 a. unprof.; 430 a. prof.
BSD post-Cromwellian	Moggarra: 276 a. prof.: Lord Kingston
Petty's map	Moygara
Census 1659	Moygara: 38 Irish
Hearth Roll 1665	Cluane, William, Moygara, Kilfree Connellane, Patrick, Moygara, Kilfree Gara, Connor, Moygara, Kilfree Gara, Fardinando, Moygara, Kilfree Hagane, William, Moygara, Kilfree Mc Kae, Moragh, Moygara, Kilfree Linch, Edmond, Moygara, Kilfree O Lunine, Donnell, Moygara, Kilfree Mc Mullroinfyn, Cahall, Moygara, Kilfree

72 Griffiths (ed.), *Calendar of the Irish patent rolls of James I*, p. 475.   **73** MacLysaght (ed.), 'Seventeenth century hearth money rolls with full transcript relating to County Sligo', pp 26, 28, 46, 54, 68, 70, 75, 79.

	Mc Mullroinfyn, Terlagh, Moygara, Kilfree
	Raghtagane, Rory, Moygara, Kilfree[73]
ASE 1667	Carrowlassan, Moygarrow, and Lisornagh or Killscornagh, 2 qrs 276 a. prof. 81 a. unprof.: John Lord Kingston
	In first group of lands worth 17*l* 12s. 1¼ d. rent *per annum*
BSD post-1688	69 a. of the 276 a. of Moygara and the 176 a. of Cloonsillagh went to Trustees of the Barracks
TFE 1703	Moygarra, 4 qrs: George Gore
TAB 1834	Moygara: 710 a.
COMMENT:	The modern townland of Moygara corresponds to the early modern quarters of Carrowcaslane and Killeskorny.

Mullaghroy   (alias Kilmacrowhie)

MODERN EQUIVALENT:	Mullaghroe
CIVIL PARISH:	Kilfree
Inq. 1614 (a)	de castro (etc.) de Moygarra cum 3 qr. viz qr de **Mullaghroy**, qr de Kyleskorny, qr de Carronamahowny …' Irriel O'Gara
Inq. 1614 (b)	the 3 qr of Moagh Igara viz. the qr of the Castle, Carrownakylly-skornii, Carrowna Mahanii, **Carroan Mullaghroy**: Irriel O'Gara let to Taaffe
Inq. 1615	de castro et vill. de Moygara, ac de 3 qr, viz. **qr de Mullaghroy**, qr de Carrownemahawny, qr de Killeskarny ac de qr de Carrowndowne, et de qr de Carroreogh quod praemiss. tenentur de Rege in capite per servic. militare: Irriel O'Gara held by knight's service.
	(Possible separate entry further down in text)
	? qr voc. Carrowkillinacrowhie: Irriel O'Gara
TCD Survey 1617	the quarter called Carrowanmullagh roe als killmcruohe: Fergal O'Gara
Cal. Pat. Rolls Jas. I	To Ferral O'Gara of Moygara … The castle, manor, town, and lands of Moygara; Carowcaslane, Carownakilskorny, **Carrownamullaghroe or Kilmacruahy**, Carownameahany, 1 qr each
1635 Strafford Survey	Carowmullgroe .1. qr.
	The inheritance of ffarrell o Gara whoe setts it to undertenna*n*ts for 10 li. it is some p*ar*te arr. lande et heathey grounde, it hath good turffe et shelter, it will grase .100. cowes, et it is worth .10. li. p*er* Annu*m*.
BSD pre-1641	Mullaghroe 1 qr: ffarrell O'Gara
	6 a. unprof.; 30 a. prof.
	p*ar*cell of Bogg to the same: 16 a. prof.
BSD post-Cromwellian	30 a.: Lord Kingston
Petty's map	Mullatow
Census 1659	Mullaghroe: 34 Irish
ASE 1667	Molloroe, 1 qr 30 a. prof. 16 a. unprof.: John Lord Kingston
	In first group of lands worth 17*l* 12s. 1¼d. rent *per annum*
TFE 1703	Moygarra, 4 qrs: George Gore
TAB 1834	Mullaghroe: 227 a.
COMMENT:	The modern townland of Moygara encompasses the early modern quarters of Carrowcaslane and Killeskorny.

Mweelroe – not mentioned in the early modern sources. See entry for Carrowreagh for mention of Mweelroe in the Tithe Applotment Books.

Ramadder

MODERN EQUIVALENT:	Rathmadder
CIVIL PARISH:	Kilfree
Inq. 1614 (a)	qr de Ramadder: Irriel O'Gara
Inq. 1614 (b)	Carro Ramedder: Irriel O'Gara let to Taaffe
Inq. 1615	qr voc. Carrowramaddir: Irriel O'Gara
TCD Survey 1617	The qrter of Rathmadder: Fergal O'Gara
Cal. Pat. Rolls Jas. I	Rathmadder … 1 qr each: Ferrall O'Gara
BSD pre-1641	Rathmadder 1 qr: ?ffarrell O'Gara[74]
	62 a. prof.
	Bogg belonging to the same
	35 a. unprof.
BSD post-Cromwellian	Bryan Magrath: 62 a.
ASE 1667	Rosmader or Rahinader, 1 qr 62 a. 12s. 6¾d.: Bryan Magrath
	(Listed within a group of lands collectively worth 8*l.* 6s. 7½d. rent *per annum.*)
TAB 1834	Rathmadder: 101 a.

Rinnasharragh

MODERN EQUIVALENT:	Cuilmore
CIVIL PARISH:	Kilfree
Inq. 1614 (b)	Laghvuline Killemore viz Carro Rugnnesharragh, Carron Tyan: Irriel O'Gara let to Taaffe
Inq. 1615	2 qr. de Koylmore vocat Carrowrummesharragh et Carrowentyhane: Irriel O'Gara
TCD Survey 1617	the qrter of Rinnasharagh: Bryan MacDonagh
Cal. Pat. Rolls Jas. I	Grant from the King to sir Arthur Savage, knt, privy councillor … SLIGO Co'. In Coilmore, Shean, and Rinsharragh, 1 qr; the estate of Teig O'Gary otherwise Teig ne Gann, slain in rebellion; rent, 5s. – To hold for ever, as of the castle of Dublin, in common soccage.
	(This entry appears 3 years before the reference below to Carrowntihannacuilmore within the general lists of Sligo landownership, p. 265.)[75]
	towns, lands, and qrs of … Carrowantihannacoilmore; Rinnasharragh, 1 qr: Bryan McDonogh[76]
1635 Strafford Survey	[Collemore .2. qrs
	The inheritance of Mr Dodwell whoe lett this (?) for .30. li. p*er* Annu*m*. it is some p*ar*te good arr. lande, it hath good wood, et turffe, some 8. dayes mowinge, it will grase .300. cowes et are worth .30. li. per Annu*m*.]

---

74 It is uncertain from the layout of the text who owned the land, but it was likely owned by Fergal O'Gara, or possibly jointly owned by Fergal O'Gara & Owen O'Gara. NAI, Books of Survey and Distribution: Sligo (microfilm), p. 132.   **75** Griffiths (ed.), *Calendar of the Irish patent rolls of James I*, p. 265.   **76** Griffiths (ed.), *Calendar of the Irish patent rolls of James I*, p. 321.

BSD pre-1641	Killmore als Carrowintihan 2 qrs
	228 a. prof.
	p*ar*cell of mountaine graseable in summer belonging to Kilmore etc.:
	?fferall O'Gara (ownership not explicitly stated)
	102 a. prof.; 35 a. unprof.
	An other p*ar*cell of Boggy mount: belonging to Killmore
	259 a. unprof. : ?fferrall O'Gara[77]
BSD post-Cromwellian	263 a.: Lord Kingston
Petty's map	Killmore
TAB 1834	Kilmore: 596 a.
COMMENT:	• Together with Carrowantihane, Rinnasharragh comprised the modern townland of Cuilmore.
	• A Crown Rental says the lands of Coilemore Risharragh et Shean were confiscated from Teige O'Gary als Teige ne Gannie, who was attainted for rebellion, and assigned to Arthur Savage at 5 shillings per year rent.[78] This statement is in line with the first entry for Coilmore in the *Calendar of Irish patent rolls* noted above.

Sephin

Sephin	(See entry for Clooneagh)
MODERN EQUIVALENT:	Seefin
CIVIL PARISH:	Kilfree
1635 Strafford Survey	Soyfin*n* & Cloneagh (2 .qrs.)
	The inherit. of ffarrell o Gara whoe setts them towe qr for .16. li it is all wood et mounteyns as aforsd. it will grase .30. cowes, et is worth .16. li. p*er* Annu*m*.
BSD pre-1641	Sephin 1 qr: ffarrell & Owen O'Gara
	99 a. prof.
	Several p*ar*cells of Bogg to the same: ffarrell & Owen O'Gara
	42 a. unprof.
	(A second entry relating to Seefin occurs after entry for Carrowreagh)
	p*ar*cel of Bog belonging to Sephin Moydow & Carrowreagh
	157 a. unprof.
BSD post-Cromwellian	59 a. Bryan Magrath
	54 a. Lord Kingston
Petty's map	Sephen
Census 1659	Sexifind: 71 Irish
ASE 1667/ASE 1678	Shiffin, 1 qr 54 a. prof. 199 a. unprof.: John Lord Kingston
	(Listed within a group of lands collectively worth 11*l* 8s. 7¾d. rent *per annum*.)
	in Sheerohin or Sheephin, 1 qr 59 a. 11s. 11¼d.: Bryan Magrath
	In group of lands worth 8*l*. 6s. 7½d. rent *per annum*
TAB 1834	Seefin: 113 a.

---

77 It is uncertain from the layout of the text who owned the land, but it was likely owned by Fergal O'Gara, or possibly jointly owned by Fergal O'Gara & Owen O'Gara. NAI, Books of Survey and Distribution: Sligo (microfilm), p. 132.   **78** TCD, MS 570, f. 285v.

Sragh – not mentioned in the early modern sources; see entry for Carrowreagh for mention of Sragh in the Tithe Applotment Books.

ADDITIONAL LAND DENOMINATIONS NOTED IN KILFREE BY SEVERAL SOURCES

Islands

MODERN EQUIVALENT:	?
CIVIL PARISH:	Kilfree
BSD pre-1641	A small Island called (name left blank) being pt. of (left blank): ffarrell O'Gara
	6 a. prof. An Island called (name left blank): Sir Robert King
	15 a. prof.
BSD post-Cromwellian	21 a.: Bryan Magrath
ASE 1667	Two small islands, 21 a. 4s. 2¾d.: Bryan Magrath
	(Listed within a group of lands collectively worth 8*l*. 6s. 7½d. rent *per annum*.)

Wooded Mountain

MODERN EQUIVALENT:	?
CIVIL PARISH:	Kilfree
BSD pre-1641	A parcell of grazeable mount: & woods in the possn. of ffarrell O Gara & claimed by Sr. Rob. King sd. to be of Kilfree parish cont:
	349 a.: unprof; 116 a. prof.
	more by Distribucon:
	10 a. prof.

The regional affiliations of Killaraght

ANNE CONNON

During the medieval and early modern periods, control of the Killaraght region appears to have oscillated between the O'Gara lordship of Coolavin and the Mac Diarmaida (Mac Dermot) lordship of Moylurg. The earliest documentary evidence, though, links Killaraght to Coolavin and Luighne.

In the Ecclesiastical Taxation of 1306–7, the parish of Killaraght was listed as part of Achonry, the medieval diocese whose borders were felt to correspond to those of the kingdom of Luighne.[1] Although the taxation's evidence does not constitute absolute proof that the parish was part of Achonry when diocesan borders were decided upon in the mid-twelfth century, it does strongly suggest that the Killaraght area was part of pre-Norman Luighne.

Further evidence linking Killaraght to Luighne is found within the early thirteenth-century literary text, *Acallam na senórach*. The *Acallam* is the first text to mention the place-name 'Cúil Ó bhFind', which it locates within Luighne.[2] The text's references to Cúil Ó bhFind occur within the context of an episode that centres around the site of *Lis na mBan*, 'the enclosure of the women'.[3] It is almost certain that the name *Lis na mBan* here is a coded reference to Ceall Athractha, an important medieval nunnery which lent its name to Killaraght.[4] Just as the *Acallam* places Cúil Ó bhFind within Luighne, so does it place *Lis na mBan* within Cúil Ó bhFind / Coolavin.

By the beginning of the fifteenth century, however, control of Killaraght appears to have shifted from the O'Gara lordship of Coolavin to the Mac Diarmada lordship of Moylurg. This surmised shift is suggested by evidence found in the Registry of Clonmacnoise, a seventeenth-century English translation of a text which may have been written in the early thirteenth century but revised in the late fourteenth century.[5] The Registry claims that a Mac Diarmada lord donated '48 daies' from Killaraght (presumably the fruits of 48 days of work) to Clonmacnoise, a gift which would seem to indicate that Killaraght was at that time under Mac Diarmada control.[6]

Late sixteenth- and early seventeenth-century documents provide more conclusive evidence regarding Moylurg's control of Killaraght. As noted in the body of the text, the cartographic evidence indicates that in this period almost all of Killaraght was considered part of Co. Roscommon;[7] this arrangement would suggest that when the counties were created in the

---

1 H.S. Sweetman and G.F. Handcock (eds), *Calendar of documents relating to Ireland preserved in her majesty's Public Record Office, London 1302–1307* (London, 1866; reprint Nendeln, Liechtenstein, 1974), p. 291. 2 W. Stokes (ed.), 'Acallamh na senórach' in W. Stokes and E. Windisch (eds), *Irische Texte*, series 4, volume 1 (Leipzig, 1900), p. 207; A. Dooley and H. Roe (eds and trans.), *Tales of the elders of Ireland: a new translation of Acallamh na senórach* (Oxford, 1999), p. 208. 3 Stokes, 'Acallamh na senórach', p. 205; Dooley and Roe, *Tales of the elders of Ireland*, p. 206. 4 Anne Connon 'The use of *Acallam na senórach* as an historical source for the political history of Connacht', paper read at the Irish Conference of Medievalists, Galway, Ireland, June 2011. 5 A. Kehnel, *Clonmacnois – the church and lands of St Ciarán* (Münster, 1997), pp 210–19. 6 J. O'Donovan, 'The Registry of Clonmacnoise. With notes and introductory remarks', *Journal of the Kilkenny and South-East of Ireland*

sixteenth century, Killaraght was not under the sway of the O'Gara dynasty whose holdings were in Co. Sligo. Further evidence indicating that at least part of the Killaraght area was under Mac Diarmada's sway is found in *The Compossicion Booke of Conought*, dated to 1586; this text lists fifteen quarters of 'The Ranna' – the alternative name for Killaraght – as part of the territory belonging to the barony of Moylurg.[8] 'Na Ranna' means 'the divisions' and the name possibly reflects some sort of land division arrangement between the lordships of Moylurg and Coolavin concerning the Killaraght region.

Conversely, an indication that the O'Garas of Coolavin still retained some sort of –possibly overlapping – claim in the Killaraght area is found in a 1586 record of Irriel O'Gara's granting five *baile* of The Ranna to Theobald Dillon. Included within the grant was Derrymore castle, a fortification on the Killaraght island of Derrymore Big.[9] Then, in 1603, Irriel O'Gara was said to have granted Derrymore Castle, along with Cuppanagh Castle, another fortification in Killaraght, to O'Conor Sligo.[10] Furthermore, when Irriel died 10 years later, he was said to have owned several townlands in Killaraght.[11] Irriel's grandson and heir, Fergal O'Gara, was to expand the O'Gara holdings in Killaraght, and is named as the owner of a number of further Killaraght townlands, mostly in the northern section of the parish.[11]

Archaeological Society, 1 (1856/7), pp 444–60, at 451.   **7** See chapter 2, figs. 2.2–2.3.   **8** A.M. Freeman (ed.), *The compossicion booke of Conought* (Dublin, 1936), p. 158.   **9** *ALC* 1586.   **10** M.C. Griffiths (ed.), *Calendar of the Irish patent rolls of James I* (Dublin, 1965), p. 475.   **11** NAI, MS RC 9/15, nos. 17 and 19.   **12** NAI, Books of Survey and Distribution: Sligo (microfilm); BL, MS 2048, under the heading 'Coolavin'.

Bibliography

MANUSCRIPT SOURCES

Brussels
Archives Generales du Royaume
Solicitors of Brabant, Deed No. 51, 17 Apr. 1776.

Department des Imprimes, Bibliotheque Royale
Will of Count Charles O'Gara, 1773.

Dublin
Genealogical Office
Registered Pedigrees, vol. 5, MS 162
MSS 482–5

National Archives of Ireland
Books of Survey and Distribution: Sligo (microfilm)
MS RC 9/15, Inquisitions 17 and 19.
Tithe Applotment Books 1834 (microfilm).

National Library of Ireland
MS 21 F 13, no. 39 (Kingston estate maps)
MS 2165 (Hearth Money Roll, Co. Sligo)
MS 3649: 'A statistical account of the county of Roscommon by the Reverend John Keogh,
    drawn up by Sir William Petty, Superintendent of the Down Survey Anno Domino 1683'
    (copy of the original)

Registry of Deeds
O'Gara to Barnewall et al., no. 39572, book 57

Royal Irish Academy
MS 23 F 16 (Book of O'Gara)
MS 23 L 44 (George Petrie, Diary of a tour of Longford and Sligo)
MS 23 N 29, f. 4r
MS 535 (23 P 2: Book of Lecan)
MS 536 (23 P 12: Book of Ballymote)
MS 1220 (C iii 3: Annals of the Four Masters)
MS D II 1 (Leabhar Uí Maine)

Trinity College Dublin
MS 570, ff 36v, 285v.
MS 831, f. 68v.
MS 1209/68 (John Browne's map of Connaught and Thomond, AD 1591)

University College Dublin
UCD-OFM, MS A 13 (Louvain copy of the Annals of the Four Masters)

London
British Library
Harleian MS 2048, Coolavin barony

Public Record Office
SP 63/379

Madrid
Archivo Historico Nacional
Microfilm Exp. 1085, Alcántara, ff 49r–50r, 53r, 35v 21 47, 50v
Micros 112 NP/377 exp. 5854, MM Santiago, f. 9r

Sligo
Sligo Public Library
Co. Sligo Microfilm, MF/R.18 (Books of Survey and Distribution: County of Sligo)
'Down Survey Co. Sligo parish maps (1654–7): 38 Sheets'
'Surveys and rentals of lands in Sligo in the 17th & 18th cc', McDonagh MS xiii S/R

EDITED SOURCES

'Abstracts of grants of lands and other hereditaments, under the Acts of Settlement and Explanation, A.D. 1666–1684', *Record Commissioners Report*, 15 (London, 1825), pp 130, 258.

'Abstracts of the conveyances from the trustees of the forfeited estates and interests in Ireland in 1688', *Record Commissioners Report*, 15 (London, 1825), p. 370.

Bieler, Ludwig (ed. and trans.), *The Patrician documents in the Book of Armagh* (Dublin, 1979).

Bliss, William Henry and Jesse Alfred Twemlow (eds), *Calendar of papal registers relating to Great Britain and Ireland*, iv: *1362–1404* (London, 1902).

Bliss, William Henry and Jesse Alfred Twemlow (eds), *Calendar of entries in the papal registers relating to Great Britain and Ireland*, v: *1396–1404* (London, 1904).

Brewer, John Sherren and William Bullen (eds), *Calendar of the Carew manuscripts, 1515–1574* (London, 1867).

Brewer, John Sherren and William Bullen (eds), *Calendar of the Carew manuscripts, 1575–1588* (London, 1868).

Carney, James (ed.), *Topographical poems by Seaán Mór Ó Dubhagáin and Giolla-Na-Naomh Ó hUidhrín* (Dublin, 1943).

Cunningham, Bernadette (ed.), *Calendar of state papers, Ireland: Tudor period, 1566–1567* (Dublin, 2009).

Dooley, Ann and Harry Roe (eds and trans.), *Tales of the elders of Ireland: a new translation of Acallamh na senórach* (Oxford, 1999).

Freeman, A. Martin (ed.), 'The Annals in Cotton MS Titus A. XXV', *Revue Celtique*, 41 (1924), pp 301–30.

Freeman, A. Martin (ed.), 'The Annals in Cotton MS Titus A. XXV', *Revue Celtique*, 42 (1925), pp 283–305.

Freeman, A. Martin (ed.), 'The Annals in Cotton MS Titus A. XXV', *Revue Celtique*, 43 (1926), pp 358–84.

Freeman, A. Martin (ed.), 'The Annals in Cotton MS Titus A. XXV', *Revue Celtique*, 44 (1927), pp 336–61.

Freeman, A. Martin (ed.), *The compossicion booke of Conought* (Dublin, 1936).

Freeman, A. Martin (ed.), *The Annals of Connacht* (Dublin, 1944).

Giblin, Cathaldus (ed.), 'Vatican archives', *Archivium Hibernicum*, 31 (1973).

Griffiths, Margaret C. (ed.), *Calendar of the Irish patent rolls of James I* (Dublin, 1965).

Griffiths, Margaret C. (ed.), *Irish patent rolls of James I: facsimile of the Irish Record Commission's calendar prepared prior to 1830* (Dublin, 1966).

Hamilton, Hans-Claude (ed.), *Calendar of state papers, Ireland: Elizabeth, 1586–1588,* 126 (London, 1877).

Hamilton, Hans-Claude (ed.), *Calendar of state papers, Ireland: Elizabeth, 1588–92,* 146 (London, 1885).

Hennessey, William M. (ed.), *Chronicum Scotorum: a chronicle of Irish affairs from the earliest times to A.D. 1135: with a supplement containing the events from 1141 to 1150* (London, 1866).

Hennessey, William M. (ed.), *The Annals of Lough Cé*, 2 vols (Dublin, 1871).

Hennessey, William M. and Bartholomew McCarthy (eds), *The Annals of Ulster*, 4 vols (Dublin, 1887–1901).

Hogan, James (ed.), *Letters and papers relating to the Irish rebellion between 1642–46* (Dublin, 1936).

Hogan, Edmund, *Onomasticon Goedelicum locorum et tribuum Hiberniae et Scotiae: an index, with identifications, to the Gaelic names of places and tribes* (Dublin, 1910; 1993).

Lyle, J.V. (ed.), *Acts of the privy council of England, 1621–1623*, vol. 38 (London, 1932).

Mahaffy, Robert Pentland (ed.), *Calendar of state papers relating to Ireland 1633–47* (London, 1901).

MacLysaght, Edward (ed.), 'Seventeenth-century hearth money rolls with full transcript relating to County Sligo', *AH*, 24 (1967), pp 1–89.

Morrin, James (ed.), *Calendar of patent and close rolls of chancery in Ireland; from the 18th year to 45th of Queen Elizabeth*, vol. 2 (Dublin and London, 1862).

Mulchrone, Kathleen (ed.), *Bethu Phátraic: the tripartite life of Patrick* (Dublin, 1939).

Nicholls, Kenneth W. (ed.), *The Irish fiants of the Tudor sovereigns: during the reigns of Henry VIII, Edward VI, Philip and Mary and Elizabeth I*, 4 vols (Dublin, 1994).

Ó Donnchadha, Tadhg (ed.), 'Cin Lae Uí Mhealláin', *AH*, 3 (1931), pp 1–61.

O'Donovan, John (ed.), *The Annals of the Kingdom of Ireland by the Four Masters*, 7 vols (Dublin, 1848–51).

O'Dowd, Mary (ed.), *Calendar of state papers, Ireland: Tudor period, 1571–1575* (Dublin, 2000).

O'Ferrall, Roger, *Linea Antigua* (Dublin, 1709).

O'Flanagan, Fr Michael (ed.), *Letters containing information relative to the antiquities of the county of Sligo* (Bray, 1927).

O'Flanagan, Fr Michael (ed.), *Ordnance Survey Name Books, Sligo, volume 1, from Achonry to Killaraght* (Bray, 1927).

Ó hInnse, Seamus (ed.), *Miscellaneous Irish annals* (Dublin, 1947).

Ohlmeyer, Jane and Éamonn Ó Ciardha (eds), *The Irish statute staple books, 1596–1687* (Dublin, 1998).

Ó Muraíle, Nollaig (ed. and trans.), *An leabhar mór na ngenealach: the great book of Irish genealogies, by Dubhaltach Mac Fhirbhisigh*, 5 vols (Dublin, 2004).

Ó Murchadha, Diarmaid, Kevin Murray and Pádraig Ó Riain (eds), *Historical dictionary of Gaelic placenames/Foclóir stairiúil áitainmneacha na Gaeilge*, vol. 1 ['Letter A' of revised *Onomasticon*] (London, 2003).

Ó Raithbheartaigh, Toirdhealbhach (ed. and trans.), *Genealogical tracts 1* (Dublin, 1932).

Ó Riain, Pádraig (ed.), *Corpus genealogiarum sanctorum Hiberniae* (Dublin, 1985).

Pender, Seumas (ed.), *A census of Ireland circa 1659, with supplementary material from the poll money ordinances, 1660–1661* (Dublin, 1939).

Pender, Seumas (ed.), 'The O'Clery Book of Genealogies', *AH*, 18 (1951), pp i–xxxiv, 1–198.

Record Commissioners Report 15 (London, 1825).

Stokes, Whitley (ed. and trans.), *The tripartite life of Patrick*, 2 vols (London, 1887).

Stokes, Whitley (ed.), 'Acallamh na senórach' in Whitley Stokes and Ernest Windisch (eds), *Irische Texte*, series 4, (Leipzig, 1900), i, pp 1–438.

Stokes, Whitley (ed.), 'The Annals of Tigernach', *Revue Celtique*, 18 (1897), pp 9–95, 150–97, 267–303.

Simmington, Robert C. (ed.), *Books of Survey and Distribution, being abstracts of various surveys and instruments of title, 1636–1703*, i: *Roscommon* (Dublin, 1949).

Sweetman, Henry Savage and Gustavus Frederick Handcock (eds), *Calendar of documents relating to Ireland preserved in her majesty's Public Record Office, London 1302–1307* (London, 1866; Nendeln, Liechtenstein, 1974).

Taaffe, Karl, *Memoirs of the family of Taaffe* (Vienna, 1856).

Twemlow, Jesse Alfred (ed.), *Calendar of papal registers relating to Great Britain and Ireland*, vi: *1404–1415* (London, 1904).

Twemlow, Jesse Alfred (ed.), *Calendar of papal registers relating to Great Britain and Ireland*, vii: *1417–1431* (London, 1906).

Twemlow, Jesse Alfred (ed.), *Calendar of papal registers relating to Great Britain and Ireland*, viii: *1427–1447* (London, 1909).

Twemlow, Jesse Alfred (ed.), *Calendar of papal registers relating to Great Britain and Ireland*, ix: *1431–1447* (London, 1912).

Twemlow, Jesse Alfred (ed.), *Calendar of papal registers relating to Great Britain and Ireland*, x: *1447–1455* (London, 1915).

Twemlow, Jesse Alfred (ed.), *Calendar of papal registers relating to Great Britain and Ireland*, xiv: *1484–1492* (London, 1960).

Ward, Catherine Coogan and Robert E. Ward (eds), *The letters of Charles O'Conor of Belanagare*, 2 vols (Ann Arbor, MI, 1980).

Ward, Robert E., John F. Wrynn, SJ and Catherine Ward (eds), *The letters of Charles O'Conor of Belanagare: a Catholic voice in eighteenth-century Ireland,* 2 vols (Washington, 1988).

SECONDARY SOURCES

Alcock, N.W., 'Tree-ring date lists 2010', *Vernacular Architecture*, 41 (2010), pp 84–122.

Anderson, Hans, Barbara Scholkmann and Mette Svart Kristiansen, 'Medieval archaeology at the outset of the third millenium: research and teaching' in James Graham-Campbell with Magdalena Valor (eds), *The archaeology of medieval Europe*, i: *eighth to twelfth centuries AD* (Aarhus, 2007), pp 19–45.

Andrews, John H., 'Ordnance Survey' in Brian Lalor (ed.), *The encyclopaedia of Ireland* (Dublin, 2003), p. 840.

Andrews, John H., 'Sir Richard Bingham and the mapping of western Ireland', *PRIA*, 103C (2003), pp 61–95.

Anon., *The compleat gunner in three parts* (London, 1672).

Ashmore, P.J., 'Radiocarbon dating: avoiding errors by avoiding mixed samples', *Antiquity*, 73 (1999), pp 124–30.

Aspinall, Arnold, Chris Gaffney and Armin Schmidt, *Magnetometry for archaeologists* (Lanham, 2011).

Barry, Terence B., *The archaeology of medieval Ireland* (London and New York, 1987).

Barry, Terence B., 'Rural settlement in Ireland in the Middle Ages: an overview', *Ruralia,* 1 (1996), pp 134–41.

Barry, Terence B., 'Late medieval Ireland: the debate on the social and economic transformation, 1350–1550' in Brian J. Graham and Lindsay J. Proudfoot (eds), *A historical geography of Ireland* (London, 1993), pp 99–122.

Barton, Kevin, 'Control station layout and geo-referenced outline castle plan of Moygara Castle', Landscapes and Geophysical Services report 06/76/01 (2006).

Barton, Kevin and Joe Fenwick, 'Geophysical investigations at the ancient royal site of Rathcroghan, County Roscommon, Ireland', *Archaeological Prospection*, 12:1 (2005), pp 3–18.

Beglane, Fiona, 'Theatre of power: the Anglo-Norman park at Earlspark, Co. Galway, Ireland', *Medieval Archaeology*, 58 (2014), pp 307–16.

Berger, Rainer, '14C dating mortar in Ireland', *Radiocarbon*, 34 (1992), pp 880–9.

Berger, Rainer, 'Radiocarbon dating of early medieval Irish monuments', *PRIA*, 95C (1995), pp 159–74.

Blake-Forster, Charles F., *The Irish chieftains, or a struggle for the crown* (Dublin, 1872).

Brady, Niall, 'The Medieval Rural Settlement Project: an overview for 2002–2004', *Discovery Programme Reports 7* (Dublin, 2005), pp 1–2.

Brady, Niall, *Discovering Irish medieval landscapes* (Dublin, 2003).

Brady, Niall, Ann Connon, Rory McNeary, Brian Shanahan and Robert Shaw, 'A survey of the priory and graveyard at Tulsk, Co. Roscommon', *Discovery Programme Reports 7* (Dublin, 2005), pp 40–64.

Brady, Niall and Paul Gibson, 'The earthwork at Tulsk: topographical and geophysical excavations and preliminary excavations', *Discovery Programme Reports 7* (Dublin, 2005), pp 65–76.

Brady, Niall and Kieran O'Conor, 'The later medieval usage of crannogs in Ireland', *Ruralia*, 5 (2005), pp 127–36

Breen, Colin, *The Gaelic lordship of the O'Sullivan Beare: a landscape cultural history* (Dublin, 2005).

Breen, Colin, *Dunluce Castle: archaeology and history* (Dublin, 2012).

Brown, R. Allen, *English castles* (London, 1976).

Byrne, Frances John, *Irish kings and high-kings* (London, 1973; Dublin 2001).

Cairns, Conrad, *Irish tower houses: a Co. Tipperary case study* (Athlone, 1987).

Campbell, Eve, Elizabeth FitzPatrick and Audrey Horning (eds), *Becoming and belonging in Gaelic Ireland, AD c.1200–1600: essays in identity and cultural practice* (Cork, 2018).

Casey, Markus, 'Archaeological report Moygara Castle, 1992' (unpublished report, Galway 1992).

Clark, Anthony, *Seeing beneath the soil: prospecting methods in archaeology* (London, 1996).

Coey, A., B. Turner and E. Flegg, *An introduction to the architectural heritage of County Sligo* (Dublin, 2007).

Comber, Michelle, *Caherconnell Archaeological Project: summary of fieldwork to date* (Burren, 2014).

Comber, Michelle, 'Central places in a rural landscape', *Journal of the North Atlantic*, 36 (2018), pp 1–12.

Comber, Michelle, 'The tale of items lost … what items tell us about the life of a medieval family at Caherconnell Cashel, Co. Clare' in Joe Fenwick (ed.), *Lost and found III* (Dublin, 2018), pp 95–102.

Comber, Michelle and Graham Hull, 'Excavations at Caherconnell Cashel, the Burren, Co. Clare: implications for cashel chronology and Gaelic settlement', *PRIA*, 110C (2010), pp 133–73.

Connon, Anne, 'The Roscommon *locus* of *Acallam na senórach* and some thoughts as to *tempus* and *persona*' in Aidan Doyle and Kevin Murray (eds), *In dialogue with the Agallamh: essays in honour of Seán Ó Coileáin* (Dublin, 2014), pp 21–59.

Conyers, Laurence B., *Ground-penetrating radar for archaeology* (Lanham, 2004).

Craig, Maurice, *The architecture of Ireland from the earliest times to 1880* (London and Dublin, 1982).

Creighton, Oliver H., *Castles and landscapes: power, community and fortification in medieval England* (London, 2005).

Creighton, Oliver, *Designs upon the land: elite landscapes of the Middle Ages* (Woodbridge, 2009).

Cunningham, Bernadette, *The Annals of the Four Masters: Irish history, kingship and society in the early seventeenth century* (Dublin, 2010).

Cunningham, Bernadette, *Clanricard and Thomond, 1540–1640: provincial politics and society transformed* (Dublin, 2012).

Curley, Daniel, 'Observations from remote sensing of the earthwork at Dundonnell Castle, Co. Roscommon' in Richie Farrell, Kieran O'Conor and Matthew Potter (eds), *Roscommon history and society: interdisciplinary essays on the history of an Irish county* (Dublin, 2018), pp 133–56.

Curley, Daniel, 'Reconstructing the Lough Croan *cenn áit* of the medieval Ó Cellaig lordship of Uí Maine', *JRSAI*, 150 (2020), pp 201–24.

Curley, Daniel, '*Le triúcha chéd in Chalaidh a màeraidecht idir mincís mórthobach:* multi-disciplinary approaches to recovering an Ó Cellaig *cenn àit* in later medieval Uí Maine', *Eolas: the Journal of the American Society of Irish Medieval Studies*, 13 (2021), pp 2–42.

Curley, Daniel, 'A multi-disciplinary study of lordly centres in the later medieval Uí Chellaig lordship of Uí Maine, *c.*1100–1600 AD' (PhD, NUI Galway, 2022).

D'Alton, John, *The history of Ireland, from the earliest period to the year 1245, when the Annals of Boyle, which are adopted and embodied as the running text authority, terminate: with a brief essay on the native annalists, and other sources for illustrating Ireland, and full historical notices of the barony of Boyle* (Dublin, 1845).

D'Alton, John, *Illustrations, historical and genealogical of King James's Irish army list (1689)* (Dublin, 1855; Limerick, 1997).

Daubjerg, Thomas S. et al., 'A field guide to mortar sampling for radiocarbon dating', *Archaeometry*, 63:5 (2021), pp 1121–40.

Dempsey, Karen, 'Understanding "hall-houses": debating seigneurial buildings in Ireland in the 13th century', *Medieval Archaeology*, 61 (2017), pp 372–99.

Dempsey, Karen, '"Making a House a Home": odd deposits in ordinary households in later medieval Ireland 1200–1600 AD' in Catarina Tente and Claudia Theune (eds), *Household goods in the European medieval and early modern countryside*, Ruralia, 14 (Leiden, forthcoming).

Egan, Ursula, Elizabeth Byrne and Mary Sleeman, *Archaeological inventory of County Sligo*, Vol. 1: *South Sligo* (Dublin, 2005).

Fenlon, Jane (ed.), *Clanricard's Castle; Portumna House, Co. Galway* (Dublin, 2012).

Finan, Thomas (ed.), *Medieval Lough Cé: history, archaeology and landscape* (Dublin, 2010).

Finan, Thomas, 'Introduction: Moylurg and Lough Cé in the Middle Ages' in Thomas Finan (ed.), *Medieval Lough Cé: history, archaeology and landscape* (Dublin, 2010), pp 11–14.

Finan, Thomas, 'Moated sites in County Roscommon, Ireland: a statistical approach' in Peter Ettel, Anne-Marie Flambard-Héricher and Kieran O'Conor (eds), *Château Gaillard, 26: L'environment du château* (Caen, 2014), pp 177–80.

Finan, Thomas, *Landscape and history on the medieval Irish frontier: the King's Cantreds in the thirteenth century* (Turnhout, 2016).

Finan, Thomas, 'The Rock of Lough Key and the moated site at Rockingham: components of a lordly landscape' in Peter Ettel, Anne-Marie Flambard-Héricher and Kieran O'Conor (eds), *Château Gaillard, 28: L'environment du château* (Caen, 2018), pp 143–45.

Finan, Thomas, 'Living in Gaelic castles: inter-disciplinary advances in 13th-century Irish castle studies' in Peter Ettel, Anne-Marie Flambard-Héricher and Kieran O'Conor (eds), *Château Gaillard, 29: Vivre au château* (Caen, 2020), pp 107–13.

Finan, Thomas and Kieran O'Conor, 'The moated site at Cloonfree, Co. Roscommon', *JGAHS,* 54 (2002), pp 72–87.

FitzPatrick, Elizabeth, *Royal inauguration in Gaelic Ireland, c.1100–1600* (Woodbridge, 2004).

FitzPatrick, Elizabeth, 'Native enclosed settlement and the problem of the Irish "ringfort"', *Medieval Archaeology*, 53 (2009), pp 271–307.

FitzPatrick, Elizabeth, '*Formaoil na Fiann*: hunting preserves and assembly places in Gaelic Ireland', *Proceedings of the Harvard Celtic Colloquium*, 32 (2013), pp 95–118.

FitzPatrick, Elizabeth, 'The landscape and settlements of the Uí Dhálaigh poets of Muinter Bháire' in Sean Duffy (ed.), *Princes, prelates and poets in medieval Ireland: essays in honour of Katharine Simms* (Dublin, 2013), pp 460–80.

FitzPatrick, Elizabeth, 'Assembly places and elite collective identities in medieval Ireland', *Journal of the North Atlantic*, 8 (2015), pp 52–68.

FitzPatrick, Elizabeth, 'The last kings of Ireland: material expressions of Gaelic lordship, *c.*1300–1400' in Kate Buchanan, Lucinda H.S. Dean and Michael Penman (eds), *Medieval and early modern representations of authority in Scotland and the British Isles* (Oxford, 2016), pp 197–213.

FitzPatrick, Elizabeth, Eileen Murphy, Ronan McHugh and Colm J. Donnelly, 'Evoking the White Mare; the cult landscape of Sgiath Gabhra and its medieval perception in Gaelic Fir Mhanach' in Roseanne Schot, Conor Newman and Edel Bhreathnach (eds), *Landscapes of cult and kingship* (Dublin, 2011), pp 163–9.

Fitzpatrick, J.E., 'Ballymote Castle', *JRSAI*, 57 (1927), pp 81–99.

Foley, Clare and Colm J. Donnelly, *Parke's Castle, Co. Leitrim: archaeology, history and architecture* (Dublin, 2012).

Foley, Clare and Brian Williams, 'The crannogs of County Fermanagh' in Marion Meek (ed.), *The modern traveller to our past* (Belfast, 2006), pp 53–64.

Fredengren, Christina, *Crannogs* (Dublin, 2002).

Gaffney, Chris and John Gater, *Revealing the buried past: geophysics for archaeologists* (Stroud, 2003)

Galloway, James A., 'The economic hinterland of Drogheda in the later Middle Ages' in Victoria McAlister and Terence B. Barry (eds), *Space and settlement in medieval Ireland* (Dublin, 2015), pp 167–85.

Gallwey, Hubert Dayrell, 'Irish officers in the Spanish service', *Irish Genealogist*, 6 (1981), pp 204–11.

Gardiner, Mark and Kieran O'Conor, 'The later medieval countryside lying beneath' in Michael Stanley, Ronan Swan and Aidan O'Sullivan (eds), *Stories of Ireland's past: knowledge gained from the NRA roads archaeology* (Dublin, 2017), pp 133–52.

Garvey, Maire, *Mid-Connacht: the ancient territory of Sliabh Lugha* (Dublin, 1995).

Gibbons, Luke and Kieran O'Conor, 'Introduction: Charles O'Conor of Ballinagare (1710–91)' in Luke Gibbons and Kieran O'Conor (eds), *Charles O'Conor of Ballinagare, 1710–91: life and works* (Dublin, 2015), pp 19–27.

Gillespie, Raymond, *Seventeenth-century Ireland: making Ireland modern* (Dublin, 2006).

Goblet, Yann M., *A topographical index of the parishes and townlands of Ireland in Sir William Petty's MSS barony maps (c.1655–9)* (Dublin, 1932).

Goodwin, G., 'King, Robert (d. 1693)' in Sidney Lee (ed.), *Dictionary of national biography*, 31 (1885–1900), pp 155–6.

Grose, Francis, *The antiquities of Ireland*, 2 vols (London, 1791).

Guest, Edith, 'Irish Sheela-na-Gigs in 1935', *JRSAI*, 66 (1936), pp 107–29.

Gwynn, Aubrey and R. Neville Hadcock, *Medieval religious houses: Ireland* (London, 1970).

Hansson, Martin, *Aristocratic landscape: the spatial ideology of the medieval aristocracy* (Lund, 2006).

Hayden, Alan R., *Trim Castle, Co. Meath: excavations 1995–8* (Dublin, 2011).

Henry, Christopher and Brian Delf, *English Civil War artillery, 1642–51* (Oxford, 2005).

Higham, Robert and Philip Barker, *Hen Domen, Montgomery: a timber castle on the English-Welsh border: a final report* (Exeter, 2000).

Hill, George, *An historical account of the Plantation in Ulster at the commencement of the seventeenth century, 1608–1620* (Belfast, 1877).

Holland, Patrick, 'The Anglo-Normans and their castles in Co. Galway' in Gerard Moran and Raymond Gillespie (eds), *Galway history and society: interdisciplinary essays on the history of an Irish county* (Dublin, 1997), pp 1–26.

Horning, Audrey, 'Challenging colonial equations? The Gaelic experience in early modern Ireland' in Neal Ferris, Rodney Harrison and Michael V. Wilcox (eds), *Rethinking colonial pasts through archaeology* (Oxford, 2014), pp 293–314.

Hunter, Robert J., 'Plantation in Donegal' in William Nolan, Liam Ronayne and Mairead Dunlevy (eds), *Donegal history and society: interdisciplinary essays on the history of an Irish county* (Dublin, 1995), pp 283–324.

Hunter, Robert J., 'Sir William Cole, the town of Enniskillen and Plantation County Fermanagh' in Eileen Murphy and William J. Roulston (eds), *Fermanagh history and society: interdisciplinary essays on the history of an Irish county* (Dublin, 2004), pp 105–45.

Jennings, Brendan, *Michael Ó Cleirigh, chief of the Four Masters and his associates* (Dublin, 1936).

Kalkreuter, Barbara, *Boyle Abbey and the School of the West* (Bray, 2001).

Kelly, Eamonn P., *Sheela-na-Gigs: origins and functions* (Dublin, 1996).

Kenyon, John R., *Medieval fortifications* (Leicester and London, 1990).

Kerrigan, Paul M., 'Seventeenth-century fortifications, forts and garrisons in Ireland: a preliminary list', *Irish Sword*, 14 (1980), pp 3–24, 135–56.

Kerrigan, Paul M., *Castles and fortifications in Ireland, 1485–1945* (Cork, 1995).

Knox, Hubert Thomas, 'Occupation of Connaught by the Anglo-Normans after A.D. 1837 – Part III', *JRSAI*, 33 (1903), pp 58–74.

Lacey, Brian, *Archaeological inventory of County Donegal* (Lifford, 1983).

Lart, Charles Edmund, *Jacobite extracts, registers of Saint Germain-en-Laye*, 2 vols (London, 1910–12).

Leask, Harold G., *Irish castles and castellated houses* (Dundalk, 1941).

Leask, Harold G., *Irish churches and monastic buildings*, vol. 3 (Dundalk, 1960).

Lenihan, Padraig, 'War and population, 1649–52', *Irish Economic and Social History*, 24 (1997), pp 1–21.

Lenihan, Padraig, '"That most wasted country"; wartime Roscommon 1641–47' in Richie Farrell, Kieran O'Conor and Matthew Potter (eds), *Roscommon history and society: interdisciplinary essays on the history of an Irish county* (Dublin, 2018), pp 259–78.

Lenihan, Padraig, 'War in the Gap, Sligo 1641–91' in Kieran O'Conor (ed.), *Sligo history and society: interdisciplinary essays on the history of an Irish county* (Dublin, forthcoming).

Lennon, Colm, *Sixteenth-century Ireland* (Dublin, 1994; 2005).

Liddiard, Robert, '*Landscapes of lordship': Norman castles and the countryside in medieval Norfolk, 1066–1200*, BAR (Oxford, 2000).

Liddiard, Robert, *Castles in context: power, symbolism and fortification in medieval England* (Macclesfield, 2005).

Lodge, John, *The peerage of Ireland: or, a genealogical history of the present nobility of that kingdom,* vols 6 (Dublin, 1789).

Loeber, Rolf, *Irish houses and castles, 1400–1700* (Dublin, 2019).

Lydon, James, *The lordship of Ireland in the Middle Ages* (Dublin, 2003).

Lynn, Christopher J., 'The excavation of Rathmullan, a raised rath and motte in Co. Down', *Ulster Journal of Archaeology*, 44–5 (1981–2), pp 65–171.

Lynn, Christopher J., 'Some 13th-century castle sites in the west of Ireland: notes on a preliminary reconnaissance', *JGAHS*, 40 (1985–6), pp 90–113.

Lyttleton, James, *Blarney Castle: an Irish tower house* (Dublin, 2011).

Lyttleton, James, *The Jacobean Plantations in seventeenth-century Offaly* (Dublin, 2013).

Mac an Ghallóglaigh, Domhnaill, 'Sir Frederick Hamilton', *Breifne*, 3:9 (1966), pp 55–99.

McAlister, Victoria L., *The Irish tower house: society, economy and environment, c.1300–1650* (Manchester, 2019).

McCarthy, Daniel P., *The Irish annals: their genesis, evolution and history* (Dublin, 2008).

MacCotter, Paul, 'Diocese of Achonry: church, land, and history', *Peritia*, 24–5 (2013–14), pp 241–65.

MacCotter, Paul, *Medieval Ireland: territorial, political and economic divisions* (Dublin, 2014).

McCracken, Eileen, *The Irish woods since Tudor times* (Dublin, 1971).

McCracken, Eileen, 'The Irish timber trade in the seventeenth century', *Irish Forestry Journal*, 21:1 (1964), pp 7–20.

Mac Dermot, Betty, *Ó Ruairc of Breifne* (Manorhamilton, 1990).

Mac Dermot, Dermot, *Mac Dermot of Moylurg: the story of a Connacht family* (Manorhamilton, 1996).

MacDermott, Anthony, 'The Irish regiments in the Spanish service', *Irish Genealogist*, 2:9 (July 1952), pp 259–68.

McDermott, John James and Kieran O'Conor, 'Rosclogher Castle: a Gaelic lordship centre on Lough Melvin, County Leitrim', *Breifne*, 13:50 (2015), pp 470–97.

McDermott, Siobhan, 'The archaeology of the Twelve Tates of McKenna, c.1591', *Clogher Record*, 20:2 (2010), pp 373–406.

McErlean, Thomas, 'The Irish townland system of landscape organization' in Terence Reeves-Smyth and Fred Hamond (eds), *Landscape archaeology in Ireland*, BAR 116 (1983), pp 315–39.

McEvoy, Brian, 'Genetic investigation of Irish ancestry and surname history' (PhD, TCD, 2004).

McEvoy, Brian and Daniel G. Bradley, 'Y-chromosomes and the extent of patrilineal ancestry in Irish surnames', *Human Genetics*, 119:1–2 (2006), pp 212–19.

McKenzie, Catriona, Eileen M. Murphy and Colm J. Donnelly (eds), *The science of a lost medieval graveyard: the Ballyhanna Research Project* (Dublin, 2015).

McKenzie, Caitriona and Eileen M. Murphy, *Life and death in medieval Gaelic Ireland* (Dublin, 2018).

MacLysaght, Edward, *Irish families: their names, arms, and origins* (Dublin, 1991).

McNeary, Rory and Brian Shanahan, 'Medieval settlement, society and land use in medieval Roscommon, 1100–1650AD', *Discovery Programme Reports 7* (Dublin, 2005), pp 3–22.

McNeary, Rory and Brian Shanahan, 'Settlement and enclosure in a medieval Gaelic lordship: a case study from the territory of the O'Conors of north Roscommon' in R. Compatangelo, J.-R. Bertrand, J. Chapman and P.-Y. Laffont (eds), *Landmarks and socio-economic systems: constructing of pre-industrial landscapes and their perception by contemporary societies* (Rennes, 2008), pp 187–97.

McNeary, Rory and Brian Shanahan, 'Roscommon landscape' in *The Discovery Programme/An Clár Fionnachtana: 2008 annual report* (Dublin, 2008), pp 22–4.

McNeary, Rory and Brian Shanahan, 'The March in Roscommon, 1170–1400: culture, contact, continuity and change' in Jenifer Ní Ghrádaigh and Emmett O'Byrne (eds), *The March in the islands of the medieval West* (Leiden and Boston, 2012), pp 195–226.

MacNeill, John (Eoin), 'Early Irish population-groups', *PRIA*, 29C (1911–12), pp 59–114.

McNeill, Thomas E., *Castles in Ireland: feudal power in a Gaelic world* (London, 1997).

Maginn, Christopher and Steven Ellis, *The Tudor discovery of Ireland* (Dublin, 2015).

Maguire, William A., 'The land settlement' in William A. Maguire (ed.), *Kings in conflict: the revolutionary war in Ireland and its aftermath, 1689–1750* (Belfast, 1990), pp 139–56.

Manning, Conleth, 'The date of the round tower at Clonmacnoise', *Archaeology Ireland*, 11:2 (1997), pp 12–13.

Manning, Conleth (ed.), *Excavations at Roscrea Castle* (Dublin, 2003).

Manning, Conleth, *The history and archaeology of Glanworth Castle, Co. Cork* (Dublin, 2009).

Manning, Conleth, *Clogh Oughter Castle, Co. Cavan: archaeology, history and architecture* (Dublin, 2013).

Markley, Shirley, 'Unearthing a forgotten medieval-building technique: an examination of earth-mortared stone construction in later medieval Ireland, 1100–1600AD' (PhD, TCD, 2018).

Meyer, Werner, 'Castle archaeology – an introduction' in Martin Carver and Jan Klápště (eds), *The archaeology of medieval Europe*, ii: *twelfth to fifteenth centuries* (Aarhus, 2011), pp 230–43.

Moore, Eoghan, 'Foibrén in Mide', *JRSAI*, 142–3 (2012–13), pp 188–90.

Moore, Michael, *Archaeological inventory of County Leitrim* (Dublin, 2003).

Moore, Sam, 'The Bealach Buidhe, the Red Earl's Road and Bóthar an Corann in Counties Sligo and Roscommon: an overview', *Journal of the Sligo Field Club,* 1 (2015), pp 65–88.

Moss, Rachel, 'Exhibitionist figures' in Rachel Moss (ed.), *Art and architecture of Ireland*, i: *Medieval, c.400–c.1600* (Dublin and New Haven, 2014), pp 77–8.

Mulchrone, Kathleen, Thomas F. O'Rahilly, Elizabeth Fitzpatrick and A.I. Pearson, *Catalogue of Irish manuscripts in the Royal Irish Academy* (Dublin, 1926–70).

Murphy, Margaret and Kieran O'Conor, *Roscommon Castle: a visitor's guide* (Roscommon, 2008).

Murtagh, Harman, 'Boating on Lough Ree' in Bernadette Cunningham and Harman Murtagh (eds), *Lough Ree: historic lakeland settlement* (Dublin, 2015), pp 192–219.

Naessens, Paul, 'Gaelic lords of the sea: the coastal tower houses of south Connemara' in Linda Doran and James Lyttleton (eds), *Lordship in medieval Ireland: image and reality* (Dublin, 2007), pp 217–35.

Naessens, Paul, 'Murchadh Ó Flaithbheartaigh and the aggrandizement of Aughanure Castle' in Richard Oram (ed.), *Tower Studies 1 & 2 – 'A house that thieves might knock at': proceedings of the 2010 Stirling and 2011 Dundee conferences* (Donington, 2015), pp 214–30.

Naessens, Paul and Kieran O'Conor, 'Pre-Norman fortification in eleventh- and twelfth-century Connacht' in Peter Ettel, Anne-Marie Flambard-Héricher and Kieran O'Conor (eds), *Château Gaillard, 25: l'origine du château médiéval* (Caen, 2012), pp 259–68.

Newman, Conor, 'Castlederg Castle' in Isabel Bennett (ed.), *Excavations 1991: summary accounts of archaeological excavations in Ireland* (Bray, 1992), pp 43–4.

Nicholls, Kenneth W., 'Rectory, vicarage and parish in the western Irish dioceses', *JRSAI*, 101 (1971), pp 53–82.

Nicholls, Kenneth W., 'Some Patrician sites of eastern Connacht', *Dinnsenchas*, 5 (1972–3), pp 114–18.

Nicholls, Kenneth W., 'Gaelic society and economy in the high Middle Ages' in A. Cosgrove (ed.), *A new history of Ireland*, ii: *Medieval Ireland, 1169–1534* (Oxford, 1987), pp 397–408.

Norton, Robert, *The gunner shewing the whole practice of artillery* (London, 1628).

O'Brien, Caimin and P. David Sweetman, *Archaeological inventory of County Offaly* (Dublin, 1997).

O'Callaghan, John Cornelius, *History of the Irish brigades in the service of France* (Dublin, 1869).

Ó Catháin, Diarmuid, 'Some account of Charles O'Conor and literacy in Irish in his time' in Luke Gibbons and Kieran O'Conor (eds), *Charles O'Conor of Ballinagare, 1710–91: life and works* (Dublin, 2015), pp 28–51.

Ó Ciardha, Eamonn, *Ireland and the Jacobite cause, 1685–1766* (Dublin, 2004).

O'Connell, Patricia, *The Irish College at Alcala De Henares, 1649–1785* (Dublin, 1997).

O'Connor, Peter, *The royal O'Connors of Connaught* (Swinford, 1997).

O'Conor, Charles Owen (O'Conor Don), *The O'Conors of Connaught* (Dublin, 1891).

O'Conor, Kieran, 'The origins of Carlow Castle', *Archaeology Ireland*, 11:3 (1997), pp 13–16.

O'Conor, Kieran, *The archaeology of medieval rural settlement in Ireland* (Dublin, 1998).

O'Conor, Kieran, 'The morphology of Gaelic lordly sites in north Connacht' in Patrick J. Duffy, David Edwards and Elizabeth FitzPatrick (eds), *Gaelic Ireland, c.1250–c.1650: land, lordship and settlement* (Dublin, 2001), pp 329–45.

O'Conor, Kieran, 'Housing in later medieval Gaelic Ireland', *Ruralia*, 4 (2002), pp 197–206.

O'Conor, Kieran, 'Sligo Castle' in Martin Timoney (ed.), *A celebration of Sligo: first essays for Sligo Field Club* (Carrick-on-Shannon, 2002), pp 183–92.

O'Conor, Kieran, 'Introduction' in Ursula Egan, Elizabeth Byrne and Mary Sleeman, *Archaeologial inventory of Co. Sligo*, i: *South Sligo* (Dublin, 2005), pp ix–xii.

O'Conor, Kieran, 'Gaelic lordly settlement in 13th- and 14th-century Ireland' in Ingunn Holm, Sonja Innselet and Ingvild Øye (eds), *'Utmark': the outfield as industry and ideology in the Iron Age and the Middle Ages* (Bergen, 2005), pp 209–21.

O'Conor, Kieran, 'English settlement and change in Roscommon during the late sixteenth and seventeenth centuries' in Audrey Horning, Ruairi Ó Baoill, Colm J. Donnelly and Paul

Logue (eds), *The post-medieval archaeology of Ireland, 1550–1850* (Dublin, 2007), pp 189–205.

O'Conor, Kieran, 'Castle studies in Ireland – the way forward' in Peter Ettel, Anne-Marie Flambard Héricher and Thomas E. McNeill (eds), *Château Gaillard,* 23: *bilan des recherches en castellogie* (Caen, 2008), pp 329–38.

O'Conor, Kieran, 'Fortifications in the North (1200–1600)' in Martin Carver and Jan Klápště (eds), *The archaeology of medieval Europe*, ii: *twelfth to sixteenth centuries AD* (Aarhus, 2011), pp 243–60.

O'Conor, Kieran, 'Castles' in Rachel Moss (ed.), *Art and architecture of Ireland*, i: *Medieval, c.400–c.1600* (Dublin and New Haven, 2014), pp 341–5.

O'Conor, Kieran, '*Crannóga* in later medieval Ireland' in Eve Campbell, Elizabeth FitzPatrick and Audrey Horning (eds), *Becoming and belonging in Gaelic Ireland, AD* c.*1200–1600: essays in identity and cultural practice* (Cork, 2018), pp 148–66.

O'Conor, Kieran, 'Settlement in Gaelic Ireland, 1100–1350', *Eolas: the Journal of the American Society of Irish Medieval Studies*, 13 (2021), pp 43–71.

O'Conor, Kieran, Niall Brady, Ann Connon and Carlos Fidalgo-Romo, 'The Rock of Lough Cé, Co. Roscommon' in Thomas Finan (ed.), *Medieval Lough Cé: history, archaeology and landscape* (Dublin, 2010), pp 15–40.

O'Conor, Kieran and Thomas Finan, 'Medieval settlement in north Roscommon, c.1200AD–c.1350AD' in Richie Farrell, Kieran O'Conor and Matthew Potter (eds), *Roscommon history and society: interdisciplinary essays on the history of an Irish county* (Dublin, 2018), pp 105–32.

O'Conor, Kieran and Christina Fredengren, 'Medieval settlement in Leitrim, 1169–c.1380AD,' in Liam Kelly and Brendan Scott (eds), *Leitrim history and society: interdisciplinary essays on the history of an Irish county* (Dublin, 2019), pp 79–101.

O'Conor, Kieran and Paul Naessens, 'Temple House: from Templar castle to New English mansion' in Martin Browne and Colman Ó Clabaigh (eds), *Soldiers of Christ: the Knights Hospitallers and the Knights Templar in medieval Ireland* (Dublin, 2016), pp 124–50.

O'Conor, Kieran and Paul Naessens, 'The medieval harbour beside Rindoon Castle, Co. Roscommon' in Peter Ettel, Anne-Marie Flambard-Héricher and Kieran O'Conor (eds), *Château Gaillard*, 27: *château et commerce* (Caen, 2016), pp 237–42.

O'Conor, Kieran, Paul Naessens and Rory Sherlock, 'Rindoon Castle, Co. Roscommon: a border castle on the Irish frontier' in Peter Ettel, Anne-Marie Flambard-Héricher and Kieran O'Conor (eds), *Château Gaillard, 26: l'environment du château* (Caen, 2014), pp 313–23.

O'Conor, Kieran, Paul Naessens and Rory Sherlock, 'Rindoon Castle, Co. Roscommon: an Anglo-Norman castle on the western shores of Lough Ree' in Bernadette Cunningham and Harman Murtagh (eds), *Lough Ree: historic lakeland settlement* (Dublin, 2016), pp 83–109.

O'Conor, Kieran and Brian Shanahan, *Roscommon Abbey: a visitor's guide* (Roscommon, 2013).

O'Conor, Kieran and Brian Shanahan, *Rindoon Castle and deserted medieval town* (Roscommon, 2018).

O'Conor, Kieran and Jeremy Williams, 'Ballinagare Castle, Co. Roscommon' in Luke Gibbons and Kieran O'Conor (eds), *Charles O'Conor of Ballinagare, 1710–91: life and works* (Dublin, 2015), pp 52–71.

O'Conor, Matthew, *Military history of the Irish nation; comprising memoirs of the Irish Brigade in the service of France, with an appendix of official papers relative to the Brigade from the archives at Paris* (Dublin, 1845).

Ó Corráin, Donnchadh, *Ireland before the Normans* (Dublin, 1972).

Ó Corrain, Donnchadh, 'Historical need and literary narrative' in David Ellis Evans, John G. Griffiths and Edward Martyn Jope (eds), *Proceedings of the Seventh International Congress of Celtic Studies* (Oxford, 1986), pp 141–58.

O'Dowd, Mary, 'Landownership in the Sligo area, 1585–1616' (PhD, UCD, 1978).

O'Dowd, Mary, *Power, politics and land: early modern Sligo, 1568–1688* (Belfast, 1991).

Ó Duigeannáin, M., 'Three seventeenth-century Connacht documents', *JGAHS*, 17 (1936–7), pp 147–61.

O'Dwyer, Peter, 'Carmelites in Pre-Reformation Ireland', *Carmelus*, 16 (1969), pp 264–78.

O'Gara-O'Riordan, Maura, 'Births, baptisms and deaths in the exiled O'Gara family after the Jacobite defeat', *Corran Herald*, 42 (2009–10), pp 25–9.

O'Gara-O'Riordan, Maura, 'Charles O'Conor and the Annals of the Four Masters' in Luke Gibbons and Kieran O'Conor (eds), *Charles O'Conor of Ballinagare, 1710–91: life and works* (Dublin, 2015), pp 227–43.

O'Keeffe, Tadhg, *The Gaelic peoples and their archaeological identities, AD1000–1650* (Cambridge, 2004).

O'Keeffe, Tadhg, 'Building lordship in thirteenth-century Ireland: the donjon of Coonagh Castle, Co. Limerick', *Journal of the Royal Society of Antiquaries of Ireland*, 141 (2011), pp 91–127.

O'Keeffe, Tadhg, 'Lohort Castle: medieval architecture, medievalist imagination', *Journal of the Cork Historical and Archaeological Society*, 118 (2013), pp 24–34.

O'Keeffe, Tadhg, *Medieval Irish buildings, 1100–1600,* Maynooth Research Guides for Irish Local History 18 (Dublin, 2015).

O'Keeffe, Tadhg, *Ireland encastellated, AD 950–1550: insular castle-building in its European context* (Dublin, 2021).

Ó Lochlainn, Colm, 'Roadways in ancient Ireland' in J. Ryan (ed.), *Féil-sgríbhinn Eoín Mhic Néill: essays and studies presented to Professor Eoin MacNeill on the occasion of his seventieth birthday, May 15th 1938* (Dublin, 1940), pp 465–74.

Ó Macháin, Padraig, '"One glimpse of Ireland": the manuscript of Fr Nicolás (Fearghal Dubh) Ó Gadhra' in Raymond Gillespie and Ruairí Ó Huiginn (eds), *Irish Europe, 1600–1650: writing and learning* (Dublin, 2013), pp 135–62.

Ó Muraíle, Nollaig, 'The townlands of Bekan' in Michael Comer and Nollaig Ó Muraile (eds), *Béacán/Bekan: portrait of an east Mayo parish* (Ballinrobe, 1986), pp 36–64.

Ó Muraíle, Nollaig, 'The autograph manuscripts of the Annals of the Four Masters', *Celtica*, 19 (1987), pp 75–95.

Ó Muraíle, Nollaig, *The celebrated antiquary Dubhaltach Mac Fhirbhisigh (c.1600–1671): his lineage, life and learning* (Maynooth, 1996).

Ó Muraíle, Nollaig, 'The manuscripts of the Annals of the Four Masters since 1636' in Edel Bhreathnach and Bernadette Cunningham (eds), *Writing Irish history: the Four Masters and their world* (Dublin, 2007), pp 61–4.

Ó Riain, Padraig, *A dictionary of Irish saints* (Dublin, 2011).

O'Rorke, Terence, *The history of Sligo: town and county*, 2 vols (Dublin, 1889).

Orpen, Goddard H., *Ireland under the Normans, 1169–1333* (Dublin, 2005).

O'Sullivan, Aidan, *The archaeology of lake settlement in Ireland* (Dublin, 1998).

O'Sullivan, Aidan, 'Crannogs in late medieval Gaelic Ireland, *c.*1350–*c.*1650' in Paul Duffy, David Edwards and Elizabeth FitzPatrick (eds), *Gaelic Ireland,* c.*1250–*c.*1650: land, lordship and settlement* (Dublin, 2001), pp 397–417.

Pollock, David, *Barryscourt Castle, Co. Cork: archaeology, history and architecture* (Dublin, 2017).

Richard-Maupillier, Frederic, 'The Irish in the regiments of Duke Leopold of Lorraine 1698–1729', *Archivium Hibernicum*, 67 (2014), pp 285–312.

Rooney, Dominic, 'Sir Frederick Hamilton (1590–1647), Leitrim planter' in Liam Kelly and Brendan Scott (eds), *Leitrim history and society: interdisciplinary essays on the history of an Irish county* (Dublin, 2019), pp 259–78.

Ruckley, Nigel A., 'Water supply of medieval castles in the United Kingdom', *Fortress*, 7 (1990), pp 14–26.

Salter, Michael, *The castles of Connacht* (Malvern, 2004).

Salter, Michael, *The castles of Ulster* (Malvern, 2004).

Schiffer, Michael B., 'Radiocarbon dating and the "old wood" problem: the case of the Hohokam chronology', *Journal of Archaeological Science*, 13 (1986), pp 13–30.

Schmidt, Armin, *Earth resistance for archaeologists* (Lanham, 2013).

Scott, Brendan, 'Seventeenth-century Leitrim: plantation to rebellion' in Liam Kelly and Brendan Scott (eds), *Leitrim history and society: interdisciplinary essays on the history of an Irish county* (Dublin, 2019), pp 279–96.

Sergeant, Philip Walsingham, *Little Jennings and Fighting Dick Talbot: a life of the duke and duchess of Tyrconnel,* 2 vols (London, 1913).

Sherlock, Rory, 'An introduction to the history and architecture of Bunratty Castle' in Roger A. Stalley (ed.), *Limerick and south-west Ireland: medieval art and architecture*, Transactions of the British Archaeological Association, XXXIV (Leeds, 2011), pp 202–18.

Sherlock, Rory, 'Using new techniques to date old castles', *Archaeology Ireland*, 27 (2013), pp 19–23.

Sherlock, Rory, 'Tower houses' in R. Moss (ed.), *Art and architecture of Ireland*, i: *Medieval, c.400-c.1600* (Dublin and New Haven, 2014), pp 354–5.

Sherlock, Rory, 'The evolution of the Irish tower house, 1400–1650' in Richard Oram (ed.), *Tower Studies, 1 &2: 'A house that thieves might knock at'* (Donington, 2015), pp 258–69.

Shingurova, Tatiana, '"This is why it is unlawful for a man from the Eóganachta to kill a man from the Crecraige": the origins and status of the Crecraige in medieval Ireland', *Eolas: the Journal of the American Society of Irish Medieval Studies,* 12 (2019), pp 26–42.

Simms, John G., 'Connacht in the eighteenth century', *IHS*, 42 (1958), pp 116–33.

Simms, John G., *Jacobite Ireland* (London, 1969; Dublin, 2000).

Smyth, William, 'Property, patronage and population: reconstructing the human geography of mid-17th-century County Tipperary' in William Nolan (ed.), *Tipperary history and society: interdisciplinary essays on the history of an Irish county* (Dublin, 1985), pp 118–30.

Smyth, William, *Map-making, landscapes and memory: a geography of colonial and early modern Ireland, c.1530–1750* (Cork, 2006).

Stalley, Roger A., *The Cistercian monasteries of Ireland* (New Haven, 1987).

Stout, Matthew, *The Irish ringfort* (Dublin, 1997).

Sweetman, P. David, 'Archaeological excavations at Ballymote Castle, Co. Sligo', *JGAHS*, 40 (1985–6), pp 114–24.

Sweetman, P. David, *The medieval castles of Ireland* (Cork, 1999).

Swift, Michael, *Historical maps of Ireland* (London, 1999).

Taaffe, Karl, *Memoirs of the family of Taaffe* (Vienna, 1856).

Taylor, George and Andrew Skinner, *Maps of the roads of Ireland, surveyed 1777* (1st ed., London and Dublin, 1778).

Taylor, George and Andrew Skinner, *Taylor and Skinner's maps of the roads of Ireland, surveyed 1777 and corrected down to 1783* (London and Dublin, 1783; Shannon, 1969).

Timoney, Martin, 'Where are they now? The Knockmore early Christian slabs', *Corran Herald*, 30 (1997), pp 3–4.

Tsokas, Gregory N., Panagiotis I. Tsourlos and Nikos Papadopulos, 'Electrical resistivity tomography: a flexible technique in solving problems of archaeological research' in Stefano Campana and Salvatore Piro (eds), *Seeing the unseen: geophysics and landscape archaeology* (London, 2008), pp 183–204.

Wakeman, William F., 'The church on White Island, Lough Erne, parish of Magherculmoney, county of Fermanagh', *JRSAI*, 15 (1879–82), pp 276–92.

Walsh, Micheline, 'A Galway officer of the Spanish Navy', *JGAHS* 26 (1954–5), pp 30–4.

Waterman, Dudley M., 'Some Irish seventeenth-century houses and their architectural ancestry' in E. Martin Jope (ed.), *Studies in building history: essays in recognition of the work of B.H. St J. O'Neil* (London, 1961), pp 251–74.

Witten, Alan, *Handbook of geophysics and archaeology* (London, 2006).

Wood-Martin, William G., *Sligo and the Enniskilliners from 1688–1691* (Dublin, 1880).

Wood-Martin, William G., *History of Sligo, county and town, from the earliest ages to the close of the reign of Queen Elizabeth* (Dublin 1882).

Wood-Martin, William G., *History of Sligo, county and town, from the accession of James I to the revolution of 1688* (Dublin, 1889).

ONLINE SOURCES

Ask About Ireland, 'Griffith's Valuation', askaboutireland.ie/griffith-valuation, accessed 8 Feb. 2023.

British History Online, 'Calendar of Papal Registers', british-history.ac.uk/cal-papal-registers/brit-ie, accessed 8 Feb. 2023.

Clavin, Trerry, 'Sir John King', Dictionary of Irish biography, dib.ie/biography/king-sir-john-a4563, accessed 8 Feb. 2023.

CELT (Corpus of Electronic Texts), 'Homepage', ucc.ie/celt/publishd.html, accessed 8 Feb. 2023.

DIAS (Dublin Institute of Advanced Studies), 'Irish script on screen', isos.dias.ie, accessed 8 Feb. 2023.

MacDermot of Coolavin, 'Geneaology of the MacDermot family', catalogue.nli.ie/Record/vtls000752120, accessed 8 Feb. 2023.

Moygara Pedigree Livestock, 'Homepage', moygara.com, accessed 8 Feb. 2023.

McEvoy, Brian Patric, 'Genetic investigation of Irish ancestry and surname history' (PhD, TCD, 2004), tara.tcd.ie/bitstream/handle/2262/77578/McEvoy%2C%20Brian%202005.pdf, accessed 8 Feb. 2023.

McEvoy, Brian and Daniel G. Bradley, 'Y-chromosomes and the extent of patrilineal ancestry in Irish surnames', Human Genetics, 119 (2006), pp 212–19, doi.org/10.1007/s00439-005-0131-8, accessed 8 Feb. 2023.

NAI, 'Census of Ireland', census.nationalarchives.ie, accessed 8 Feb. 2023.

NAI, 'The Tithe Applotment Boooks', titheapplotmentbooks.nationalarchives.ie/search/tab/home.jsp, accessed 8 Feb. 2023.

Wikipedia, 'Old wood', en.wikipedia.org/wiki/Old_wood, accessed 8 Feb. 2023.

Index

Achonry diocese, 30

Aghalane, Co. Fermanagh, 97

Anglo-Normans, 15, 24, 36–7

Annals of the Four Masters, 129–32, 187

apotropaic carvings, 201–4

Ardconnell, Co. Sligo, 122, 126, 204

Ardtarmon Castle, Co. Sligo, 104–7, 194

Aughrim, Battle of, 123

Balllinafad Castle, Co. Sligo, 104

Ballintober Castle, Co. Roscommon, 15

Ballyhanna, Co. Donegal, 22

Ballymooney Castle, Co. Offaly, 53, 103

Ballymote Castle, Co. Sligo, 15, 19, 106, 118, 120, 126

barony formation and creation, 26–7

Barryscourt Castle, Co. Cork, 21

Benburb, Co. Tyrone, 96

Bingham, George, 119

Bingham, Sir Richard, 42, 69–71, 118–19

Blarney Castle, Co. Cork, 21

Blayney, Sir Edward, 99–100

Books of Survey and Distribution, 50

Boyle Abbey, Co. Roscommon, 15, 19, 38, 40, 60, 63, 115, 200

Boyle River, 66, 70, 187, 195

Boyle Town, 200, 205, 208

Boyne, Battle of the, 52

Brady, Niall, 22

Breen, Colin, 22

Browne, John I, 69–71, 77

Browne, John II, 71–2

building stone, Moygara Castle, 173–4, 180

Caherconnell cashel, Co. Clare, 22

Callow, Co. Roscommon, 33

Campbell, Eve, 24

cannon, 197

Carlow Castle, 68

Carrowntemple, 47, 57

Carrowcaslan (Moygara townland today), 40, 43, 50, 52

Carrownekillskorny, 49

Casey, Markus, 79

Castleblayney, Co. Monaghan, 97, 99–100, 103

Castlecoote, Co. Roscommon, 201

Castlederg, Co. Tyrone, 95–7

Castlemore, Co. Roscommon, 37, 42, 54

castle life, 46

castle studies in Ireland, 20–1

Charles I, 198

Charlotte, princess of Lorraine, 124

Clara Castle, Co. Kilkenny, 162–3

Clanricarde Burkes, 199

Clegna, Cootehall, Co. Roscommon, 97

Clogh Oughter Castle, Co. Cavan, 21

Clooncunny, 27, 46, 52

Clooneagh, 52

Cloontycarn, 52, 119

Cloonmacmullan, 33

Cloonsillagh, 52

Cocking, Thomas, 109

Cole, Captain William Cole, 98

Composition of Connacht (*The compossicion booke of Conought*), 44, 50, 113

Confederate forces, 5

Confederate War, 59, 121, 198–9, 205

Connon, Anne, 198–9, 204

Coolavin (*Cúil Ó bhFind* – lordship and later barony), 18, 22, 26–31, 34, 37, 40–1, 43–5, 48–9, 52, 56–8, 65, 112, 115, 118, 122, 125, 186, 195–6, 204–7

Coolavin woodlands, 53

Cooper, Edward, 15, 19, 55

Corran (*Corann*), 33–6

Corcu Fhir Trí, 33

Costello (barony), 27

Craig, Maurice, 17

crannogs, 42, 68–9

Cromwellian War and confiscations, 59, 121, 198–9, 205, 207

Cuilprughlish (Clonehagglishe), 31, 47, 52

Culmullen mill, 47

Cuppanagh, Co. Sligo, 41–2, 49, 52, 58, 69, 71, 109, 119–22, 127, 186, 195, 199, 208

Curlew Mountains, 31, 38, 40, 66, 74, 105

Cushing (*Cúisín*), 37–8

Davies, Sir John, 95

de Burgh, Richard I, 36, 111

de Burgh, Richard III (*an Iarla Rua*), 15, 106

d'Exeter, Jordan, 36

de Lacy, Hugh, 36

de Nangle (de Angulo), 36

de Nangle, Miles, 37

Derrymore (castle and manor), 42, 45, 57–8, 69, 71, 109, 186

Dillon family, 126

Dillon, Sir Theobald, 44–5, 54, 119–20

Discovery Programme, Dublin, 22, 24

DNA-testing project, 128–9

Down Survey, 57–8, 63

Dromahair, Co. Leitrim, 94, 106

Dunluce Castle, Co. Antrim, 21

Eaghra (mac Saergusa), 109

earth resistance survey, 138–42

Eleanor, Countess of Desmond, 120

electrical resistivity tomography survey, 142–6

Elphin, Co. Roscommon, 201

Emmel West Castle, Co. Offaly, 104–6

Fairymount, Co. Roscommon, 15

Falleens, 52

Faugher, Co. Donegal, 53–4, 97–9, 103, 107

Finan, Thomas, 22

fitz Gerald, Maurice, 36

FitzPatrick, Elizabeth, 22, 24

Five Cantreds, 36

Foyren (*Foibrén*), 32

Frenchpark, 32

Gadhra, 109–10

Gaelic Ireland (the development of the study), 22–4

Gaelic Resurgence, 112

Garvey, Máire, 37

geophysical survey, 133–54

Glanworth Castle, Co. Cork, 21

Glenfarne, Co. Leitrim, 100–1

Gore, George, 52, 61

Gortygara, 41–2

Greagraighe, 31–2

ground penetrating radar survey, 149–52

Hamilton, Sir Frederick, 100–2, 199–200

Hannay, Sir Robert, 56

Hansard, Sir Richard, 99

Hartley, L.P., 188

Hen Domen motte castle, Powys, 68, 183

Horning, Audrey, 24

Jacobites, 56, 60, 65, 206–7

James II, 52, 123

Jamestown, Co. Leitrim, 201

Jones, Roger, 43, 120

Kerrigan, Paul, 17, 62

Kilcolgan More Castle, Co. Offaly, 106–7

Kilcolman, 27, 30, 44, 57

Kilcorkey, Co. Roscommon, 32

Kilfree, 26, 30–1, 44, 57

Kilkea Castle, Co. Kildare, 202–3

Killaraght (*na Ranna*), 26–31, 41, 44, 52–3

Kilnamanagh, Co. Roscommon, 33–4

Kilnaskorny, 43, 52

King family, 44, 60, 208

King, Captain Francis, 206

King, Sir John, 45, 50, 205

King, Sir Robert (afterwards Lord Kingston – d. 1707), 45, 51–2

Kingston, Lord John (d. 1676), 47, 50–2, 56, 60–1, 64, 121–2, 127

Kingston, Lord Robert (d. 1693), 60, 206–7

Knockmore friary, 112

Knockvicar, 200

Leopold Joseph, duke of Lorraine, 124

Leyny, 32, 34, 36–7

Lime mortars, Moygara Castle, 175–7

Lindsay, Jerome (Jeremy), 98

Lismore, Co. Tyrone, 97

Loeber, Rolf, 18

Lomcloon, 27, 46, 52

Lough Gara (*Loch Techet*), 15, 26, 31–4, 37–8, 66–7, 73, 108, 187, 195

Luighne (kingdom and tribe), 26, 32, 33–6, 109–11, 129

Lyttleton, James, 21, 53, 102–3

MacCostello dynasty, 27, 37

MacCotter, Paul, 32, 34

MacDermot dynasty of Moylurg, 15, 22, 27, 44, 114–15, 121, 126–7, 189

MacDonagh dynasty, 117, 119

Mac an Leagha medical family, 47

magnetic gradiometer survey, 146–9.

Magrath, Bryan, 50–1, 122

Mahanagh, 43, 52

Malby, Nicholas,

Manorhamilton, C. Leitrim, 97, 100–3, 199–200

McAlister, Victoria, 18, 21

McEvoy, Brian, 129

McFearagheir, Owen Boy, 47

McNeill, Thomas E., 15, 20

McSweeney dynasty, 99

McSweeney, Sir Mulmory, 99

McSweeney, Walter McLaughlin, 99

Meyer, Werner, 192

moated sites, 41–2

Monaghan, Co. Monaghan, 99

Mortar-dating at Moygara Castle, 171–3, 177–80, 190–4

Mountjoy, Co. Tyrone, 103

Moygara townland, 47–52, 58–61, 75–6, 121–2

Moygara Castle, 15, 17–9, 21–2, 24–6, 37, 39–40, 42–3, 47–50, 52, 54–74, 76–94, 97, 102–3, 107–9, 119, 133–81, 183–8, 190–203, 205, 207–8

Moygara Castle Research and Conservation Project, 7, 13, 23, 171, 181

Moylurg (*Magh Luirg* – kingdom and later lordship), 22, 27, 32, 38

Mullaghroe, 43, 52

Mullaghthee Mountain, Co. Sligo, 26, 66–7

multi-disciplinary approach, 24–5, 181

Newman, Conor, 96

Nine Years War, 45, 187

Nugent, Christopher, 44

O'Boyle, Tirlagh Roe, 53, 99

O'Carroll, Donnell, 53, 103

O'Concannon (Ó Con Cheannáin), 33

O'Conor dynasty (Ó Conchobhair), 22, 33, 36, 112, 114, 119, 121, 126, 189

O'Conor, Aodh (Hugh), 37

O'Conor, Charles of Ballinagare, 123, 125, 205

O'Conor Don, 121

O'Conor, Felim, 37

O'Conor, Hugh (O'Conor Don), 182

O'Conor, Mary, 123, 204

O'Conor Sligo, 43, 45, 47, 112, 115, 117, 121
O'Conor (Sligo), Cathal Óg, 39–40
O'Conor (Sligo), Sir Donal, 116, 118
O'Conor (Sligo), Donogh, 42–3, 119–20
O'Conor, Rory, 182
O'Conor (Sligo), Tadgh MP, 121
O'Conor, Turlough, 111, 182
Ó Corráin, Donnchadh, 32
O Doibhiléin lineage, 35
O'Donnell dynasty, 96, 109, 115, 188, 191
O'Donnell, Hugh McHugh Duffe, 99
O'Donnell, Manus, 38
O'Donnell, Colonel Manus, 61–2
O'Donnell, Niall Garbh, 38
O'Donnell, Rory, 40
O'Donnell, Rory (father of Colonel Manus O'Donnell), 61
O'Donovan, John, 130
O'Dowd dynasty of Tireragh 117, , 121
O'Dowd, Mary, 43, 53
O'Duignenan family, 47
Ó Finn (Finn) lineage, 31, 34
O'Flaherty dynasty, 121
O'Gara, Bernard, archbishop of Tuam, 126–7
O'Gara clerics, 113
O'Gara (Ó Gadhra) dynasty, 15, 18, 22, 25–7, 35–7, 40, 42–3, 47, 50–1, 54, 58, 71, 76, 88, 91, 108, 110–19, 121, 126, 128–9, 131, 193, 195, 201, 203–4, 208
O'Gara, Charles (son of Fergal), 126
O'Gara, Count Charles, 124–5, 132, 205
O'Gara, Diarmait mac Eoghan, 64
O'Gara, Diarmait mac Eogan, 114, 191
O'Gara, Diarmait Óg, 40
O'Gara, Edmund Óg, 45
O'Gara, Eogan I (d. 1469), 114, 191
O'Gara, Eogan II (d. 1537), 191
O'Gara, Fergal, 38, 43–5, 47, 49–50, 53–4, 56, 59–60, 64–5, 109, 114, 119–23, 126–7, 130–2, 187, 195–6, 198–201, 204–6, 208

O'Gara, Irriel, 42–7, 50, 52–4, 64, 109, 118–20, 187
O'Gara, Colonel James Oliver, 123–4
O'Gara, Captain John (eldest son of Fergal), 27, 121, 123, 204
O'Gara, Lt Colonel John, 123
O'Gara, Colonel Joseph, 124
O'Gara, Kean of Tirerrill, 117–18
O'Gara, Mary, 123, 125
O'Gara, Michael, archbishop of Tuam, 126–7
O'Gara, Colonel Oliver (Fergal's grandson), 123, 126, 204
O'Gara, Owen, 45, 122
O'Gara, Tadg or Tadgh (Fergal's father), 54, 119
O'Gara, Tadg ne Gann, 44
O'Gara, Tadg Bane, 44
O'Gara, Tomaltach, 47
O'Gara-O'Riordan, Maura, 7, 171
O'Grady, John, 118
O'Hara (Ó hEaghra) dynasty, 35, 37, 110–11, 115, 121, 128–9
O'Hara Boy dynasty (Buí), 117
O'Hara, Kean, 132
O'Hara Roe dynasty, 117
O'Hart, Cormac, 47
O'Hart family, 119
O'Higgins family, 46–7
O'Keeffe, Tadgh, 18, 21
O'Kelly dynasty, 189
old wood effect, 178–80, 191–2, 194
Ó Mothláin (O'Mullen) lineage, 33–4
Ó Muraíle, Nollaig, 131
Ordnance Survey, 75
O'Neill dynasty, 96
O'Neill, Frank, 7, 171
O'Neill, P.J., 171, 181
Ormsby, Philip, 122
O'Rorke, Canon Terence, 54, 62, 201–2
O'Rourke dynasty, 94, 119, 121
O'Spillane (Spellman) family, 46

Pallas Castle, Co. Galway, 196
pardons (1604), 46
Parke's Castle (Newtown), Co. Leitrim, 21, 94
Parke, Captain Robert, 94
Penal Laws, 125, 205
Perrot, Sir John, 117
Plunkett family, 125
Portora, Co. Fermanagh, 97
Portumna Castle, Co. Galway, 21
prehistoric activity at Moygara Castle, 169

Raphoe, Co. Donegal, 103
Rathcroghan, Co. Roscommon, 15
Rathfarnham, Co. Dublin, 103
Rathmullan motte castle, Co. Down, 183
Read, Christopher, 91, 190, 194, 197
Restoration period, 204, 207–8
Richard de Burgh III (*an Iarla Rua*), 15, 182
Rindoon Castle, Co. Roscommon, 182
river transport, 66–7
Rock of Lough Key, Co. Roscommon, 22
Roscommon, 75
Roscommon Castle, 182
Roscrea Castle, Co. Tipperary, 21

Salter, Mike, 17
Sheela-na-Gigs, 202–4
Siege of Limerick, 52
Síl Muireadhaigh, 32–3
Sliabh Lugha, 29, 31, 35, 36–9, 66, 74, 111
Sligo Castle, 38, 115
Sligo Hearth Money Roll, 40, 58–9, 63
Sóergus (son of Bécc), 34
St Athracht (Attracta), 31
St Germain, 205
Strafford Survey, 48–9, 56
Stukeley, Thomas, 118
Sweetman, David, 15
Sydney, Sir Henry, 115

Taaffe family, 126, 132, 204
Taaffe, Elizabeth (wife of Fergal O'Gara), 120, 122–3
Taaffe, Count Francis, 124
Taaffe, Viscount John, 126
Taaffe, Major General Luke, 121
Taaffe, Viscount Theobald (d. 1664), 122, 126, 201
Taaffe, William, 43, 53, 118–20
Taichleach (son of Cenn Faoledh), 34, 109–10
Talbot, Sir Richard (later earl of Tyrconnell), 52, 60–2, 121–2
Talbotstown, Co. Wicklow, 60
Tawnymucklagh, 52
Taylor and Skinner maps, 65, 72–4
Templehouse Castle, Co. Sligo, 190
Templeronan, 127
timber trade, 194–5
Tirerrill (*Tír Ailella*), 32
tower houses, 19, 184–90
townlands, 44
Trim Castle, Co. Meath, 21
Trinity College Dublin, 54
Tulsk, 201

Uí Dhiarmaida, 33–4

village / hamlet beside Moygara Castle, 75–6, 187
Villiers family, 95, 106

Wakeman, William Frederick, 15, 19, 55
water supply to castles, 67–8
Wentworth, Thomas, 198–9
Williamites, 206–7
Williamite War (1689–91), 56, 60, 62, 65, 123, 206, 208
Wingfield, Sir Richard, 96
Wood-Martin, William, 111